Bonding, Bridging, & Bypassing

Bonding, Bridging, & Bypassing

Understanding Ethnic Politics in Diverse Societies

COLM A. FOX

OXFORD
UNIVERSITY PRESS

Oxford University Press is a department of the University of Oxford. It furthers
the University's objective of excellence in research, scholarship, and education
by publishing worldwide. Oxford is a registered trade mark of Oxford University
Press in the UK and certain other countries.

Published in the United States of America by Oxford University Press
198 Madison Avenue, New York, NY 10016, United States of America.

© Oxford University Press 2024

All rights reserved. No part of this publication may be reproduced, stored in
a retrieval system, or transmitted, in any form or by any means, without the
prior permission in writing of Oxford University Press, or as expressly permitted
by law, by license, or under terms agreed with the appropriate reproduction
rights organization. Inquiries concerning reproduction outside the scope of the
above should be sent to the Rights Department, Oxford University Press, at the
address above.

You must not circulate this work in any other form
and you must impose this same condition on any acquirer.

CIP data is on file at the Library of Congress

ISBN 978–0–19–774396–6 (pbk.)
ISBN 978–0–19–774395–9 (hbk.)

DOI: 10.1093/oso/9780197743959.001.0001

Paperback printed by Marquis Book Printing, Canada
Hardback printed by Bridgeport National Bindery, Inc., United States of America

For Zeno, Ash, and Sayaka.

Contents

Acknowledgments	ix
Maps	xiii
Glossary of Indonesian Political Parties	xvii
1. Introduction	1

I. THEORY

2. What Is an Ethnic Appeal?	23
3. The Logic of Ethnic Appeals	42

II. DATA

4. Electoral Reform in Indonesia	67
5. Measuring Ethnic Appeals	92

III. EVIDENCE

6. Electoral Rules	123
7. Viable Ethnic Groups	146
8. Party Ideology	177

IV. IMPLICATIONS

9. Religious Polarization in Indonesia	197
10. Conclusion	224
Appendix A: Statistical Analysis	237
Appendix B: Newspaper Data	253
Appendix C: Election Poster Data	257
Notes	263
References	285
Index	305

Acknowledgments

Election posters were scattered across our living room floor. They featured large images of Charlie Haughey, the colors of the Irish flag, and a caption that read "Fianna Fáil, The Republican Party." Ireland's 1981 election campaign was in full swing, and my father was putting up campaign posters around our village. Little did I know that 30 years later, I would be on a motorbike in the jungles of Indonesia, photographing a myriad of colorful election posters—for a book on political campaigns. I'm pretty sure the odd endeavor of studying Indonesia election posters puzzled my dad too.

This book began as my doctoral dissertation in the Department of Political Science at George Washington University (GWU). I am deeply indebted to my dissertation advisor, Henry Hale, and my committee members, Susan Sell, Eric Lawrence, Nathan Brown, and Bill Liddle. Much of what I know about ethnic politics—and about how to be a scholar—I have learned from Henry. Throughout the research process, he gave me ample space to explore, but also gently guided me back on track when necessary.

Beyond her incisive comments, Susan supported me in surviving the rigors of graduate school and in my development as a teacher—all with a great sense of humor. Eric allowed me to take his statistics classes multiple times until I finally (more or less) got it, and he also helped me understand how to use statistics to communicate ideas meaningfully. Nathan, an expert on the Middle East, helped me consider the bigger picture and identify where my work fits in. Finally, with regard to Indonesia specifically, Bill has been a great inspiration, due to his extensive scholarship and his selfless dedication to nurturing scholars of Indonesia over five decades.

The decision to go to graduate school was not easy, but I thank Patrick Dorey, Gary Gartlan, Eoin McGrath, David McManus, Eugene Mulligan, Conor Smith, and in particular, Marianna Betti for encouraging me to give up the comfortable life as a graphic designer in NYC for something just a bit different.

At GWU, I was fortunate to have a remarkable group of supportive friends who have (sometimes unwittingly) served as sounding boards for ideas contained in this book. For their advice and friendship, I thank Davy Banks,

Dina Bishara, Enze Han, Michele Jorkovich, Brian Karlson, Inwook Kim, Craig Kaufman, Joey O'Mahoney, Lilian Ting, and Ajay Vergese.

This book would not have been possible without the kindness of many Indonesians who helped me during my travels and research in their country. My initial trips to Indonesia were for language training. My homestay families, Bapak and Ibu Trisoyno and Bapak and Ibu Sulis Krave, introduced me to life in Indonesia and gave me welcoming homes. I also thank the whole team at the United States–Indonesian Society's sponsored language program at Universitas Gadja Mada and at the Consortium for the Teaching of Indonesian and Malay at Universitas Kristen Satya Wacana. In particular, my teachers and tutors, Bapak Basuki, Taufik Nur, Ibu Rio Rini, Christian Rudianto, Ibu Sugihastuti, and Toar Sumakul, were unfailingly patient and encouraging.

Syarif Hidayat at the Indonesian Institute of Sciences (LIPI) graciously served as my Indonesian counterpart and offered advice and introductions during fieldwork. I received superb research assistance from Ines Cute, Husnul Isa Harahap, Shobiburrohmah, and Ibrahim Zafar. They taught me much about the ethnic geography, culture, and politics of different regions of Indonesia.

A number of Indonesians and foreign researchers helped me immensely in gathering thousands of election posters across the country. These Indonesians include the many motorbike drivers who drove me around for hours while I photographed election posters, as well as networks of researchers who took the time to photograph posters and send them to me. I thank Firman Witoelar and his network of researchers at SurveyMeter, along with Dani Alfah, Abdullah Alwazin, Alpha Amirrachman, Colin Cahill, Erica Copeland, Kevin Fogg, Jesse Gerstin, Ruth Hastutiningsih, Bettie Landauer Menchik, Taufiq Nur, Christina Pomianek, Lacey Raak, Jacob Ricks, Megan Ryan, Danau Tanu, Bart Thanhauser, and Muslim Zainuddin. Without them, the data in this book would have been far less comprehensive.

Over the years, numerous Indonesian candidates, campaign workers, political analysts, journalists, and regular Indonesians carved time out of their busy schedules to help me understand local politics, elections, and campaign materials in North Sumatra, Java, and Maluku. In particular, I thank Taufan Damanik, Andreas Maryoto, Ali Murthado, Herlen Tampubolon, and Warjio for their time and generosity in sharing their insights. Also I thank J. Anto who helped me understand the Indonesian media and provided access to the wonderful archive of North Sumatran papers at his media NGO, KIPPAS.

During field research, I enjoyed being accompanied by a group of wonderful fellow researchers: En-Chieh Chao, Kevin Fogg, Jeremy Menchik, Sandeep Ray, Mark Renner, Sarah Shair-Rosenfield, and Danau Tanu. In particular, Jeremy's insight into the potential of studying election posters proved invaluable, and we collaborated in gathering and coding the Indonesian election poster dataset. In addition, our numerous conversations in Jakarta helped me hone my research methodology. As the book began to take shape, I also benefitted greatly from the writings of Kanchan Chandra, Daniel Posner, and Matthew Shugart. As will become evident, their scholarship has provided much of the intellectual inspiration underlying the book's main argument.

Over the years, I presented aspects of the book through numerous presentations. I would like to thank attendees for their comments and suggestions during presentations in Jakarta (at CSIS and the Freedom Institute), Vietnam (at the Southeast Asia Research Group meeting), Australia (at the Australian National University), Canada (at the University of Toronto), and the United States (at UCLA, AAS, and APSA). Aside from those mentioned, in writing this book, I have benefited from comments and advice from Kuskridho Ambardi, Paddy Barron, Shane Barter, Jacque Bertrand, Michael Buehler, Robin Bush, Robert Cribb, Greg Fealy, Sydney Jones, Amy Liu, Marcus Mietzner, Eddy Malesky, Steven Oliver, Kai Ostwald, Blair Palmer, Benjamin Reilly, Joel Selway, Stephen Sherlock, Aim Simpeng, Dan Slater, Alfred Stepan, Sunny Tanuwidjaja, Ross Tapsell, Risa Toha, Dirk Tomsa, and Meredith Weiss.

The book has been thoroughly reworked during my years at the School of Social Science at Singapore Management University, with excellent research assistance from Victorial Birrell and Eugene Tan. Working within Southeast Asia and being surrounded by so many scholars of the region has enriched my understanding of Southeast Asia immensely. Our dean, Chandran Kukathas, has been instrumental in supporting my research, including a book workshop. I thank my colleagues, Jake Ricks, Sebastian Dettman, and Charlotte Setijadi, for participating in the workshop and for their insightful comments and enthusiasm for the project. I am also indebted to Edward Aspinall, Jamie Davidson, Allen Hicken, and Tom Pepinsky for their participation. Ed has offered some of the best comments on contemporary ethnic politics in Indonesia (as well as plenty of encouragement over the years); Jamie's close reading and detailed comments helped me iron out inconsistencies and add richness to the text; and Allen and Tom contributed to a more precise argument and conceptual framework. Having this set of talented and experienced scholars read the full manuscript and provide comments helped me refine and extend the book into something far better than I could have achieved alone.

While intellectual stimulation is vital for any in-depth piece of research, so too is funding. I thank the Sigur Center for field research grants in 2008 and 2009 and the Matsushita International foundation for a field research grant from 2009 to 2011. Kimberly Morgan provided invaluable support for my fieldwork research during her years as GWU's director of graduate studies. Melissa Van and the late Alfred Stepan facilitated my stay as a visiting research scholar at the Institute for Religion, Culture, and Public Life at Columbia University. Additionally, Al Stepan was doing fieldwork in Indonesia at the same time as me, and he graciously drew on his vast knowledge to advise me on how to proceed when it felt as if my research was going nowhere.

My editor, Bruce Barron, was meticulous in ironing out inconsistencies and adding clarity to the book's text, resulting in far more readable prose. I thank Angela Chpnako at OUP for taking on this project and shepherding me through the process. She and her team helped a first-time author pull everything together.

I am very sure my parents and my siblings Margot, Kate, and David would never have expected me to write a book on Indonesia. However, our family holidays abroad fostered a curiosity about countries far beyond our Irish village. Their support and the independence my parents instilled in me allowed me to pursue my creative and intellectual interests in places far from home and laid the foundation for my academic work. Having said that, I'm sure my mother would have preferred to see me write something just a bit funnier.

Finally, I would like to thank my wife, Sayaka Chatani. We met in the early years of graduate school at GWU, and over the years she has made innumerable sacrifices and put up with long periods of being apart. From writing our dissertations in Bali through the last few years in Singapore, she has always been there to help me sound out ideas and has had a considerable impact on this book and my intellectual journey. I am quite certain that I never would have completed graduate school, let alone the book, without her encouragement, support, and love. In the process of writing this book, two little rascals, Zeno and Ash, arrived to complete our family. They don't really care about this book, they just want me to come home and play. I dedicate this book to Zeno, Ash, and Sayaka.

Maps

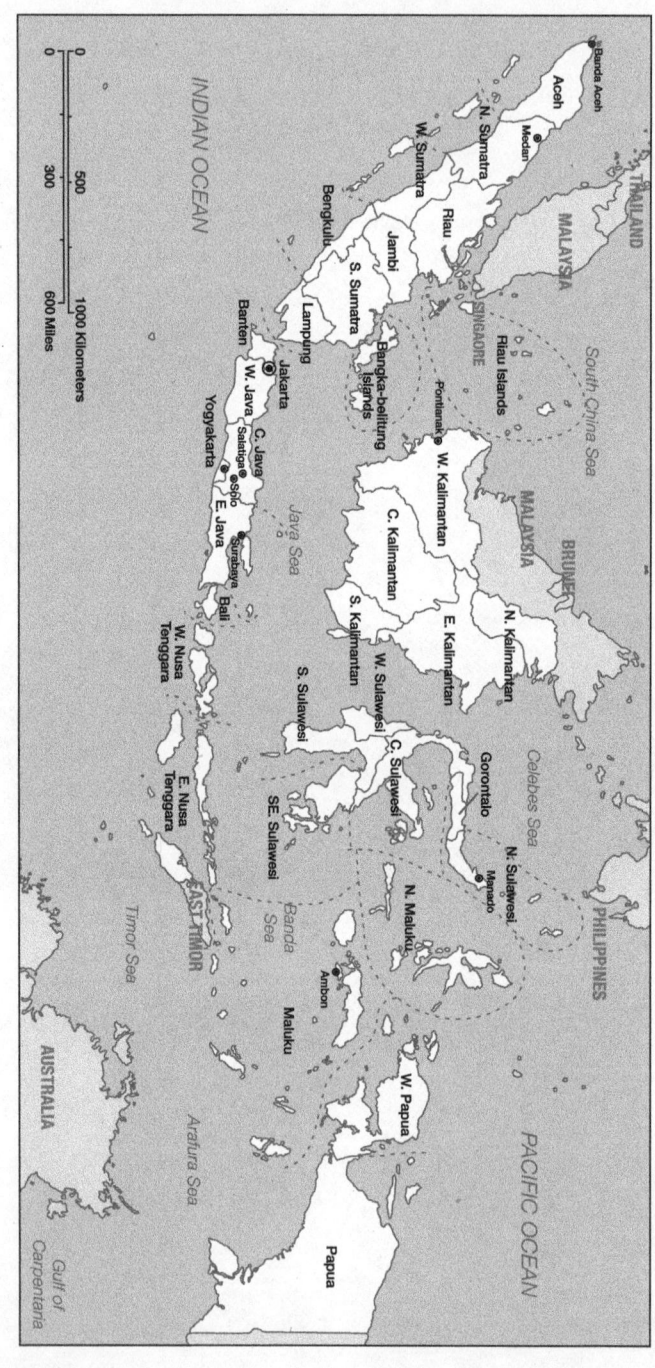

Map of Indonesia.

Map of North Sumatra.

Glossary of Indonesian Political Parties

Barnas   Partai Barisan Nasional (National Front Party). A small, nationalist party founded in 2007 by Vence Rumangkang, a former member of Partai Demokrat. Competed in the 2009 election.

Demokrat   Partai Demokrat (Democratic Party). A nationalist party founded in 2001 as an electoral vehicle for the retired general, Susilo Bambang Yudhoyono. Competed in every election since 2004.

Gerindra   Partai Gerakan Indonesia Raya (Great Indonesia Movement Party). A nationalist party founded in 2008 as an electoral vehicle for the former general, Prabowo Subianto, shortly before he resigned from Golkar. Competed in every election since 2009.

Golkar   Partai Golongan Karya (Party of Functional Groups). A nationalist party, which was initially founded in 1964 as a social and political organization. From the 1970s, it became the pro-government organization that mobilized the vote for Suharto. In 1999 it officially became a political party. Competed in every election since 1971.

Hanura   Partai Hati Nurani Rakyat (People's Conscience Party). A nationalist party founded in 2006 by Wiranto, a retired army general, after he resigned from Golkar. Competed in every election since 2009.

Masyumi   Partai Majelis Syuro Muslimin Indonesia (Council of Indonesian Muslim Associations). An Islamist party founded in 1945 by Muslim leaders. Competed in the 1955 election. It was banned in 1960 by Sukarno. In 2020, a new party revived its name, claiming to be its successor.

NasDem	Partai NasDem (National Democratic Party). A nationalist party founded in 2011 by media mogul Surya Paloh, shortly before he resigned from Golkar. Competed in every election since 2014.
NU	Nahdlatul Ulama (Revival of the Ulama). A Muslim democrat party founded in 1952 by leaders from the Nahdlatul Ulama organization who were unhappy with their lack of influence in Masyumi. Competed in the 1955 and 1971 elections. Forcibly fused into PPP in 1973.
PA	Partai Aceh (Aceh Party). A regional, Acehnese party founded in 2007 by Gerakan Aceh Merdeka (The Free Aceh Movement, GAM), a separatist group that fought for Acehnese independence from 1976 to 2005. Competed in every election in Aceh since 2009.
PAAS	Partai Aceh Aman Sejahtera (Prosperous and Safe Aceh Party). A small, regional, Islamist party founded in 2007 by Ghazali Abbas, a singer, and former PPP member. Competed in the 2009 election in Aceh.
Pakar Pangan	Partai Karya Perjuangan (Functional Party of Struggle). A small, nationalist party founded in 2007 by retired Lieutenant General Muhammad Yasin. Competed in the 2009 election. Merged into Partai Demokrat in 2012, but taken over by Partai Kebangkitan Nusantara in 2022.
PAN	Partai Amanat Nasional (National Mandate Party). A Muslim democrat party founded in 1998 by Amien Rais, the chairman of the Muhammadiyah organization. Competed in every election since 1999.
Parkindo	Partai Kristen Indonesia (Indonesian Christian Party). Founded in 1945 by several Christian politicians. Competed in the 1955 and 1971 elections. Forcibly fused into PDI in 1973.
Partai Katolik	Partai Katolik: (Catholic Party). Founded in 1949 when Partai Katolik Republik Indonesia merged with a number of Catholic organizations. Competed in the 1955 and 1971 elections. Forcibly fused into PDI in 1973.

Patriot	Partai Patriot (Patriot Party). A small, nationalist party founded in 2001 by Pancasila Youth who left Golkar. Competed in the 2004 and 2009 elections. Joined PPN in 2011.
PBA	Partai Bersatu Atjeh (Aceh United Party). A small, regional, Islamist party founded in 2007 by Farhan Hamid, an academic and former PAN member. Competed in the 2009 election in Aceh.
PBB	Partai Bulan Bintang (Crescent Star Party). An Islamist party founded in 1998 by Yusril Ihza Mahendra and supporters of the former Masyumi party. Competed in every election since 1999.
PBN	Partai Buruh (Labour Party). A small, nationalist party founded in 1998 by a labor union, Serikat Buruh Sejahtera Indonesia, and its chairman Muchtar Pakpahan. Competed in the 1999, 2004, and 2009 elections. In 2021 the party reformed itself and joined forces with several labor organizations.
PBR	Partai Bintang Reformasi (Reform Star Party). A small, Islamist party founded in 2002 by Zainuddin MZ, an Islamic preacher and other members of PPP. Competed in the 2004 and 2009 elections. Joined Gerindra in 2011.
PDA	Partai Daulat Atjeh (Aceh Sovereignty Party). An Islamist party founded in 2007 by Muslim clerics and graduates of local Islamic boarding schools. Competed in every election since 2009. In 2021 it changed its name to Partai Darul Aceh.
PDI	Partai Demokrasi Indonesia (Indonesian Democratic Party). A nationalist party founded in 1973 when all nationalist and non-Islamic parties were forced to merge. Competed in every election from 1977 to 1999. One faction broke off in 1999 to form PDI-P; the remnants formed PPDI in 2003.
PDI-P	Partai Demokrasi Indonesia Perjuangan (Indonesian Democratic Party of Struggle). A nationalist party founded in 1999 by Megawati Sukarnoputri and her faction from PDI. Megawati had previously been forced out of PDI's leadership position. Competed in every election since 1999.

PDK	Partai Demokrasi Kebangsaan (Democratic Nationhood Party). A small, nationalist party founded in 2002 by a group of intellectuals. Competed in the 2004 and 2009 elections. Joined PPN in 2011.
PDP	Partai Demokrasi Pembaruan (Democratic Renewal Party). A small, nationalist party founded in 2005 by former PDI-P members. Competed in the 2009 election. Joined PPN in 2011.
PDS	Partai Damai Sejahtera (Prosperous Peace Party). A small party founded in 2001. While widely viewed as a reincarnation of Parkindo, it projected a nationalist ideology. Competed in the 2004 and 2009 elections. Joined Hanura in 2013.
Pelopor	Partai Pelopor (Pioneers' Party). A small, nationalist party founded in 2002 and initially led by Sukarno's daughter, Rachmawati Sukarnoputri. Competed in the 2009 election. Joined PPN in 2011.
PIS	Partai Indonesia Sejahtera (Prosperous Indonesia Party). A small, nationalist party founded in 2007. Competed in the 2009 election. Joined PPN in 2011, but eventually merged with Hanura in 2013.
PK	Partai Kedaulatan (Sovereignty Party). A small, nationalist party founded in 2006 by Ibrahim Basrah, a former PPP member. Competed in the 2009 election. Joined PPN in 2011, but eventually merged with Hanura in 2013.
PKB	Partai Kebangkitan Bangsa (National Awakening Party). A Muslim democrat party founded in 1998 by Islamic clerics from Nahdlatul Ulama. Competed in every election since 1999.
PKDI	Partai Kasih Demokrasi Indonesia (Indonesian Democratic Party of Devotion). A small, nationalist party founded in 2006 when several small Christian parties joined together. Competed in the 2009 election. Joined PPN in 2011.
PKI	Partai Komunis Indonesia (Indonesian Communist Party). A communist party whose origins go back to the establishment of a socialist association in Indonesia in 1914. In 1924 it was renamed Partai Komunis Indonesia. Competed in the 1955 election. Violently disbanded in 1965 and banned in 1966.

PKNU	Partai Kebangkitan Nasional Ulama (Ulama National Awakening Party). A small, Muslim democrat party founded in 2006 by Nahdlatul Ulama Islamic clerics and former PKB members. Competed in the 2009 election. Joined a new party, Partai Kedaulatan Rakyat, in 2022.
PKPB	Partai Karya Peduli Bangsa (Concern for the Nation Functional Party). A small, nationalist party founded in 2002 by former members of Golkar and Suharto supporters, including his daughter. Competed in the 2004 and 2009 elections.
PKPI	Partai Keadilan Dan Persatuan Indonesia (Indonesian Justice and Unity Party). A small, nationalist party founded in 1999 by Golkar members. Changed its name to Partai Keadilan Dan Persatuan in 2021. Competed in all elections since 1999.
PKS	Partai Kedadilan Sejahtera (Prosperous Justice Party). An Islamist party founded in 1998 by Islamic activists. It was originally named Partai Keadilan, before taking its current name in 2002. Competed in all elections since 1999.
PM	Partai Merdeka (Freedom Party). A small, nationalist party founded in 2002 by Adi Sasono, a former minister in Habibie's cabinet. Competed in the 2004 and 2009 elections. Joined PPN in 2011.
PMB	Partai Matahari Bangsa (National Sun Party). A small, Islamist party founded in 2006 by activists from PAN. Competed in the 2009 election.
PNBKI	Partai Benteng Kerakyatan Nasionalis Indonesia (Indonesian National Populist Fortress Party). A small, nationalist party founded in 2002 as Partai Nasionalis Bung Karno. Competed in the 2004 and 2009 elections. Joined PPN in 2011.
PNI	Partai Nasional Indonesia (Nationalist Party of Indonesia). A nationalist party founded in 1927 by Sukarno. The party was dissolved, but revived again in 1946. Competed in the 1955 and 1971 elections. Forcibly fused into PDI in 1973. A number of parties claiming to be PNI's heir, formed after the fall of Suharto.

PNIM   Partai Nasional Indonesia Marhaen (Indonesian National Party of Marhaenism). A small, nationalist party founded in 2002 by Sukarno's daughter Sukmawati Sukarnoputri. Competed in the 2004 and 2009 elections.

PPD   Partai Persatuan Daerah (Regional Unity Party). A small, nationalist party founded in 2002 by several members of the unelected upper house, which was being replaced by an elected body. Competed in the 2004 and 2009 elections. Joined PPN in 2011.

PPDI   Partai Penegak Demokrasi Indonesia (Indonesian Democratic Vanguard Party). A small, nationalist party founded in 2003 from PDI. Competed in the 2004 and 2009 elections. Joined PPN in 2011, but eventually merged with Hanura in 2013.

PPI   Partai Pemuda Indonesia (Indonesian Youth Party). A small, nationalist party founded in 2007 by a group of youth activists. Competed in the 2004 and 2009 elections. Joined PPN in 2011, but eventually merged with Hanura in 2013.

PPIB   Partai Perjuangan Indonesia Baru (The New Indonesian Struggle Party). A small, nationalist party founded in 2002 by a prominent economist, Sjahrir, as Partai Perhimpunan Indonesia Baru. Competed in the 2004 and 2009 elections. Joined with another party to become Partai Kedaulatan Bangsa Indonesia Baru in 2012.

PPN   Partai Persatuan Nasional (National Unity Party). A small, nationalist party founded in 2011 through the merger of 12 small parties that previously competed in the 2009 election. Registered for the 2014 election, but was not allowed to compete by the General Election Commission.

PPNUI   Partai Persatuan Nahdlatul Ummah Indonesia (Indonesian Nahdlatul Community Party). A small, Islamist party founded in 1998 by NU Islamic clerics as Partai Nahdlatul Ulama. Changed to its current name in 2003. Competed in the 1999, 2004, and 2009 elections.

PPP	Partai Persatuan Pembangunan (United Development Party). An Islamist party founded in 1973 when all Islam-based parties were forced to merge by Suharto. Competed in every election since 1977.
PPPI	Partai Pengusah Dan Pekerja Indonesia (Indonesian Workers and Employers Party). A small, nationalist party founded in 2002 by several trade unions and business associations. Competed in the 2009 election.
PPRN	Partai Peduli Rakyat Nasional (National People's Concern Party). A small, nationalist party founded in 2006 by a palm oil plantation baron Sutan Raja DL Sitorus. Competed in the 2009 election. Joined Hanura in 2013.
PRA	Partai Rakyat Aceh (Aceh People's Party). A small, regional party founded in 2006 by leftist activists. Competed in the 2009 election in Aceh.
PSI	Partai Sarikat Indonesia (Indonesian Unity Party). A small, nationalist party founded in 2002 by a number of micro political parties. Competed in the 2004 and 2009 elections.
RepublikaN	Partai Republika Nusantara (Archipelago Republic Party). A small, nationalist party founded in 2007 by high ranking military officials Syahrir MS and Djasri Marin amongst others. Competed in the 2009 election. Joined Hanura in 2013.
SIRA	Partai Suara Independen Rakyat Aceh (Independent Voice of the Acehnese Party). A small, regional party founded in 2007 by activists and Aceh's then Vice Governor Muhamad Nazar. Changed its name to Partai Soliditas Independen Rakyat Aceh in 2012. Competed in the 2009 and 2019 elections in Aceh.

1
Introduction

Political leaders of the most diverse ideological strains have been mindful of the common blood component of ethnonational psychology and have not hesitated to appeal to it when seeking popular support.
—Walker Connor, 1993: 382

The idea that ethnicity and democracy don't mix is a widely held assumption. Particularly during elections, it is expected that politicians will mobilize ethnic identities such as race, religion, or tribe, thereby polarizing societies and fostering interethnic strife. Media reports in such countries as India, Iraq, Malaysia, Kenya, and Ghana often describe elections as tense struggles for power and domination between opposing ethnic groups. Sensational statements make the headlines, with leaders valorizing their ethnic kin while denigrating other groups. Popular fears are raised and the risk of interethnic violence increases.

To explain this dire turn of events, the standard narrative blames politicians for politicizing ethnicity, but it also excuses them, claiming that the temptation to "play the ethnic card" during elections is too great. After all, it is natural and easy for leaders to draw on emotional attachments and to use beloved ethnic symbols, myths, and the belief in a common blood to rally fervent support. Stoking fear and prejudice toward an outgroup can be even more effective. Political speeches imbued with historical narratives of persecution, economic hardship, and political discrimination at the hands of a malicious other resonate at a far deeper level than the relatively dull details of policies and platforms. Ultimately, ethnicity is seen as a fixed, unidimensional, and inherently divisive force.[1] So should we just assume that politicians will inevitably exploit ethnic bonds and inherent intergroup prejudice in search of electoral victory?

No, we should not. The actual day-to-day practice of campaigning in ethnically diverse societies is much more complex. A mayoral election in Medan, a provincial city in Indonesia, illustrates this point. Medan is large and ethnically diverse; most of its residents are Muslim, Christian, or Buddhist and indigenously Batak, Javanese, Minangkabau, or Chinese Indonesian. Religious and indigenous events, activities, and rituals form an important part of social life in Medan, and associational life in the city is vibrant. Interreligious and inter-indigenous relations are generally harmonious, although there have been some tensions and incidents of violence in the past. Elections are festive events in the city, and the 2010 mayoral campaign was typical. Colorful rallies took place in Freedom Square, and the city was blanketed with posters of smiling candidates, often dressed in their religious or indigenous garb. While campaigning, candidates spent much of their time canvassing communities door to door, meeting with religious and indigenous associations, and seeking media coverage. Religious and indigenous appeals were prevalent, but the standard narrative of opposing groups facing off in a hostile electoral battle fails to capture the various ways in which religion and indigeneity was actually deployed.

Four observations on the election are noteworthy. First, for most of the campaign it was difficult to recognize any direct competition between identity groups. The ten candidate tickets (for mayor and deputy mayor) that competed in the first round came from various religious and indigenous groups, and most mayoral candidates choose deputies who belonged to indigenous and religious groups different from their own. Second, candidates appealed to a wide variety of groups. Occasionally, a candidate made a narrow appeal to a single indigenous group; others largely targeted their religious identity group; but many chose to reach out, to varying degrees, to religious or indigenous groups to which they did not belong. Complicating things still further, a few candidates largely avoided these identities altogether, and promoted their party label instead. Third, religious and indigenous appeals allowed candidates to connect with their constituents and show that they identified with those citizens' group commitments; they were not used to publicly denigrate outgroups. Finally, although some tensions were raised in the second round of the election, as a Muslim Batak and a Buddhist Chinese were the remaining two candidates, the campaign took place without any violent incidents.

Overall, as an election with an ethnically diverse constituency, Medan's mayoral race was very much intertwined with ethnicity, but in a less conflictual way than we might expect. It illustrated that candidates do indeed seek to connect with groups in ethnic terms, but in many different ways. It also showed that candidates have numerous ethnic cards to play, not just one. Viewed from this perspective, ethnicity appears far less fixed, multidimensional, and not necessarily a divisive force in electoral competition.

1.1. Innovations

In recent years, the literature on ethnic politics has presented new arguments that emphasize the instrumental nature of ethnicity and how politicians and voters mobilize along ethnic lines to gain control of scarce resources such as jobs, patronage, and government revenues. This literature also views ethnicity from a constructivist perspective, taking into account its multidimensional and somewhat fluid nature. According to this approach, individuals have a repertoire of ethnic identities—such as their religion, language, or region—that may be activated in certain situations or at certain times.

In relation to electoral competition, two important arguments have emerged. The first contends that candidates and voters mobilize around one of their ethnic identities if that ethnic group is large enough to achieve electoral victory but avoid politicizing their other ethnic identities that have too little representation in the populace to enable success.[2] Second, when voters and candidates have multiple ethnic identities around which they can mobilize to achieve electoral victory, they will choose the one that is of "minimum winning size." This allows candidates and voters to form a group capable of electoral victory while sharing the economic and political spoils with the smallest possible number of group members.[3] Thus, for example, if a mayoral candidate has a religious affiliation shared by 90% of the population and a language-group affiliation shared by 60%, he or she will tend to mobilize voters around the language-group identity.

In studying Indonesia, I found that these arguments overestimate the effect of "minimum winning size" groups and ethnic group size. Very often, there are not two potentially winning groups from which a candidate can choose the minimum one. They may belong to just one winning group, or maybe even none. But even when there is a minimum winning group, often too much uncertainty surrounds whether one can attain the required high degree of support from the minimum sized group. This uncertainty is exacerbated when more than one candidate is appealing for support from the same ethnic group. Meanwhile, insights on group size—candidates appeal to ethnic groups that are large enough to secure victory but avoid politicizing ethnic groups that are too small—may seem valid. However, in Indonesia, I found that candidates often avoided appealing to their winning ethnic group. This was puzzling. Why would a candidate avoid appealing to a ready-made ethnic group of winning size? Clearly, ethnic group size alone could not explain candidates' choice of ethnic appeals.

In my effort to explain this phenomenon, I found that two additional factors must be considered along with ethnic group size. First, sometimes social constraints, such as stigmas and norms, make it difficult for candidates to explicitly appeal to particular ethnic groups, even if they are of winning size. Some ethnic groups themselves may be uncomfortable with overt ethnic appeals that attempt to mobilize them as a group. These social constraints can vary from country to country or across regions. In the case of Indonesia, I found broad social constraints preventing candidates from making non-Islamic religious appeals publicly.

Second, candidates are often constrained in how they campaign by their political party and its leaders. Some electoral rules give party leaders the power to nominate and allocate party seats. This ability allows them to control candidates' careers and influence their campaigns. Leaders are often thinking more broadly about the party's success, so they may persuade a candidate to emphasize the party's platform rather than appealing to a winning ethnic group in their constituency.

In this book, I build on previous insights regarding ethnic demographics, but I develop an innovative argument that shows how social and political factors can either constrain or encourage candidates' politicization of ethnicity. Another innovation relative to previous research involves how I conceptualize and measure the politicization of ethnicity, and specifically the use of ethnic appeals. Trying to capture campaign appeals in an election, particularly one in a developing country, is challenging. As the example from Medan illustrates, multiple candidates may make a variety of religious, indigenous, and partisan appeals through both paid and earned media—which can be overwhelming for a researcher. As a result, scholars pursuing large systematic studies have usually relied on ethnic voting data to measure the politicization and mobilization of ethnicity. However, voting data tell us more about voter behavior than candidate behavior. If we use ethnic voting to understand candidates, we will need to assume that if a candidate was supported by their ethnic kin, the candidate made ethnic appeals *and* those appeals were successful. Although this assumption might be true, voting data tell us nothing about what appeals candidates actually made—whether they appealed to one of their own ethnic groups, or across ethnic lines, or avoided ethnic appeals altogether.

In developing this book, I took a different approach. First, I created a new classification of the different ways candidates can appeal to ethnic groups. Second, I developed a new argument to explain when, how, and why candidates choose to appeal to particular ethnic groups. Third, I tested this argument using original evidence, gathered from thousands of Indonesian candidates competing in local and national elections in one of the largest and most ethnically diverse democracies in the world. Ultimately, using a methodologically individualist approach, I seek to identify and test the microfoundations that guide candidates' decisions on how and whether to politicize ethnicity.[4]

1.2. The Logic of Ethnic Appeals

1.2.1. Ethnic Appeals

In this book, I employ the convention of using ethnicity as an umbrella term, one that "easily embraces groups differentiated by color, language, and religion; it covers 'tribes,' 'races,' 'nationalities,' and 'castes'" (Horowitz 1985: 53). Ethnicity is viewed as multidimensional, encompassing such dimensions as language and religion, with the number and type of dimensions varying by country. Within each dimension of ethnicity, there are particular ascriptive ethnic categories that individuals are usually born into—for example, Muslim or Christian. I use "ethnic categories" synonymously with "ethnic groups." While "ethnic groups" is an intuitive term, it does have a more unidimensional and fixed connotation. As a result, I will refer to "categories" when I want to emphasize the multidimensional nature of ethnicity.

I define ethnic appeals as campaign messages or signals that invoke ethnicity. They can be deployed explicitly through the use of verbal messages that advocate for an ethnic group or denigrate outgroups. They can also be deployed in subtle ways through the use of ethnic signs, symbols, or coded messages. There are two main varieties of ethnic appeals: bonding and bridging.[5] Bonding describes appeals to ethnic categories to which the candidate belongs. Due to the multidimensional nature of ethnicity, candidates may invoke their religious, linguistic, tribal, or racial identity. When candidates make ethnic bonding appeals, they tend to narrow the breadth of their potential support, but simultaneously tap into ingroup solidarity and the norms of intraethnic reciprocity. Ethnic bonding does not necessarily entail negativity toward outgroups, though that unfortunate feature is sometimes present.

On the other hand, the term "ethnic bridging" describes appeals to ethnic categories to which the candidate does not belong. Bridging also includes appeals to broader identities (such as nationalism in Indonesia) that encompass various religious, indigenous, and regional groups. Bridging appeals usually expand a candidate's potential support, but there is a greater risk of desertion because candidates cannot rely on the bonding effect of shared ethnicity.

Of course, candidates may also make appeals that have nothing to do with ethnic affiliation, such as to women or based on a particular policy stance. I call these appeals "ethnic bypassing."

Often, candidates use a mixture of all three types of appeals. But viewing ethnic appeals in this nuanced way accounts for the multidimensional nature of ethnicity and the varied appeal options available to candidates, and it enables us to understand why candidates tend to focus on some kinds of ethnic appeals more than others.

1.2.2. Candidates

To explain when and why candidates choose to make ethnic appeals, this book places candidates at the center of the analysis. Whereas many studies focus on parties or party leaders, candidates are typically at the forefront of voter mobilization—going door to door, distributing campaign materials, making campaign speeches, and conveying what electing them or their party would mean for local communities. The ethnicization of campaigns is often a local affair, with candidates politicizing ethnicity in some locations but not in others. In addition, when ethnic electoral politics does turn violent, it usually happens in certain locations and is often instigated by local candidates. Our knowledge regarding these actors is particularly sparse in developing countries, due to a lack of systematic studies of local candidates.[6] Overall, an understanding of these actors and how they campaign is critical to understand discern the microfoundations of ethnic politicization during elections.

To study candidates, I first explore the impact of electoral rules on their campaign behavior. To date, a large body of work has focused on the effects of proportional representation (PR) and majoritarian rules on ethnic politics. Although the general theoretical argument has predicted that PR systems should politicize ethnicity more than majoritarian systems, the empirical evidence has been mixed.[7] This book moves beyond the PR/majoritarian debate and draws on insights from the personal vote literature,[8] which has shown that the degree to which the electoral system promotes personal vote strategies affects candidates' behavior in predictable ways. I demonstrate how the electoral system can have far-reaching impact on candidates' decisions to use particular types of ethnic appeals.

From the personal vote literature, we know that electoral rules form a continuum from candidate-centric to party-centric, with personal vote strategies mattering most when the rules are highly candidate-centric. We also know that under candidate-centric rules, such as nonpartisan rules and open-list PR, candidates' success depends on their reputation among voters in their constituency. Voters are most concerned about the candidate's character, responsiveness, and ability to respond to their interests. Meanwhile, party leaders lack mechanisms to reward candidates for their loyalty to the party or to sanction those who don't toe the party line. These rules offer candidates considerable independence as to how they run their campaigns.

In contrast, party-centric rules offer candidates incentives to promote the reputation of their party. Under party-centric rules, such as closed-list PR, candidates' success depends on the attractiveness of their political party and the candidate's loyalty to the party. Party leaders can sanction candidates who veer from the party line and can reward faithful party members. What matters most for voters is the reputation, ideology, and platform of the candidate's party, so voters want to know about parties, not candidates. Under party-centric rules, candidates are less well connected with constituents, and they primarily promote their political party and broader programmatic policies. In contrast, under candidate-centric rules, candidates emphasize their personal attributes, develop close relationships with constituents, pursue particularistic policies, and engage in pork-barrel politics.[9]

Although the personal vote literature has produced a wealth of insights into candidate behavior, it has, surprisingly, not been applied to ethnic politics. This book, however, will show that the personal vote literature, and specifically the distinction between party-centric and candidate-centric elections, provides a valuable conceptual lens through which to understand how candidates use ethnicity in election campaigns.

1.2.3. The Argument

My argument starts with the impact of electoral rules. I argue that the degree to which the electoral rules are candidate- or party-centric affects how ethnicized campaigns are and, ultimately, the kinds of ethnic appeals they make (see Figure 1.1). When campaigning under candidate-centric rules, candidates have incentives to promote their personal reputation among voters in their constituency. To do so, they will often appeal to salient local identity groups. In many multiethnic democracies around the world, particular ethnic identities are the most salient. As a result, candidates will spend much of their time appealing directly to these local ethnic groups. Their ethnic appeals draw on voters' religious, tribal, and regional loyalties. Such candidates frequently visit local ethnic leaders and associations to emphasize their support for those groups. In addition to their ethnic rhetoric, candidates also engage in distributing "pork," or patronage, along ethnic lines. This helps establish a reputation for responsiveness and builds trust with the group. Ultimately, candidates competing under highly candidate-centric rules in countries with salient ethnic identity will tend to make more ethnic appeals.

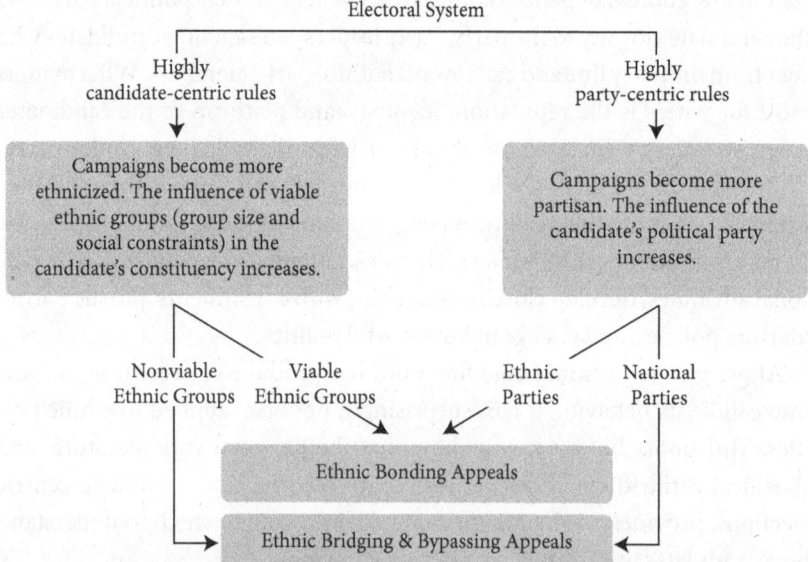

Figure 1.1 The logic of ethnic appeals.

In contrast, under party-centric rules, candidates have greater incentives to emphasize their party affiliation and promote the party's reputation. As a result, these candidates will spend more time and resources appealing to voters' allegiance to, or identification with, their political party. Candidates promote the party by emphasizing its platform and quality of leadership. Some campaigns of this type may contain explicit appeals to ethnic groups that form their party's support base; for example, candidates from Islamic parties might appeal explicitly to Muslims. However, this behavior still derives from the need to campaign on the party label and appeal to party supporters. Overall, candidates competing under highly party-centric rules craft more partisan campaigns.

Although the electoral rules help us understand when a candidate might target local ethnic groups versus party supporters, it doesn't explain whether a candidate will appeal to one or more particular ethnic groups. For example, will a candidate choose to make ethnic bonding appeals based on a shared religious, linguistic, or indigenous identity? Or will the candidate instead make ethnic bridging appeals, trying to reach out to nonethnic kin? To answer this question, we cannot rely on the electoral rules alone. Ethnic appeal choice is also affected by the viability of ethnic groups in the candidate's constituency and by the ideological position of the candidate's party on ethnic issues.

Under candidate-centric rules, candidates can increase their chance of electoral success by appealing to local ethnic groups. However, they need a critical mass of support to win. Due to the multidimensional nature of ethnicity, each candidate has a repertoire of ethnic identities they can appeal to (such as religion, language, or region) and searches this repertoire for an ethnic group that is politically *viable*. An ethnic group is viable when it is large enough to enable the candidate to win the election *and* there are no social constraints on appealing to that group. Social constraints represent any social taboos, stigmas, or norms that place restrictions on the politicization of certain groups. They are important because they can prevent a candidate from appealing to a winning ethnic group. Ultimately, candidates who belong to viable ethnic groups have strong incentives to make ethnic bonding appeals; in all other cases, candidates must expand their support through ethnic bridging or bypassing appeals. We can extend this logic when we consider that candidates operate within societies that have multiple ethnic dimensions (e.g., religion and indigeneity). Take a candidate who is from a large (and viable) Muslim group and also a small (and non-viable) Javanese group. Here, the candidate can engage in both bonding and bridging strategies. However, I argue that candidates in this situation will tend to follow a *bonding-trumps-bridging* heuristic—that they will put more effort into bonding with their religious group compared to bridging across the indigenous dimension.

Under party-centric rules, candidates can also make ethnic appeals, but these appeals are not influenced by the size of local ethnic groups in their constituency. Instead, candidates' ethnic appeals are shaped by their party's *ideology*—by which (unless otherwise indicated) I mean the party's ideological stance on ethnic issues, not its position from left to right on the political spectrum. In multiethnic countries, parties are often rooted in either national or ethnic ideologies. National parties have a multiethnic stance on ethnic issues, so a loyal national party candidate will favor ethnic bridging or bypassing appeals that reach out across ethnic groups. Conversely, ethnic parties define themselves as representatives of a particular ethnic group. Given the broad use of the term *ethnic*, this can include parties defined not only by ethnicity but also by religion, tribe, or race. A loyal candidate from the ranks of one of these parties will tend to bond with the party's favored ethnic group. Figure 1.1 illustrates this argument.

As noted previously, the argument places candidates at the center of the analysis. Their campaigns and ethnic appeals can be influenced by their constituency, specifically by the availability of viable ethnic groups, or by their political party, through its stance on ethnicity. Critically, the degree to which either constituencies or parties shape candidates' appeals is mediated by the political system's position on the continuum from highly candidate-centric to highly party-centric. As the rules become more candidate-centric, the influence of the constituency rises and that of their political party falls; in contrast, more party-centric rules maximize the impact of the party and minimize that of the constituency on campaign appeals. In this respect, the electoral rules act like a dial, turning the influence of the constituency versus the political party up or down.

This argument draws on research that has highlighted the importance of ethnic group size, but it proposes a more dynamic explanation of when, how, and why candidates choose to politicize particular ethnic identity groups in their electoral campaigns. Three factors—electoral rules, ethnic group viability, and party ideology—interact to guide candidates' behavior and provide the microfoundations for their ethnic appeal strategy.

While maintaining parsimony, the argument can explain much of the variation in ethnic appeals. However, to supplement the main argument,

I present three second-level factors that can result in fewer bonding appeals than we would initially expect. First, candidates with a *strong ethnic reputation* for representing a particular (viable) ethnic group may reduce their ethnic appeals so as not to scare off moderates or potential support from other ethnic groups. Second, candidates competing in a *crowded field of co-ethnic candidates* will be concerned that the ethnic vote will be split, so they may use alternative appeal strategies to build support and make themselves stand out. Finally, candidates in *uncompetitive elections* may see less need to mobilize voters along ethnic lines. These three second-level factors can reduce candidates' incentive to bond with their viable ethnic group and instead prompt them to (1) make more bonding appeals that target nonviable groups, or (2) make more bridging appeals, or (3) bypass ethnic appeals.[10] Overall, the main argument coupled with these three important second-level factors explains much of the variation in how and why ethnicity is politicized across different constituencies and institutional environments.

1.2.4. Implications

This research has great practical importance because it shows how institutional design can be used to affect the influence of ethnicity on electoral competition in ethnically diverse societies. This is particularly important when we want to curb contentious ethnic politics. Two institutional mechanisms are important. First, to affect the influence of local ethnic groups vis-à-vis party ideologies regarding ethnic politicization, we can change the degree to which electoral rules are candidate-centric versus party-centric. More candidate-centric rules can often result in the politicization of multiple dimensions of ethnicity because candidates appeal to ethnic groups specific to their constituency, potentially resulting in a greater variety of appeals within and across constituencies. This multiple ethnic politicization can prevent polarization of the electorate along a single gaping cleavage, thereby curbing the most contentious and damaging forms of ethnic politics. Second, to alter in a more targeted way what cleavages (if any) become politicized, we can restrict the formation of ethnic parties or modify the electoral boundaries of constituencies. Changing the boundaries of particular constituencies with contentious ethnic polarization can affect what candidates run for the office and the appeals they make. These implications of the argument offer valuable practical advice on institutional design in ethnically diverse societies.

Finally, we turn to the case of Indonesia, where three qualifications of the argument are warranted. First, it applies to the use of overt, public appeals to mobilize ethnicity. While candidates may make private campaign appeals that are hidden from public view, it is unlikely that these kinds of appeals will seriously affect political competition. Second, the argument applies to elections that require a candidate to mobilize larger networks beyond one's personal network of extended family and friends. Finally, ethnic appeals do not necessarily involve polarizing ethnic rhetoric. Very often, they are used in more benign ways to connect with constituents. However, what causes polarizing forms of ethnic rhetoric to emerge is a crucial issue. Later, in Chapter 9, I will discuss how a culmination of factors that foster ethnic bonding appeals can help to explain why some campaigns become polarized along ethnic lines while others don't. Specifically, I use this extended argument to explain religiously polarizing campaigns in Indonesian elections.

1.3. Why Indonesia?

I test my thesis using electoral campaigns in Indonesia, a tropical archipelago of over 17,000 islands spanning more than 3,000 miles. With a population of over 270 million, Indonesia is the largest country in Southeast Asia, the fourth most populous country in the world, the third-largest democracy, and the largest Muslim-majority democracy. Aside from its sheer size, Indonesia offers an excellent testing ground due to within-country variations in its electoral rules, party ideologies, and ethnic diversity.

The different electoral rules used in Indonesia in recent years enable us to compare and contrast the effect of these rules on candidate behavior. After an armed and diplomatic struggle with the Dutch Empire, Indonesia gained its independence in 1949. Sukarno, the leader of the independence movement, was appointed president, and preparations were made for the first legislative elections, which were held in 1955 under party-centric rules.

These elections, however, did not produce a clear winner, and divisive ideological competition continued over the years, resulting in a slow decline of democracy. This culminated in the rise to power of Suharto, an autocrat who would maintain power for over three decades, an era known as the New Order. During this time, six more legislative elections were held, from 1971 to 1997. These elections remained party-centric, but the system ensured that one hegemonic political party, Golkar, would dominate. A major change came in 1998 with the fall of Suharto and a transition to democracy. In the 1999 and 2004 elections, the rules remained party-centric, but they allowed for genuine multiparty competition.

In 2009, key changes in the electoral rules made the elections more candidate-centric. In addition, Indonesia introduced highly candidate-centric regional head elections at the provincial and sub-provincial district levels in 2005.[11] Since there are differences in the candidate-centric nature of Indonesian elections, I use three terms to describe them. I use the term "party-centric" for the legislative elections before 2009, "semi-candidate-centric" for the legislative elections since 2009, and "candidate-centric" for the regional head elections.

These recent moves toward more candidate-centric legislative and regional head elections allow me to make two main comparisons. First, I can compare legislative campaigns before and after the shift to a semi-candidate-centric formula in 2009. Second, I can compare appeals in these legislative elections with those in the more highly candidate-centric regional head elections. These two comparisons offer an ideal opportunity to study the impact of candidate-centric rules on candidates' campaign strategies and appeals.

A second reason why Indonesia provides a good test of my argument is the presence of political parties with different identity commitments. Specifically, Indonesian parties have either a nationalist, multiethnic ideology or an Islamic ideology. Moreover, the Indonesian party system is primarily defined along these lines. Unlike the West, where parties generally split from left to right on economic ideology, Indonesian parties are centrist on economics. Without the complication of differences in economic ideology, we can see more clearly if and when the party's ideological stance affects candidates' appeals. During the period of study, over 40 nationalist and Islamic Indonesian parties competed for power in legislative and regional head elections. This diversity allows me to test the impact of party ideology on candidates' bonding, bridging, and bypassing appeals across numerous national and Islamic parties.

Finally, Indonesia has a very diverse ethnic landscape of religious, indigenous, and regional identity groups. In Indonesian culture and literature, the term *suku* (ethnicity) is used to refer to groups such as the Batak, Madurese, and Javanese. In this book I use the term *indigenous* for these identities, and I follow the convention in studies of ethnic politics of reserving ethnicity as an umbrella term for descent-based identities.

The emergence of ethnic consciousness and the development of regional and national identities in Indonesia are relatively new. In an early study of local ethnic politics in Indonesia, Liddle (1970: 57) wrote,

> Prior to the twentieth century the ethnic group as a self-perceived, coherent social unit did not exist in Simalungun or in North Sumatra as a whole. Individuals had relations with individuals, lineage groups with lineage groups, and villages with villages, but few regular patterns of interaction existed above this level and there was little sense of belonging to larger social or political units.

Liddle explained that ethnic consciousness developed during the colonial era when modernization—specifically, economic change—improved communications, and missionary activity brought different ethnic groups into contact with each other for the first time. Indigenous and religious identities intensified, but the supraethnic identities of regionalism and nationalism also emerged.[12]

Today, religion and indigeneity are prominent forms of ethnic identification in Indonesia. Practically all Indonesians identify with a religious and an indigenous ethnic category.[13] Social life often revolves around religious and indigenous rituals, ceremonies, festivals, and prayer groups. Ethnic relations have not always been harmonious. Between 1997 and 2002, unprecedented levels of ethnic violence occurred as Indonesia passed through a turbulent transition to democracy, and at least 10,000 people were killed in various conflicts across the country. These conflicts included urban anti-Chinese riots, clashes between indigenous Dayaks and Madurese in Kalimantan, conflicts in Maluku and Sulawesi that fell along Christian–Muslim lines, as well as separatist conflicts in East Timor, Aceh, and Irian Jaya (Papua). The causes of the violence were diverse and tended to be localized, but in a broad sense they were related to a reconfiguration of Indonesia's institutions and the introduction of a new, competitive political system.[14] Although these conflicts have largely been resolved, interreligious and inter-indigenous tensions still exist, particularly in the postconflict regions.[15] Overall, elections have been relatively peaceful, but they have served as triggers for incidents of ethnic and communal violence.

Indonesians have broad regional identities, which are usually associated with one's province or island and often encompass multiple ethnic groups. However, their national identity is even more encompassing. Under the motto of "Unity in Diversity," Indonesians espouse an inclusive national identity that does not exclude groups based on their indigenous language, religion, or regional ancestry.

Given the multiple dimensions of ethnicity, Indonesian candidates have various options in choosing ethnic appeals; the argument outlined above allows us to predict which options they are most likely to pursue. However, to test these predictions, we need to compare appeals across constituencies that vary in terms of indigenous and religious group size. Fortunately, there is plenty of variation across Indonesian constituencies. Most constituencies have a Muslim majority, but many others are mixed or have Christian or Hindu majorities. Nationally, as of 2010, 88% of the population was Muslim, while Christians (Catholics and Protestants) represented 9.8%, and there were small numbers of Buddhists, Hindus, and followers of Confucianism.[16] Indigenous ethnic groups, on the other hand, are more diverse; in fact, the 2010 census identified over 1,000 distinct indigenous ethnic groups. Many are very small, but there are 15 indigenous groups with at least two million members.[17] Most indigenous groups have their own unique language and are concentrated in a regional homeland. However, due to urbanization, internal migration, and state-led transmigration over the years, many regions are inhabited by a variety of indigenous groups. Ultimately, the significant variation in the size of religious and indigenous groups across hundreds of constituencies in Indonesia allows us to determine how ethnic group size affects candidates' ethnic bonding, bridging, and bypassing strategies.

1.4. Research Materials

One of the biggest problems in testing a theory on the politicization of ethnicity during elections is the lack of data on candidates' ethnic appeals. Research that has systematically gathered a significant amount of data on local candidates' ethnic appeals is very rare.[18] To date, measures of the politicization of ethnicity have relied primarily on ethnic vote-share data and political parties' stances on ethnic issues as coded from party manifestos.[19] Neither of these data sources actually measures the appeals made by candidates; rather, they describe voter behavior and party leaders' views. To apply these data to candidate appeals, we would have to assume that all candidates make appeals that are in line with their party's manifesto or that ethnic voting is neatly correlated with ethnic appeals. These assumptions are a bit of a stretch, particularly in large countries with candidate-centric systems and weakly institutionalized parties. To address the lack of data on candidates' appeals, I compiled original datasets of campaign appeals for elections held in Indonesia, using two main sources: newspaper reports and election posters. These datasets were supplemented by qualitative evidence on the politicization of ethnicity in Indonesia, drawn from secondary scholarly research and NGO reports.

To study changes in campaign appeals over time, I analyzed and coded newspaper reports on election campaigns published during five legislative election campaigns from 1997 to 2014. The reports were drawn from the provincial press in North Sumatra. In contrast to national newspapers, which are Jakarta-centric and focus on party leaders, provincial newspapers offer a wealth of information on local candidates' campaigns. These reports are often written by, or in conjunction with, candidates and campaign managers, so they have little editorial voice or political analysis. In this respect, the reports are a good reflection of how candidates appeal to voters from one election cycle to the next.

I coded each report for identity-related appeals, the type of campaign event, and candidate endorsements. This approach provided me with comparative measures of candidates' appeals before and after Indonesia's democratic transition in 1999 as well as before and after the system became more candidate-centric in 2009. The analysis from newspaper reports was confined to North Sumatra, where a number of the same candidates competed repeatedly in legislative elections. Comparing these candidates' campaigns over time helped me control for regional differences and identify how institutions affected candidates' appeals.

In addition to studying provincial press coverage of campaigns over time, I also lived in the province of North Sumatra for a year, traveling to numerous regional head elections and doing extensive interviews. Two important factors drove me to choose this province as a key research site to study ethnic politics up close. First, with a population of almost 14 million, North Sumatra is the most populous province outside of Java, and during the time of fieldwork many regional head elections were scheduled to occur across its 33 constituencies. Second, compared to all other provinces, there was far more variation in the degree of indigenous and religious diversity across North Sumatra's constituencies.

To study the impact of ethnic group size, I needed to gather data on candidate campaign appeals from a large number of constituencies that varied in terms of religious and indigenous diversity. To do so, I used a unique and underutilized source of campaign appeals: election posters. With the assistance of other researchers, I obtained photographs of election posters across the country during the 2009 legislative election and then during the regional head elections held in 2010 to 2012. Additionally, I photographed thousands more posters during elections across the country. This dataset contained over 25,000 poster images. After processing, I identified almost 4,000 uniquely designed campaign posters from 2,152 candidates competing in 129 constituencies across Indonesia. This is the largest collection of unique election posters that has ever been systematically gathered in any country.[20]

In Indonesia (as in many other countries), a proliferation of elaborate, colorful election posters appears on the streets during campaign seasons. Both major and minor candidates use them. Although some posters contain brief textual content, they are primarily a visual medium, communicating through images of the candidate's clothing, background imagery, signs, and symbols. To quantify various aspects of the campaign appeals from the election posters, I coded the clothing, background imagery, and textual messages for each poster. Based on the indigenous and religious identity of the candidate and the content of the posters, I calculated the degree to which each candidate bonded with their own ethnic group (or groups), bridged across other ethnic groups, or bypassed ethnicity by making nonethnic appeals. I used these appeal data to compare the semi-candidate-centric legislative elections with the more fully candidate-centric regional head elections. This allowed me to test the mediating role of party- and candidate-centric rules on party ideologies and ethnic group sizes and, ultimately, their effect on candidates' choice of ethnic bonding or ethnic bridging appeals.

To supplement my newspaper and poster data, I also gleaned information on campaigns from secondary sources. In particular, to understand polarizing ethnic campaign rhetoric in Indonesia's gubernatorial elections held from 2017 to 2020, I drew on an array of scholarly works and NGO reports.

I test my argument against three competing explanations (described in detail in Chapter 3). They focus on the impact of ethnic attachment, cultural modernization, and critical junctures on the politicization of ethnicity. To test my argument and the competing explanations, I had to gather extensive demographic, social, economic, and political data from across Indonesia. This included measures of religious and indigenous diversity, ethnic attachment, economic development, and election results. Furthermore, to test my predictions as to what ethnic appeals a particular candidate would make, I needed fine-grained ethnic demographic data at the constituency level. Fortunately, the Central Agency on Statistics (Badan Pusat Statistik) possesses this information. In the 2010 census, individuals were allowed to self-identify according to ethnicity, offering a truer picture of Indonesia's ethnic landscape. The availability of such data is rare in developing countries.

To attain a broader grounded understanding of Indonesian elections, I made frequent fieldwork trips. On these visits, I attended campaign events and interviewed candidates, campaign managers, journalists, religious and indigenous leaders, and voters during numerous elections in Sumatra, Java, Maluku, and Bali.

Overall, this book differs from other studies that draw on ethnic voting or party manifestos to measure ethnic politicization. Here, I measure and analyze the ethnic appeals of thousands of candidates and how they are affected by electoral rules, ethnic group viability, and party ideology. With this methodology, I can hold country-level variables constant and conduct multiple tests to rigorously evaluate the evidence for each part of the argument.

1.5. Organization of the Book

This book is organized into four main sections: Theory, Data, Evidence, and Implications. Section 1 (Theory) presents the theoretical foundation for the book. In Chapter 2, I discuss different approaches to understanding and measuring ethnic politicization. As I have found no good guides on how to define or measure ethnic appeals, I conceptualize what an ethnic appeal is, in both its explicit and implicit forms. I also introduce the concepts of bonding, bridging, and bypassing as a way to understand ethnic and nonethnic appeals. I show how these categories can facilitate meaningful description of ethnic appeals across various identity categories (e.g., tribe, religion, language) and different types of media.

Having established these concepts, in Chapter 3 I present the main argument, which explains why candidates choose to politicize ethnicity in their election campaigns. First, I review studies on ethnic demographics and the personal vote. Then, building on insights from this review, I introduce my argument that electoral rules, ethnic group viability, and party ideology affect candidates' campaigns and their choice of ethnic appeals. I then examine how the three second-level factors discussed above affect appeals. Finally, I review the three competing explanations.

Section 2 (Data) introduces the Indonesian case and describes my methods of gathering and coding campaign appeals. Chapter 4 provides an overview of Indonesia's elections from 1955 to 2020. Breaking with the conventional approach of comparing Indonesian elections under authoritarian versus democratic regimes, I instead consider the candidate-centric nature of elections. Studying legislative and regional head electoral elections over time, I identify which elections operated under party-centric, semi-candidate-centric, and candidate-centric rules. This three-way classification sets the stage for my comparisons of campaigns under different electoral rules.

Chapter 5 explains how I gathered and coded unique datasets on ethnic appeals. First, I present my approach to sampling newspaper election reports between 1997 and 2014, and explain how I coded these reports with regard to campaign events, endorsements, and appeals. Second, I explain how I gathered and coded election posters from 2,152 candidates competing in elections between 2009 and 2012. After presenting an overview of the ethnic appeal data, I conclude by highlighting and explaining a critical social constraint on appeals to non-Islamic religious groups in Indonesian elections.

Section 3 (Evidence) presents the empirical evidence used to test the argument. It is organized into three chapters, one for each of the key driving factors: the electoral rules, ethnic group viability, and party ideology. Chapter 6 considers the impact of electoral rules on ethnic and partisan appeals. I use two tests to analyze the effect of electoral rules in making campaigns more ethnicized or partisan. First, I draw on the newspaper reports dataset (1997–2014) and examine changes over time in campaign events, endorsements, and appeals. Second, I use the election poster dataset to compare appeals in regional head elections with those in legislative elections. The chapter goes on to show that while the candidate-centric nature of the electoral rules can explain when campaigns become ethnicized, the competing explanations cannot.

Chapter 7 examines how ethnic group viability affects ethnic appeals. First, it demonstrates that in candidate-centric elections, candidates were very sensitive to the influence of ethnic group viability, and that they made ethnic bonding appeals if they were members of a viable ethnic group; otherwise, they chose ethnic bridging or bypassing appeals. Second, I show that across constituencies with varying levels of diversity, the argument can predict the kinds of ethnic identities and cleavages that will become politicized. Third, I explain how the three second-level factors can affect expected ethnic appeals. All these dynamics are illustrated through statistical analysis of the election poster appeals, as well as a number of qualitative examples (including some rather colorful ones) and controlled comparisons between individual candidates.

Chapter 8 analyzes how party ideology can influence ethnic appeal choice. I find that whereas candidates from Islamic parties tended to make religious bonding appeals, nationalist party candidates espoused ethnic bridging and bypassing appeals far more frequently. More importantly, this effect is mediated by the electoral system. Under party-centric rules, candidates looked largely to the party and its ideology to inform their campaign, rather than to the ethnic groups in their constituency. In addition, focusing on the province of Aceh, I find that the ideology of regional parties had a particularly strong impact on ethnic bonding appeals.

Section 4 (Implication) explores several implications of the argument. Chapter 9 focuses on religiously polarizing election campaigns. It begins by recounting the massive, religiously inspired mobilization against the leading candidate in Jakarta's 2017 gubernatorial election—a minority Chinese Christian candidate, Basuki "Ahok" Purnama. Building on the key factors from the main argument, I explain why religious polarization occurs. To test this explanation, I analyze the gubernatorial elections that took place in every province between 2017 and 2020. Finally, I assess the repercussions of Jakarta's election and suggest which constituencies may be most prone to religious polarization in the future.

The concluding chapter highlights the importance of understanding the microfoundations that underlie candidate behavior. It also assesses how Indonesia's candidate-centric system has contributed to the politicization of ethnicity. I close the book with some insights on ways to curb contentious ethnic politics.

I
THEORY

2
What Is an Ethnic Appeal?

Over the last few decades, studies have highlighted the impact of ethnic appeals on many important outcomes. In Africa and Asia, scholars of ethnic politics have shown how appeals can be used to mobilize political support by co-ethnics, sometimes with deadly consequences.[1] In the United States, over the last two decades, scholars of political communications have studied the racially charged rhetoric or "dog whistles" used by politicians to activate racial attitudes. More recently, racial appeals in the United States have been deployed with a veritable bullhorn rather than a dog whistle, and their use has expanded to target Arab Americans, Latinos, and immigrants.[2] Similarly, in Europe, scholars have documented the rise of right-wing populist parties and movements characterized by xenophobic and anti-immigrant sentiments. To garner support, these parties and movements have used text and imagery emphasizing the threat posed by immigrants to the native population's economic well-being, security, culture, and traditional way of life.[3]

However, despite the pressing importance of and the growing literature on ethnic appeals, few scholars have tried to explain precisely what an ethnic appeal is. As yet, there is no standard definition, and we still largely approach the issue of ethnic appeals with an "I-know-it-when-I-see-it" logic.[4]

Before presenting, in Chapter 3, a theory to explain why candidates make ethnic appeals, this chapter conceptualizes what an ethnic appeal is. The chapter contains four parts. Part I defines ethnicity and presents an approach to understanding ethnic identity as composed of different dimensions, such as religion, race, and tribe. Part II, building on studies of racial appeals in the United States and ethnic appeals in other countries, offers a comprehensive definition of an ethnic appeal. In Part III, I argue that ethnic appeals have important bonding and bridging functions for candidates and I describe the steps involved in identifying these types of appeals. Finally, in Part IV, I discuss issues related to the quantitative aggregation of ethnic appeals and the impact of ethnic appeals on political behavior.

Bonding, Bridging, & Bypassing. Colm A. Fox, Oxford University Press. © Oxford University Press 2024.
DOI: 10.1093/oso/9780197743959.003.0002

2.1. Ethnic Identity

Before I present a definition of an ethnic appeal, I must define ethnic identity. There is broad agreement within the field of political science on the use of "ethnicity" as an umbrella term. Horowitz (1985: 53) stated that ethnicity "easily embraces groups differentiated by color, language, and religion; it covers 'tribes,' 'races,' 'nationalities,' and 'castes.'" In this book, I use the "ethnic group" as an umbrella term and draw on a modified version of Chandra's definition.[5] I define an ethnic group as *an identity category in which descent-based attributes are necessary for membership, and one large enough that all members of the group cannot personally know each other*.[6] The central part of this definition is the emphasis on descent-based attributes, which most group members acquire at birth and which are relatively difficult or impossible for individuals to change. This is a minimalist definition; other definitions add features beyond descent-based attributes.[7] Common ethnic identities that contain descent-based attributes are region, religion, language, race, clan, indigeneity, tribe, caste, and nationality. The one difference between my definition and Chandra's is that I include nationality as an ethnic identity category.[8] Beyond their alignment with Horowitz's broad conception of ethnicity, appeals to national identities play an important role in candidates' appeal strategies. As I will explain below, within an ethnically diverse country such as Indonesia, where broadly positive views of nationalism predominate, appeals to national identities are a particular kind of ethnic appeal (akin to patriotism) that enables candidates to reach multiple ethnic groups.

Although this approach to conceptualizing ethnic identity is regularly used by scholars working on comparative ethnic politics, it does have critics.[9] Conceptualizing ethnicity in such an inclusive way may sacrifice important differences between the various dimensions of ethnicity.[10] In Indonesia, for instance, communal conflicts along religious lines have been found to last longer than those occurring along indigenous lines (Davidson 2008a). Meanwhile, in Ghana, Langer (2010) found that religion was particularly important with regard to private life and marriage, but ethnicity (narrowly defined) was more important in public life.

However, although there might be differences between dimensions of ethnicity, the core commonality of having descent-based attributes is key. This feature binds groups together in similar ways, providing a powerful base of identity and group formation. Scholars of ethnic politics have found that politicians can draw on this sense of group cohesion to mobilize support among many descent-based groups.[11] My argument in this book on why candidates make ethnic appeals rests on similar assumptions. However, we must be open to the possibility that different dimensions of ethnicity may affect political competition in unexpected ways. For that reason, in this study I measure and analyze various kinds of appeals (specifically, religious, indigenous, and nationalist appeals) that candidates make.

The following discussion draws on insights from recent constructivist scholarship to offer a clear conceptualization of ethnic identity that lends itself to measurement and comparative analysis.[12] One approach to understanding ethnicity's role in political competition is to differentiate between the structure and activation of ethnicity (Chandra and Wilkinson 2008). Ethnic *structure* is the distribution of populations in different categories, such as religions, tribes, and clans. This structure is reflected in the kinds of demographic data contained in census datasets. With respect to individuals, ethnic structure represents the full repertoire of ethnic categories to which they belong (e.g., Christian, Javanese, Asian). Although ethnic categories can be used to sort individuals, they do not indicate how strongly an individual is attached to a particular ethnic category. In contrast, *activation* of an ethnic category indicates a stronger level of attachment. The activated category is a subset of an individual's overall repertoire of ethnic categories and is often referred to as a salient, mobilized, or politicized ethnicity.

The activation of ethnic categories is strictly contextual. A religious ethnic category, such as Christian, might be activated in private life—for example, in choosing a marriage partner or through participation in religious rituals—but not in political life, such as one's selection of a presidential candidate. In political life, indigenous ethnic categories might be especially activated within societies where employment, political discourse, electoral campaigning, and voting are driven by indigeneity. Importantly, ethnic structure remains relatively fixed but ethnic activation can change (often rapidly) over time, in different contexts, and through the instrumental action of individuals and elites.

This clear distinction between ethnic structure and activation allows us to analyze how structural aspects of ethnicity, such as the size of an ethnic group, can impact the activation of an ethnic category. Drawing on this conceptualization, ethnic appeals by candidates may be viewed as a way to activate particular ethnic categories.

Mapping out the structure of ethnic identity is helpful to understand the range of ethnicities that can be activated. Figure 2.1 illustrates the structure of ethnic identity. Using examples from Indonesia, it shows the hierarchy of ethnic dimensions, categories, and subcategories. Ethnic dimensions are the broadest classification and include examples such as religion and indigeneity. The number and types of dimensions can vary between countries. For example, religion, nation, and region are prominent dimensions in the United States, Thailand, and Indonesia; however, race is more prominent in the United States, language in Thailand, and indigeneity in Indonesia.

Under each ethnic dimension, there exist a number of ethnic categories, which in turn often contain subcategories. For example, the

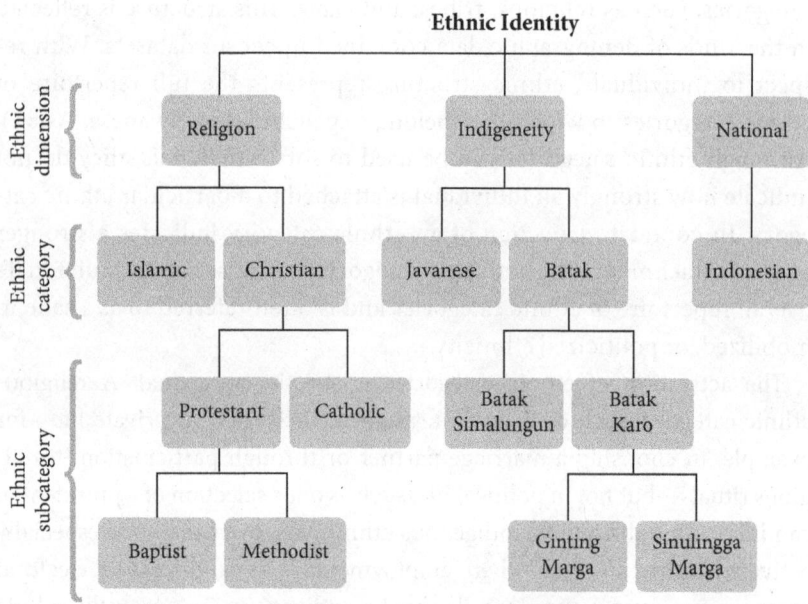

Figure 2.1 Illustration of ethnic dimensions, categories, and subcategories in North Sumatra, Indonesia. The ethnic categories used are for illustration purposes and are not exhaustive; i.e., not all ethnic dimensions and categories are fully mapped into the various ethnic subcategories. Although the Javanese are prominent in North Sumatra, they originate from the island of Java. The Batak originate from North Sumatra and are composed of different subgroups such as the Batak Simalungun and Batak Karo. Within each of these groups are different *Margas* (or clans) distinguished by a family name, such as Ginting and Sinulingga in the case of the Batak Karo.

dimension of religion includes a Christian category, with Protestant and Catholic subcategories, and the Protestant subcategory can be further divided into Methodists, Baptists, and other denominations. An individual's identity is multidimensional, including various ethnic categories that may overlap. Perfect overlap exists if, for example, all individuals who belong to the Islamic religious category also belong to the Javanese indigenous category, and vice versa. Partial overlap, or crosscutting, would occur if members of the Islamic religious category come from two or more indigenous groups. This presentation of ethnic structure is not new, but it helps to clarify the range of ethnic dimensions and categories to which candidates can appeal in their election campaigns.[13]

2.2. Ethnic Appeals

2.2.1. The Study of Ethnic Appeals

Tali Mendelberg is probably the best-known scholar who has informed our understanding of ethnic appeals—specifically, racial appeals. In *The Race Card*, Mendelberg (2001) makes a broad distinction between explicit and implicit racial appeals. She defines an explicit racial appeal as one that uses racial nouns or adjectives to support white privilege, to make anti-Black, racially stereotypical, or derogatory statements, or to portray African Americans as threatening (Mendelberg 2001: 8). As of that time, explicit racial appeals had nearly disappeared in the United States, so Mendelberg's main focus was on implicit appeals.

Implicit racial appeals (or "dog whistles") do not overtly mention race and generally are not consciously recognized as racial in nature. Mendelberg (2001: 9) found that implicit appeals are most effective when they combine language and images to present a conservative stance on an issue that only incidentally implies racial stereotypes or threats from African Americans. In the United States, certain conservative policy stances, such as being tough on crime or the anti-welfare stance, have taken on a racial dimension over time. Mendelberg (2001) argued that candidates can couple these policy stances with racial images to trigger unconscious racial thinking among voters. The most famous example was the 1988 advertisement in which George H. W. Bush's presidential campaign accused opponent Michael Dukakis of being weak on crime. The ad recalled how Willie Horton, a Black convicted murderer, had been released on a weekend furlough in Massachusetts while Dukakis was governor of that state. Horton subsequently escaped, stabbed and bound a man, and raped his fiancée. The narrative, coupled with mugshot images of Horton, played into a racist depiction of Blacks as vile and violent rapists. Over the last few decades, many scholars have studied these kinds of implicit appeals and the gradual racialization of U.S. policy issues, including crime, drugs, welfare, and capital punishment.[14] More recently, Haney López (2015) studied the U.S. Republican Party's use of coded racial appeals to garner support for anti-crime, anti-immigration, and anti-Muslim policies.

In recent years, racial appeals have become increasingly visible in U.S. politics. Although Americans have become more adept at recognizing the coded racial content of implicit appeals, explicit, racially charged discourse has re-emerged since the election of Barack Obama as the first Black U.S. president in 2008. Through a series of experiments, Stephens-Dougan (2020) has shown how Black and white candidates from both major parties use racial rhetoric and imagery to tap into racial stereotypes and to attract support from racially moderate and conservative whites. Moreover, studies have found that negative racial rhetoric describing Arab Americans and Latinos has risen sharply in frequency and that many citizens are no longer angered or disturbed by explicit racial rhetoric.[15]

This literature has informed our understanding of racial appeals by emphasizing the explicit or implicit nature and by showing how they can be effectively deployed through policy messaging using a combination of text and visuals. However, for the purpose of describing what an ethnic appeal is, this literature is limiting for two reasons. First, this line of scholarship has concentrated primarily on racist appeals to whites that draw on a negative or threatening view of another race. McIlwain and Caliendo (2011: 16–17), however, have argued that appeals to race can be either *racist* or *racial*; the difference is that racial appeals do not use anti-minority sentiments. Similarly, Chandra (2011: 161) argued that in making an ethnic appeal, a candidate or party does not have to express opposition to another group. An ethnic appeal merely requires a candidate to identify an ethnic category to champion, in such a way as to prompt other individuals to identify with the category. In run-of-the-mill politics, candidates' ethnic appeals can be more positive, serving to bind groups together through "ingroup love" rather than "outgroup hate."[16] The second critique of the U.S. scholarship is that it has focused largely on race rather than on other ethnic dimensions. However, beyond the United States, research on ethnic mobilization has considered appeals along a wider variety of ethnic dimensions. Kuenzi and Lambright (2015), for instance, studied both ethnic and religious appeals in a study of Nigeria's 2007 gubernatorial election.

Among political scientists working on ethnic politics in countries outside the United States, Gadjanova (2013) has gone farthest in conceptualizing ethnic appeals. She considers ethnic appeals to be a part of ethnic rhetoric, but also linked to ethnic references (e.g., mentions of a group language) and ethnic claims (e.g., a right to speak their own language). Specifically, ethnic appeals are the policies and actions that politicians use to address their ethnic group's grievances. These actions and policies might seek more equality among ethnic groups, call for greater autonomy, or even advocate for outright independence through violent opposition. In this sense, Gadjanova makes a valuable contribution in showing how leaders and parties can appeal to an ethnic group for support by transforming their ethnic grievances into concrete promotion of policy positions or certain political acts.

However, while this approach is useful for finding ethnic appeals in party platforms and leaders' speeches, debates on such issues as ethnic language rights or regional autonomy are rarely central to local candidates' campaigns. Additionally, research has shown that candidates in developing countries tend to campaign less on distinct policy positions and more on valence issues—efforts to distinguish themselves based on their identity, sincerity, and competence (Bleck and Van de Walle 2013). As a result, focusing too heavily on policy positions runs the risk of underestimating the degree to which candidates use ethnicity to mobilize support.

A final critique of previous studies is that they have often ignored cross-ethnic appeals, instead prioritizing politicians' appeals to their ethnic kin.[17] Fortunately, this trend is changing, with some exciting new work on cross-ethnic appeals in recent years. For instance, Collingwood (2020) studied how white Democratic legislators in the United States reached out across racial lines to mobilize Latinos. Meanwhile, Horowitz (2016) and Gadjanova (2017) examined how African presidential candidates appealed to other ethnic groups by holding campaign rallies in these groups' ethnic homelands or by raising ethnic wedge issues and proposing actions to resolve their grievances.

2.2.2. Defining Ethnic Appeals

To provide a comprehensive understanding of ethnic appeals, I discuss four important aspects that characterize them: their mode of perception, means, tone, and ultimate goals. Perceptibility relates to the explicit or implicit nature of appeals. Explicit appeals are clear, direct, and perceived easily; implicit appeals are perceived either unconsciously or only by select individuals who understand the coded nature of the appeal. Candidates and parties can make explicit appeals when they advocate on issues that clearly relate to and offer definable advantages for a particular ethnic category or categories—for instance, a policy to allow the use of an ethnic language in schools or more political autonomy for the ethnic group's homeland. In contrast, implicit appeals are often ambiguous and open to multiple interpretations. This offers candidates a certain amount of leeway or deniability, particularly if the content of a message is interpreted as disparaging by another ethnic group. When challenged on the use of an implicit appeal, a candidate can claim that the disparaging interpretation was not intended. Drawing a firm distinction between explicit and implicit appeals can be difficult, as ethnic appeals lie on a continuum (see Table 2.1).

Ethnic appeals can be expressed implicitly or explicitly in different means: words, visuals, or actions. Speeches, interviews, newspaper articles, online messaging, and party manifestos are common ways in which parties and candidates can make ethnic appeals in verbal and textual forms. Gadjanova (2015), for instance, studied relatively explicit ethnic appeals by coding the ethnic issues that parties promoted in their written manifestos. These issues included language rights, minority rights, affirmative action, the preservation of traditions, territorial rights, secession, and policies to remedy past injustices suffered by ethnic groups. As for more implicit appeals, candidates may discuss their involvement with particular ethnic organizations or make passing references to their clan name, religion, birthplace, the school they attended, or a sports team they support. Or they

Table 2.1 Aspects of Ethnic Appeals

Mode of Perception	Means	Tone	Goal
Explicit	Verbal/textual	Positive	Invoke an ethnic dimension
Implicit	Visual	Negative	Invoke an ethnic category
	Action		Invoke an ethnic subcategory

might use an ethnic language in their messaging, in which case the language itself, not the substance of the message, carries the ethnic appeal. Ricks (2020), for instance, showed how the mere use of an ethnic language by Thai politicians, regardless of the message, powerfully affected constituents' political opinions.

Candidates and parties can also make ethnic appeals through the use of visual images, which can be negative (e.g., images of outgroups such as minorities or immigrants) or more positive (displaying members of the ethnic group from which the candidate is seeking support). Other ethnic-related imagery might include houses of worship, indigenous dwellings, or ethnic designs. A candidate's choice of clothing can also provide an ethnic visual cue.

Another means of making ethnic appeals is actions. This can include personal actions by a candidate, such as eating certain types of food, praying, or engaging in some type of ritual. Strategic campaign actions can also send strong ethnic signals. This category includes selecting campaign locations populated by particular ethnic groups,[18] posting election posters in particular ethnic neighborhoods, seeking ethnic endorsements, and choosing certain media outlets that primarily serve the targeted ethnic group.

Moving to the third category, ethnic appeals can have a positive or negative tone. Candidates and parties can use positive words associated with group stereotypes, advocate for an ethnic group, or valorize a group's achievements and attributes by praising their history, art, culture, or other accomplishments. Alternatively, they can use negative words associated with outgroup stereotypes and make appeals that stigmatize outgroups, denigrate them, or cast them as a threat.

Regardless of the perceptibility, means, or tone of ethnic appeals, their ultimate goal in political competition is to mobilize ethnic support. Building on our understanding of how ethnicity is structured, these appeals can invoke ethnic dimensions, categories, or subcategories. Appeals to an ethnic dimension can be quite inclusive. For instance, in countries where a large majority of the population are religious, though from different faiths, an appeal to religion can potentially target a wide range of individuals. Ethnic appeals may also serve to invoke an ethnic category or subcategory, such as Protestant or Baptist.

Based on this discussion, we can now characterize an ethnic appeal as *an explicit or implicit message, deployed through words, visuals, or actions, in positive or negative ways, with the goal of mobilizing support by invoking an ethnic dimension, category, or subcategory*. This is a comprehensive definition that captures the various ways in which ethnic appeals can function.

2.3. Bonding, Bridging, and Bypassing

When making ethnic appeals, candidates have choices regarding the ethnic dimensions and categories to which they appeal. Their decision allows them to mobilize some groups but not others. As such, ethnic appeals have a delimiting function on the size of a candidate's support base. Posner (2005: 4) in particular emphasized the importance of delimiting the size of a candidate's support base. He argued that candidates (and voters) want to constrain their support to a "minimum winning coalition." In this way, they can share the spoils of victory with the smallest possible group or coalition of groups.

At the most basic level, candidates may use ethnic appeals to mobilize support from their own ethnic group, defining themselves as champions of their ethnic kin through exclusive ethnic appeals. I use the term *ethnic bonding* to describe these appeals. Alternatively, candidates may reach out beyond their ethnic group and take on a more pluralistic image by using inclusive, though still ethnic, appeals.[19] I refer to this approach as *ethnic bridging*. Of course, candidates might eschew ethnic appeals altogether; I call this *ethnic bypassing*. Bonding, bridging, and bypassing are central terms in this book and require further elaboration.

2.3.1. Social Capital and Political Parties

Bonding and bridging are important terms within the social capital literature. Putnam (2002) considered bonding and bridging social capital as the main lines along which social capital varies. As Putnam (2002: 11) explained:

> Bridging social capital refers to social networks that bring together people of different sorts, and bonding social capital brings together people of a similar sort. This is an important distinction because the externalities of groups that are bridging are likely to be positive, while networks that are bonding (limited within particular social niches) are at greater risk of producing externalities that are negative.

So while bonding social capital reinforces homogeneous groups and exclusive identities, bridging social capital fosters heterogenous collectives and inclusivity. Although Putnam measured social capital in various ways (e.g., political participation, group membership, religious participation, informal socializing), he never explicitly explained how these measures of social capital relate to bonding or bridging. This is because, as Putnam explained, he could not find reliable, comprehensive, and nationwide measures that distinguish between bonding and bridging. Ultimately, he concluded that social networks could not be neatly divided into two types but, instead, are at various points on a continuum.

Norris (2004) used the concepts of bonding and bridging to describe the campaign strategies of political parties around the world. Drawing on Norris's work, Reilly (2006a: 18–23) specifically related bonding and bridging to parties and party systems in the Asia-Pacific region. Both Norris and Reilly began by distinguishing between centripetal and consociational political systems. Centripetal systems, which use majoritarian institutional rules, lead to centrist governments and large catch-all parties, which tend to engage in bridging campaign strategies. Parties in such systems depoliticize ethnic identity by reaching out across social cleavages and appealing to multiple identity groups. Norris (2004: 10) defined the bridging campaign strategies of these parties as "designed to gather votes promiscuously and indiscriminately wherever campaign support can be found among diverse sectors of the electorate." She explained that bridging strategies involve building "broad coalitions across diverse social and ideological groups . . . linking different generations, faiths and ethnic identities, thereby aggregating interests and creating crosscutting allegiances."

In contrast, consociational political systems, which use multiparty proportional and consensual institutional rules, lead to greater minority representation and the proliferation of smaller parties, often with an ethnic support base. These parties engage in bonding campaign strategies, mobilizing narrower and more homogeneous social groups such as farmers, ethnic minorities, and environmentalists. Members of such groups usually belong to the same social category and share a religious faith, tribe, class, or ideological beliefs. Bonding strategies use targeted appeals that address the ingroup's interests and values while disregarding other groups or broader kinds of appeals (Norris 2004: 10).

Norris (2004) and Reilly (2006a) used voting and survey data to measure the extent to which parties bond or bridge. They presented anecdotal evidence on bonding and bridging appeals, but neither author systematically measured the appeals themselves. To my knowledge, no prior study has attempted to do so either. In addition, both authors focused on parties rather than local candidates. The broad definitions used in their work make it difficult to measure bonding and bridging in a fine-grained, systematic way. To overcome these challenges, I narrow the focus of bonding and bridging to ethnic dimensions and specify how candidates (rather than parties) bond with or bridge across ethnic groups.

2.3.2. Candidates' Ethnic Appeals

In this book, I apply the concepts of bonding and bridging to individual ethnic appeals made by candidates. One key difference between parties and candidates lies in how they define their identity. A party's identity is defined by the party's platform, the kinds of appeals it makes, and its support base. To identify ethnic bonding and bridging appeals made by a party, we would need to look at the distribution of ethnic appeals and consider the ethnic makeup of the party's traditional support base. With this information, we could determine whether a specific appeal qualifies as ethnic bonding (appealing to the party's ethnic base) or bridging (reaching out to other ethnic groups).

In contrast, the identity of candidates is separate from their campaign platform and appeals. Once we know an individual candidate's ethnicities, identifying whether a particular ethnic appeal qualifies as bonding or bridging is far more clear-cut. An ethnic bonding appeal is aimed at one of the candidate's own ethnic groups to secure their political support; an ethnic bridging appeal targets an ethnic group or groups to which the candidate does not belong so as to achieve broader support. An appeal with no recognizable ethnic content is classified as ethnic bypassing.

The specific process of identifying appeals as ethnic bonding, bridging, or bypassing is shown in Figure 2.2. It illustrates the application of three questions to define an appeal as one of four possible types (there are two types of ethnic bridging appeals).

Ethnic Bypassing Appeals
An answer of "no" to the first question identifies an ethnic bypassing appeal. This type encompasses all nonethnic appeals—for instance, appeals to

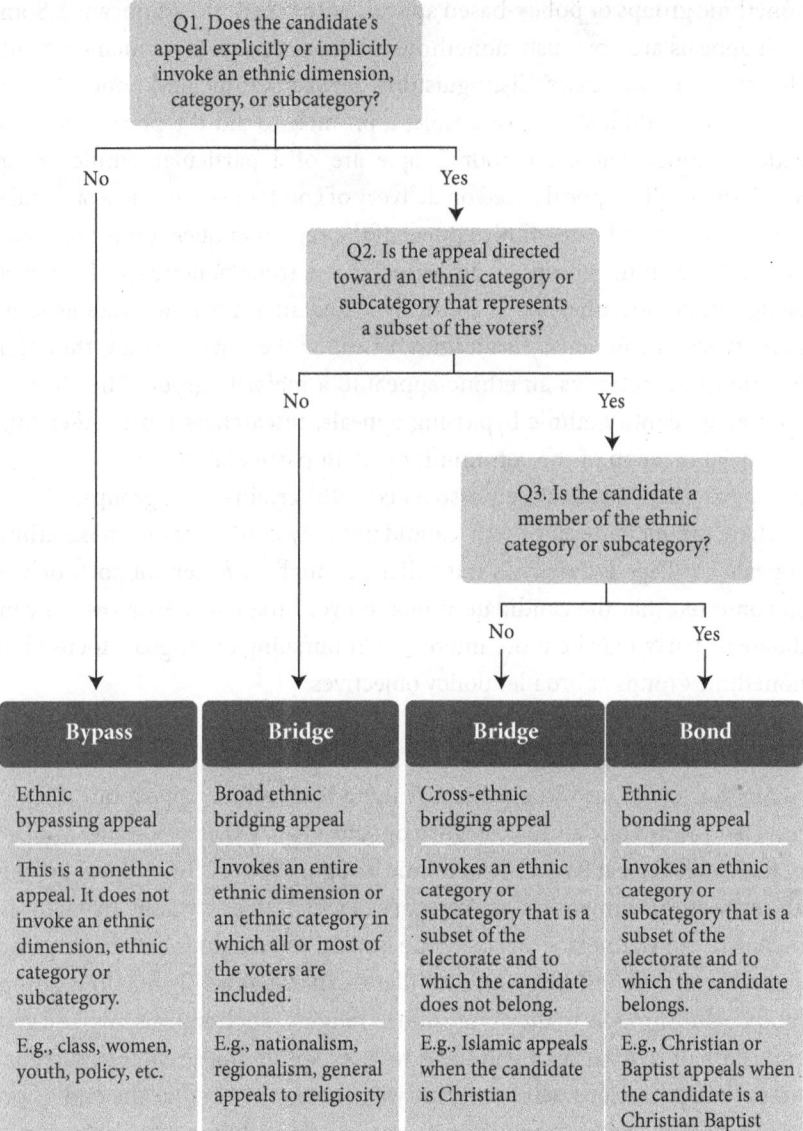

Figure 2.2 Classifying appeals in terms of bonding, bridging, or bypassing functions.

nonethnic groups or policy-based appeals with no ethnic significance. Some such appeals are obviously nonethnic, such as appeals to women or youth. However, in other cases, distinguishing between ethnic and nonethnic appeals is more difficult—for example, a promise to aid the poor, when it is widely known that most poor people are of a particular ethnic group. Similarly, a policy appeal based on delivery of goods or services to a particular region could also be an ethnic appeal, if the region in question is populated by a specific ethnic group. As discussed above, some policy appeals, such as being tough on crime, are often thinly veiled attempts to activate negative stereotypes of migrants, ethnic minorities, or the lower classes; they thus function in practice as an ethnic appeal to a majority group. Therefore, to accurately identify ethnic bypassing appeals, researchers must understand the social makeup of the community and, in particular, the socioeconomic groups or policy issues closely associated with certain ethnic groups.

There are many reasons why candidates may choose not to make ethnic appeals. Perhaps ethnicity is not salient enough to foster support, or it is so contested that the candidate wants to avoid the issue. Moreover, a candidate or party may be more interested in pursuing other goals focused on nonethnic groups or broader policy objectives.

Broad Ethnic Bridging Appeals

In answer to the second question, if there is an ethnic appeal but it is not directed toward any ethnic category or subcategory that represents a subset of the voters, I treat it as a broad ethnic bridging appeal. This appeal invokes an entire ethnic dimension or a category in which all or virtually all voters are included. For example, if an electorate is relatively religious but encompasses a number of different religions, candidates can bridge across religious groups by appealing broadly to the dimension of religion. Such appeals invoke a general sense of religiosity or godliness without specifying a religious category. Many U.S. politicians behave in this way, invoking "God" at the end of political speeches without referring to any specific religion. Similarly, during field research in Indonesia, I found that candidates often made broad appeals to religion without specifying a category such as Islam, Christianity, or Hinduism. In Indonesia, where religious identity is strong across all religious groups, this approach represents a broad ethnic bridging appeal. However, in countries where large sections of the electorate are not religious, an appeal to religiosity would not be a broad ethnic bridging appeal because it would exclude a large number of voters.

In multiethnic countries, an appeal to national identity can have a broad ethnic bridging function. This is particularly true in countries where nation-building emphasizes national identity as a new identity category that includes, but does not try to assimilate, existing ethnic categories. Wimmer (2013: 51) referred to this as a "frequent variant of nation-building [that] proceeds by emphasizing a higher layer of ethnic differentiation that corresponds to the population of a state and thus superposes existing ethnic, regional, or racial divisions."

Examples of multiethnic countries with an encompassing national identity include the three largest democracies in the world: the United States, India, and Indonesia. In these countries, candidates can reach out across a diverse electorate of multiple races, religions, language groups, and indigenous groups by appealing to their one commonality: a shared national identity. In the United States, this sentiment is commonly referred to as patriotism, but in Indonesia the term "nationalism" has similar positive connotations.[20] The Indonesian national motto is "Unity in Diversity," and national holidays are reserved for all state-sanctioned religions.[21] In this context, where the vast majority of voters have a strong national identity[22] but can still maintain separate religious and indigenous ethnic identities, Indonesian candidates can use nationalist appeals to bridge religious and indigenous divides in their constituencies. Moreover, beyond mobilizing voters, broad ethnic bridging can have positive effects on interethnic relations. Studies have found that priming nationalism can help to soften boundaries between ethnic groups, foster altruism across ethnic lines, and focus ethnic members' attention on national policies that benefit the broader group.[23]

Regional appeals by a candidate can also constitute broad ethnic bridging if voters in the region are from different ethnic groups but share a regional ethnic identity. Unless there has been recent large-scale regional migration, voters in the constituency will tend to share the regional identity. Within these regions, candidates can reach out across ethnic groups by appealing to this common regional identity.

In sum, broad ethnic bridging appeals are appeals to ethnic dimensions or categories that are widely held and shared by voters within the constituency. These kinds of appeals are relatively safe for risk-averse candidates because they pursue support from multiple ethnic groups without running the risk of antagonizing any particular group. In contrast, cross-ethnic bridging is a riskier tactic.

Cross-Ethnic Bridging Appeals

A cross-ethnic bridging appeal invokes an ethnic category or subcategory that is a subset of the electorate and to which the candidate does not belong. Cross-ethnic bridging appeals enable candidates to reach beyond their ethnic groups. It may involve campaigning in the neighborhoods of other ethnic groups, placing advertisements in newspapers read primarily by other ethnicities, or seeking endorsements from other ethnic leaders. Cross-ethnic bridging can be a difficult campaign strategy because of the possibility that appeals to other ethnic groups might reduce support from the candidate's own ethnic group. Accordingly, we might expect this tactic to be more common among ethnic minority candidates who, out of necessity, must appeal to the majority and to multiethnic constituencies.

Ethnic Bonding Appeals

Finally, ethnic bonding appeals are the core of ethnic politics. They invoke an ethnic category or subcategory that is a subset of the electorate and of which the candidate is a member. Ethnic bonding appeals draw on ingroup solidarity and tap into a ready-made support base, particularly when candidates have grown up in a relatively homogeneous ethnic region and have strong personal ties with the community. In these cases, candidates may also feel an inner sense of obligation to represent their group in government, as well as a sense of legitimacy in doing so (Lindberg 2010). However, there is a potential risk that other ethnic groups (or members of the candidate's own group who disapprove of their ethnicity being used for political purposes) may be antagonized by ethnic bonding appeals.

2.4. Aggregating and Quantifying Ethnic Appeals

Candidates have choices as to when they will make ethnic bonding appeals. First, they choose the ethnic dimension to which they will appeal. In Indonesia, the primary choice is between religion and indigeneity. Candidates can make broad appeals to religiosity that are inclusive of all those who are attached to any major religion. Within an ethnic dimension, candidates can then choose an ethnic category or subcategory to which they will appeal (e.g., Christian or Islamic, or a particular Christian denomination). However, it is often more advantageous to broaden the appeal to a higher-level ethnic category (e.g., Christian), as these appeals unite subgroups under a larger shared ethnic category. In particular, candidates tend to appeal to higher-level ethnic categories when constituencies are enlarged, when the electoral rules require broad support, and when ethnic categories contain many ethnic subcategories.

Ethnic appeals can be measured in various quantitative ways. For example, after coding a candidate's speech for religious bonding, bridging, and bypassing appeals, we could then report the proportion of each type. Alternatively, we could code ethnic appeals from each ethnic dimension in the speech and calculate the proportion of appeals along each ethnic dimension. We could also aggregate proportions of ethnic appeals across candidates, parties, or constituencies; alternatively, we could look for changes over time.

In contrast to such quantitative approaches, some scholars believe that discursive analysis and thick description provide a more fruitful way to understand the politicization of ethnicity.[24] Indeed, studies employing such approaches have offered tremendous insights into ethnic politics, using narrative formats and multiple interpretations that draw on stories of heroes and villains, national monuments, history, past battles, engagement in rituals, and so forth.[25] These different methods can also be combined. An edited volume on measuring identity (Abdelal et al. 2009) argued that we can effectively engage in quantification through diverse methods, such as surveys, content analysis, and experiments. Laitin (1998) used a combination of content and discursive analysis to study changes in identity terms used in newspapers. Various authors cited in this chapter employed content analysis of campaign materials to measure the ethnic, multiethnic, or nonethnic identities of political parties.[26] Also, many studies of U.S. politics have quantified issue-based, racial, and ethnic campaign appeals from newspapers and television advertisements.[27]

One reason for the larger number of quantitative studies in the United States is the availability of campaign data. Many local newspapers are available online, and campaign television advertisements have been collected and transcribed for researchers by initiatives such as the Wisconsin Advertising Project. In later-developing countries, researchers often must painstakingly gather these data themselves, which is not always feasible, so they rely on voting data or illustrative evidence of campaign appeals.[28] Overall, the problem is not that we are unable to quantifiably measure ethnic appeals, but that we usually lack comprehensive data from which to make measurements.

Some might contend that even if ethnic appeals could be quantified, such measures are worthless because campaign appeals are merely empty rhetoric with little persuasive effect.[29] However, given that candidates continue to spend considerable time and resources crafting and communicating ethnic appeals, the suggestion that ethnic appeals have no persuasive effect is difficult to support. On the whole, candidates know their audience; therefore, it is not unreasonable to assume that ethnic appeals have some persuasive value. As Riker (1990: 57) explained, "We assume that experienced rhetors know something about how persuasion works.... If they then use a particular technique frequently, we can infer that this technique is believed to be persuasive. Furthermore if many rhetors use the technique, it is then widely believed to be persuasive."

Beyond these assumptions, a number of laboratory and real-world survey experiments have confirmed that candidates' campaign messages do affect electoral support. Studies have found that the use of particular kinds of imagery, music, and repetitive messaging can foster participation, persuasion, and increase candidate support.[30] In addition, racial and anti-immigrant appeals by candidates have been shown to activate racist attitudes and subsequently increase candidate support.[31]

Moreover, the importance of campaign rhetoric and appeals can go beyond influencing voting behavior by affecting policy preferences and interethnic relations. McCauley (2014) found that priming ethnicity tended to evoke concerns for access to material goods whereas priming religion caused individuals to prioritize policies related to behavior and morals. Also, Helbling et al. (2013) found that party rhetoric regarding cultural diversity had an effect on generalized trust between a nation's native-born and immigrant populations.

2.5. Conclusion

The information in this chapter offers two broad contributions to our understanding of and ability to measure ethnic campaign appeals. First, this chapter has presented a clear definition of an ethnic group and has laid out the structure of ethnicity. It has explained how ethnic appeals vary in terms of their mode of perception, means, tone, and goals. This information reveals the complex nature of ethnic politicization and the various ways candidates can invoke ethnicity in their campaigns.

Second, the chapter has introduced the important bonding and bridging functions of ethnic appeals. It has explained how to identify the different types of appeals and their functions, along with why these functions are important. Bonding and bridging functions allow us to summarize and compare ethnic appeal strategies, regardless of the particular ethnic categories to which candidates appeal. In this approach, important ethnic categories are not identified a priori; instead, politically salient ethnic categories become evident from the distribution of ethnic appeals made by candidates.

These measures allow us to summarize and compare candidates' ethnic appeals in different contexts, across regions, by political party, and over time. Such analyses paint a more realistic picture of the variation in their ethnic appeals. Furthermore, they enable us to answer important questions about the kinds of ethnic appeals candidates use to mobilize ethnic groups in particular times and places. Last but not least, these analyses help us understand why candidates choose to politicize some ethnic categories but not others.

3
The Logic of Ethnic Appeals

The use of ethnic rhetoric to mobilize groups is often a prominent part of election campaigns in old and new democracies alike. Importantly, the mobilization of ethnic groups through targeted rhetoric can polarize societies along ethnic lines and can have detrimental effects on a number of important outcomes, such as economic growth, political stability, interethnic relations, democratization, and conflict.[1] So why do electoral candidates make ethnic appeals, and how do they decide whether to appeal exclusively to their ethnic kin, reach out across ethnic lines, or avoid ethnic appeals entirely?

Ethnic politicization has been a major area of academic study for decades, with much research revolving around the proposed inherent detrimental effects of ethnic diversity and the relevance of institutional design. Several prominent early works found that ethnically diverse societies were associated with lower levels of democracy and higher levels of instability and conflict.[2] Rabushka and Shepsle (1972) contended that in multiethnic societies, ethnic groups become polarized due to enduring differences over public policy, and that they are unwilling to share power. Electoral contests tend to spiral out of control as leaders woo ethnic groups through a process of "ethnic outbidding," whereby they take on increasingly extremist policy positions and rhetoric. This ultimately results in ethnic conflict and the demise of democratic governance. Although this argument has received some criticism, policymakers and journalists still frequently contend that ethnically diverse countries (and the ethnic hatreds they allegedly spawn) are the main cause of democratic decline and conflict.[3]

Another large body of literature has looked at institutional design, particularly the choice between proportional representation (PR) or majoritarian electoral systems and how each interacts with ethnic diversity. One view is that PR politicizes ethnicity because it fosters ethnic parties, whereas majoritarian rules depoliticize ethnicity by encouraging more nationally oriented parties.[4] However, the empirical evidence to support this view is mixed.[5] In addition, much of the PR–majoritarian debate has focused on governance and conflict *after* elections and not on election campaigns themselves.[6]

Moving beyond previous work on ethnic diversity, in this chapter I build on newer constructivist work that considers how the multidimensional nature of ethnic demographics affects the mobilization of ethnicity. In addition, rather than engaging with the PR-majoritarian debate, I draw on the personal vote literature to understand how electoral systems affect candidate behavior.

This chapter contains three parts. In Part I, I discuss findings from the ethnic demographic and personal vote literatures and how they can help us interpret candidates' ethnic appeals. In Part II, I present my argument, which is composed of three main explanatory factors—electoral rules, ethnic group viability, and party ideology—and three second-level factors. I explain how these factors guide candidates' behavior, providing the microfoundations for their ethnic appeal strategy. Finally, in Part III, I present some competing explanations for how candidates choose to make particular types of ethnic appeals.

3.1. Ethnicity and Electoral Competition

3.1.1. Ethnic Demographics

Ethnic demographics, especially the size of ethnic groups, is an important factor in explanations of conflict. Studies have found that multiethnic countries with a majority ethnic group were more likely to experience the politicization of ethnicity, leading to violence, civil war, and even state collapse.[7] These studies suggest that in situations of ethnic dominance, the government and the ethnic majority often cannot credibly commit to protecting ethnic minorities; rather, they often have incentives to politicize ethnicity and exploit minorities. In contrast, other studies have found relatively low levels of ethnic politicization, instability, and conflict in countries with higher levels of ethnic diversity, such as India, Papua New Guinea, and Indonesia (Hardgrave 1994; Reilly 2000, 2001). Large-N studies have also found that very ethnically diverse societies are no more prone to conflict than highly homogeneous ones (Collier and Hoeffler 1998; Collier 2001).

In recent years, research on the politicization of ethnicity during electoral competition has taken into account the multidimensional nature of ethnicity. This approach considers how individuals have a repertoire of ethnic identities—such as their religion, language, or region—that may be activated in certain situations or times. Importantly, these studies have found that politicians and voters strategically choose which of these ethnic identities to politicize.[8]

Two important arguments have emerged from studies of electoral competition. First, it has been argued that candidates and voters mobilize around one of their ethnic identities if that ethnic group is large enough to achieve electoral victory, but avoid politicizing their other ethnic identities that are too small to attain success.[9] Second, it has become widely accepted that when candidates and voters can choose from two or more possible winning groups, they will choose the one that is of "minimum winning size."[10] For example, a white Protestant candidate in a single-member district composed of 80% whites and 60% Protestants would be expected to appeal to voters based on the candidate's Protestant identity. This allows the candidate and supporters to form the smallest possible group capable of electoral victory, thereby sharing the economic and political spoils with the smallest possible number of group members.

Although the study of ethnic politicization has provided important insights, various concerns remain, particularly with regard to the empirical findings. First, to date, research has relied largely on ethnic voting data or anecdotal evidence as proof of the politicization of ethnicity. There are virtually no systematic studies of what ethnic appeals candidates actually make. As a result, we are unable to understand when candidates actively politicize particular ethnic categories. I will return to this point in Chapter 5.

Second, and as mentioned in Chapter 2, until recently research on ethnic politics has tended to focus narrowly on the politicization of candidates' ethnic kin.[11] Scholars have rarely considered how ethnic demographics might affect candidates' efforts to reach out to groups they do *not* belong to. Some new research, however, has begun to correct this oversight. Collingwood (2020), for instance, argued that as the U.S. population has grown more diverse, there has been an increase in white candidates' bridging appeals to Latinos. In addition, Horowitz (2016, 2022) contended that the high level of diversity in Kenya has prompted presidential candidates to appeal to ethnic groups without a candidate in the race. Similarly, Gadjanova (2017) argued that in elections in Kenya and Zambia, presidential candidates appeal to ethnic groups to which they do not belong when these groups are a regional majority and when they can be targeted with a salient ethnopolitical wedge issue.

Besides these concerns, the situations where the "minimum winning size" logic works are actually quite limited. Seldom are there two groups large enough to be considered winning from which a candidate can choose the minimum one. This is particularly true in constituencies with a few ethnic groups and when elections require candidates to win a large portion of the vote (e.g., single-member districts). But even when a candidate has the option to choose the "minimum winning group," there is often simply too much uncertainty in electoral outcomes to select the minimum winning group and feel confident of victory. This uncertainty is heightened when other candidates are also seeking support from the same ethnic group. Notably, the concept was initially proposed by Riker (1962) to explain the formation of minimum winning governing coalitions *after* elections.[12] Its application to the mobilization of ethnic groups *before* elections is quite risky because one cannot know in advance if one will get full support from the selected "minimum winning group."

Finally, although it may seem logical to rely on the basic insight that candidates appeal to ethnic groups large enough to secure victory and avoid politicizing smaller ethnic groups, there are two good reasons why candidates may not appeal explicitly to a winning ethnic group: social constraints on appealing to particular groups and the influence of a candidate's political party.

As for social constraints, various kinds of restrictions, rooted in history or social norms, can block the politicization of a specific ethnic dimension or category, preventing candidates from appealing to particular ethnic groups. For example, Laitin (1986) showed how colonial discourse restricted the politicization of religious identities among the Yoruba in Nigeria. Moreover, in Chandra's (2012) edited volume, scholars described various restrictions on the politicization of ethnic groups and coalitions. Petersen (2012), for instance, demonstrated that social stigmas and negative emotional content attached to an identity group can prevent those ethnic identities from becoming politicized.

Social constraints can also affect how appeals are conveyed. Mendelberg (2001) argued that norms of equality in the United States constrain the use of explicitly racist appeals. As a result, politicians sometimes turn to implicitly racist appeals, which are not consciously interpreted by voters as racist. Mendelberg found that implicit racist appeals were more effective in mobilizing white support because they can trigger unconscious racial thinking. However, as noted in Chapter 2, Valentino et al. (2018) have argued convincingly that Mendelberg's model of implicit racial appeals no longer holds, as many U.S. citizens are no longer angered or disturbed by explicitly racial appeals. This example reminds us that social constraints and the forms they take are not fixed; they can be challenged and can change over time.

In addition, social constraints vary not only across countries but also across constituencies. Collingwood (2020) highlights how particular U.S. constituencies' tendency toward racial intolerance can constrain white candidates from appealing to Latinos. Although these candidates may desire to pursue Latino votes, they fear that appealing to Latinos might incite underlying racial hostility among their base and result in a backlash. More particularly, in recent years, Republican candidates, relative to Democrats, have become more constrained as their base has grown increasingly hostile to Latinos and illegal immigration (Reny et al. 2019; Valentino et al. 2013).[13] In sum, social constraints rooted in particular histories and social norms can shape the kinds and forms of ethnic appeals that candidates can make.

Political parties can also influence candidates' campaigns. In particular, when the party and its leaders wield significant power over a candidate's electoral success and career, they can greatly shape the candidate's campaigns and appeals. Often, parties want to mold candidates' campaigns so that they are more in line with the party's platform and ideological outlook. In taking this direction, candidates might have to forgo a campaign targeting a winning ethnic group in his or her constituency. To understand when political parties might influence candidates' campaigns, I draw on insights from the personal vote literature. This literature focuses on the effect of electoral rules on candidate behavior—specifically, whether candidates promote themselves rather than the party's collective identity.

3.1.2. The Personal Vote

The personal vote literature helps us understand how electoral rules structure competition in a way that also affects the attractiveness of parties and candidates in the eyes of voters and, in response, how candidates mobilize support. The spectrum of electoral rules ranges from highly candidate-centric at one end to highly party-centric at the other. Compared to party-centric rules, candidate-centric rules increase the importance of candidates among voters, and these rules offer candidates more independence in their campaigns by reducing party leaders' ability to reward or sanction candidate behavior.

The degree to which elections are candidate- or party-centric is largely defined by a number of electoral rules that affect how candidates are nominated, how voters vote, and how seats are allocated. Carey and Shugart (1995) ranked legislative electoral systems along a continuum in terms of the degree to which they encourage candidates to invest in their personal reputation. To do so, the authors used a discrete number of variables to create an ordinal ranking system. Each variable affects the degree to which an electoral system is candidate-centric or party-centric.

The first variable considers how candidates are nominated. Elections are more candidate-centric when party leaders have less control over nomination and ranking—for example, if independent candidates can get on the ballot by collecting signatures and if party leaders do not control the ranking. In contrast, elections are more party-centric when party leaders control the endorsement of candidates and their ranking in electoral list systems. The second variable concerns how votes are counted and how seats are allocated. When all candidates win seats based entirely on their own votes, the system is more candidate-centric. In contrast, if votes are first pooled within parties to determine who wins seats, the system is more party-centric. The third variable focuses on how voters vote. When they can vote for a specific candidate, the electoral system is more candidate-centric; when they can cast their vote only for a political party, the system is more party-centric.[14]

I should note that using these variables to measure the degree to which electoral rules are candidate-centric is not an exact science. Cary and Shugart (1995) added that other factors besides electoral rules can affect the candidate-centric nature of elections. Meanwhile, other scholars have used somewhat different approaches to measuring candidate-centric systems. For instance, Samuels (1999) highlighted additional rules in studying the candidate-centric nature of Brazilian elections, while Norris (2004) put more emphasis on the structure of the ballot and the voting options available to voters in a comparative study.

Evidence from the personal vote literature shows that voters' expectations and candidates' level of independence can affect candidate behavior in predictable ways. Under candidate-centric electoral rules, the candidate's personal reputation is most important, and voters are most concerned with the candidate's character, responsiveness, and ability to meet their needs. Candidates in this situation enjoy greater independence in how they campaign. They have strong incentives to use personal vote strategies, tending to highlight their personal attributes, develop close relationships with constituents, help solve constituents' problems with the government bureaucracy, pursue particularistic policies for their constituency, and engage in pork-barrel politics.[15] Under these rules, candidates' success depends largely on their ability to develop highly personalistic relationships with their constituency.

Under party-centric rules, on the other hand, the party's reputation, ideology, and platform are most important. Voters want to know about parties, not the individual candidate, and the success of candidates depends heavily on the party's performance. Therefore, candidates have less independence as to how they campaign; they have strong incentives to toe the party line and to build strong relationships with party leaders. They are also less closely connected with constituents, and they primarily promote their political party and broader programmatic policies.

Most of these findings come from developed countries such as the United States, and the studies have not explicitly examined the effect of candidate-centric rules on ethnic politics.[16] However, research suggests that candidate-centric rules might have an important effect on ethnic politics in the developing world. First, in many developing countries, pork-barrel spending and patronage are frequently distributed based on ethnic affiliation. Moreover, scholars have argued that the politics of pork and patronage is well suited to ethnic politics and the organization of electoral competition along ethnic lines.[17] Laitin and Van Der Veen (2012: 341) summed it up: "If pork is up for grabs, ethnic identities become more politically salient." Second, we know that candidate-centric elections offer strong incentives for pork-barrel spending and patronage. Combining these two insights suggests that in countries where ethnicity is salient, candidate-centric elections could exacerbate an already ethnicized politics of pork, thus increasing the politicization of ethnic identities.

Pomper (1966) offered some empirical evidence that connects candidate-centric rules and the politicization of ethnicity more directly. He compared nonpartisan (candidate-centric) and partisan (party-centric) U.S. municipal elections, finding that under candidate-centric rules, the candidates were responsible for financing and organizing their own campaigns. Untethered from the party label, they more frequently engaged in ethnic mobilization to attain support, campaigning through ethnic associations such as Italian social organizations, Black churches, and local ethnic media. This pattern ultimately resulted in higher levels of ethnic voting.

3.2. The Argument

My argument takes a methodologically individualist approach, focusing on candidate decision-making. It identifies three important factors that largely determine whether and how candidates appeal to ethnic groups: the electoral rules, the viability of ethnic groups in the candidate's constituency, and the ideology of the candidate's political party. Each will be discussed in turn.

3.2.1. Electoral Rules

Distinguishing between candidate-centric and party-centric electoral systems can help us understand candidates' ethnic campaign strategy. Under candidate-centric rules, candidates have more freedom to control their campaigns and tend to look to their constituents' concerns. They have strong incentives to promote their personal reputation and to mobilize members of organized groups at the local community level. In contrast, under party-centric rules, a candidate's campaign strategy is largely dictated by the political party.

These incentives result in either candidate-centric or party-centric campaign strategies. Under candidate-centric rules, candidates appeal directly to members of organized local groups. Depending on the society, these groups may be ethnic or nonethnic. However, in many multiethnic democracies around the world, ethnic groups are the most organized and salient groups at the local level, with the result that candidates have strong incentives to appeal to ethnicity. Campaign strategies in these contexts stress ethnic identity, character, work experience, local community service, and personal connections with local groups and institutions. Candidates also organize more intimate campaign events with particular ethnic and community associations, seek endorsements from the leaders of these entities, and verbally emphasize their support for such groups. Candidates appeal for votes based on their personal success stories; they display their image prominently in campaign materials, openly express their individuality, and stress their personal connections with local ethnic and community groups. Appealing to local groups and emphasizing personal attributes help to establish a personal reputation as responsive and build trust with the targeted groups.

Under party-centric rules, candidates' campaigns emphasize their connection to the political party along with the party's performance, platform, ideology, and quality of leadership. They participate in rallies with party leaders and fellow candidates, seek endorsements from regional and national party leaders, and make verbal appeals to the party faithful. These appeals can come in various verbal, visual, and symbolic forms. For example, they may reiterate the party's successes in their political speeches or newspaper interviews, prominently display the party's logo, color, and symbols in their campaign literature; dress in party clothing while campaigning; or appeal directly to party leadership by reproducing the leader's image and statements in their campaign materials.

For an illustration of this argument regarding candidate-centric and party-centric campaigning, see Figure 3.1.

Of course, candidates can and do use both types of appeals in their campaigns. However, they place greater emphasis on party-centered campaign strategies when the rules are highly party-centric. Conversely, as the rules become more candidate-centric, candidates de-emphasize the party; in addition to promoting their personal attributes, they direct their campaigns towards organized groups (often including ethnic groups) at the local level.

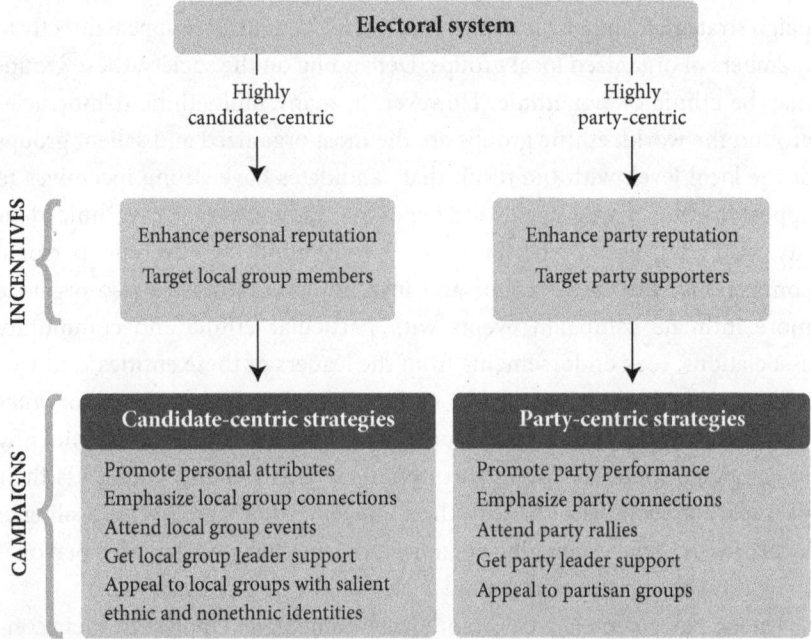

Figure 3.1 Electoral rules and candidates' campaign strategies.

THE LOGIC OF ETHNIC APPEALS 51

Electoral rules can be used not only to explain candidate-centric and party-centric campaign strategies, but also as a starting point to explain the types of ethnic appeals that candidates make—specifically ethnic bonding, bridging, or bypassing appeals. In the next two sections, I further discuss how the candidate/party-centric nature of electoral rules shapes the types of ethnic appeals candidates make.

3.2.2. Viable Ethnic Groups

Figure 3.2 (left side) illustrates the conditions under which candidates, operating under candidate-centric rules, can either bond with their ethnic group,

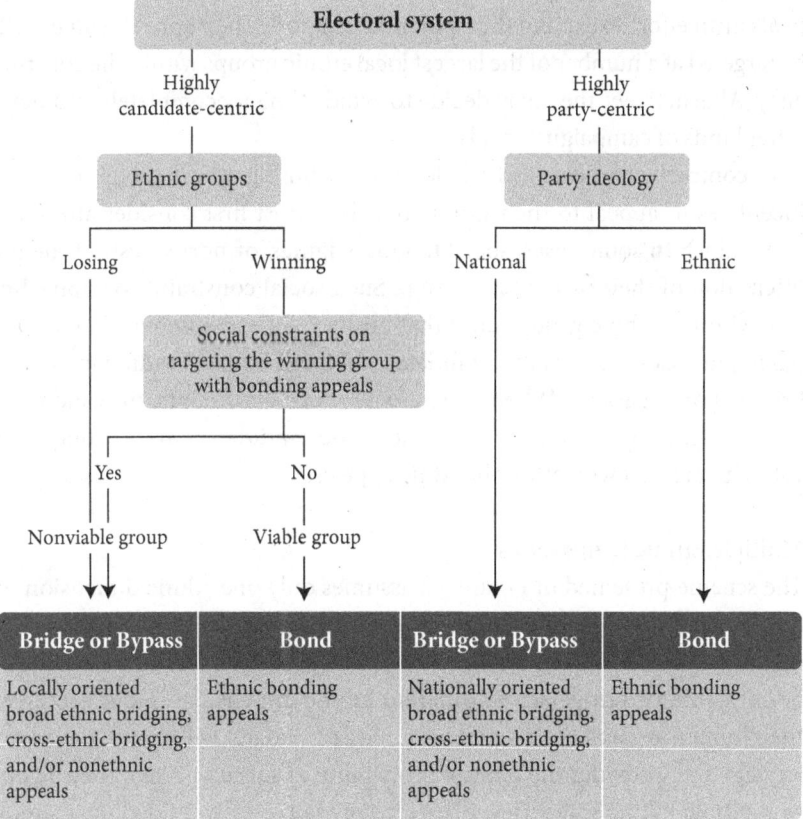

Figure 3.2 How candidates choose ethnic bonding, bridging, or bypassing appeals.

build bridges to other ethnic groups, or bypass ethnicity altogether in their campaigns. The figure depicts a candidate belonging to either a losing ethnic group (i.e., one whose support is insufficient to decide an election) or a winning ethnic group that could, by itself, propel the candidate to victory. The actual size of a winning ethnic group depends largely on the electoral system.[18] Candidates competing in majoritarian electoral systems with single-member districts and runoffs will generally need support from a larger ethnic group than candidates in proportional systems with multimember districts; in the latter type of system, a candidate can win a seat with a smaller proportion of the district's vote.

Once an estimation is made of what percentage size constitutes a winning or losing ethnic group, a candidate can determine whether an ethnic group is viable. Candidates who belong to a losing ethnic group must seek support from other ethnic groups; therefore, they tend to make ethnic bridging appeals in an effort to expand their potential support. Their appeals will usually be targeted at a number of the largest local ethnic groups within the constituency. Alternatively, they may decide to avoid ethnicity completely and make other kinds of campaign appeals.

In contrast, candidates who belong to a winning ethnic group may have incentives to appeal to their group, but they must first consider any social constraints. In some cases, social taboos, stigmas, or norms restrict the politicization of their own ethnic group. Such social constraints on appealing to a winning ethnic group cause that group to become nonviable for campaign purposes. As a result, candidates will forgo ethnic bonding in favor of bridging or bypassing. When there are no social constraints, the candidate's winning ethnic group is politically viable, and candidates have a strong motivation to target it with ethnic bonding appeals.

Multiple Ethnic Dimensions

The scheme presented in Figure 3.2 assumes only one ethnic dimension. In reality, candidates belong to multiple ethnic categories (e.g., religious, indigenous, linguistic) and can draw on this repertoire of ethnic categories to bond within or bridge across different ethnic dimensions. However, given their limited amount of time and resources, candidates will choose the appeal strategy that provides the highest probability of success. When they belong to multiple ethnic categories, their strategy is typically guided by a simple heuristic: *bonding-trumps-bridging*. If, for example, a candidate belongs to a politically viable religious group and a nonviable indigenous group, that candidate will focus on bonding with the religious group. Less time will be spent bridging across indigenous groups, because appealing across ethnic lines is a particularly demanding and risky strategy, for multiple reasons.

First, material factors can inhibit the success of cross-ethnic bridging. Due to expectations of ethnic favoritism, candidates often struggle to effectively or credibly target non-co-ethnics with material benefits (Huber 2017: 3–4) or policy objectives. With regard to patronage, clientelistic appeals and vote buying are more effective with members of one's own group (Kramon 2017; Wantchekon 2003). In addition, co-ethnic candidates can more credibly communicate that they are informed about and committed to advancing any specific policy interests that are important for their ethnic groups (Collingwood 2020).

Second, in-group social and psychological factors can also inhibit cross-ethnic bridging. Often, politicians face social pressures to take care of their own ethnic group and lose status and prestige if they fail to do so (Lindberg 2010). Voters also have a psychological predisposition to vote for their ethnic kin due to an expressive voting logic (Barreto 2007; Horowitz, 1985). Studies have found that voters have a strong interest in electing candidates who look like them and share their ethnic identity (e.g., Barreto, 2010).[19] Additionally, the social environment of networks can influence voting choices (Nickerson 2008; Sokhey and McClurg 2012). These findings suggest that individuals may be influenced to vote for co-ethnics by the ethnic networks in which they are embedded. In contrast, when candidates appeal to nonethnic kin, they cannot rely on shared psychological ethnic attachments or social networks, so the chances of voter desertion are greater.

Third, intergroup rivalries, competition, and distrust may undermine the effectiveness of cross-ethnic bridging, as an appeal to one group may antagonize another group from whom the candidate is also seeking support (Nteta and Schaffner 2013). Bridging appeals are inherently risky in that they might be viewed as threatening by the candidate's co-ethnic base and result in a backlash.[20]

Having established the impact of viable group membership and the bonding-trumps-bridging heuristic, we can now characterize the expected appeal strategies of candidates in a multidimensional ethnic setting under candidate-centric rules. Consider the example of an environment with two salient ethnic dimensions, labeled A and B, where each candidate is from a particular A group and B group. Table 3.1 distinguishes the four possible scenarios for candidates based on the viability of their ethnic groups. In the

Table 3.1 Candidates with Two Ethnic Identities and Their Appeal Strategies

Viable Groups	Candidate Type	Dominant Appeal	Secondary Appeal
A and B	Viable dual-group candidate	Bond with group A and/or B	
A	Viable A group candidate	Bond with group A	Bridge across or bypass B dimension
B	Viable B group candidate	Bond with group B	Bridge across or bypass A dimension
None	Nonviable dual-group candidate	Bridge across or bypass A and B dimensions	

first scenario, the candidate belongs to a viable A group and a viable B group; this candidate has incentives to bond with either group or both groups. I refer to this category as "viable dual-group candidates." In the second scenario, the candidate belongs to a viable A group only. Considering the bonding-trumps-bridging heuristic discussed above, the dominant strategy for this candidate is to bond with the A group, and a secondary appeal is to bridge across ethnic groups in the B dimension, or to bypass ethnic appeals in the B dimension altogether. The same logic applies to the third scenario, except the candidate's B group but not the A group is viable. In the final scenario, the candidate belongs to no viable ethnic groups and thus has no incentive to make any bonding appeals. Instead, these candidates will engage in ethnic bridging strategies or bypass ethnicity altogether.

Table 3.1's illustration of an environment with two salient ethnic dimensions is relatively simple, but it demonstrates how the viability of candidates' ethnic groups can be used to predict not only whether they will make ethnic bonding or bridging appeals, but also with which ethnic groups they will seek to bond or bridge. The scheme can be modified by including additional ethnic dimensions to which candidates belong. Also, in determining ethnic group viability in a particular context, other group parameters, such as social constraints and the estimated percentage of the population that constitutes a winning group, can be considered.

I should also note, that while I expect the bonding-trumps-bridging heuristic to apply in the vast majority of instances, it is not an iron-clad rule. In certain situations, other factors can prompt candidates from viable groups to choose more bridging or bypassing strategies than we would expect. Below, I discuss three second-level factors that can produce this result.

Ethnic Diversity

A further implication of the logic of ethnic appeal strategies concerns how they help to explain patterns of ethnic appeals across districts with different levels of ethnic diversity. Knowing the sizes and viability of ethnic groups within constituencies allows us to predict ethnic appeal dynamics even when we don't know the identities of individual candidates. This is because the size and viability of groups will tend to result in particular kinds of candidates, who will make predictable appeals when running for election.

The key is to know the size of the largest ethnic group (with no social constraints on appealing to it) and whether it is of winning size. Figure 3.3 illustrates the range of possibilities. The horizontal axis represents the size of the largest ethnic group and whether it is of losing or winning size. The vertical axis measures the degree to which candidates in the constituency will make ethnic bonding, bypassing, or bridging appeals. On the left of the figure, the size of the largest ethnic group is small. Consequently, all ethnic groups in these constituencies will also be small and of losing size, so no candidate will be a member of a viable ethnic group. The argument predicts that candidates facing this situation will usually engage in bridging appeals or bypass ethnicity altogether. To illustrate this expectation, the solid bonding line in the figure is low, while the dotted bridging and bypassing lines are higher.

As we move from left to right in Figure 3.3, we arrive at constituencies that have an ethnic group of potentially winning size. In these constituencies,

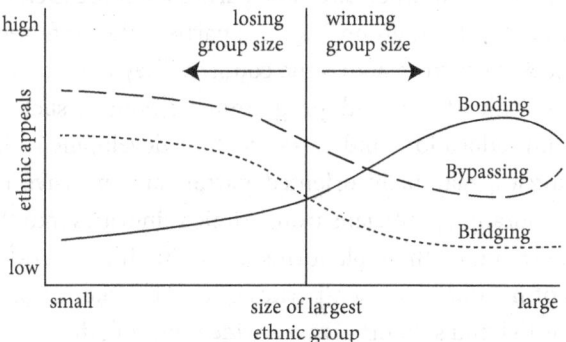

Figure 3.3 Expected change in ethnic appeals across constituencies, based on the size of the largest ethnic group. Constituencies range from ethnically diverse to homogeneous along any ethnic dimension. The figure assumes no social constraints on appealing to the largest ethnic group.

more candidates from the larger ethnic group will enter the race, and they will have incentives to increasingly target their ethnic kin with bonding appeals and to abandon bypassing and bridging strategies. Once we approach the right edge of Figure 3.3, where one group constitutes a large majority of the population, I postulate a change in the trajectory of appeals. In this case, all candidates in the race will likely come from the same dominant ethnic group. Since candidates can no longer use their ethnicity to differentiate themselves from their competition, some will make nonethnic appeals, possibly based on policy, gender, occupation, or party affiliations. Therefore, bonding appeals plateau and eventually begin to decrease as the dominant ethnic group becomes larger. Conversely, ethnic bypassing appeals will bottom out and then begin to rise. Meanwhile, ethnic bridging appeals will bottom out and stay flat, as there are no incentives to appeal to small ethnic groups when one ethnic group is so dominant.

3.2.3. Party Ideology

Figure 3.2 (right side) illustrates the bonding, bridging, and bypassing appeals we can expect from candidates operating under party-centric rules. In this system, party ideology is key. At a most basic level, the ideological nature of parties can be differentiated in terms of how ethnically inclusive or exclusive they are.

National parties in ethnically diverse countries usually have an inclusive, multiethnic orientation, whereas ethnic parties are more exclusive, oriented toward a particular ethnic group. National parties (often referred to as catch-all parties) seek votes from across the country. They tend to be centrist and to promote middle-of-the-road, programmatic policies such as economic growth, health, education, and infrastructure development. In ethnically diverse countries, nationally oriented parties are inclusive of all ethnic groups, incorporating politicians from ethnic minorities into the party and campaigning on multiethnic platforms. In multiethnic countries that have civic forms of nationalism, such parties often promote nationalism or patriotism so as to build support across a wide range of ethnic groups. Studies have found that priming a positive sense of nationalism can help to soften boundaries between ethnic groups, foster altruism across ethnic lines, and focus ethnic members' attention on national policies that benefit the broader group.[21] Scholars generally have a positive view of national parties, because they foster interethnic peace and function as the glue that holds ethnically diverse countries together.[22]

Under party-centric rules, candidates in national parties have strong incentives to draw on the party's national and multiethnic ideology and make nationally oriented appeals. One option for candidates from these parties it to highlight broad programmatic policies and bypass ethnic appeals altogether. Another option is to make ethnic bridging appeals in search of support from multiple ethnic groups across the country. In ethnically diverse societies, celebrating the country's ethnic diversity is often a cornerstone of national party ideology and commonly shows up as part of campaign appeals. Candidates use cross-ethnic bridging appeals and invoke multiple ethnic groups so as to make a favorable impression on a diverse population. Additionally, in diverse countries where nationalism has wide positive connotations, national parties and their candidates use nationalist appeals as a form of broad ethnic bridging aimed at many groups at once. By using nationalist symbols (e.g., the flag, a map of the country, national monuments) and nationalist rhetoric, and by emphasizing a national identity, national parties and candidates can expand their potential support base. In fact, Norris (2004) explicitly defined national parties as bridging parties.

We must exercise care in categorizing political parties as national. There is a crucial distinction between *national* parties, which often use nationalism to invoke a broad positive and inclusive sense of national pride within a multiethnic society (as described above), and more radical *nationalist* parties that make nationalist appeals in an exclusionary fashion, casting outgroups, such as immigrants and minorities, as outsiders. These nationalist parties are effectively ethnic parties, presenting themselves overtly as champions of a particular ethnic group to the exclusion of others. In this respect, the behavior of nationalist parties is actually in line with Chandra's definition and discussion of what constitutes an ethnic party.

Chandra (2004:3) defines an ethnic party as "a party that overtly represents itself as a champion of the cause of one particular ethnic category or set of categories to the exclusion of others, and that makes such a representation central to its strategy of mobilizing voters." This more exclusionary stance informs ethnic (or nationalist) parties' strategy of mobilizing voters. In contrast to national parties, being more ethnically exclusive narrows ethnic parties' potential support base but allows them to draw on a shared ethnic identity, which may foster high loyalty among their target group. Such parties act as representatives of the group and pursue policies that cater to the ethnic group's cultural, political, and economic interests. They promote an ethnic ideology and invariably nominate candidates with the same ethnic background. The symbols associated with the party (such as the party's color and logo) often have ethnic connotations.[23] In addition, ethnically oriented parties advocate for their ethnic group in campaigns, emphasize group-specific issues, and often use the group's language in their campaign messages.

Under party-centric rules, candidates in these parties have strong incentives to draw on ethnic ideology and to make appeals to the favored ethnic group. These ethnic appeals have a bonding function, targeting members of the same ethnic group and playing on their sense of attachment to the group.[24] Candidates incorporate ethnic appeals by reiterating the party's ethnic slogans, repeating the party's stance on ethnic issues, and replicating the party's ethnic symbols and use of ethnic language in their campaign materials. As a result, ethnic parties are bonding parties. Even among ethnic parties, some will engage in ethnic bonding more than others. Evidence suggests that regionally-based ethnic parties are particularly prone to mobilizing ethnic groups (Brancati 2006). Meanwhile, ethnic parties that compete nationally will have more incentives to somewhat moderate their ethnic appeals.

In sum, under party-centric rules, candidates' ethnic appeals are guided by the ideology of their political party. Candidates in national parties will make appeals that bypass ethnicity or bridge across ethnic groups; those from ethnic parties will make appeals that bond with the favored ethnic group.

3.2.4. Second-Level Factors

I expect that a candidate's choice of ethnic appeals will be largely explained by the three factors discussed above—electoral rules, ethnic group viability, and party ideology. These factors and their interaction constitute a relatively parsimonious argument. However, it is still probabilistic in nature and will not explain every candidate's choice of ethnic appeals. Candidates can use a range of appeals, which may include ones that the argument doesn't predict. To supplement the argument and add some nuance, I highlight three additional factors that, for candidates in certain contexts, can have a second-level effect on appeals. All three factors will encourage more bonding with nonviable groups, as well as more bridging and bypassing, than we might expect from the main argument.

The first factor concerns candidates who enter a race with a *strong ethnic reputation* for representing a particular (viable) ethnic group who loyally supports them. Candidates with this reputation may fear scaring off moderates or potential voters from other ethnic groups. As a result, they have incentives to reduce their ethnic bonding appeals. The second factor concerns competing in a *crowded field of co-ethnic candidates*. When multiple co-ethnic candidates are all appealing to the same (viable) ethnic voting bloc, they have incentives to try to stand out from the crowd by appealing to voters in alternative ways. The third factor concerns competing in an *uncompetitive electoral contest*. Intuitively, one would expect that in a tight race, a candidate may be prone to "play the ethnic card" through ethnic bonding appeals.[25] Conversely, uncompetitive electoral contests should make ethnic bonding appeals less necessary.

These three second-level factors can offer incentives for candidates to abandon or at least reduce their ethnic bonding appeals. Instead, candidates can make three other kinds of appeals. First, they can make bonding appeals targeting an alternative, nonviable ethnic group to which they belong. For instance, a candidate from a viable Muslim group might choose to appeal to indigenous kin, even though the group is too small to be politically viable by itself. Second, candidates may reach out to other ethnic groups with bridging appeals,[26] as long as they believe that those appeals won't prompt a backlash from their co-ethnics.[27] This can be a particularly good option if the other ethnic group does not have a candidate in the race.[28] Finally, perhaps the safest approach is to bypass ethnicity altogether and appeal to voters based on a nonethnic identity category (e.g., youth or women), a partisan identity, or more programmatic policy appeals.[29] Candidates may combine several such strategies.

Before I turn to competing explanations for ethnic appeal choice, three qualifications of the argument are warranted. First, the argument applies to the use of overt, public appeals to mobilize ethnicity.[30] Candidates' private campaign appeals might be different. In the presence of a small, receptive audience, and when out of earshot of other groups, a candidate might feel more able to ignore social constraints on certain kinds of appeals. However, this qualification is of relatively limited significance, because if a form of ethnic rhetoric must be continually hidden from public view because of the risk of backlash, it is unlikely to seriously affect political competition or cause interethnic strife. Second, the argument applies to elections in which candidates need a significant number of votes. In situations where 500 or 1,000 votes are enough to secure a seat, mobilizing personal networks of extended family, friends, and colleagues, or even vote buying, would likely be a more effective and reliable strategy. Appealing to ethnicity is useful when candidates need to mobilize larger networks that they cannot reach through personal contacts or vote buying alone. Finally, the argument applies to ethnic bonding, bridging, and bypassing appeals as defined in Chapter 2. These appeals do not necessarily involve negative or polarizing ethnic rhetoric. In fact, in most cases, no polarizing rhetoric is present. However, in Chapter 9 I will apply my main argument to explain when ethnic bonding appeals can become divisive and polarizing.

3.3. Competing Explanations

There exist competing explanations of why candidates politicize ethnicity in particular ways. I organize them around three prominent driving forces: ethnic attachment, cultural modernization, and critical junctures. Scholars who have written on these factors take a largely constructivist view of ethnicity, which contends that identities are constructed at some point, that they can change to some degree over time, and that one's level of attachment to ethnicity can also vary.[31] However, there is some disagreement among scholars as to the relative ease and speed with which ethnic identity can change over time. Most students of ethnic attachment and cultural modernization see ethnicity as quite durable once it has been constructed. In contrast, scholars writing on the impact of critical junctures view ethnicity as more fluid, suggesting that given certain constraints, there is greater opportunity to instrumentally alter ethnic identities.

3.3.1. Ethnic Attachment

Journalistic accounts of interethnic contestation have popularized the notion that ethnic attachment can lead to divisive ethnic politics and violence.[32] Scholars from the fields of anthropology, sociology, and psychology have also emphasized the importance of ethnic attachment, or the salience of ethnicity, and how it can be politicized. In the political sociology of Weber and

Geertz, ethnic identities are seen as reflections of traditional loyalties. Ethnic identities are always culturally relevant, and this naturally flows into being politically relevant. From this perspective, culture and politics are inherently interconnected.[33]

Other scholars who take socio-psychological approaches have emphasized the importance of ethnic attachments and their impact on the behavior of politicians and the electorate. According to this perspective, forms of ethnic identification are driven by an inherent need for group formation and are passed down through a process of socialization in early childhood (Elliott 1986; Volkan 1988). Consequently, the essence of ethnicity is a psychological bond that joins and differentiates groups of people; it is a subconscious conviction of its members and an intrinsic part of our makeup. Connor (1993) emphasized that ethno-nationalist leaders know this and elicit support by appealing to these emotional attachments through ethnic symbols, music, and poetry. Accordingly, people respond to the emotionally potent ethnic symbols that politicians evoke (Kaufman 2001).

Moreover, prominent psychological research by Tajfel (1982) claimed that people have strong tendencies to compare their group to others in order to find a basis for favoring their own group and thereby raise their self-esteem. Drawing on these insights, scholars such as Horowitz (1985) argued that ethnic groups are inherently competitive and that the political behavior of groups is often driven by concern not just for self-esteem but for the group's very survival. This level of concern makes it easy for politicians to mobilize the electorate for ethnic voting and other forms of divisive behavior.

One problem with these theories is that they draw a direct line from the social salience of ethnicity to its political salience. As a result, they have difficulty explaining why some socially salient ethnic identities become politicized while others do not. For instance, in Nigeria, Laitin (1986) found that the religious faith of Christian and Muslim Yoruba was an important part of social life and socially salient. As a result, he expected that a contentious religious wedge issue (a parliamentary debate on a proposal for a Sharia Court of Appeal) would politicize religion among the Yoruba. However, a religious divide among the Yoruba did not occur; in other words, social salience did not lead to political salience. Another issue concerns the scholarly works which highlight the competitive and conflictual aspects of ethnic groups. Most of this research was written in the 1970s and 1980s and based on Tajfel's (1982) claims that ethnic groups inherently reflect discriminatory urges to gain self-esteem. Hale (2008: 17–20) points out that these claims have been undermined by more recent research in psychology. Despite these critiques, the view that socially salient ethnic identities become readily politicized remains an intuitive alternative explanation of why candidates make ethnic appeals.

3.3.2. Cultural Modernization

One of the older explanations of the politicization of ethnicity comes from cultural modernization theorists.[34] Although modernization arguments vary in their emphasis on particular aspects of economic change (e.g., industrialization, the spread of capitalism, or the rise of mass print media), they are all rooted in the impact of structural economic change on culture. This cultural transformation, in turn, affects forms of identification and has a profound effect on political competition and electoral behavior. The main structural economic change is a shift from a traditional agrarian society to an industrial society.

Traditional agrarian societies survive primarily on farming, fishing, and unskilled work; literacy rates are low, and few opportunities exist for social mobility. Individuals are closely connected to their family and local community and have strong ethnic and religious identity attachments. A shift toward capitalism and the manufacture of industrial goods results in migration to cities, urbanization, social mobility, an expansion of the middle class, an increase in prosperity, higher levels of literacy, and growth in mass media. As workers move to the cities, they mix with people from different backgrounds. This leads to the development of a common language and a common national identity that unite the workforce. Modernization theorists posit that these experiences gradually reshape forms of identification. Traditional ethnic identities, such as local indigenous, religious, and linguistic identities, weaken and are replaced by class, occupational, and national identities.[35]

One critique of modernization theory states that the slow rate of change in forms of identification cannot explain rapid changes in the politicization of ethnicity. In particular, the gradual move from indigenous and religious identities to class-based and national ones is not consistent with the experiences of postcolonial countries. After successful wars for independence and the colonial powers' withdrawal, many independence movements split along ethnic and religious lines.

In addition, other scholars have challenged the older modernization arguments that workers living and working in modern cities have weaker ethnic and religious identities than those in the rural hinterland. These scholars have argued that, because industrialization and urbanization entail more competition for jobs, workers and leaders in modern sectors and living in urban areas have greater incentives to exploit ethnic group membership to attain economic resources and political power. Thus, modernization can actually strengthen and politicize ethnic identities.[36] In one way or another, modernization may result in different identity attachments for individuals working in traditional sectors and living in rural areas compared with those employed in modern sectors and living in urban areas. This claim may provide an alternative explanation of why candidates make certain kinds of ethnic appeals in some districts but not others.

3.3.3. Critical Junctures

Finally, some scholars have argued that critical junctures can have dramatic effects on the politicization of ethnicity. Critical junctures—times of abrupt structural shocks such as economic collapse, social upheaval, regime change, and war—are particularly detrimental to interethnic relations.[37] These turning points can alter intergroup power relations, intensify contestation over differing cultural values, and increase competition over policy and access to resources.

Many scholars have focused on the transition to democracy as a major critical juncture that triggers ethnic mobilization and conflict. Mansfield and Snyder (1995, 2002, 2005), who have done the most prominent work in this area, connect democratization with the politicization of nationalism and ethnicity through the actions of aspiring politicians. In emerging democracies with weak institutions, politicians use belligerent ethnic and nationalist rhetoric to mobilize electoral support along ethnic lines. Although this rhetoric helps politicians to attain support, it also increases the risk of ethnonationalist conflict.[38]

Other scholars have reported similar findings. Examining transitions to democracy in multiethnic states in Africa, Asia, and the former Soviet Union, Reilly (2006b) highlighted the emergence of ethno-nationalist parties—that is, parties that drew their support from one ethnic group or region and espoused nationalist or separatist agendas. Meanwhile, several works have linked democratization with ethno-nationalist mobilization and ethnic conflict in multiethnic countries.[39]

In sum, these scholars' work suggests that at critical junctures in multiethnic countries, politicians frequently appeal to voters' fears and turn electoral politics into a competition between ethnic groups. Although critical junctures may not always result in the politicization of ethnicity, we can test whether it created incentives for politicians to appeal to ethnicity during Indonesia's turbulent transition to democracy in 1999. This alternative explanation, along with the other two discussed above, will be explored in Chapter 6.

3.4. Conclusion

Using a methodologically individualist approach, this book presents a parsimonious argument composed of three explanatory factors: electoral rules, ethnic group viability, and party ideology. I have explained in this chapter how these factors plus the bonding-trumps-bridging heuristic guide candidates' behavior and provide the microfoundations for their ethnic appeal strategy. As a result, the theory can be used to predict what ethnic cleavages will become politicized in particular constituencies.

As electoral rules become more candidate-centric, the influence of ethnic groups within a constituency increases while the influence of the party decreases. Ultimately, electoral rules function like a dial, causing the relative importance of ethnic groups and political parties, respectively, on a candidate's campaign and ethnic appeals to move up or down. This argument goes beyond looking simply at ethnic group size and offers a more dynamic approach to understanding when, how, and why candidates choose to politicize particular ethnic identity groups in their electoral campaigns.

The argument is particularly powerful because it explains how the politicization of ethnicity may change quite rapidly over time. Any changes in the electoral rules, ethnic group viability, or the ideologies of competing parties can affect how ethnicity is politicized and can result in the formation of new, salient ethnic cleavages.

II
DATA

4
Electoral Reform in Indonesia

Over the last two decades, a number of landmark books on institutional reform in Indonesia have been published. In a seminal account of the transitional period, King (2003) studied the reforms implemented during the turbulent years between 1998 and 2001 and provided some historical context regarding Indonesia's electoral institutions from 1955 through Suharto's New Order. Crouch's (2010) highly readable manuscript extended this analysis of electoral reform and examined the implementation of political and financial decentralization. Both Horowitz (2013) and Shair-Rosenfield (2019) presented meticulously detailed accounts of the reform process. Explaining Indonesia's distinctive process of holding elections before reforming the system, they showed how various actors created a complex electoral system by gradually introducing reforms over the years. Horowitz credited Indonesia's elite consensus-building approach to constitutional design with helping to avert conflict and producing a thoroughly democratic document. Shair-Rosenfield used extensive interviews and process tracing to provide a day-to-day account of how the negotiations and decision-making of inexperienced elites helped to consolidate Indonesia's democracy while unintentionally constraining their self-interest.

Although Indonesia's initial democratic reforms were viewed as surprisingly successful, more recent research has indicated democratic regression and a rise in polarization. Drawing on an array of scholarship, Davidson (2018) charted these trends, categorizing them into three distinct eras of innovation (1998–2004), stagnation (2004–2014), and polarization (2014–2018). Expanding on the most recent era, Power and Warburton (2020) presented the first comprehensive study of signs of decline in Indonesia's democratic institutions. While this might be a worrying trend, Fossati's (2022) book argues that Indonesia's religiously divisive politics has actually fostered more meaningful political participation and consequently increased Indonesians' support for, and satisfaction with, the democratic process.

These books have given us a rich and detailed understanding of institutional reform in the post-transition era. Additionally, numerous journal articles have been written on the topic. Building on the existing scholarship, this chapter more specifically focuses on the change in electoral rules from party-centric to candidate-centric, through an examination of key electoral reforms from 1955 to 2020. From the writings of Clifford Geertz and Indonesia's first democratic election in 1955 through the authoritarian years of Suharto's New Order and on into the post-transition era of *Reformasi*, there has been a long tradition of studying Indonesian political parties—their ideologies, their national leaders, and their social bases of support. This emphasis made sense when political power was centralized in Jakarta and when political competition was structured around national political parties. Today, however, Indonesia's political landscape has shifted. The regions have wrested significant power from Jakarta, and party politics has been supplanted by a politics of personality.

This chapter serves two main goals. First, it illustrates how and why Indonesia's electoral system moved from a party-centric to a candidate-centric system. The effects of this change have been wide-ranging—influencing how candidates enter politics, how campaigns are run, how constituents are mobilized, and how votes are cast. Second, and more specifically, I characterize the party-centric versus candidate-centric features of different Indonesian elections over the years. Defining elections in this way is a critical prerequisite for testing how electoral rules affect the politicization of ethnicity.

The chapter contains three parts. In Part I, I present a general framework for measuring how party-centric or candidate-centric an election is, and explain how I apply this framework to Indonesian elections. In Part II, I discuss Indonesia's legislative elections from 1955 to 2020, highlighting the reform efforts that eventually shifted these elections in a candidate-centric direction. Finally, in Part III, I describe the regional head elections that were introduced in 2005, in the context of prior reforms that expanded regional autonomy, and the highly candidate-centric rules that govern these elections.

4.1. Comparing Elections

To judge how party- or candidate-centric Indonesian elections are, I compare features of the electoral rules that foster the personal vote—campaigning and voting based on a candidate's individual characteristics rather than party affiliation. To do so, I focus on the formal and informal rules that empower or constrain candidates' ability to campaign independently. In particular,

I consider how candidates are nominated, how voters vote, and how seats are allocated. This analysis is based largely on the key features of the electoral rules that offer incentives for the personal vote as identified by Carey and Shugart (1995) and discussed in Chapter 2.[1]

The first important feature concerns the degree to which party leaders control the nomination of candidates and the rankings of candidates on party lists. Elections are more candidate-centric when party leaders have less control over nomination and ranking procedures. For instance, nonpartisan rules are candidate-centric because they allow independents to run and thus reduce the ability of party leaders to control candidate entry. Second, with regard to voting, whether constituents can vote directly for a candidate is key. PR systems with open rather than closed lists are more candidate-centric because constituents can reject candidates favored by party leaders and choose a candidate of their own preference. Third, how seats are allocated determines whether votes are first pooled across candidates from the same party. Elections are more candidate-centric when candidates are elected based solely on their personal votes and not on party votes, or even on votes cast for other candidates from the same party.

Using this framework, I place different Indonesian elections over the years on a continuum from party-centric to candidate-centric. Figure 4.1 provides a visual estimation of the position of each Indonesian election on this continuum. This figure is mainly for illustrative purposes, as there is no precise method for placing elections on the continuum. However, I believe that the approximate placements are adequately justified by this chapter's discussion of the rules governing each election.

Figure 4.1 shows that Indonesia's legislative elections were at the party-centric end of the spectrum for the first democratic election in 1955, through the authoritarian elections from 1971 to 1997, and into the *Reformasi* era of

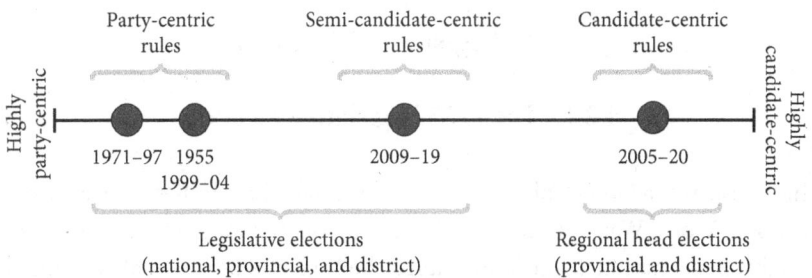

Figure 4.1 Indonesian elections on the continuum from party-centric to candidate-centric.

1999–2004. These elections were held for legislatures at the national, provincial, and district levels and used the same electoral rules—PR and closed (or effectively closed) lists. The elections under Suharto's authoritarian regime are defined as slightly more party-centric due to constrained party competition and the high degree of centralized control by leaders of the governing party, Golkar, during these elections. Other countries that have similar party-centric PR electoral systems with closed lists include Italy, South Africa, Spain, and Argentina.

Indonesia made a major change in 2009, retaining PR but switching to fully open instead of closed lists. This change shifted the electoral system closer to the center of the continuum; I define the resulting system as semi-candidate-centric. The 2014 and 2019 elections used the same rules. Brazil, Peru, Switzerland, and Iraq have similar electoral systems with PR and open lists. These systems are often described elsewhere as simply candidate-centric, but I use "semi-candidate-centric" to distinguish these elections from both the highly party-centric rules used in 1997 and the highly candidate-centric rules used in the regional head elections since 2005.

Finally, executive elections for regional head elections were introduced in 2005 and are positioned at the candidate-centric end of the spectrum due to key features of the rules. Specifically, party leaders largely lack control of the nomination process, constituents vote for individual candidates, and candidates are elected based entirely on their personal votes.

The rest of this chapter describes the reforms of Indonesian legislative and regional head elections implemented from 1955 to 2020. Over these years, election procedures have been revised several times. At each of these time points, I provide an overview of the reform process, why revisions were made, what rules resulted, and how these rules affected the party-centric or candidate-centric nature of the elections that followed.

4.2. Legislative Elections

4.2.1. The 1955 Legislative Election

Indonesia was a Dutch colony known as the Dutch East Indies before the outbreak of World War II. In the two decades before the war, the colonial regime established a national legislature called the Volksraad, or "People's Council." It had no real power and was not a democratic institution, with many appointees and substantial representation of Dutch officials and plantation owners. A version of the Volksraad remained in place during the Japanese occupation of Indonesia, but it had even less power (Anderson 1996: 26–27).

After the Japanese surrender in August 1945, Indonesian nationalists declared independence. A war with the returning Dutch ensued. During the war, President Sukarno and Vice President Hatta appointed a revolutionary parliament with representatives from all major Indonesian political groups (Anderson 1996: 28). The Indonesian army together with various militias and youth groups finally prevailed in what had turned into a guerrilla war by 1948. A settlement with the Dutch was signed in 1949, and preparations for Indonesia's first election began.

Electoral Reforms
King (2003: 16) explains that there was little debate surrounding the choice of PR for the 1955 national legislative elections. This was seen as the best option for a few reasons, including the highly decentralized way in which the war of independence had been fought, a strong participatory ethos that had developed during the war, and the fact that Indonesian nationalists had prior exposure to PR from their travels to the Netherlands or interactions with Dutch politicians. Beyond these influences, another relevant factor is that the rules were written by a legislature composed of many small political parties whose representatives were appointed by the president (Feith 1954: 246). Although many of them knew they had little chance of holding their seats in the upcoming election, PR was likely seen as their only hope for survival. There was more debate over the number of constituencies. Different political parties proposed amendments that they believed would benefit them at the polls— ranging from a single national constituency up to 33 separate constituencies. In the end, they settled on 16 (Feith 1954: 250).

The elections were designed to be free and fair and had few restrictions on political parties and individuals standing for election. By some estimates, at least 172 parties or individuals competed (King 2003: 16). The major parties, including Partai Nasional Indonesia (PNI), Partai Komunis Indonesia (PKI), and two Islamist parties (Masyumi and Nahdlatul Ulama) competed alongside dozens of other small parties.

After a number of delays, elections to replace the provisional national legislature were set for September 29, 1955. Political parties, organizations, officials, and local elites mobilized Indonesians to come out to vote by declaring that since Indonesia was now independent, it must have its own elections, and, moreover, that elections would also bring greater stability (Feith 1957).

Electoral Rules

In the election for the national legislature, party leaders first nominated candidates and drew up ranked party lists for each of the 16 multimember constituencies. A few candidates ran as independents. All constituents at least 18 years old had the right to vote, and upon arriving at the polls they were presented with a list of parties and their logos, as well as the names of the independent candidates, plus space to write in another candidate's name if they wished (King 2003: 29). Effectively, this was a closed-list system because when voters chose a party (as the vast majority did), they could not express a preference for individual candidates. To calculate the number of seats for each party, votes were pooled across candidates from the same party in each constituency. Party seats were then allocated in the order of the party lists. Independent candidates needed a full seat quota to win a seat. To calculate the number of votes a candidate would need to win a seat with a full seat quota, you divide the total number of votes by the number of available seats in the candidate's constituency. This was a substantial proportion of the vote, given the large numbers of parties and candidates running in each constituency.

Overall, the electoral rules for Indonesia's inaugural election were highly party-centric. Party leaders largely controlled party nominations and the ranking of candidates, constituents generally voted for parties, and votes were pooled across candidates from the same party.

The 1955 electoral results did not produce a clear winner, and divisive ideological interparty competition continued. A number of regional rebellions erupted, and in 1957 President Sukarno initiated martial law. Elections for regional legislatures at the provincial and district levels were held in 1957 and 1958 using the same party-centric rules, but due to the rebellions, they took place only in Java, South Sumatra, Riau, and Kalimantan. Support for the Communist party, PKI, surged. Its emergence as Indonesia's largest party resulted in more forceful opposition from the other parties and stiffened the military's determination to destroy the party system altogether (Lev 1966: 104–121). As the instability escalated, Sukarno and army leaders instituted a semi-authoritarian system they called Guided Democracy in 1958. However, in 1965 the crisis culminated in a coup, a counter-coup by Major General Suharto, the extermination of the PKI, and the massacre of hundreds of thousands of suspected communists. Sukarno was forced to transfer power by Suharto, who was appointed president in 1967.

4.2.2. The 1971–1997 Legislative Elections

Suharto's authoritarian government, self-titled the New Order, ruled Indonesia from 1966 to 1998. The regime destroyed democratic institutions to the point at which the legislative elections held in 1971, 1977, and then every five years until 1997 bore little resemblance to the competitive multiparty democratic regime that had flourished during the 1955 election campaign. Institutional reforms and the coercive apparatus produced an authoritarian regime with an empowered hegemonic political party, Golkar.

Electoral Reforms
During the New Order, elections were used to legitimize Suharto's rule. Prior to the 1971 election, the first under the New Order regime, two major decisions regarding the electoral rules were discussed. First, in terms of the electoral system, a majoritarian single-member district system was considered, but Suharto and the other political parties settled on a closed-list PR system and disallowed independent candidates. Second, as for regional representation, the constituencies were based on Indonesia's 27 provinces, with the number of seats per constituency reflecting the size of the province's population. However, because Java had a slight majority of the total population and would consequently get a majority of these legislative seats, there were fears that this arrangement could be perceived as facilitating Javanese political domination over the peripheries. Indeed, major rebellions had previously erupted in Sumatra and Sulawesi, in part due to perceptions of Javanese dominance. To assuage these fears, the number of seats per province was adjusted so that the total number allocated to constituencies in Java would be equal to those outside Java (Ellis 2000: 241; King 2003: 28).

More far-reaching, however, were reforms that created a hegemonic party system with severe restrictions on opposition parties. The governing party, Golkar, was founded in 1964 by the military as an umbrella social and political organization for various anti-communist groups and became the government's electoral vehicle for the 1971 election.[2] Although multiple political parties competed, Golkar won over 60% of the vote, enabling Suharto to consolidate his power and increasingly restrict competition in future elections.[3]

Golkar was not a political party in the traditional sense. As Liddle (1996: 44–45) wrote, "Golkar is not a political party at all, in the sense of an organization in society that competes electorally with similar organizations for control of the government. It is rather the electoral face of the civilian bureaucracy and the armed forces, mobilized every five years to get out the vote for the ruling group led by Suharto." Under the New Order, Golkar could mobilize state officials and use the state's powers of coercion. Most important, it could tap into the state's administrative structure, which stretched from Jakarta right down to the village and neighborhood level. This provided Golkar with a permanent local presence that could be exploited to influence voters at any time. All civil servants and local officials were required to be members of Golkar, to vote for Golkar, and to mobilize support during elections. These officials wielded power over ordinary Indonesians because they issued permits and clearances that were important for everyday life. In addition, Golkar could draw on its connections with the army and on loyal youth groups, such as the paramilitary organization, Pemuda Pancasila, to intimidate reluctant voters. Anyone who questioned the legitimacy of the election process could be detained and threatened with a trial.[4] Since many people did not believe that votes were secret, a vote against Golkar entailed high risks.

Golkar could also use state resources in exchange for votes. A common tactic was to promise to build a mosque or a road in a village if the people delivered 90% of the vote to Golkar.[5] More broadly, Golkar's legitimacy was built on its ability to improve the economy. As Liddle (1996: 34–35) observed, "[The New Order's] primary or first-line claim is that it is a developmental regime, dedicated to the achievement of a modern industrial economy, including a high standard of living for all Indonesians." Liddle explained that although few believed the regime was truly democratic, Golkar was successful in convincing many Indonesians that it was responsible for providing economic development and stability.

Beyond empowering Golkar, the political system severely constrained the development of opposition parties. In 1973, all of them were forced to combine into two parties. Partai Demokrasi Indonesia (PDI) was formed from five nationalist and Christian parties, and Partai Persatuan Pembangunan (PPP) was a fusion of four Islamic parties. These mergers forced the two new opposition parties to incorporate some very diverse and often antagonistic groups. But the government did not envision that they would act as traditional opposition parties. Rather, their official role was to seek solutions to the country's development problems and support a broad national consensus on the government's policies (Eklöf 1997: 1182). Unlike Golkar, which had a permanent presence in villages (via the government bureaucracy), the opposition parties were not allowed to maintain organizations below the district level (i.e., at the subdistrict and village levels). Lacking a support base, the parties were dependent on direct grants from the government to survive.

During election campaigns, opposition parties lacked media access, as all television stations were controlled by the state or the president's children (Schiller 1999: 4). Moreover, they were constrained by regulations against criticizing the government and president (Crouch 2010: 44). This effectively meant they were not allowed to criticize Golkar. If all that wasn't enough, the period for opposition parties to campaign was reduced from 60 to 25 days during the elections of 1971 to 1997, and each party could campaign only every third day (King 2003: 26). Finally, the opposition or independent monitors had little or no oversight of the process of counting and tallying votes, which was conducted primarily in private by government officials, offering plenty of opportunity for ballot stuffing.

Electoral Rules
Similar to the 1955 election, the New Order elections used PR and closed lists, although independent candidates were excluded. Elections for the national, provincial, and district legislatures used the same rules and were held concurrently. The government tightly controlled who could stand as a candidate. All opposition leaders had to be officially approved, and all candidates on their party lists had to be screened by military intelligence for their formal qualifications and ideological correctness before they could be nominated.[6] After candidates were approved, party leaders then drew up fixed lists of candidates for each constituency. For the national legislature, Indonesia was divided into 27 multimember constituencies (which were based on the provinces).[7] All candidates had to run with a party, but they did not have to reside in their constituency. Many didn't, preferring to live in the capital city of Jakarta. In the 1997 elections, for instance, 60% of candidates lived in the capital, putting them in closer proximity to party leaders than to their constituents (Horowitz 2013: 60).

In terms of voting, constituents could choose only a party name on the ballot. Seats were awarded to parties in proportion to each party's vote share in the constituency. Parties were then expected to allocate their seats to candidates in the order of the party's fixed list. In actual practice, party leaders—especially Golkar—often changed the lists after the election. Many candidates on the initial lists were there to promote the party's image, not to actually occupy the seats.[8]

The New Order elections operated under highly party-centric rules that ensured a win for the hegemonic party. Furthermore, they were tightly controlled by a highly centralized state and its leaders, who concurrently led Golkar—the hegemonic government party that acted as a thin facade for authoritarian state control. For aspiring Golkar candidates, although being liked by voters was nice, what really mattered was to be on good terms with Golkar party leaders, which may explain why so many politicians lived in Jakarta. Party leaders, not voters, selected the candidates, and these leaders completely controlled the allocation of party seats, even after the election.

In each of the six elections from 1971 to 1997, Golkar won between 62.1% and 74.5% of the vote, and its domination was further enhanced by the military appointees who made up one-fifth of the national legislature during most of the New Order period. Given the elaborate political system the government had constructed, it is surprising that Golkar didn't win by an even wider margin. Ultimately, the number of seats won by the two opposition parties had no effect on the election of the executives and little impact on government policy (King 2003: 33).

4.2.3. The 1999 Legislative Elections

In the second half of 1997, the Asian financial crisis hit Indonesia. With capital flight, a plummeting rupiah, and panic setting in, vocal criticism of Suharto and his government increased. Student demonstrations, counter-violence by the security forces, and extensive rioting in Jakarta and other cities around Indonesia followed. Having lost the support of the military, Suharto resigned on May 21, 1998, and was replaced by his vice president, B. J. Habibie.[9] Faced with continuing demonstrations, the new president lacked legitimacy and needed to win public support quickly. In his first week in office, Habibie declared that he would support new electoral legislation, allow the formation of new political parties, and hold a general election no later than June 1999.[10]

Electoral Reforms

In preparation for new democratic elections, electoral reforms were rushed through. A team of experts consisting mainly of American-trained political scientists, popularly known as the Team of Seven (*Team Tujuh*), was given the responsibility to draft new electoral legislation. The group proposed a radical change from PR to a mixed-member proportional (MMP) system. Under this system, 75 candidates would be elected using PR and 420 would win their seats in single-member districts (SMDs). The Team of Seven hoped that this more candidate-centric system, with its high proportion of SMDs, would make representatives more responsive and accountable to constituents and would also help larger political parties to win more seats, creating a party system with a limited number of competing parties (King 2003: 55–56; Crouch 2010: 47).

The draft bill was debated by a legislature still dominated by Golkar. While initially hesitant to drop a PR system that had served them well in the past, Golkar eventually supported MMP after calculating that they could win 30% of the vote nationwide due to the large number of SMDs (Ellis 2000). However, the other parties were fearful the new system would allow Golkar to entrench its power, and they resisted it. PPP went so far as to threaten to walk out if Golkar used its majority power to pass the legislation. Fearing that a walkout would undermine its electoral prospects and potentially spark more street demonstrations, Golkar accepted PR but proposed that electoral constituencies be based on the existing 314 districts (*Kabupaten/Kota*). This was a crafty move, since most constituencies would end up only having one seat—similar to the high number of SMDs in the proposed MMP system. The PPP and PDI promptly resisted this proposal, and Golkar relented. In the end, the previous system of PR with multimember districts based on the province prevailed (Crouch 2010: 48–49).

Although the Team of Seven's MMP system was rejected, legislators compromised by supporting a rule that would benefit locally popular candidates and potentially foster stronger connections between candidates and constituents. This was done by first assigning each nominated candidate to one of the districts (*Kabupaten/Kota*) within the larger, multimember provincial constituency. In each constituency, voters voted for a party and parties won seats proportional to their votes. Seats would then be allocated to the candidates assigned to districts where the party performed best.[11]

Along with changing the electoral system, the reforms removed restrictions on political party formation and campaigning. Forming a new political party required just 50 or more signatures from citizens age 21 or over, and parties could form around any principle or aspiration as long as it did not conflict with the national ideology, Pancasila.[12] Parties could extend their organization down to the village level and were protected against government interference. In addition, Golkar's monopoly on support from civil-service employees ended.[13]

Although it became far easier for parties to form and campaign, the Team of Seven developed stringent requirements for parties wishing to compete in the 1999 election. These restrictions were driven by a goal to build large strong national parties and shut out small political parties, particularly those based on a single ethnic group, a region, or separatist claims.[14] This suppression of political parties with separatist aspirations was particularly pressing, as East Timor was moving toward independence while Aceh and Papua had active separatist movements. The Team of Seven created two sets of requirements for parties to demonstrate that they had a national support base. First, parties were required to establish branches with governing boards in at least half of Indonesia's 27 provinces and in half of the districts within those provinces. Second, parties were required to meet a threshold of 10% in 1999 to be eligible for the next election in 2004. Although parties agreed to the rules requiring sufficient provincial and district branches, they pushed back against the registration threshold until it was reduced to 2% of seats in national parliament.[15]

Electoral Rules
The 1999 elections allowed multiple parties to compete and used PR with effectively closed lists. Parties nominated candidates and controlled their ranking by largely ignoring the rule meant to favor candidates in districts where the party performed well. Constituents could vote only for a party, and each party was assigned seats proportional to its vote percentage in the constituency. In each multimember constituency, parties were awarded seats proportional to their votes. Party leaders then assigned the seats to their preferred candidates. In violation of the rules, over 20% of the candidates awarded national legislature seats were not attached to the district where the party performed the best, and two candidates even switched provinces (Ellis 2000).

After several decades of rigged elections, the democratic election of 1999 was greeted with great fanfare and high voter turnout across the country.[16] As expected, when finally facing genuine competition, Golkar suffered huge losses. However, it still won 22.5% of the vote, placing second behind only Partai Demokrasi Indonesia Perjuangan (PDI-P) led by Megawati Soekarnoputri, which won 33.8%. Three other Islamic parties also received significant support.[17]

4.2.4. The 2004 Legislative Elections

During the 1999 election, a number of problems arose with the electoral rules that needed to be addressed before the 2004 election. Accordingly, the government established another team of experts to draft new electoral legislation.

Electoral Reforms
The first concern of the reform team, as with the Team of Seven, was to tighten the relationship between legislators and constituents, shifting the elections in a more candidate-centric direction. This concern arose partly because the one candidate-centric feature of the 1999 rules, designed to benefit candidates assigned to districts where their party performed well, was complicated and poorly implemented. Confusion surrounding the rule offered party leaders leeway to allocate seats to any candidate they wished, and electoral authorities ignored violations of the intended procedure. In addition, since the 1999 election, NGOs and media commentators had become very critical of the power of parties and their leaders, which fed into a growing anti-party public sentiment (Tan 2002).

Given these concerns, the government's team of experts proposed open-list PR for the 2004 election. This would allow constituents to choose a candidate on the ballot rather than a party. A major argument in favor of open lists was that it would loosen the grip of party leaders in Jakarta and the provincial capitals and force candidates to appeal for support from constituents directly. Initially, PDI-P and Golkar resisted, while smaller parties were more open to the idea. After some haggling, a compromise was reached whereby constituents would have a choice—they could vote for a party alone, or they could choose a candidate and their party. Candidates who received enough personal votes to fill a full seat quota would be awarded a seat. In practice, however, the quota was so high that the elections were effectively closed-list.[18]

Another reform that the team of experts proposed to bring legislators closer to constituents was an increase in the number of constituencies, combined with a decrease in the number of seats per constituency. This move was popular with the larger parties because it made winning seats harder for smaller parties. In 1999, the number of seats per constituency ranged from four to 82; for 2004, it was allowed to vary only between three and 12.[19]

Changes were also made to increase the numbers of branches parties were required to maintain across the country. In 1999, the electoral authorities were rather loose in implementing the branch rule, with the result that 48 political parties competed in the election.[20] However, the larger parties recognized that stricter requirements on branches and registration thresholds could help them increase their vote share by reducing the number of small parties allowed to compete. Consequently, before the 2004 election, new reforms required parties who wanted to contest the election, to establish party branches in at least two-thirds of all provinces. Also, in order for parties who compted in the 2004 election to be eligible to participate in the 2009 election, they now needed to achieve a thresholds of 3% of seats in the national parliament.[21] These thresholds still had little practical impact, however, since parties could merge with each other or dissolve and reassemble as "new" parties for the 2009 election.

Finally, an upper house for the national legislature was established in 2004. Its role was to increase the regions' participation in governance, though it acts only as an advisory body and lacks veto power over bills passed by the lower house. I do not analyze the campaigns of upper-house candidates in this book, but they have also contributed to Indonesian's overall shift to more candidate-centric elections because members of the upper house are elected using the single nontransferable vote (SNTV) and nonpartisan ballots.[22]

Electoral Rules
All candidates were nominated by parties, and party lists were drawn up for each constituency. But many party leaders disliked the rule that allowed candidates to win a seat based on their personal votes, so they called on supporters to vote for the party only. Moreover, the full seat quota threshold was so high that only two candidates out of 548 won a seat based on their personal votes (Crouch 2010: 65). Effectively, this made it a closed-list PR system where party leaders controlled both nomination and the ranking of candidates. In terms of voting, constituents could choose either a party

or a candidate on the ballot. As many as 52% of voters voted for individual candidates instead of parties, indicating a strong demand among constituents to choose their representative, even if it ultimately had little effect on who won seats.[23] In the allocation process, parties won seats proportional to their vote in each constituency and assigned them according to the party list.

In 2004, Golkar maintained 21.5% of the vote and actually emerged as the largest party, slightly ahead of PDI-P whose support had declined. A number of Islamic parties continued to attract votes, as did Partai Demokrat, a new party led by a former general, Susilo Bambang Yudhoyono (SBY). He would go on to win Indonesia's first direct presidential election a few months after the legislative elections.

Although the new political system used in the 1999 and 2004 elections allowed for multiple parties and enabled genuine democratic competition, it was still highly party-centric. Efforts by the two government-appointed teams of experts charged with electoral reform did not succeed in altering this feature. As in the old system, party leaders maintained control of nominations and ranking, voters effectively cast ballots for parties, and party leaders had considerable discretion in selecting the candidates who would fill the earned seats.

4.2.5. The 2009–2019 Legislative Elections

After two democratic elections, Indonesian democracy entered its consolidation phase, and government reforms slowed. However, the electoral laws did undergo some additional revisions, one of which, implemented before the 2009 election, would have a dramatic effect on Indonesian politics for years to come.

Electoral Reforms
A new law introducing incremental revisions for the 2009 election was debated in the national legislature and eventually adopted. Under continuing pressure from NGOs and commentators to create incentives for candidates to be more responsive to constituents rather than beholden to party leaders, the parties compromised, agreeing to a partially open-list system. Voters could vote for a candidate or a party in a multimember constituency, and seats would be allocated to candidates in the order of their personal votes, as long

as they received more than 30% of the seat quota for their constituency. All other seats would be allocated according to the party list. This increased the possibility that popular (and ideally responsive) candidates would be elected, but it also allowed parties to secure seats for their preferred candidates by placing them high on the party list.[24]

The law, however, was criticized as not meeting the standards of an open-list system, and a number of candidates challenged the law before the Constitutional Court.[25] To the surprise of many, they were successful. In December 2008, the court ruled that all seats must be allocated to candidates based on their personal votes rather than their position on the party list. Horowitz (2013: 185-186) explained the decision: "The court held that awarding seats to candidates based on their rankings on the parties' lists, when other, lower-ranked candidates had actually won more individual votes, violated the sovereignty of the people." To Horowitz, declaring the closed list unconstitutional was an extraordinary act for the Constitutional Court. Moreover, as he noted, the court didn't seem to appreciate that the 30% seat quota rule would have significantly increased the number of candidates elected by their personal votes. Nevertheless, this ruling suddenly scrapped the closed-list system that had been used since 1955 in favor of a fully open-list system. With less than four months before the 2009 elections, the effect was immediate. Candidates scrambled to mobilize personal support from their constituencies, while those who had already paid their parties for high positions on the candidate list wrangled with party leaders to retrieve some of the costs.

Beyond this important change, other incremental reforms implemented before and after the 2009 election continued to squeeze Indonesia's struggling small parties. The number of required branches was not increased for the 2009 election, but before the 2014 election it was raised to all provinces, 75% of all districts, and 50% of the sub-districts (*Kecamatan*) in those districts. Second, district magnitude (i.e., the number of seats per constituency) was decreased from a range of three to 12 seats to a maximum of 10 seats before the 2009 election. Third, a new rule on electoral thresholds was also introduced before the 2009 elections. The larger parties proposed that parties could be assigned seats in the national parliament only if they received more than 5% of the national vote.[26] Predictably, the smaller parties resisted and the threshold was lowered to 2.5%, but it increased to 3.5% in 2014.

Finally, some initially promising reforms regarding women's representation were introduced before the 2009 election. Women's representation in the national legislature was just 8.8% in 1999, barely above the 7% of seats won by women in 1955. Before the 2004 election, international NGOs and Indonesian women's groups argued that electoral laws disadvantaged women and advocated for measures to support female candidates. The political parties eventually agreed to a law stating that they should "give consideration" to having 30% women among their nominated candidates. As a result, some parties did nominate more female candidates, but because the law did not stipulate where on the list they could be placed, most women languished at the bottom of the lists. Predictably, the 2004 election saw only a modest increase in women's representation, to 11.8%. Before the 2009 election, a stronger law on gender quotas required parties to nominate 30% female candidates and required that one in every three list spots should be awarded to a female. Ironically, the advantages of this "zipper system" for women were undermined by the last-minute introduction of an open-list system. Nonetheless, women's representation in the national legislature reached 18.3% in 2009, 17.3% in 2014, and an all-time high of 20.5% in 2019.[27]

Electoral Rules
In the 2009 election, party leaders could still control the nomination of candidates, but for the first time, voters controlled which candidates would be allocated party seats. Voters could vote for either a party or a candidate, and 70% chose to vote for a candidate. In each multimember constituency, votes were first pooled across all candidates from the same party to determine how many seats that party had won. Parties winning seats in a constituency then had to assign them to the candidates on their list in the order of who had won the most personal votes.

The same open-list PR rules were used in the 2014 and 2019 legislative elections. This change undermined the ability of party leaders to control candidates, introduced competition between candidates in the same party, and gave candidates incentives to manage their personal campaigns more fully. As Aspinall (2010: 108) explained, "This decision radically altered the nature of campaigning, with legislative candidates now pouring their resources and efforts into promoting their own individual candidacies, rather than those of their parties." Moreover, the impact of open-list PR on candidates' campaigns was swift. As Sherlock (2009: 7) noted, "There were reports of candidates demanding that their party return the money paid for their position on the list because the funds were now required for the candidate's own personal campaign. And since they were now running their own campaign they were less interested in being directed by the central party board."

The candidate-centric nature of the 2009 and 2014 elections should not be overstated, however. Candidates still had to belong to and be nominated by a party in order to compete in the legislative elections. Also, securing a high position on the list was still valuable, as it offered a somewhat better chance of winning. Additionally, even popular candidates continued to rely on their party and its candidates to perform well in the constituency so that the party would receive at least one seat. Winning seats in a constituency became a difficult task for parties since district magnitude had been reduced to a maximum of 10 seats. The smaller parties struggled to win even one seat in a constituency, while the larger parties would be doing well if they secured two. Moreover, the ability of popular leaders to energize their base and get them out to vote could greatly increase the chance that a party seat might be available for a candidate. For instance, Partai Demokrat and its popular leader and sitting Indonesian president (in 2009), SBY, could mobilize sizable support on election day. Meanwhile, parties with more ideological and historical roots, such as PDI-P, could also rely on the support of loyal followers.

Table 4.1 summarizes the rules for legislative elections based on the features that determine the extent to which they are candidate-centric—specifically, the rules governing nomination procedures, voting, and the allocation of seats. A party-centric system prevailed from 1955 until 2004. As noted above, I describe the electoral system since 2009 as semi-candidate-centric to contrast them with the highly candidate-centric rules for regional head elections, discussed below.

4.3. Regional Head Elections

Direct regional head elections were introduced in 2005 as part of a broader effort to decentralize governance that began during the transition to democracy. These reforms aimed to deepen democracy, reduce corruption, bring government closer to the people, and make regional heads more responsive

Table 4.1 Legislative Elections

Party-Centric System

Years	Regime	Rules
1955	Multiparty democracy	**System:** PR with effectively closed lists. **Nomination:** Party leaders controlled party nominations and candidate rankings on the party lists. Independents could self-nominate. **Voting:** Constituents could vote for (a) a party, (b) a self-nominated candidate, or (c) a write-in candidate. **Seats:** In each multimember constituency, parties were awarded seats proportional to their votes. Parties then allocated their seats to candidates in the order of the party's fixed list. Independent candidates needed to win a full seat quota.
1971–1997	Authoritarian with a hegemonic party	**System:** PR with closed lists. **Nomination:** Party leaders controlled nominations and candidate rankings. **Voting:** Constituents could vote only for a party. **Seats:** In each multimember constituency, parties were awarded seats proportional to their votes. Parties were then expected to allocate their seats to candidates in the order of the party's fixed list. However, party leaders often changed these lists after the election.
1999	Multiparty democracy	**System:** PR with effectively closed lists. **Nomination:** Party leaders controlled nominations and effectively controlled candidate rankings. **Voting:** Constituents could vote only for a party. **Seats:** In each multimember constituency, parties were awarded seats proportional to their votes. Seats should then have been allocated to candidates assigned to districts where their party performed best. In practice, seats were allocated to the parties' favored candidate.
2004	Multiparty democracy	**System:** PR with effectively closed lists. **Nomination:** Party leaders controlled nominations and effectively controlled candidate rankings. **Voting:** Constituents could vote for (a) a party or (b) a candidate and their party. **Seats:** In each multimember constituency, parties were awarded seats proportional to their votes. Seats were allocated to candidates in the order of the fixed list, except for candidates who won a full seat quota (only two did).

Semi-Candidate-Centric System

Years	Regime	Rules
2009–2019	Multiparty democracy	**System:** PR with fully open lists. **Nomination:** Party leaders control party nominations but not list rankings. **Voting:** Constituents could vote for (a) a party or (b) a candidate. **Seats:** In each multimember constituency, votes were pooled across candidates from the same party. Party seats were then allocated to candidates with the most personal votes.

Note. In 1955, the election was only for the national legislature. Elections for some provincial and district legislatures used the same electoral rules, but were held in 1957 and 1958. For all the other elections, members of the national, provincial, and district legislatures were elected at the same time and using the same rules.

to constituents. Below, I briefly describe the regional autonomy reforms and then the electoral reforms that followed subsequently.

4.3.1. Regional Autonomy Reforms

During the New Order, governance was highly centralized and regional governments were an extension of central authority emanating from Jakarta. However, when the economic crisis hit and the movement to bring down Suharto gained steam, calls for regional autonomy also came to the fore. When Habibie became president, he was too weak to use repression against regional dissension, as Suharto had done in the past. This opportunity prompted regional leaders to push harder for regional autonomy. Elites were quite aware that other similar multiethnic states, such as the Soviet Union and Yugoslavia, had fallen apart, so regional discontent raised real fears of national disintegration. Many in the military and bureaucracy viewed regional autonomy as a likely stepping stone to disintegration, but others saw it as the only way to hold the country together. With East Timor moving toward independence and with militant separatist movements active in Aceh and Papua, the Habibie government anticipated dissent from other regions in the future and decided to move quickly with an extensive decentralization program (Crouch 2010: 90–92).

Time was a factor, however. The decentralization laws had to be drafted and passed while Golkar was still in power. If nothing happened until after the 1999 election, a new government might have different ideas and a dragged-out process could offer opportunities for centrist elites to resist significant reforms. Due to this urgency, Indonesia pursued a "Big Bang" approach, decentralizing governance in one blow rather than in increments.

In late 1998, Habibie again called on the Team of Seven to draft regional autonomy legislation. The team completed a draft in less than four months and sent it to the legislature, where it was passed with no substantial changes and then signed into law in May 1999—just a month before the election.[28] One particularly unusual feature of the decentralization program was that it bypassed the provinces, devolving power to district governments. This decision was born out of a fear that large provinces with a strong sense of communal identity might be prompted to push for independence after they experienced some regional autonomy. Districts, however, were far too small to even consider such a move.

This reform, described as the world's largest decentralization program, took effect in January 2001. Almost two million civil servants were reassigned from the central government to help run enlarged district governments, which now had wide-ranging powers in such areas as government services, agriculture, communications, industry, trade, investment, labor, and the environment (Smith 2008: 212). To fund local governance, huge transfers of revenue flowed to the districts, which were also allowed to keep larger proportions of revenues raised in the district—a particular boon for resource-rich regions.

As part of the reforms, new provinces and districts were allowed to form—and they did, in dramatic fashion. In the 10 years after the transition, the number of districts doubled to over 500, and eight new provinces were established, in a process commonly referred to as *pemekaran* (blossoming). Though the intended goal of *pemekaran* was to make local governance and development more efficient, in reality new districts and provinces were created largely for political and financial reasons: they offer new power bases for politicians and new revenue flows from the central government (Pierskalla 2016; Kimura 2013).

4.3.2. Regional Head Elections Since 2005

Electoral Reforms
During the New Order, regional heads were formally elected by their local legislatures. However, in reality, governors were chosen by the central government, and district heads were chosen by the provincial governments. Most regional heads were drawn from the ranks of military officers or the government bureaucracy (Crouch 2010: 89).

Between 1999 and 2004, electoral reforms gave regional legislatures the power to elect regional heads with a simple majority vote. However, it soon became apparent that legislative members were accepting bribes for these appointments. Because the elections were by secret ballot, legislators often deceived the regional head candidates who paid them and voted for someone else anyhow. A sense of betrayal and financial loss resulted in court cases and demonstrations. Beyond that, the corrupt spectacle revealed to the public that the process wasn't working, prompting calls for reforms (Aspinall and Berenschot 2019: 76). The decision to hold direct presidential elections, as well as its runoff format, also influenced regional head electoral reform. In the past, political parties in the legislature elected presidents, but since 2004, Indonesians have directly elected their presidents. Reforms established that presidential candidates must be nominated by a party or coalition and are elected in a two-round system in which the winner must receive a majority of the vote.[29] Popular with the public, direct presidential elections have contributed to the candidate-centric turn in Indonesian elections. In the past, backroom dealings among party leaders largely decided who became president. Today, presidential contests are far more personalistic, with candidates drawing on their character, experience, and ideas to foster support.

All parties agreed to direct regional head elections, commonly referred to as *pilkada*.[30] Like the presidential elections, candidates ran in pairs (i.e., for governor and deputy governor) in a two-round system which was held outside of the legislative elections. Held on a rolling basis every five years, the first round occurring between 2005 and 2008. In general, the large parties tried to shape the rules in ways that they believed would be beneficial to their candidates. First, to increase their candidates' chance of winning in the first round, the large parties successfully pushed for a rule to allow the leading candidate to avoid a runoff if he or she had 25% or more of the vote (later raised to 30%), rather than the 50% that presidential candidates needed in order to win in the first round. Second, to restrict small-party candidates from running, the large parties pressed for a requirement that all candidates must be nominated by a party, or a coalition of parties, that at the time of nomination held at least 15% of the seats in the regional legislature (or, alternatively, 15% of the votes). Finally, by rejecting a proposal by the Department of Home Affairs, the large parties initially prevented independent from running. However, a Constitutional Court ruling in 2007 overturned that provision, allowing independents to enter regional head races if they could collect signatures from 3% of the constituency's population.[31]

In 2015, the large political parties passed new legislation in another attempt to reshape the rules so as to help their candidates and squeeze out independents. Three key changes were introduced. First, the level of political party support required of nominated candidates was increased to 20% of seats or 25% of votes. Second, the number of signatures required of independent candidates was increased from 6.5% to 10% of the constituency's population, depending on the size of the population. And finally, the two-round system was dropped; only a plurality of the vote was required to win. The only exception to this rule was the capital, Jakarta, where the winning candidate still needed more than 50% of the vote. In addition, simultaneous elections would be held on a single day of the year in 2015, 2017, 2018, and 2020.

Electoral Rules

Despite the large parties' efforts to shape the rules in their favor, the connections between regional head candidates and political parties are weak. Most candidates secure party nominations from multiple political parties on a transactional basis. Parties usually auction off nominations to the highest bidder, with little concern for the candidate's ideological affinity or loyalty (Hendrawan et al. 2021; Aspinall and Berenschot 2019: 78). Indeed, candidates are rarely even members of the parties whose nomination they seek. Since 2007, candidates could enter as independents, bypassing the political parties completely. For many, running as an independent was a popular option, despite the arduous registration process and the large number of signatures required. Approximately one-sixth of all regional head candidates ran as independents by 2015.[32] Overall, compared to the legislative elections, party leaders had far less control of the nomination process.

When voting, constituents are presented with a list of candidates and choose a candidate name, not a party name. At the polling booth, therefore, voters do not need to know which party or parties support their candidate. This situation is in contrast with the legislative elections, in which a voter first needs to find the party name and then look down though the party list to find the candidate's name.

Competing in a single-seat election, regional head candidates win or lose based solely on the personal votes cast for them. Before 2015, to win the seat in the first round, the leading candidate needed to win at least 30% of all votes. If no candidate was elected in the first round, the top two candidates competed in a runoff election a few weeks later. Since 2015, the candidate with a simple plurality of personal votes wins. This again contrasts with legislative elections, where candidates are dependent on fellow candidates' votes because votes are pooled within parties before seat allocation. See Table 4.2.

These rules have contributed to the highly candidate-centric nature of regional head election campaigns. They are more candidate-centric than the 2009–2019 legislative elections because party leaders have less control over the nomination of candidates, voters can vote only for a candidate, and there is no pooling of votes across multiple party candidates.

Table 4.2 Regional Head Elections

	Candidate-Centric System	
Years	Regime	Rules
2005–2020	Multiparty democracy	**System:** Two-round system. **Nomination:** Candidates can be nominated by one or more parties. Independent candidates have been eligible to run since 2007. **Voting:** Constituents can vote only for a candidate. **Seats:** Allocation of a seat is based entirely on the candidate's vote. Up until 2015, the leading candidate won the seat in round one if he or she had at least 30% of the total vote. Otherwise, the top two candidates competed in a runoff. Since 2015, candidates won with a simple plurality of the vote. The gubernatorial election in Jakarta is the one exception, where the winning candidate needs 50%+ of the vote.

4.4. Conclusion

This chapter has presented an overview of electoral reform in Indonesia, focusing on actors and justifications behind revisions of the electoral law at various points in time since 1955. A major opportunity for institutional change arose with the fall of Suharto. At that time, the Team of Seven, with broad ambitions to bring the government closer to the people, drafted new legislative electoral rules. Although the Team's proposal of a more candidate-centric MMP system was thwarted by the political parties, the idea foresaw a shift in public opinion. In the years that followed the euphoria of the 1999 election, an anti-party sentiment and a desire for reforms that could hold politicians more accountable to their constituency emerged. However, despite increasing public pressure, party leaders successfully blocked moves to make the system more candidate-centric for almost a decade. Then, in 2008, the Constitutional Court stepped in with a surprise ruling that required fully open lists—a move that dramatically shifted legislative elections in a candidate-centric direction for the foreseeable future.

The Team of Seven also designed Indonesia's extensive regional autonomy laws, which, along with the introduction of direct presidential elections, led eventually to the introduction of candidate-centric regional head elections in 2005. Although political parties tried to control the candidate nomination process and prevent independents from entering these races, the Constitutional Court intervened in 2007 to allow independent candidates.

These changes show how reformers, such as the Team of Seven, as well as the general public have pushed to make the government more responsive to the people's aspirations. However, both the reformers and the political parties have also restricted certain aspirations that they considered dangerous. Since 1999, the reforms have increasingly sought to discourage political parties that could represent the particular interests of an ethnic group or region. Here lies an inherent tension in Indonesian electoral reform—driven on one hand by highly democratic motives to fulfill the people's aspirations for a meaningful role in government, but on the other hand by an effectively anti-democratic impulse to restrict certain ideas and forms of representation.

This tension aside, for the purposes of this book, the variation in electoral rules provides an excellent opportunity to understand the impact of party-centric versus candidate-centric rules on ethnic appeal strategies. By comparing ethnic appeal strategies across elections held under different rules, we can assess whether ethnic appeal strategies vary in ways that my argument would predict. Before testing the argument, in Chapter 5 I discuss my approach to measuring ethnic appeals in Indonesian election campaigns.

5
Measuring Ethnic Appeals

By far, the most challenging part of studying the politicization of ethnicity has been figuring out how to systematically gather ethnic campaign appeals. Early in my research, I realized that no other studies had gathered ethnic appeals from candidates at any significant scale. Some early observations of elections in Indonesia, however, offered possible options.

In Indonesia, one of the best ways to get information on candidates and campaign events in local elections is from the regional press. Because the nation is so vast, the regional press has played a critical role in delivering local news; it became more fully empowered to do so with the transition to democracy and a loosening of restrictions on the media. Examining regional media publications over an extended time period would enable me to identify changes and continuities in campaigns over time.

In addition, a colleague suggested the novel approach of examining Indonesian election posters.[1] In Indonesia, the streets are blanketed with election posters during election seasons. The posters are adorned with colorful imagery and symbols. They feature larger-than-life candidates dressed in all types of garbs, and contain messages and slogans in numerous languages spoken across the archipelago. They radically alter the urban and rural landscape temporarily and then vanish with little trace after polling day. Photographing posters during this window of opportunity and then coding their appeals would provide an excellent way to study hundreds or even thousands of candidates across constituencies.

This chapter contains four parts. In Part I, I discuss how other scholars have measured the politicization of ethnicity. Next, I introduce my method of gathering ethnic appeals from the regional press in Part II, and from election posters in Part III. In Part IV, I discuss social constraints on appealing to non-Muslim groups in Indonesia—a phenomena observed from the newspaper reports and poster data.

5.1. Measuring the Politicization of Ethnicity

A number of quantitative studies have measured the politicization of ethnicity and ethnic appeals used by political parties and their leaders. They have largely employed one of two approaches. The first measures ethnic politicization broadly by drawing on data on either ethnic voting or the ethnic composition of political party members and leaders. The second approach more specifically measures ethnic appeals by drawing on reports and campaign materials.

To understand ethnic politicization, Horowitz (1985) looked at the emergence of ethnic political parties in multiethnic societies and at ethnic voting. Since then, others (e.g., Houle 2017; Huber 2012) have frequently drawn on ethnic vote share data to study the politicization of ethnicity. To study ethnic vote shares, scholars consider two interconnected measures.[2] First, in defining a party as ethnic, the *percentage of a party's vote* that comes from a specific ethnic group is critical. If a high percentage of its support comes from one ethnic group, then it is an ethnic party. However, to understand the politicization of ethnicity across a whole party system, a second measure must also be considered, namely the *percentage of an ethnic group* that votes for a political party. A system in which each political party is largely supported by one ethnic group and each ethnic group generally supports only one party is a highly ethnicized system.

Beyond the ethnicity of voters, another measure of ethnic politicization is the ethnic composition of the government or of political party candidates. The Ethnic Power Relations (EPR) dataset focuses on ethnic groups in government and has been used to study ethnic conflict and civil war.[3] It draws on expert surveys in multiple countries to identify all politically relevant ethnic groups—i.e., those that have a political actor representing them in national politics and those that suffer systematic and intentional discrimination. It then codes the degree to which government representatives (the president, cabinet, and senior posts in the administration, including the army) come from each ethnic group. An ethnic group's power can range from total control of the government to total exclusion. At the time of writing, the EPR dataset covered all countries in the world with a population of at least 250,000 from 1946 to 2019.[4]

The ethnic background of party leaders and candidates is a further indicator of ethnic politicization. Political parties often carefully consider the ethnicity of the candidates they nominate because it sends a signal to voters regarding the party's ethnic or multiethnic nature (Chandra 2011: 162).

There are two advantages of using ethnic vote share and the ethnic composition of governments and parties to measure ethnic politicization: the data are relatively easy to acquire, and the measures are reasonably effective in identifying politically salient ethnic groups.[5] However, these measures do not determine whether ethnicity was *actively* politicized, because they do not capture the appeals actually made by candidates. They provide no information regarding the content of campaigns or the types of ethnic appeals made by parties.

The other, more direct, approach is to study the active politicization of ethnicity by analyzing ethnic party platforms and the actual ethnic appeals they make. This can be done by drawing on party manifestos, country reports, newspaper articles, and campaign speeches. For example, the Manifesto Project provides a dataset of coded party manifestos from around the world. It primarily covers developed democracies in the West but has expanded its scope to political parties in several Asian and Latin American countries. Over the years, the Manifesto Project has become one of the most popular sources for party positions on left/right and other ideological and policy dimensions.[6] However, scholars using the database have paid little attention to analyzing the ethnic messages in party manifestos, even though ethnocultural issues are coded in the Manifesto Project. One exception is Gadjanova (2015), who developed a novel approach to measuring ethnic appeals from the Manifesto Project's database. She identified policy and issue positions that reflected appeals to ethnic communities. These stances could then be quantified and compared across parties using standard methods of estimating policy positions.

Daniel Posner's Politically Relevant Ethnic Groups (PREG) dataset also uses qualitative materials. Rather than drawing on manifestos, PREG includes country reports and other sources that determine when ethnic categories are used as the basis for political parties. The data were gathered from 42 African countries and coded over time to generate a list of politically relevant ethnic groups. Posner (2004) used this dataset to create a new ethnic fractionalization index and tested its impact on economic growth in Africa.

Finally, the Constructivist Dataset on Ethnicity and Institutions (CDEI), created by Kanchan Chandra, draws on the ethnic rhetoric of political parties—that is, what parties actually say to voters during their campaigns. The CDEI covers 100 countries for elections that took place in or soon after

1996. Its extensive array of source materials includes reference guides, political speeches, and translated news articles for the three months prior to an election. Data for each political party are qualitatively assessed, and parties are coded as ethnic, multiethnic, or nonethnic. Measuring political parties according to these criteria allows for the identification of parties that politicize ethnicity in their campaigns.[7]

The methodologies used by the Manifesto Project, PREG, and CDEI provide direct measures of ethnic politicization from campaign materials. However, the data come primarily from political party platforms and appeals made by national party leaders. As such, they treat political parties as homogeneous groups with unified campaign appeals. This approach bypasses the reality that individual candidates in a party often make appeals that diverge from the official party line—especially when the electoral rules are candidate-centric, when political parties are undisciplined, and when there are significant regional differences. As discussed in Chapter 3, the appeals made by local candidates provide critical information in understanding campaigns. These candidates are closest to the voters and are often at the front lines of ethnic mobilization.

To test a theory on why local candidates make ethnic appeals, two potential sources of their ethnic appeals are worth exploring: election coverage of candidates in the media and candidates' campaign materials. First, election news coverage in print, on TV or radio, or online is a useful source of ethnic campaign appeals. It often provides comprehensive information on campaigns, rallies, and debates, as well as interviews, statements, and profiles of candidates. Second, ethnic appeals can be gathered directly from candidates' campaign materials, which range from the premodern fliers and election posters to traditional print, TV, and radio ads, to more modern digital media approaches. Increasingly, candidates are advertising online, as well as building their own websites and promoting themselves though online platforms such as Facebook, X (previously Twitter), and Instagram, which will continue to evolve over time.

For this project, I applied three main criteria in selecting Indonesian media sources. To qualify for consideration, a source needed to (1) contain information on candidates who ran large as well as more limited campaigns, (2) provide access to data on a significant number of candidates (given time and resource constraints), and (3) facilitate gathering appeal data from past elections so as to study the impact of changes in the Indonesia's electoral rules. These criteria considerably narrowed down the choice of sources. They ruled out TV and radio, since poorer candidates tended to get very little coverage in those media. Printed candidate campaign fliers were also not feasible, because there was no way to gather them on any kind of large scale. I explored online media sources during my field research by attempting to gather appeal data from candidates' websites, Facebook, Twitter, and other platforms. Unfortunately, the vast majority of the legislative or regional head candidates had no online presence at all, so this option was deemed infeasible.[8]

Ultimately, newspaper reports and election posters remained the best options as sources for ethnic appeals. Newspapers had the advantage in that I could gather appeal data over time. Election posters, as discussed further below, were an excellent source of campaign appeals by both wealthy and poor candidates—in fact, virtually all candidates had posters that could be gathered and analyzed. Also, with help from research assistants, I could photograph thousands of posters across the country, covering a significant number of candidates. Each election poster came from a specific geographic location—a useful feature in studying variations in appeals across different demographics. I now turn to how I gathered and coded newspaper reports and campaign posters.

5.2. Campaigning in the Press

Newspapers often play a central role in election campaign coverage. Not surprisingly, numerous studies in various countries have analyzed newspapers to uncover a wealth of detailed information on many aspects of campaigns. Often employing content analysis, these newspaper studies have examined the location of campaign events, candidate endorsements, the salience of candidate attributes, and the prevalence of particular issues.[9] More specifically, newspapers have been used to study identity politics[10] and ethnic campaign appeals.[11]

5.2.1. Campaign Coverage in the Indonesian Press

As in other countries, campaign press coverage in Indonesia has been extensive since the country's first election in 1955. Two prominent scholars of Indonesian media, Sen and Hill (2000), wrote that when Indonesia transitioned to democracy in 1999, newspapers employed more journalists and spent more time gathering and disseminating news than any other media. Despite the fact that Indonesian newspapers reached a smaller audience than television,[12] they have largely determined what constitutes news in Indonesia. As a result, the Indonesian newspapers have been an important source of information for researchers, who have relied on this source to examine such issues as the news coverage of political parties; matters of war, defense, and diplomacy; the content of the national news; news coverage of development issues; ethnic conflict; and election campaign rhetoric.[13]

I quickly determined that the regional press (i.e., newspapers printed outside the capital city of Jakarta) would be the best source of campaign data on individual candidates. First, due to Indonesia's size, the regional press has played an important role in delivering news on local politics. This role has expanded further with the introduction of decentralization and the development of a less Jakarta-centric media space. Since the introduction of democracy, the number of regional papers has grown exponentially, and they operate in a more free and competitive media environment, offering detailed coverage of local politics and elections. Moreover, democratic competition and the general move toward a candidate-centric system have made media exposure in the regional press a critical part of campaigns. As a result, the regional press provides the most extensive local coverage, in a report-length format that offers great detail on a large number of candidates and how they appeal to voters. In addition, regional press reports are a very good reflection of what candidates want to say and how they desire to be seen by voters. Often these reports are written by, or in conjunction with, candidates and campaign managers.[14] These reports are also characterized by minimal editorial voice, political analysis, or criticism. To a large extent, they capture the candidate's direct and unfiltered message, making them a valuable source of information on candidate appeals.

5.2.2. Gathering Press Reports in North Sumatra

A main criterion for selecting a regional newspaper was that it had to serve a multiethnic community. Examining campaigns in a multiethnic environment can shed light on the main question of this book—namely, under what conditions candidates make ethnic appeals and how they choose the ethnic identities to which they appeal. This criterion ruled out the more homogeneous provinces in Indonesia. After surveying a number of provinces, I chose to investigate the regional press in North Sumatra, an ethnically diverse region with particularly salient indigenous and religious identity groups and a strong regional press.[15]

North Sumatra is located in western Indonesia,[16] with the Strait of Malacca to the east and the Indian Ocean to the west. It is sandwiched between the provinces of Aceh to the north and West Sumatra and Riau to the south. It is a large province (approximately the size of South Carolina or Ireland) and the most populous one outside Java. During my fieldwork, it had a population of 13 million, higher than that of most countries, and was religiously diverse: 66% of residents were Muslim and 31% Christian, with a small number are Hindu and Buddhist followers.[17] In contrast, Indonesia overall was 87% Muslim and 10% Christian. In North Sumatra, indigeneity is fragmented: the Javanese were the largest single indigenous group (33% of the population) and a number of Batak indigenous groups combined to constitute 45% of the population. There were also smaller numbers of ethnic Chinese and other indigenous groups, including Mandailing, Nias/Kono Niha, Malay, and Minangkabau. Medan, the provincial capital, was the fifth-largest city in Indonesia, with a population of 2.1 million. Religious and indigenous demographics in the city reflect those of the overall province, though Medan had a higher percentage of ethnic Chinese (9.7%).

Not only is North Sumatra diverse, but religious and indigenous identities are also salient there. Indigenous and religious ceremonies, festivals, and prayer groups are common everyday activities. Although interethnic relations have generally been harmonious, interethnic tensions have occasionally come to the fore. For example, in 1998, protests calling for reform turned into riots that targeted the Chinese minority in Medan with looting.[18] Also, Christian churches' attempts to acquire operating permits in Muslim-majority communities are sometimes a source of tension, and in recent years some churches have been burned down. Overall, this rich array of ethnic groups and the salience of these identities offer candidates many options in their choice of ethnic appeals.

North Sumatra has historically had a vibrant and independent press. During the New Order, five to ten regional newspapers operated in the province. Medan's *Waspada* and *Mimbar Umum* dailies, in particular, were prominent for their longevity and independence (Hill 2006: 119). They persisted despite the fact that the military and police had far-reaching powers to control the press, with the authority to approve or censor individual reports. Since the transition to democracy and the concomitant rise in press freedom, newspapers have flourished in the province, with approximately 120 daily and weekly papers operating by 2010.[19]

Although papers no longer need to seek approval before publishing stories, they do engage in self-censorship to some degree. For example, the newspaper *Analisa*, among others, declines to identify the religious or indigenous identity of groups involved in acts of violence.[20] This policy was put in place to avoid inflaming social tensions by framing conflicts in terms of identity groups. The intentions are good, but the practice is reminiscent of Suharto's SARA restrictions on reporting on religious, ethnic, and group conflicts.[21] With media liberalization, there has also been a rise in publications in indigenous languages. For example, two magazines, *Sora Mido* and *Maranata* (a local Batak Karo Church newsletter), began publishing in the Karo language soon after the transition to democracy. Beyond using the national language, Bahasa Indonesia, many newspapers in North Sumatra publish sections in indigenous languages and Chinese.

To study election coverage in North Sumatra's regional press, I gathered and reviewed election-related reports in various regional papers. This review, plus interviews with journalists and constituents in North Sumatra, led me to choose *Waspada* for detailed content analysis. First, *Waspada* is the oldest daily newspaper in North Sumatra and one of the oldest in Indonesia, having begun publishing in January 1947. Founded by H. Mohammad Said and H. Ani Idrus, it remains under Said family ownership. Published in Medan, it has a primarily city and provincial focus. Second, *Waspada* has a large, multiethnic readership. Interviewees indicated that *Waspada* was popular among Medan's Muslim population, but was also widely read by other religious and indigenous groups in North Sumatra. My observations confirmed that it was available at all newsstands and appeared to be popular across different classes. Third, compared to other newspapers, *Waspada* had the most extensive coverage of politics in Medan and North Sumatra. Finally, on a more practical level, archives of *Waspada* issues were available from before and after Indonesia's transition.

At archives in Indonesia and the United States, I photographed or scanned the entire *Waspada* newspaper for the month before and two weeks after the legislative elections in 1997, 1999, 2004, 2009 and 2014.[22] These years covered critical periods of electoral reform, highlighted in Chapter 4, that occurred before the 1999, 2004, and 2009 elections. To select a sample of pre-election reports to code, I looked for stories that fell into one or more of three types: (1) interviews with candidates, (2) profile

Table 5.1 Number of Coded Reports by Political Party

	1997	1999	2004	2009	2014	Total
Gerindra	0	0	0	2	4	6
Golkar	38	10	12	21	27	108
Hanura	0	0	0	3	3	6
NasDem	0	0	0	0	8	8
PAN	0	10	8	17	7	42
PBB	0	1	3	2	2	8
Demokrat	0	0	2	8	7	17
PDI	10	1	0	0	0	11
PDI-P	0	3	10	4	2	19
PDS	0	0	0	3	0	3
PKB	0	2	0	2	4	8
PKPI	0	3	1	1	7	12
PKS	0	0	2	3	9	14
PPP	16	8	9	6	2	41
Other minor parties	0	35	21	8	0	64
Total	64	73	68	80	82	367

pieces on candidates, and (3) reports on campaign events, such as a party rally, a community event, or a candidate's door-to-door campaign. These kinds of reports constituted most of *Waspada*'s election coverage.[23] I included all pre-election reports of these types for every day during the three weeks preceding each election. The three-week window was chosen because the bulk of reports on campaigns appeared during this time, which covered almost the whole official campaign period. Campaigns are relatively short in Indonesia—only 17 to 24 days for the elections covered in this study. Using a systematic random sampling technique, I then selected half of the articles for coding. Table 5.1 shows the number of reports coded for each political party per year.

5.2.3. Coding Press Reports

Chapter 2 defined an ethnic appeal as an explicit or implicit message, deployed through words, visuals, or actions, in positive or negative ways, with the goal of mobilizing support by invoking an ethnic dimension, category, or subcategory. With this definition in mind, I developed a codebook to code ethnic appeals from newspaper reports during my fieldwork. In the process, I identified four ways in which candidates could invoke ethnicity in the reports. The first and second ways concerned the types of campaign events and endorsements described in the reports. Events or endorsements targeting a particular ethnic group can be viewed as actions intended to invoke ethnicity, albeit in a somewhat implicit manner. The third and fourth ways were more explicit, as they represented candidates' verbal appeals to particular ethnic groups, as well as references to their own attributes, specifically their identity, work experience, and any particular traits. Although in theory these group appeals could be negative (denigrating an outgroup), in all the reports I read they were positive (i.e., verbally lauding or in some way showing support for an ethnic group).

In the final codebook, these events, endorsements, appeals, and attributes were coded according to particular categories (e.g., religious, indigenous, occupational) as well as more detailed subcategories. The categories and subcategories were developed from reading the reports during codebook development. The codebook enabled the coding of multiple campaign events, elite endorsements, verbal group appeals, and candidate attributes in each report. You can see some details on these coding procedures below.[24]

1. *Events.* The main categories of campaign events coded consisted of party, religious, indigenous, community, and occupational events. Each main category had more specific subcategory codes (e.g., "Islamic" for a religious event, or "farmers" for an occupational event). Newspaper reports usually focused on a single campaign event, such as a political rally, a meeting with an indigenous youth group, or a candidate's participation in a community-level mosquito eradication event. Any social or ethnic identity associated with the event could also be coded: e.g., Buddhist, Acehnese, farmers, youth.
2. *Endorsements.* Elite support and endorsements were defined broadly for coding purposes. Although there were some explicit and official endorsements by associations and elites, implicit support in the form of attendance by particular elites and institutional leaders at a candidate's campaign event was more common. As with campaign events, the main endorsement categories were "party," "religious," "indigenous," "community," and "occupational." Also, any associated social or ethnic identity was coded.

3. *Group appeals.* Verbal group appeals to ethnic and nonethnic social groups were defined as positive statements of support or admiration for a particular religious, indigenous, occupational, or other social group by a candidate. For such an instance to be coded as an appeal to a group, the candidate had to mention the group by name or use a term closely related to the group. In some cases, a candidate was quoted as simply lauding a particular group. In other cases, the candidate promoted particular issues or policies related to a particular group. For example, if a candidate called for increasing teachers' salaries to improve the quality of education, this was coded as an appeal to teachers. The main categories for group appeals were religious, indigenous, and occupational groups, as well as the poor. Within each category, I created more specific subcategory codes such as "Islamic," "Acehnese," or "fishermen."

4. *Candidate attributes.* Candidate attributes consisted of two basic forms: references to candidates' identity and work, and references to their character traits. This information was usually provided at the end of reports by candidates, their supporters, or reporters. Candidates often referred to aspects of their own identity, such as their religion or the region where they were born, as well as their professional work and any organizations in which they were involved. To code these kinds of references from the reports, I used the categories "religious," "indigenous," "regional," "occupational," "political," and "other" (such as sex and age). Finally, candidate traits of leadership, compassion, honesty, intelligence, and morality were occasionally mentioned.

A total of 367 pre-election reports were coded. Figure 5.1 presents the percentage of reports over the five legislative elections that contained each type of event, endorsement, appeal, and candidate attribute. Overall, party events (mostly party rallies) were the most commonly reported type of campaign event. Among the endorsements, support from party leaders was most prevalent. Religious appeals were the most prominent form of group appeal for candidates in North Sumatra. Finally, with regard to candidate attributes, candidates most often mentioned their political experience and sense of honesty in reports.

A closer look at the data revealed some important differences. Candidates appealed to a wide variety of indigenous groups (16). In contrast, the vast majority of religious appeals were Islamic. Over 35% of the reports contained

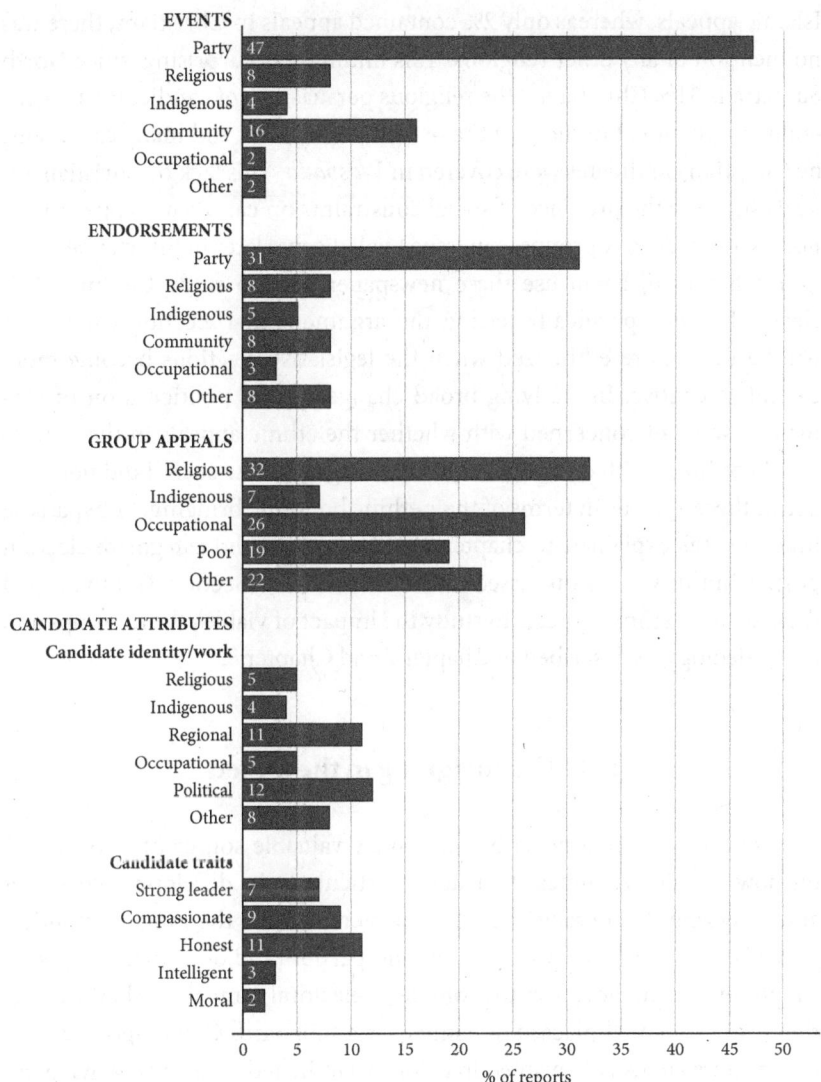

Figure 5.1 Events, endorsements, appeals, and candidate attributes in pre-election reports. The figure includes all 367 coded reports for 1997, 1999, 2004, 2009, and 2014. Some reports contained multiple types of events, endorsements, appeals, or attributes, while others had none. This explains why the percentages in each category can be up to more than 100%.

Islamic appeals, whereas only 2% contained appeals to Christians; there was no mention of any other religions. This finding was surprising, since North Sumatra is 31% Christian,[25] the religious persuasions of candidates are generally proportional to those of the overall population, and many campaigns by Christian candidates were covered in *Waspada*. This lack of Christian appeals suggests the presence of social constraints on candidates appealing to non-Islamic identity groups—an issue I will discuss later in this chapter.

In Chapter 6, I will use these newspaper data to study the impact of electoral rules, specifically testing the argument that election campaigns will become more ethnicized when the legislative elections become more candidate-centric. In studying broad changes in the politicization of ethnicity, I was not concerned with whether the ethnic appeals in the reports sought to bond with or bridge across ethnic groups. As such, I did not categorize these appeals in terms of their ethnic bonding, bridging, or bypassing functions (as explained in chapter 2).[26] However, I did categorize election posters in this way, as discussed in the next section (Section 3). I then used these data on ethnic appeals to study the impact of viable ethnic groups and party ideology, as described in Chapter 7 and Chapter 8.

5.3. Campaigning in the Streets

Election posters are a novel but extremely valuable source of information on how candidates appeal to voters, particularly in developing countries and emerging democracies. Election posters include the range of political advertisements posted by candidates and parties (and occasionally by their supporters) in public spaces to promote an electoral campaign. They can take the form of a small placard, a banner, or a billboard. Contemporary election posters are usually printed in color on laminated cardstock, vinyl, polyester, or PVC. However, candidates and parties have increasingly been using digital billboards, which can cycle through several messages (Ankario 2011; Nyczepir 2012, 2013). Election posters are often secured to posts, trees, or buildings, and they can be distributed across a wide or narrow geographic area. Posters usually contain a large, stylized image of a candidate or group of candidates and can incorporate a range of images and slogans.

Around the world, candidates frequently spend a considerable portion of their campaign budget on producing and posting many election posters across their constituencies. As a result, posters are a highly visible form of advertising in the West. In Ireland, Marsh (2004) found that 83% of respondents reported seeing election posters, a much higher figure than those who had seen newspaper campaign advertisements or election-related information on the internet. In a larger study, Norris (2000: 157) found that 22% of respondents in 12 western European countries had read an election poster in the three weeks before an election. This was only slightly less than the number of people who had read a newspaper article on the election.

Though we lack rigorous data on the prevalence and visibility of election posters outside the West, anecdotal evidence suggests that it is higher. One Malaysian commentator (Shams 2010) observed the stark difference between poster campaigns on Malaysian streets and those in Australia and the United States. Whereas in the latter countries, the streets showed little evidence of a campaign season in process, the atmosphere on the streets in Malaysia was carnival-like, with a massive proliferation of colorful election posters decorating the streets. Meanwhile, journalists reporting on Egypt's 2012 presidential campaign wrote that the country became awash with posters pasted all over walls and hanging from trees. One Egyptian candidate reportedly spent U.S. $6.4 million on 10 million posters.[27] American political consultants working on elections in other countries abroad have also been surprised by the importance of poster and billboard campaigns. In the 2010 presidential election in Ukraine, nearly every billboard had a political message, and outdoor posters and billboards rivaled television advertising as the most popular medium for candidates (D'Aprile and Jacobs 2010).

Although election posters are often viewed as dating back to the premodern era of campaign advertising, they are still popular, largely because they can appeal to voters on an emotional level through the heavy use of visuals. Their slogans can trigger emotional responses and have a particularly persuasive effect on voting behavior.[28] Also, as a largely nonverbal form of campaign advertising, posters can reach illiterate parts of the population, speak to multilingual communities, and influence voters through their use of particular colors and symbols.[29]

Given the prominence and potential persuasiveness of election posters, it is surprising that only a few systematic studies have focused on their impact. These rare studies have generated important insights. They have shown that posters can focus voter attention on local or national political agendas, signal competitiveness, raise name recognition, and ultimately increase participation and support. In Thailand, Fox (2018) explained how political parties and candidates used election posters to direct voter attention to either local or national politics. Analyzing the visual and textual content of more than 12,000 posters, he found that some of them focused on local, personalistic politics by emphasizing the image and messaging of local candidates, while others contained imagery and messaging focused on parties, leaders, and national policies. In France and Belgium, Dumitrescu (2009, 2012) analyzed hundreds of election posters and surveyed politicians. She found that election posters were an important way for candidates to signal their competitiveness to voters, supporters, and opponents. In Ireland, Marsh (2004) also observed how election posters were used as a signaling mechanism. Irish candidates reported that having numerous posters gave the impression that they were credible. Finally, in the United States, Panagopoulos (2009) as well as Kam and Zechmeister (2013) found that election posters raised name recognition and increased overall turnout and candidate support.[30]

5.3.1. Indonesian Election Posters

In Indonesia, posters have a history of being used for the purposes of political mobilization and persuasion. Between 1942 and 1945, occupying Japanese military authorities placed posters around the country, seeking to portray their enemies—the British, Dutch and Americans—as evil oppressors (Anderson 1990: 163). After the Japanese surrender in August 1945, nationalist youth used posters to promote the independence movement, placing them in markets, government offices, restaurants and cinemas, and drawing pro-independence messages with chalk or paint on vacant walls (Anderson 1972: 126; Oey 1971: 35).

Election campaign posters appeared in Indonesia's first election in 1955. These posters contained black-and-white party logos that integrated powerful religious, nationalist or socialist symbols representing alternative ideologies and forms of identification. The symbols chosen were rooted in social cleavages within Indonesian society. Similarly, during the New Order period, many posters contained a party logo and perhaps a brief text invoking Islam or nationalism, but there were some new developments. Some of Golkar's posters added printed illustrations, while the opposition parties made use of hand-drawn imagery and messaging critical of Golkar.[31] Over the years, Suharto's regime tightened regulations on the content of posters. It allowed only black-and-white posters beginning in 1976, required all visual elements in a party logo to be drawn from the symbol of the Republic of Indonesia as of 1987, and prohibited the use of pictures and slogans reflecting individual persons in 1992 (Eklöf 1997: 150). These rules forced the Islamic party PPP to change its potent Islamic Ka'bah logo to a simple star and prevented the PDI from using the image and symbolism of former president and nationalist icon Sukarno.[32]

These restrictions were lifted during the transition. Parties and candidates could now use new technologies to design and reproduce election posters as they wished, provided that they did not engage in hate speech. Specifically, posters were prohibited from insulting an individual, religion, ethnicity, race, class, or other candidate, or from pitting individuals and communities against each other. Parties and candidates also have considerable freedom in distributing election posters, which can be displayed on private property (with the owner's permission) and in any public spaces except schools, government offices, and places of worship.

In the new democratic era, the design and production of election posters have become big business. The need for election posters has been a boon for local printing companies, which often print tens of thousands of full-color posters for candidates during an election season. Also, professional graphic designers, photographers, and design firms are increasingly employed to produce multiple poster designs that feature the candidate wearing various costumes and that include buildings, landscapes, monuments, symbols and elite images—elements that often invoke various ethnic identities. Indeed, the artistry of the humble election poster has been elevated in recent years. In July 2019, an art exhibition was held in Jakarta to celebrate Joko Widodo (Jokowi) and Ma'ruf Amin's victory in the presidential election. The event brought together 44 cutting-edge graphic designers from Indonesia and abroad to exhibit their artworks—a collection of election posters that coupled stylized images of the candidates with various design elements, images and messages.[33]

Although no large systematic studies of Indonesian election posters existed before the present study, opinion surveys have indicated that posters are an important source of information and can influence voters. As Kuskridho Ambardi, the executive director of the survey firm Lembaga Survei Indonesia (LSI), explained, "According to LSI surveys, posters, billboards, and banners provide the most information concerning who the candidates are in regional executive elections."[34] Hill's (2009) voter surveys during regional head elections in Sulawesi and in the cities of Manado and Surabaya also demonstrated posters' effect on voting. In these surveys, voters were asked what communication medium most influenced their voting choice. Among those who voted for the winning candidate, taking the average across three elections, the largest portion of voters (18%) chose direct contact with the candidate or their campaign team. However, 11% said their vote choice was most influenced by the candidate's election posters and brochures—a figure on par with newspapers and TV and larger than all the other survey options.

Given these findings, it is unsurprising that candidates, campaign managers, and journalists with whom I spoke in Indonesia viewed posters as an important part of a successful campaign and spent a considerable portion of their budget on them. Echoing previous studies, they explained that producing numerous posters lent credibility to a candidate's electoral bid and signaled to the public that the candidate had money. Posters also offered face recognition, which was particularly critical for candidates who were not very well known. However, the posters also have some limitations, such as lack of space to describe a candidate's vision and mission. Accordingly, they are just one of multiple campaign activities considered critical for electoral success.

Beyond their importance as a campaign tool for candidates and a source of information for voters, election posters offer a number of advantages for researchers studying campaign appeals in a developing country like Indonesia. First, posters can be used to study appeals at the candidate level and make comparisons across candidates, since their relatively low cost causes them to be used by practically everyone. Candidates who lack the resources or popularity to have a presence in other mediums (such as TV, radio, newspapers, or online) can and do engage in some kind of poster campaign.

Second, they allow us to quickly capture the key campaign appeals that candidates want to convey to voters. With limited space on a poster canvas, candidates must carefully choose the visual and verbal elements that they believe will resonate with voters. The careful use of powerful signs, symbols, imagery, and emotive messages can define a candidate's campaign and mobilize voters around a central idea, theme, or core set of values. This brevity has advantages for research, facilitating content analysis of posters or comparisons across multiple regions and thousands of candidates.

Finally, election posters are a particularly good medium for studying ethnic and partisan appeals due to their heavy use of evocative imagery and emotive messages.[35] Invariably, Indonesian election posters feature candidates dressed in Islamic, indigenous, or political party clothing. They contain short emotive messages, identity-related words, and images of mosques, indigenous houses, regional monuments, party leaders, or the

Indonesian flag. Coding these images and messages can help us identify with reasonable certainty the ethnic and partisan groups to which candidates seek to appeal.

5.3.2. Gathering Election Posters across Indonesia

Photographing election posters in Indonesia is challenging. Campaign periods are short, candidates are numerous, and the country is large, consisting of islands stretching across an expanse of over 4,000 miles. Traveling around the country to photograph election posters is time-consuming, and they remain on display for only a few weeks (see Figure 5.2 for sample posters). Given these challenges, gathering a random sample of posters was not feasible. Instead, a convenience sample of election posters was gathered during the 2009 legislative elections and then during the regional head elections held between 2010 and 2012.

Before the 2009 legislative election, a colleague and I recruited a network of researchers in various parts of Indonesia to photograph as many election posters as they could and send them to us. They were paid a small sum for each poster. In 2010, the second round of regional head elections began, occurring on a rolling basis across the country. Again, we contacted

Figure 5.2 Posters in Salatiga, Central Java, 2011.
Source: Author.

a network of researchers and asked them to photograph regional election posters if an election was taking place in their vicinity. In addition, I spent over a year traveling to different districts in Sumatra, Maluku, and Java to photograph regional head election posters, observe elections, and gather other materials. I chose areas that varied widely in their levels of indigenous and religious diversity. In these districts, I hired motorbike drivers and spent several days or weeks, depending on the size of the district, crisscrossing the constituency and photographing posters.

All the photos of election posters were then cropped and sorted by means of photo archiving software. I excluded any posters from candidates for the national upper house (DPD), any duplicate posters with the same design, and any posters that featured a group of candidates (this last category was not helpful in interpreting the campaign behavior of individual candidates and was very rare anyhow). Each item in the dataset was therefore a uniquely designed poster for an individual legislative or regional head candidate.[36]

Although the regions, neighborhoods, or streets where we photographed posters were not randomly preselected, we made every effort to ensure that the ones photographed and used in the analysis did not differ in any significant way from those we were unable to photograph. To prevent bias produced by gathering posters from a limited number of regions, the research team photographed posters on all the main islands for the legislative and regional head elections. To avoid bias in the posters photographed within a particular constituency, researchers were not informed of any hypotheses and were paid on a per-poster basis. This arrangement gave them an incentive to photograph as many posters as possible, rather than to exclude certain posters due to personal preference or to avoid posters that might disconfirm the research hypotheses.

The final dataset of posters is representative in a number of important ways. In terms of gender, the proportions of male and female candidates were consistent with the candidates competing. All 44 political parties (38 national parties and six local Acehnese parties) that competed in the 2009 legislative elections were represented in the posters, with larger numbers of posters from the major political parties.[37] In terms of regional variation, about half the posters came from Java (where half of Indonesia's population resides) and the rest from the outer islands. Also, the number of rural and urban constituencies was roughly proportional to the national averages.

Finally, the constituencies where researchers photographed posters had levels of indigenous and religious diversity that broadly reflected the country as a whole. Unfortunately, this fact means that many posters came from constituencies with a large Muslim population or a large indigenous group. To test my argument on how viable ethnic groups affect appeals in candidate-centric elections, I needed posters from constituencies with greater variation in terms of their degree of ethnic diversity. As a result, I concentrated on gathering posters from regional head elections in constituencies with larger non-Muslim groups and with higher degrees of indigenous diversity. Many of these were in North Sumatra and Maluku. Oversampling posters from these kinds of constituencies enabled me to more effectively test the argument about the impact of viable ethnic groups on ethnic appeals (see Chapter 7).

Three years of gathering over 25,000 election posters resulted in, to my knowledge, the largest dataset of election posters ever gathered for research. It contains almost 4,000 uniquiely designed posters, photographed in 129 constituencies across 20 of Indonesia's 33 provinces. The posters feature 2,152 different candidates; 62% of the posters came from legislative elections and the remainder from regional head elections.[38] See Table 5.2 for a breakdown of the figures across legislative and regional head elections, by province.[39]

5.3.3. Coding Election Posters

In the content analysis of newspapers, reports were coded for appeals in legislative elections from 1997 to 2014 so as to look for any changes in appeals over time. In contrast, the election poster campaigns of candidates were coded for the purpose of studying how candidates' partisan appeals, as well as their ethnic bonding, bridging, and bypassing appeals, varied across constituencies, across political parties, or between legislative and regional head elections. Three steps were taken to analyze candidates' poster campaigns: (1) coding the content of each poster, (2) classifying individual posters, and (3) creating measures of candidates' poster campaigns—such as the percentage of each candidate's posters that had partisan or religious bonding appeals.

First, the content of individual posters was descriptively coded using a codebook I developed. Coding options allowed for the coding of two candidates on a poster because the regional head posters usually contained the images of the head and the deputy candidate. Each poster was first coded for the election, constituency, name and gender of the candidate(s), and

Table 5.2 Number of Posters, Candidates, and Constituencies by Election and Province

	Legislative Elections			Regional Head Elections		
	Posters	Candidates	Constituencies	Posters	Candidates	Constituencies
Aceh	217	173	3	–	–	–
North Sumatra	71	54	9	783	91	15
West Sumatra	–	–	–	112	19	4
Bengkulu	–	–	–	2	2	1
Lampung	305	229	8	–	–	–
Jakarta	168	124	6	–	–	–
West Java	365	252	7	–	–	–
Central Java	535	392	10	231	17	5
Yogyakarta	253	203	9	51	9	2
East Java	–	–	–	51	16	3
Bali	15	11	4	8	4	2
East Nusa Tenggara	121	109	3	51	35	5
West Kalimantan	–	–	–	5	3	1
South Kalimantan	32	29	3	–	–	–
East Kalimantan	–	–	–	25	8	2
North Sulawesi	29	26	4	21	12	3
South Sulawesi	42	34	3	71	22	5
West Sulawesi	41	35	5	–	–	–
Maluku	113	92	4	90	8	1
West Papua	158	143	3	–	–	–
Total	2,465	1,906	81	1,501	246	49

party. I then identified three ways in which candidates could make appeals in the posters: (1) clothing and headdress, (2) imagery, and (3) textual content. The first two ways are visual approaches to implicitly invoke ethnicity or partisanship, while textual appeals were more explicit. Predefined codes were used to code clothing and imagery; all textual content was transcribed into input boxes and machine-coded for words related to different ethnic and nonethnic groups, using a customized dictionary of Indonesian identity-related words drawn from the posters.[40]

In the next step, each whole poster was classified as to whether it contained an appeal to partisan voters and whether it contained religious and indigenous bonding, bridging, or bypassing appeals. To distinguish ethnic bonding from bridging, I needed to know each candidate's religious and indigenous identity. Aided by my research assistants, I gathered this information from national and regional electoral commissions, newspapers, online searches, and interviews with journalists and other informants across Indonesia. Examples of indigenous poster content included indigenous clothing, an image of an indigenous house, and the use of indigenous language; typical religious poster content included religious clothing, an image of a mosque, or the use of religious slogans.

Each poster was also classified with regard to whether it contained nationalist elements, such as the Indonesian flag. In the Indonesian context, these posters were interpreted as an effort to bridge across voters in a constituency, because Indonesian nationalism tends to have broad appeal. Finally, posters were classified as to the presence or absence of partisan elements, such as party clothing, use of party logos in the background imagery, or images of party leaders.[41]

Having completed these coding steps, I calculated the percentage of each candidate's posters that had each type of appeal. Indonesian candidates frequently produce multiple election poster designs, and they often appeal to different groups through different posters. Because the book's argument is based on the behavior of candidates, it was desirable to assess each candidate's entire poster campaign. This enabled me to use the candidate as the unit of analysis and resulted in a set of eight measures of appeals, which are briefly described below, for all 2,152 candidates in the dataset. On each measure, a candidate's score could range from 0% to 100%. These eight measures became the dependent variables for the analysis presented in Chapter 6, Chapter 7, and Chapter 8.[42]

1. *Indigenous bonding.* The percentage of a candidate's posters that contained elements invoking the candidate's indigeneity, but no other indigenous categories.
2. *Indigenous bridging.* The percentage of a candidate's posters that contained (1) elements invoking an indigenous category (or categories) of which the candidate was not a member or (2) elements invoking indigeneity more generally, appealing to Indonesians from different indigenous groups. I referred to these strategies as broad indigenous bridging and cross-indigenous bridging, respectively, in Chapter 2. In the analysis, I combined these two types of bridging appeals because their frequency was quite low overall. I did the same for religious bridging appeals.
3. *Indigenous bypassing.* The percentage of a candidate's posters that did not contain any elements invoking a dimension or specific indigenous category.
4. *Religious bonding.* The percentage of a candidate's posters that contained elements invoking the candidate's religion, but no other religious categories.
5. *Religious bridging.* The percentage of a candidate's posters that contained (1) elements invoking a religious category (or categories) of which the candidate was not a member or (2) elements invoking religion or religiosity more generally, appealing to Indonesians of different faiths.
6. *Religious bypassing.* The percentage of a candidate's posters that did not contain any elements invoking a religious dimension or specific religious category.
7. *Nationalist bridging.* The percentage of a candidate's posters that contained at least one element invoking nationalism.
8. *Partisan.* The percentage of a candidate's posters that contained at least one element invoking the candidate's political party.

Figure 5.3 presents an overview of these eight appeal measures of candidates' posters. Here, and in the analysis, I use the candidate's poster campaigns—rather than the individual poster—as the unit of analysis. It shows that 82% of the average candidate's poster campaign were classified as indigenous bypassing and 71% as religious bypassing. This indicates that candidates often had many posters in their poster campaign that did not invoke indigeneity or religion. Candidates most commonly included posters with partisan

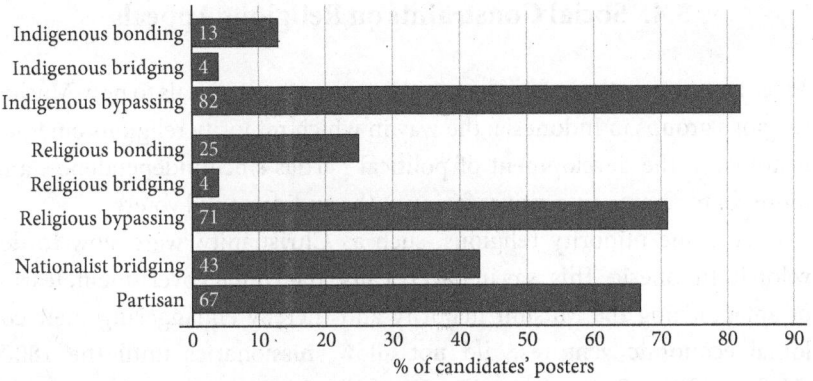

Figure 5.3 Percentages of appeals in candidates' poster campaigns. It includes all the legislative and regional head election candidates' poster campaigns, a total of 2,152 candidates. Candidates' poster campaigns often contained posters with different appeals, such as one poster with an indigenous bonding appeal, another poster with an indigenous bridging appeal, and another with a partisan appeal.

and nationalist appeals in their poster campaigns, followed by posters with religious and indigenous bonding appeals and then bridging appeals.

In terms of indigenous bonding, there was great variety in the indigenous categories to which candidates made bonding appeals. Over 30 indigenous groups are represented in the dataset. Such groups in Indonesia tend to be regionally concentrated, so indigenous bonding appeals varied depending on the region where the posters were photographed.

In contrast, religious bonding appeals were overwhelmingly Muslim (98%), and the tiny remainder were to Christians. Most of the Christian appeal posters were photographed in regional head elections, on the Christian island of Nias or deep in the jungles of Christian-majority regions of Maluku. No candidates made bonding appeals to Hindu or Buddhist religious groups on a poster. The lack of non-Muslim religious appeals was surprising, considering that many posters came from Christian-majority constituencies in provinces such as North Sumatra, Maluku, North Sulawesi, West Kalimantan, and West Papua. This finding, also observed in the newspaper reports, suggests the presence of broad social constraints on appealing to religious minorities—at least in the very public settings of newspaper reports and street-level election posters. These social constraints will be discussed next.

5.4. Social Constraints on Religious Appeals

Three factors help to explain the social constraints on appeals to non-Muslim religious groups in Indonesia: the way in which minority religions emerged historically, the development of political parties since independence, and more contemporary incentives facing both candidates and voters.

First, some minority religions, such as Christianity, were slow to develop in Indonesia. This was in part because the Dutch government, fearful of antagonizing the Muslim majority and thereby endangering their colonial economic ventures, did not allow missionaries until the 1800s (Hefner 1993). Furthermore, many of the Protestant missionaries who came to Indonesia, as well as more recent Catholic missions, engaged in acculturation—adapting to indigenous beliefs and practices so long as they do not conflict with historical Christian thinking. Today, many Christian churches still draw on indigenous beliefs and customs, deliver sermons in indigenous ethnic languages, and incorporate indigenous signs and symbols.[43] In this respect, Christianity has perhaps been grafted onto a stronger and deeper form of identification.

However, despite the diligent efforts of colonial-era missionaries, most conversions to Christianity and other minority religions have occurred after Indonesian independence (Aritonang and Steenbrink 2008: 173). Since independence, the state has played a prominent role in regulating religion and pushing Indonesians to join, often against their will, one of the religions officially sanctioned by the government. With the establishment of the Indonesian state, rules requiring Indonesians to be members of an official religion in order to acquire full citizenship rights pressurized atheists and members of unofficial religions to convert. In the 1950s, the unofficial religions included Hinduism, Confucianism, and traditional or animist religions that were tightly intertwined with indigenous identities and practices.[44]

The pressure to convert increased significantly after the 1965 attempted coup and the annihilation of the communist PKI party. Many PKI supporters had been atheists, so in its quest to eradicate any remnants of the PKI and communism, the New Order government made it mandatory for all Indonesians to have a religion and carry identification stating their religious affiliations. As a result of this policy, and to avoid being associated with the communist party, mass conversions ensued among atheists, followers of Confucianism, and members of animist religions. Many of them converted to Christianity, but a number also converted to Hinduism, which had gained state recognition in 1962 (Bertrand 2004: 74; Hefner 2004: 99–101). Therefore, many Indonesians have joined, relatively recently and often under duress, a minority religion which was intertwined with their indigeneity. Such people may be less driven to act on their religious identities, undermining the utility of efforts by candidates to mobilize support based on minority religious identities.

A second reason for constraints on minority religious appeals is related to the development of Indonesia's political parties and the fact that religious minority parties have never been prominent or popular. In the 1955 election, a number of small religious minority political parties competed unsuccessfully. The largest of these, Partai Kristen Indonesia, better known as Parkindo, and Partai Katolik won just 2.6% and 2% of the vote, respectively. Both parties preformed even worse in the first election under the New Order in 1971, receiving just 1.4% and 1.1%, respectively. Subsequently, Suharto allowed only three parties to compete in elections, and the Christian parties were absorbed into the nationalist-secular PDI.

With the transition to democracy, multiparty competition was reintroduced, and the country began to implement one of the world's most extensive financial and political decentralization programs. This prompted the formation of many new political parties. Ordinarily, open multiparty competition, combined with decentralization in a large and ethnically diverse country such as Indonesia, would lead to the formation of regional parties that could reap many of the political and financial benefits of decentralization by developing a regional power base rather than a national one (Brancati 2006). As such, we might have expected Christian parties to form and mobilize support in provinces with a high proportion of Christians, such as North Sumatra, North and South Sulawesi, East Nusa Tenggara, Maluku, Papua, and West Papua. Similarly, Hindu parties could have emerged in Bali and parts of Central and South Kalimantan.

However, as discussed in Chapter 4, the framers of Indonesia's electoral reforms put in place rules to prevent the formation of regional parties and, more broadly, to limit the number of parties that could compete in elections. Despite these rules, Partai Damai Sejahtera (PDS) formed in 2001. Although the PDS was widely seen as the reincarnation of Parkindo, it did not make overt Christian-based appeals, rooting itself instead in the national ideology of Pancasila. Its electoral results, however, were as poor as Parkindo's: 2.1% of the vote in 2004 and 1.5% in 2009. The PDS met a similar end to Parkindo when it was absorbed into the secular-nationalist Hanura before the 2014 election.

Overall, since independence there have been significant constraints on forming minority religious parties, and the few attempts to establish such parties have proved unsuccessful. During this time period, religious minorities have consistently voted for parties that appeal for support based on a nationalist-secular ideological platform rather than a religious one.

Finally, beyond historical patterns, there are more immediate reasons why voters and candidates avoid the overt politicization of minority religions. Religious minority candidates with aspirations to run for higher office will need broad support in the future from Muslim voters and party leaders, so heavy appeals to a religious minority would likely hurt their careers in the long run. Meanwhile, given the recent incidents of religious violence in Indonesia, minority voters may feel particularly vulnerable when candidates attempt to politicize their religion. Ultimately, this context constrains candidates from making minority religious appeals.

Although these social constraints reduce the likelihood that candidates will appeal to religious minorities, it has not totally eliminated this campaign strategy. Occasionally, candidates make political speeches in churches, engage in religious activities such as praying with voters, and refer to minority religious groups in their messages. However, these religious appeals are more targeted, tending to occur in private settings with smaller groups. In larger public arenas, such as on election posters or in widely read newspapers, these kinds of appeals are extremely rare. Candidates do, however, find other ways to mobilize religious minority groups. One prominent way is to appeal to their indigenous identity. This approach can work particularly well because there is significant overlap between indigenous and religious identities in Indonesia.

5.5. Conclusion

I began this chapter by reviewing approaches to studying the politicization of ethnicity and then introduced my methodological approach to measure ethnic appeals via newspaper reports and election posters. Although the use of election posters is considered a premodern mode of campaign communication (Norris 2000), I highlighted a number of advantages that election posters offer to researchers, particularly with regard to understanding local-level candidates. I further showed how coupling the ethnicity-related content of posters with the candidate's own ethnicity allows us to identify how candidates use ethnic bonding, bridging, or bypassing appeals in their campaigns. One advantage of my methodology is that it is not country-specific; it can be used to study election campaigns in countries beyond Indonesia and can be modified to study other kinds of campaign appeals.

In the upcoming chapters, I will use my measures of ethnic appeals to test the book's argument and to shed light on where and when candidates choose to make such appeals.

III
EVIDENCE

6
Electoral Rules

It was a hot, muggy day in May, two weeks before the 1997 election. Golkar was holding a rally in the coastal city of Tanjungbalai, North Sumatra. A large crowd of 10,000 gathered for the festive event. They were there to hear live music by artists from the region and Jakarta, eat the free food, and possibly get some of the gifts, such as jackets, ballpoint pens, umbrellas, foodstuffs, or even cash, that were often handed out or thrown from the stage. Marzuki, a senior Golkar politician, walked onto the large stage and spoke of Golkar's efforts to promote economic development under the leadership of *Pak Harto* (Suharto) over the last 30 years. "*Hidup Golkar, Pancasila Jaya!*" ("Long live Golkar, success for Pancasila!") the crowd roared when prompted. Quieting the throng, Marzuki asked for their support in the election and introduced the Golkar candidates waiting in the wings.[1]

One of them was Serta Ginting, a politician whose rise and fall sheds light on the evolution of Indonesia's political system. The youngest of six children, Serta grew up in a remote village, but left home at a young age after getting into fights with local youth. Soon, he settled in Rantauprapat, a town nestled among North Sumatra's palm oil plantations. Short and stocky, with his intimidating trademark sideburns and a thick mustache, he scalped tickets at the local cinemas and bus terminal, tussled with other gang members, and led a youth group that assisted a crackdown on suspected Communist party sympathizers in 1965. With these skills, he began work in security on the plantations.

Over the years, Serta became an ardent supporter of Golkar and its nationalist developmentalist ideology. Eventually he entered politics. A gregarious figure, he served three terms as a Golkar representative in the district legislature of Labuhan Batu during the 1970s and 1980s. Throughout the 1980s and 1990s, he continued to work on the plantations, doing public relations and holding leadership roles in a number of worker, youth, and sports organizations.

This background led Serta to that stage in Tanjungbalai in May 1997. Stepping forward, Serta delivered an impassioned speech on Golkar's progress in eradicating corruption—one of Golkar's talking points. No one believed his message, but that didn't matter. With the support of Golkar leaders and his ranking at the top of the party's PR list, his place in the North Sumatra provincial legislature was assured.

The following year Suharto fell, but Serta stuck with Golkar. Campaigning with them again in 1999 he regained his seat and became a leading figure in the provincial legislature. Popular among party leaders, he was encouraged to run for the national legislature. At the 2004 Golkar rallies, Serta rolled out Golkar's talking points on economic development, the rule of law, and the plight of farmers. Placed at the top spot of the party list again, Serta was one of two successful Golkar candidates in his 10-seat constituency and headed to Jakarta.

But in 2009, things changed. Getting placed high on the list of a relatively popular party was no longer enough. With the move from a closed- to an open-list proportional representation system, candidates needed personal votes, and the incumbent Serta struggled in a very competitive constituency that included other popular candidates from his own party. In an effort to adapt and boost his personal appeal, he engaged in smaller, more targeted campaign events on his own. On April 5, Serta was at a Karo Muslim association's building in the small town of Tanjung Pura, Langkat, just north of Medan. On a makeshift stage, the association's leader introduced Serta, telling the small group of members who gathered that they should be proud to have a Karo representative in the national legislature and that he was the only reliable son of Karo. Taking the microphone, Serta said he was happy to see all the cheerful faces of his brothers and sisters, and he went on to explain how, if elected, he would secure funds from the central government to build a road from Langkat to Karo and build health centers and schools in the region. The meeting ended with Serta being honored with the Karo *ulos* (traditional cloth).[2]

In the end, Serta's campaign efforts were to no avail, and his career in office ended in 2009. Golkar won two seats in his constituency that year, but they were assigned to candidates who won more personal votes than Serta.[3] Soon afterwards, he left Golkar, but his 2014 candidacy with the Hanura party was also unsuccessful.

Having spent most of his career as a member of Golkar within a party-centric system, Serta worked the system and experienced great success both during the New Order era and after the introduction of democracy. From humble origins, he embraced Golkar's anti-communist development ideology, demonstrated his support of and loyalty to the party, and, most importantly, forged close connections with its leaders. This strategy took him from the plantations of North Sumatra to the local, provincial, and eventually the national legislature. However, with the introduction of a more competitive candidate-centric system for legislative elections in 2009, Serta needed to quickly alter his approach to attract personal votes. Compared to previous campaigns, he engaged in more small events, sought endorsements from local leaders, appealed to ethnic kin, played up his ethnic identity, and ratcheted down the political party rhetoric. Ultimately, though, it was too little, too late. Serta was surpassed by fellow party candidates who better understood the new system and knew how to mobilize voters more effectively.

This chapter examines the impact of electoral rules on campaigns since 1997. More specifically, it tests the argument that when elections become more candidate-centric, as they did in 2009, the politicization of ethnicity increases and partisan appeals decline.

The chapter contains three parts. In Part I, I present the first major test of the argument. I draw on newspaper reports to compare legislative campaigns over time, presenting evidence of how candidates' campaign events, endorsements, group appeals, and references to their attributes changed after the move to semi-candidate-centric rules in 2009. Part II presents the second major test, as I use the dataset of election posters to compare campaign appeals between the semi-candidate-centric legislative elections of 2009 and the highly candidate-centric regional head elections. The evidence of campaign appeals is measured based on the levels of ethnic bonding and bridging appeals in election posters, as well as their partisan nature. In Part III, I test the three competing explanations of the politicization of ethnicity: ethnic attachment, cultural modernization, and critical junctures.

6.1. Comparing Legislative Elections over Time

6.1.1. A Content Analysis of Newspaper Reports

In Chapter 3, I proposed that party-centric rules provide candidates with incentives to enhance the party's reputation and target party supporters in their campaigns. Conversely, as the rules become more candidate-centric, candidates increasingly have incentives to enhance their personal reputation and target local, and often ethnic, group members in their campaigns. Recent changes in Indonesia's legislative electoral rules offer us an opportunity to test if this is the case. As explained in Chapter 4, Indonesia's legislative elections were party-centric beginning with its first election in 1955. But the 2009 election introduced a change from closed to open-list PR, thereby shifting to what I termed a semi-candidate-centric system. With this change, we would expect candidates' campaigns to evolve. Specifically, the argument predicts that candidates would increasingly organize their own campaign events with ethnic groups and community associations, rather than attending large party rallies with leaders and fellow party candidates. Under the new system, candidates should seek more endorsements from local ethnic and community leaders rather than from party leaders, as well as targeting appeals at local groups rather than partisan supporters. In doing so, candidates can be expected to favor promoting their personal success stories, character, and personal connections with the community rather than the party's platform, performance, and leadership.

To test the impact of a shift towards candidate-centric rules, I draw on data from the content analysis of pre-election newspaper reports described in detail in Chapter 5. To gather these data, I first sampled reports from the North Sumatra daily *Waspada* for the five legislative elections held between 1997 and 2014. I then coded references to (1) campaign events, (2) elite endorsements, (3) group appeals, and (4) candidate attributes. For the quantitative analysis below, each aspect of a campaign (a religious event, indigenous endorsement, etc.) was stored as a binary variable, equal to 1 if present in a report and 0 if not. This method allowed me to see how campaigns changed from one election to the next. For instance, I could calculate whether the percentage of reports describing religious-related campaign events increased or declined.

6.1.2. Open-List PR and the Politicization of Ethnicity

To study the impact of a shift from a party-centric to a semi-candidate-centric system, I compared campaigns before and after 2009 (see Table 6.1). The first column of figures presents the total percentage of reports from the three party-centric elections (1997–2004) that mention a type of event, endorsement, or group appeal. The second column presents the data for the semi-candidate-centric (2009–2014) reports. The "Percentage point change" column shows the degree to which these percentages rose or declined.

To see if any changes in the percentage of reports were statistically significant, I performed separate binomial logit regressions on each dependent

Table 6.1 Changes in Campaigns after the Introduction of Open-List Proportional Representation

	% of Reports		Percentage Point Change	Logit Regression Results		
	1997–2004	2009–2014		Coefficient	SE	Odds Ratio
Events						
Party	66	23	−43	−1.84**	(0.24)	0.16
Religious	5	11	6	0.89*	(0.41)	2.44
Indigenous	1	9	8	2.26**	(0.76)	9.60
Community	7	27	20	1.52**	(0.32)	4.58
Occupational	1	2	1	0.53	(0.77)	1.70
Other	3	1	−2	−0.88	(0.82)	0.41
None	21	35	14	0.69**	(0.24)	1.99
Endorsements						
Party	46	11	−35	−1.91**	(0.29)	0.15
Religious	5	12	7	0.91*	(0.39)	2.48
Indigenous	1	9	8	2.34**	(0.76)	10.36
Community	4	14	10	1.23**	(0.41)	3.42
Occupational	2	4	2	0.59	(0.60)	1.81
Other	8	8	0	0.03	(0.39)	1.03
None	45	56	11	0.45*	(0.21)	1.57
Group Appeals						
Religious	29	35	6	0.27	(0.23)	1.31
Indigenous	4	11	7	1.12*	(0.44)	3.08
Occupational	31	19	−12	−0.65**	(0.25)	0.52
The poor	20	17	−3	−0.18	(0.27)	0.84
Other	20	24	4	0.24	(0.25)	1.27
None	31	29	−2	−0.10	(0.23)	0.90
Candidate Attributes						
Candidate identity/work						
Religious	2	10	8	1.71**	(0.57)	5.51
Indigenous	1	7	6	1.68*	(0.66)	5.39
Regional	4	20	16	1.72**	(0.39)	5.57
Occupational	2	9	7	1.63**	(0.57)	5.13
Political	0	27	27	4.33**	(1.02)	76.07
Other	3	15	12	1.75**	(0.47)	5.77
None	93	46	−47	−2.69**	(0.31)	0.07

(*continued*)

Table 6.1 Continued

	% of Reports		Percentage Point Change	Logit Regression Results		
	1997–2004	2009–2014		Coefficient	SE	Odds Ratio
Candidate traits						
Strong leader	3	11	8	1.26**	(0.46)	3.54
Compassionate	2	19	17	2.44**	(0.54)	11.42
Honest	3	20	17	2.14**	(0.46)	8.48
Intelligent	1	5	4	1.25^	(0.69)	3.50
Moral	1	3	2	1.17	(0.84)	3.23
None	92	60	−32	−2.07**	(0.31)	0.13

Note. Some reports contained multiple types of events, endorsements, appeals, or candidate attributes, so the sum of the percentage may exceed 100%. I coded 205 reports from the 1997–2004 elections and 162 reports from the 2009–2014 elections. $N = 367$. The coefficients are the values from the logistic regression, and standard errors (SE) are for those coefficients. As for the p-values, $*p < .05$; $**p < .01$; $^p < 0.10$. The odds ratio is a measure of the likelihood that an event will happen. See the section entitled "Table 6.1" in Appendix A for more detail.

variable (religious event, indigenous event, etc.). The main independent variable was the electoral rules, equal to 1 for the semi-candidate-centric, open-list PR elections (2009 and 2014) and 0 for the party-centric, closed-list PR elections (1997–2004). The unit of analysis was an individual report. Results from these regressions are presented in the last three columns of Table 6.1. The coefficient figures are the logistic regression's predicted effect of the semi-candidate-centric rules on events, endorsements, appeals, or attributes. Their standard errors are in parentheses. Statistical significance, or the probability of the semi-candidate-centric rules having an effect, is indicated by the asterisks. Because the coefficients are difficult to interpret, I include the odds ratio figure, which measures the likelihood (or odds) of a report containing a given event, endorsement, appeal, or attribute in 2009–2014, relative to 1997–2004. A number greater than 1 indicates how many times more likely the item is to appear, whereas a number less than one indicates how many times less likely it is to appear. From these data, we can see that the shift toward a semi-candidate-centric system had a sweeping impact on campaigns, and in particular on the politicization of ethnicity.[4]

Events
One of the biggest changes in election campaigns was a move from large party rallies in 1997–2004 to smaller campaign events with community-based,

indigenous, and religious groups in 2009 and 2014. In the 1997–2004 period, 66% of reports discussed political party rallies, but this figure dropped by 43 percentage points for the 2009–2014 elections, a decline that was statistically significant. Meanwhile, there was a statistically significant increase of 6 to 20 percentage points in the frequency of appearances of religious, indigenous, and community events in reports. The number of constituents attending these more intimate campaign events tended to range from 20 to a few hundred—far fewer than the thousands or even tens of thousands who attended the mass rallies.

Indigenous events increased in frequency by 8 percentage points, and the odds ratio indicates that an indigenous event was 9.6 times as likely to be reported on in the 2009–2014 elections than in the 1997–2004 elections. Across North Sumatra, candidates increasingly attended indigenous ceremonies, dances, and music events; engaged in rituals such as receiving the traditional indigenous Batak cloth (*ulos*); and were occasionally accepted into the indigenous group by receiving a clan name (*marga*). Candidates also met with various religious groups, visiting women's Islamic groups, religious youth groups, Islamic schools, mosques, and church congregations. Activities involved prayers, readings from the Koran, discussions of the group's needs, and promises of financial support. The reports on indigenous and religious events were often accompanied by photos of the candidate meeting the group while wearing indigenous or religious clothing.

Community group visits were the most common type of event in 2009 and 2014. In these events, candidates typically visited a neighborhood and spoke with a small group of residents.[5] They also frequently used community service and sports events as campaign opportunities. Many reports described candidates providing free mobile medical care to poor neighborhoods, hosting sports events, or working with residents to fumigate mosquito-laden areas, clean ditches, and plant trees. Overall, the mass rallies that had been a staple of Indonesian campaigns became less prominent. With the shift to a semi-candidate-centric system, most campaign activity now involves smaller events that often target local ethnic and community groups.

Endorsements
Endorsements showed a similar pattern. In the 2009–2014 elections, there was a dramatic decline of 35 percentage points in reports with endorsements and support from party leaders, whereas the frequency of reports indicating religious, indigenous, and community leader support increased. Again, these

changes were statistically significant. Since 2009, a far more diverse range of local elites, associations, and groups has expressed candidate endorsements. The percentage of reports mentioning support from local religious leaders and associations more than doubled in the 2009–2014 period, while indigenous support increased almost tenfold. To secure support from these groups, candidates visited local religious and indigenous leaders, Islamic and indigenous youth associations, Islamic schools and foundations, and local mosques. Seeking support from Islamic women's groups—small groups of local women who often meet for Koranic recitation—also became a popular tactic in 2009 and 2014. Notably, the nationalist (non-Islamic) party candidates were the ones primarily adopting this strategy. Compared to previous years, indigenous elite support was much more diverse, with politically active elites representing Gayo, Batak Pakpak, Batak Mandailing, Batak Karo, Minangkabau, as well as Javanese and Indonesian Chinese groups.

The percentage of reports that mentioned candidate endorsements by community associations and leaders increased almost fourfold in the 2009 and 2014 elections. Community groups were involved in various aspects of local development, including the environment, health, education, and sports. Candidates also reached out to local social associations, especially alumni groups from local high schools and universities in Medan. In addition, support from occupational groups was no longer confined to civil service associations but also came from leaders in various other fields, including pensioners, teachers, agricultural workers, and transportation workers.

The 2009 and 2014, reports also specifically named the elites who supported and actively engaged with candidates—for example, at community service events. This tendency was in particularly sharp contrast with the 1997 election reports, in which elites were passive bystanders at rallies, identified simply as community, youth, religious, or indigenous leaders rather than by name. This change was not due to a sudden improvement in journalism, but because candidates actively sought to highlight the support of particular local figures. Overall, with the shift to a semi-candidate-centric system, candidates relied less on party leaders and instead sought support from a more diverse range of local elites and associations, the most prominent of these being local community, religious, and indigenous bodies.

Group Appeals

There was also a rise in group appeals to religious and indigenous groups, but only the increase in indigenous appeals (by 7 percentage points) was statistically significant. In 2009 and 2014, religious (specifically Islamic) appeals by both Islamic and nationalist party candidates increased. In addition, the percentage of reports invoking indigenous groups increased threefold, with candidates appealing to a wider range of such groups. Candidates usually emphasized their personal connection to the group or highlighted the importance of preserving the group's culture and traditions.

Meanwhile, there was a decline in appeals to class-based groups, specifically occupational groups. The vast majority of such appeals involved small farmers or the urban working class. This decline is particularly stark, considering that class was a very salient identity category during the 1999 election campaign. Notably, appeals to women increased in recent years. This rise can be attributed partly to the greater number of female candidates taking part in elections and more strenuous efforts by candidates to secure women's votes through campaign visits to women's prayer groups. In addition, female candidates received more coverage in *Waspada*. In 2009, the publication introduced a special section containing interviews with women candidates, entitled *Kasih Caleg Perempuan* ("Affection for Female Candidates"). In these reports, the candidates often emphasized the importance of voting for a female leader, the struggle for gender equality, and efforts to empower women and help female entrepreneurs.

Candidate Attributes

Finally, there was a clear shift in the focus of election coverage from parties to candidates and their attributes. From 1997 to 2004, reports usually included the party name in the headline and generally described rallies by presenting extensive quotations from party leaders on their party's platform and past achievements. From 2009 onward, the reports became centered on candidates. Headlines often contained the candidate's name, and the narrative of election reports was driven by the personal details and professional activities of individual candidates—their identity, work experience, and character traits.

In *Waspada*'s reports, references to candidates' identity and work experience increased across the board, and all such increases were statistically significant. Candidates increasingly referred to their local indigenous identity in these reports, which frequently described them as dressed in traditional or indigenous clothing. It was also commonplace for local candidates to invoke their regional identity and claim that people need a *Putra Daerah* ("son of the region") representative in the legislature. Compared to the "Jakarta drop-ins" (i.e., people who live primarily in the capital), candidates who are natives of and still live in the region can develop stronger local connections, which can help to increase their personal support.

More column-inches were dedicated to candidates' professional achievements and work experience—for example, their leadership roles in political, business, ethnic, and non-ethnic organizations, or their work experience in specific professions such as law, education, or medicine. One new development was the descriptions of candidates' constituency service. Various reports described candidates' personal efforts to help constituents, such as by providing legal and medical care for individual residents or delivering personal assistance to earthquake and flood victims. References to past political experience also rose sharply from virtually no mentions in 1997–2004 to more than one-fourth of all reports in the 2009 and 2014 elections. Increasingly, candidates attempted to persuade voters that they were qualified to lead because of their previous work experience, leadership roles, and service to the community.

Finally, references to positive character traits of candidates increased in the 2009 and 2014 elections, with 40% of reports containing some such reference, compared to only 8% previously. Candidates frequently portrayed themselves as compassionate, honest leaders who truly cared about the people, never told lies, and had never engaged in corruption. Although, in many cases, the accuracy of such claims might be questioned, the emphasis on these particular traits indicates the kinds of character traits that candidates thought voters were looking for in a political leader.

Overall, the findings offer strong support for the argument. The move from a party-centric to a semi-candidate-centric system was accompanied by a rise in the religious and indigenous nature of campaign events, endorsements, and appeals, as well as by increases in community events and endorsements. In addition, candidates rather than parties have become the main protagonists in elections, with much more attention being paid to their individual identity, work experience, and traits.

6.1.3. Confounding Factors

Several confounding factors other than the introduction of a semi-candidate-centric system could explain the decisive shift observed in campaigns from

2009 onward. One of these is decentralization, discussed in Chapter 4. After the 1999 election, an extensive decentralization program implemented across Indonesia offered substantial revenue and expenditure autonomy at the sub-provincial district level (*Kabupaten/Kota*). Conceivably, the availability of more revenues at the local level made candidates more attentive to local ethnic and community needs in the elections after 1999. Second, the number of parties has fluctuated between elections. An election with numerous parties might create incentives for candidates to appeal to smaller indigenous groups, whereas the presence of fewer parties could foster appeals to larger groups based on religion or social class. Finally, the ideology of parties—specifically, whether they are Islamic or secular-nationalist in nature—may affect campaigns. Potentially, shifts in the proportion of Islamic parties from one election to the next could increase or decrease the frequency of Islamic appeals.

To consider these confounding factors, I analyzed changes in the religious and indigenous aspects of events, endorsements, group appeals, and candidate attributes between 1997–2004 and 2009–2014. In statistical analysis, I controlled for changes in decentralization, the number of parties, and whether a party was Islamic. The results indicated that the rise in religious and indigenous aspects of campaigns was associated with a shift to a semi-candidate-centric system, and that this change could not be attributed to the confounding factors.[6]

6.2. Comparing Legislative and Regional Head Elections

6.2.1. A Content Analysis of Election Posters

Whereas Part I of this chapter focused on election campaigns over time in North Sumatra, this part analyzes the impact of candidate-centric rules across Indonesia, looking at candidates' partisan and ethnic group appeals in their election posters. Under candidate-centric rules, I argued, candidates would tailor their appeals more directly to voters and groups within their constituency. To connect directly with constituents, I expected, candidates would appeal directly to salient ethnic identities by making ethnic bonding or bridging appeals. In contrast, under party-centric rules, the candidate's party affiliation is more important, and so more partisan appeals and more ethnic bypassing appeals are anticipated.

To test these expectations, I compare candidate appeals in the 2009 legislative election and regional head elections held in 2010 and 2011. As explained in Chapter 4, in relation to the highly candidate-centric regional head elections, the legislative elections of 2009 could be defined as semi-candidate-centric. In the legislative elections, the candidate-centric aspect derived largely from the use of open lists, which generated more competition between candidates within parties and offered more incentives for candidates to run personal and localized campaigns. However, these elections still had party-centric aspects. Parties continued to control the nomination of candidates, many parties had loyal followings, and voters could simply vote for a party on the ballot rather than for specific candidates. The semi-candidate-centric nature of the legislative elections contrasted with the regional head elections, which had highly candidate-centric nomination and election procedures. These elections were not at extreme opposite ends of the party-centric/candidate-centric continuum (see Figure 4.1). As a result, they represent a challenging test for the argument.

Data on campaign appeals come from the posters of thousands of candidates competing in regional head and legislative elections across the country. Therefore, this test has a much broader geographic scope than the analysis of newspaper reports in North Sumatra. It draws on a content analysis of almost 4,000 posters from 2,152 candidates competing in 129 constituencies across 20 provinces. As explained in Chapter 5, all clothing, imagery, and textual content were coded. I paid particular attention to any poster elements that invoked religious, indigenous, nationalist, or partisan identities. After I coded poster content, each poster was classified as having an indigenous bonding, bridging, or bypassing appeal; a religious bonding, bridging, or bypassing appeal; and, potentially, a nationalist bridging appeal and a partisan appeal. Finally, I calculated the percentage of each candidate's total posters that contained each type of appeal. Each of these eight measures ranged from 0% to 100% for every candidate.

6.2.2. Regional Head Elections and the Politicization of Ethnicity

To determine whether electoral rules affected candidates' ethnic appeal strategies, I compared the poster campaigns of candidates from the candidate-centric regional head elections and semi-candidate-centric legislative elections. If the argument is correct, I would expect the regional head candidates to have more ethnic bonding and bridging appeals and fewer ethnic bypassing and partisan appeals, compared to the legislative candidates.

To test the argument, I ran regressions on the eight dependent variables—each one representing the percentage of candidates' posters that had a type of ethnic appeal or a partisan appeal. Focusing on candidate's poster campaigns rather than on individual posters fits with the argument, which is centered on the overall appeal strategies of individual candidates. The key independent variable is *Regional head election*, which represents the type of electoral rules under which a candidate was operating. It was coded as 1 for the candidate-centric regional head elections and 0 for the semi-candidate-centric legislative elections.

The argument contends that ethnic group size has an impact on ethnic bonding, bridging, and bypassing appeals, particularly in highly candidate-centric elections, so this factor must be controlled for. To do so, I used the percentage of the population from the largest indigenous group in the constituency. Using the largest religious group size, however, is not an appropriate control because of the social constraints on appealing to non-Muslims. As discussed in Chapter 5, the newspaper and poster data showed that non-Muslim appeals were extremely rare. As a result, only the size of the Muslim population had an effect on religious appeals. In constituencies with larger Muslim populations, we can expect more Islamic appeals, either by Muslim candidates (religious bonding) or non-Muslim candidates (religious bridging). In contrast, when the Muslim population is small, there should be few if any religious appeals. Given these social constraints, I included a variable for the percentage of the Muslim population in the constituency.[7]

The argument also contends that party ideology will have an impact on appeals. Unfortunately, there are some difficulties in including a variable for the Islamic or nationalist orientation of political parties in regressions on the entire database. This is due to differences in party support. In legislative elections, each candidate is supported by only one party, but in regional head elections, a candidate can be supported by one or more parties or can run as an independent. In Chapter 8, I will look more closely at the impact of party ideology by subsetting the data and using various measures of party ideology.

I also included variables to test two competing explanations—namely, the ethnic attachment and the cultural modernization explanation. For indigenous attachment, I included a variable, *Indigenous law*, representing the percentage of villages in the district that observed traditional indigenous law, more commonly known as *Adat*. Across Indonesia, *Adat* is applied to varying degrees to manage interpersonal relations and resolve conflicts. Its prevalence is an indication of salient indigenous identities. For religious attachment, I focused on the most relevant religion, Islam, and measured attachment in terms of the number of mosques per 1,000 Muslim constituents in the constituency (*Mosques*). To measure modernization, I included variables representing the percentage of people living below the poverty line (*Poverty*) and the percentage of gross regional domestic product derived from farming or fishing (*Fishing/farming GRDP*). Higher degrees of poverty and GRDP from fishing and farming implies lower levels of modernization.

I included a control variable for the candidate's gender (*Female candidate*, equaling 1 if female or 0 if male). I did so because most female candidates wore a headscarf in their posters, and although I coded the headscarf as an Islamic appeal for consistency, it is worn as a social convention and can have nuanced meanings.[8] This variable helps to control for any potential difference in appeals from female candidates. Finally, I included a variable for the natural logarithm of the population in each constituency (*Population (log)*).[9]

To test the impact of the candidate-centric electoral rules on ethnic appeals, I drew on the entire dataset, using a candidate's poster campaigns as the unit of analysis ($N = 2,152$). I used a linear probability model (OLS) with robust standard errors for each of the dependent variables, which ranged continuously from 0% to 100%.[10] To get a clear picture of the impact of candidate-centric electoral rules, I calculated the probabilities that candidates made each appeal. In Figure 6.1, the bars show the percentage of candidates' poster campaigns that contained each appeal while holding ethnic demographics, ethnic attachment, modernization, gender, and population at their mean. By comparing legislative candidates and regional head candidates, we can see the impact of candidate-centric rules on appeals. From the argument, I expected that candidate-centric electoral rules would lead to more ethnic bonding and bridging appeals, but fewer ethnic bypassing and partisan appeals. These expectations are reflected in the types of appeals made by candidates in Figure 6.1.

Ethnic Bonding Appeals
First, as expected, candidate-centric regional head elections had a significant and substantial impact on indigenous and religious bonding appeals.

ELECTORAL RULES 137

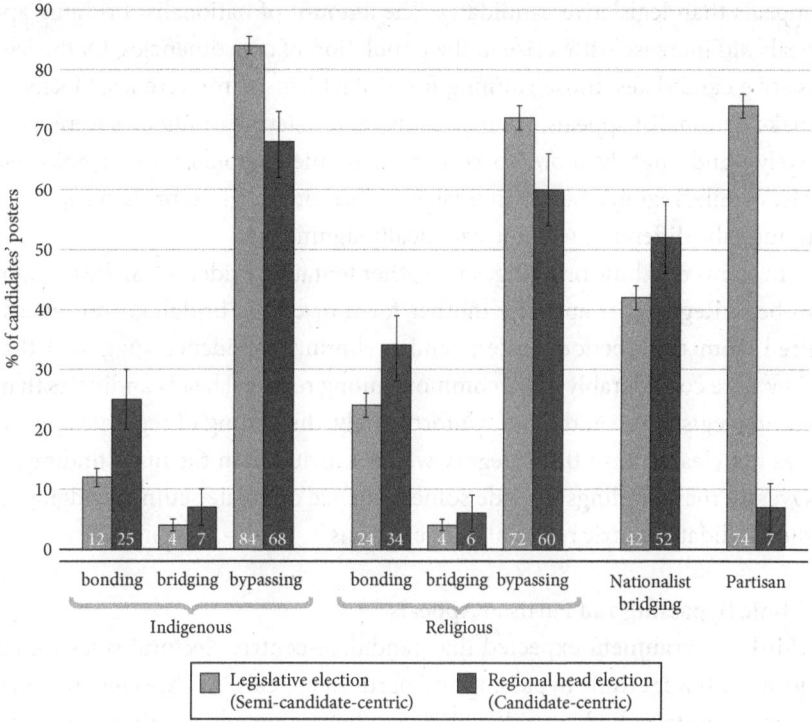

Figure 6.1 Predicted probabilities of candidate appeals for legislative versus regional head elections. Probabilities are calculated for election type (regional head election variable) while holding all other independent variables at their mean. Error bars represent 90% confidence intervals. For the regression table from which these data are drawn, see the section entitled "Figure 6.1" in Appendix A.

Regional head candidates' poster campaigns contained more than twice as many indigenous bonding appeals and approximately 40% more religious bonding appeals than those of legislative candidates. Thus, we have strong evidence indicating that candidate-centric rules in Indonesia do result in more ethnic bonding appeals.

Ethnic Bridging Appeals
Second, the argument predicted that under candidate-centric electoral rules, there would be more bridging appeals. In line with expectations, regional head candidates made significantly more indigenous and nationalist bridging

appeals than legislative candidates. The amount of nationalist bridging appeals did increase with a rise in the population of constituencies. Of the legislative candidates, those running for district legislature were least likely to make nationalist appeals, whereas national legislature candidates were most likely—and slightly more so compared to the regional head candidates. Meanwhile, regional head candidates made more religious bridging appeals, though the difference was not statistically significant.

In terms of ethnic bridging, some other tentative evidence can be brought to bear. Regionalist appeals, another form of ethnic bridging, were measured from the election posters, and preliminary evidence suggested that they were considerably more common among regional head candidates than among legislative candidates. Unfortunately, the coding of regional appeals was not clear-cut, so this category was not included in the main findings.[11] Overall, these findings provide some evidence of greater ethnic bridging in the candidate-centric regional head elections.

Ethnic Bypassing and Partisan Appeals
Third, the argument expected that candidate-centric electoral rules would generate fewer ethnic bypassing and partisan appeals. As expected, regional head candidates had considerably fewer bypassing appeals than legislative candidates, along with extremely low levels of partisan appeals. Only 7% of poster campaigns for regional head election candidates contained partisan appeals, compared to almost 75% of poster campaigns for legislative candidates. This result offers strong support for the presence of lower levels of ethnic bypassing and partisan appeals in the candidate-centric regional head elections.

An alternative interpretation of these findings may claim that the higher levels of ethnic appeals in regional head elections were not because of their candidate-centric rules, but rather because these elections occur within small constituencies where politicians engage in more personalistic campaigning. The evidence, however, indicates that this is not the case. Most of the legislative candidates actually competed for seats in the sub-provincial district legislatures, within constituencies that were smaller than the regional head constituencies. When I compared appeals by candidates competing within the (smaller) district legislative constituencies and the (larger) regional head constituencies, the regional head candidates still made more ethnic appeals.[12] Ultimately, ethnic appeals are not driven by the size of the constituency.

Endorsements

In Part I of this chapter, I compared legislative elections over time, demonstrating how candidates in the 2009 and 2014 legislative elections often engaged in local campaign events with ethnic community-based groups and sought support from local associations and elites. This pattern of connecting with local groups was even more pronounced in the regional head elections. A common tactic for regional head candidates was to include endorsements from local associations, businesses, and institutions in their election posters. The posters frequently included images of local leaders and the logos of local worker, youth, Islamic, and indigenous associations. They designed customized posters that included endorsements from business owners and posted them outside each owner's business. In addition, candidates promoted institutions they had founded that were (at least in name) engaged in community welfare. As shown in Table 6.2, over 10% of regional head candidate posters contained these kinds of local endorsements, compared to fewer than 1% of posters for candidates in the legislative elections. These public displays of local support helped candidates show that they had tight connections with local groups.

Table 6.2 Posters with Endorsements from Associations or Groups

Association or group	Legislative		Regional Head	
	N	%	N	%
Candidate institution	5	0.20%	31	2.07%
Local business	2	0.08%	31	2.07%
Indigenous association	1	0.04%	29	1.93%
Community group	1	0.04%	20	1.33%
Youth association	5	0.20%	16	1.07%
Religious association	9	0.37%	13	0.87%
Workers association	0	0.00%	12	0.80%
Regional association	0	0.00%	7	0.47%
Nationalist association	1	0.04%	2	0.13%
Total	24	0.97%	161	10.73%

Note. N = total number of posters that contained endorsements from an association or group in the regional head election or the legislative election. % = the percentage of the total number of posters in the regional head elections ($N = 1,501$) or the legislative elections ($N = 2,465$).

Candidates in the semi-candidate-centric legislative elections in Indonesia employed many of the same general tactics to connect with voters, but their election posters focused on party affiliations to a greater extent. In their election posters, legislative candidates often wore party clothing, displayed the party color and logo prominently in their poster design, included images of party leaders and rallies, and used party slogans.

The overall analysis of the election posters shows decisively that regional head candidates used a richer variety of ethnic images and messages to appeal to ethnic groups. Compared to legislative candidates, they were more likely to connect with ethnic groups by using Arabic or indigenous languages, dressing in Islamic or indigenous clothing, or including images of mosques and traditional indigenous dwellings, as well as endorsements. Regional head candidates were three to four times more likely to deploy these forms of nonverbal communication than legislative candidates.

6.3. Testing the Competing Explanations

This chapter also provides a good opportunity to test and discuss the three competing explanations presented in Chapter 3. These arguments focus on the impact of ethnic attachment, modernization, and critical junctures.

6.3.1. Ethnic Attachment

To test the first competing explanation, I assessed the impact of ethnic attachment on ethnic appeals. This explanation was based on a proposed fusion between cultural and political spheres. It contends that ethnic politicization is driven by voters' deeply rooted psychological attachment to their ethnic identity and strong allegiance to their ethnic group. If this claim is correct, candidates would appeal to the ethnic identities that are most socially salient. As a result, there should be a correlation between the strength of ethnic attachment and ethnic appeals. The findings from Indonesia, however, indicate a lack of support for this explanation.

First, in analyzing the newspaper reports for legislative elections in North Sumatra, I found a sharp rise in ethnic campaign appeals with the 2009 election. There is no reason to believe that this increase could be accounted for by a strengthening of indigenous or religious identities. No significant interethnic conflicts were occurring around that time, nor were there prevalent ethnicity-related issues in the cultural and social spheres that could have strengthened and politicized ethnic identities.

Second, in studying the election posters from legislative and regional head elections, I found that regional head candidates made higher levels of ethnic bonding and bridging appeals. In the statistical analysis, I included a number of variables including a variable for indigenous attachment and one for religious attachment. I used the *Indigenous law* variable to measure the prevalence of *Adat* in the constituency. For religious attachment, I included *Mosques*, a measure of the number of mosques, to capture the strength of Islam, the only religion that matters when it comes to campaign appeals. These variables did not have a statistically positive impact on ethnic bonding appeals, as the ethnic attachment explanation would have expected.[13]

Finally, if ethnic attachment were an important factor, we might expect at least some appeals to non-Muslim groups. In contrast, even in areas where Christians are a majority and churches abound, appeals to Christians in the press or on posters were extremely rare. The lack of these non-Muslim religious appeals casts further doubt on the ethnic attachment thesis.

6.3.2. Cultural Modernization

I also considered the impact of modernization on ethnic appeals. Cultural modernization theorists posit that modernization and the host of changes it brings about (e.g., urbanization, social mobility, increased prosperity) should undermine traditional ethnic identities and strengthen class-based and nationalist identities. Others have challenged this explanation, claiming conversely that modernization actually strengthens and politicizes ethnic identities. According to this latter account, urbanization and industrialization entail more competition for jobs. As a result, workers and leaders engaged in urban modern sectors have greater incentives to exploit their ethnic group membership as a means of attaining economic resources and political power. A traditional cultural modernization argument would then expect ethnic bonding appeals to be more prominent in less developed rural regions and nationalist appeals to be more common in the more developed urban regions. Meanwhile, those challenging this argument would expect stronger ethnic bonding in the urban regions.

Evidence from Indonesia, however, indicates that neither modernization argument explains variations in the politicization of ethnicity. First, the rise in ethnic appeals in 2009, as captured by the newspaper reports, was so sudden that it cannot be explained by a slow-moving process such as modernization. If modernization were a factor here, we might see incremental change, evidenced by a gradual decline or increase in indigenous and religious appeals, but not a swift rise.

Second, in the statistical analysis of the election posters, I included two variables associated with modernization: *Poverty* (with higher levels implying less modernization) and *Fishing/farming GRDP*, a measure of how rural the constituency is. Overall, more modern districts should have lower levels of poverty and be less reliant on fishing and farming. Findings from the regression analysis about the impact of modernization on candidates' ethnic appeals were inconsistent.[14] In support of the cultural modernization explanation, there were more nationalist appeals in urban areas. However, most of the evidence indicates that modernization cannot explain the variation in ethnic appeals. Contrary to a cultural modernization argument, there were more nationalist appeals in poorer (less modern) constituencies. More broadly, the modernization variables had no impact on indigenous or religious appeals in the statistical analysis. This finding undermines cultural modernization arguments, as well as their challengers who believe modernization politicizes ethnic identities.

Other evidence, however, potentially offers some support for the challengers. Early studies of North Sumatra by Bruner (1961) and Liddle (1970: 124) showed how indigenous identification and practices were strong in the urban areas of Medan and Pematangsiantar. Today, indigenous associational life in these cities remains vibrant. Also, in terms of religion, there has been an Islamic revival in Indonesia since the 1970s. Urban areas in particular have seen a growing number of mosques, more Muslim women wearing the jilbab, and new forms of Islamic student activity at urban university campuses (Hefner 1997; Howell 2001). Backing up these observations, a colleague and I analyzed the poster data from the Islamic party candidates, finding that they made more Islamic appeals and fewer nationalist appeals in urban than in rural constituencies (Fox and Menchik 2022).

6.3.3. Critical Junctures

Finally, I examined the impact of critical junctures on ethnic appeals. In Indonesia, the democratic transition was such a juncture. We would expect this transition to offer candidates strong incentives to politicize ethnicity and to appeal to ethnic groups. Indonesian candidates campaigning in an environment of weak institutions, strong ethnic bonds, and nascent partisan attachment would be expected to seek to bolster their support by appealing to voters' emotional allegiances to their indigenous or religious identities. However, the data from the newspaper reports indicate no evidence of a politicization of ethnicity during the 1999 election campaign.

Table 6.3 compares the *Waspada* reports from the 1997 authoritarian election campaign and the 1999 transitional election. The figures indicate the percentage of reports that mentioned (at least once) a religious or indigenous event, endorsement, group appeal, or candidate attribute. The figure for "Percentage point change" represents the increase or decrease in 1999 (in percentage points) relative to 1997. If democratization had a politicizing impact on ethnicity, we should see an increase in these percentages, but that is not the case. With the exception of religious events, the figures indicate a decline in each of the categories examined.

Table 6.3 Democratization and the Change in Religious and Indigenous Aspects of Campaigns in Reports

	% of Reports		Percentage Point Change
	Authoritarian Election 1997	Transitional Election 1999	
Events			
Religious	6.3	6.9	0.6
Indigenous	3.1	0.0	−3.1
Endorsements			
Religious	7.8	4.1	−3.7
Indigenous	3.1	0.0	−3.1
Group Appeals			
Religious	40.6	31.5	−9.1
Indigenous	6.3	4.1	−2.1
Candidate Attributes			
Religious	1.6	0.0	−1.6
Indigenous	1.6	0.0	−1.6

Note. The first column indicates the percentage of reports from the 1997 election that mentioned a type of event, endorsement, appeal, or candidate attribute. The second column indicates the percentage of the 1999 reports. "Percentage point change" denotes the percentage increase or decrease in the 1999 election. I coded 64 reports for the 1997 election and 74 for the 1999 election.

If candidates and parties were not mobilizing ethnic and religious groups in significant ways, how were they campaigning for support? In terms of events, large political rallies and street parades (*pawai*), prominent during the authoritarian years, remained the most common type of campaign event, particularly for the larger parties. Similar to previous elections, at these events constituents were entertained with *dangdut* (a genre of Indonesian music); given gifts such as party T-shirts, pens, and staple foods; and introduced to the party's new candidates. In terms of endorsements, local religious, indigenous, or community elites played little or no role; rather, regional and national party leaders voiced support for the party and their candidates.

The 1999 election, which occurred amidst the pain of a devastating financial crisis, did exhibit a shift in the kinds of appeals made. Candidates and party leaders from an array of new parties spent much of their time criticizing Golkar and its leadership, emphasizing the need for democracy to flourish, calling for political reform, and promising to stamp out corruption once and for all. When candidates did make identity-group appeals, they often appealed to working-class occupational groups and the poor, those most affected by the financial crisis. In these appeals, they emphasized issues of social justice; for example, they appealed to fishermen by criticizing the large fishing companies, to farmers by proposing land reform, and to laborers by arguing that wages were too low, and that the government had continually ignored workers and their rights.

Although many new parties formed for the 1999 election, the new party system, to some degree, reflected the system from the 1950s—one rooted in traditional sociocultural divides or what is termed *aliran* (streams) in the Indonesian literature.[15] In 1999, the political parties were largely divided in their views on the role of Islam, with the main cleavage between nationalist and Islamic parties. Candidates in these parties toed the party line, and their appeals corresponded with their party's orientation; for instance, Islamic appeals were almost totally limited to the Islamic party candidates. Meanwhile, nationalist party candidates eschewed explicit religious appeals, but would occasionally use nationalist appeals.

In the end, there is little evidence of an increase in the politicization of religious or indigenous groups during the transitional election of 1999. This finding is all the more striking when one considers the swiftness with which the transitional election was held—before democratic institution building and constitutional reform, and under a cloud of serious ethnic conflicts in various parts of Indonesia. The events, endorsements, and rhetoric of the

1999 campaign suggest that the context of the election (held during a severe national financial crisis) and the use of party-centric rules were the most powerful factors in shaping campaigns and mitigating ethnic politicization. The parties and candidates continued to engage in large party rallies, and national party leaders played prominent roles, focusing their campaigns on the immediate issues of poverty, corruption, and political reform and basing their appeals on economic interests rather than ethnic identities.

Overall, then, the competing explanations related to ethnic attachment, modernization, and critical junctures all fail to explain the observed politicization of ethnicity in Indonesian elections. Instead, the evidence presented in this chapter points to the party-centric or candidate-centric nature of elections as a better explanation of why candidates do or do not make ethnic appeals.

6.4. Conclusion

Indonesian elections have become more candidate-centric in recent years. The key changes were a move to fully open lists in the 2009 legislative elections and the introduction of direct elections for regional heads in 2005. This chapter has presented both qualitative and quantitative evidence to support the book's argument that the move toward a candidate-centric system in Indonesia has resulted in an increase in politicization of local ethnic identities and a decline in appeals to partisan identities. In Chapter 7 and Chapter 8, I test the argument further by exploring the factors that influence candidates' choice of ethnic appeals. Specifically, I use poster data to examine the effect of viable group size and party ideology on candidates' choice among ethnic bonding, bridging, and bypassing appeals.

7
Viable Ethnic Groups

In the first half of 2010, a number of regional head election campaigns took place in the ethnically diverse province of North Sumatra. I traveled to various parts of the province to observe the campaigns and gather election materials. One of my more interesting visits was to the popular tourist destination of Samosir, nestled in the heart of North Sumatra. Samosir is a large island surrounded by the massive Lake Toba. Its relatively cool climate, scenic views, and thriving Batak culture make it attractive to tourists. It is considered the ancestral home of the Batak Toba, one of the several Batak groups indigenous to Sumatra.[1] The Batak, and particularly the Batak Toba, are well-known throughout Indonesia for their gregariousness and their love of art, music, and singing. Traditionally a well-educated group, the Batak Toba have often been active in government and politics at local and national levels.

Samosir today is still inhabited almost totally by the Batak Toba, who are split between Protestants (58%) and Catholics (40%). Given these demographics, a "minimum winning size" argument would predict that candidates and voters in the election would mobilize around a religious cleavage, politicizing their Protestant–Catholic divide. That, however, did not occur. None of the Protestant or Catholic Toba candidates even alluded to a religious divide in their posters or in press reports. Instead, they overwhelmingly appealed to their indigenous Batak Toba identity through the use of traditional clothing, imagery of Batak houses, and the use of the Batak language. It appeared that social constraints on appealing to Christian identity groups left indigenous identity as the only ethnic identity available to Samosir candidates. But maybe this interpretation was mistaken. Perhaps, I wondered, these indigenous appeals were prevalent because the Batak Toba identity was so strong that *every* candidate felt compelled to appeal to it.

To explore this idea further, I traveled 50 kilometers to the provincial town of Pematangsiantar. A regional hub for transport, trade, and industry, this town is also famed for its Batak culture and has a thriving, though somewhat smaller, Batak Toba community, constituting 45% of the population.

There, I found that Batak Toba candidates campaigned very differently compared to their indigenous kin in Samosir. In Pematangsiantar, Toba candidates presented themselves in their posters and in the press in far more secular ways, dressing in suits and replacing Batak symbolism with nationalist symbols, such as the Indonesian flag. Ultimately, it didn't appear that it was a strong Batak Toba identity that was driving appeals. Since the Batak Toba were no longer a group large enough to secure electoral victory, Toba candidates in Pematangsiantar lost the incentive to politicize them and instead chose to appeal more widely.

These two examples demonstrate the importance of the size of ethnic groups, but also the critical role that social constraints can play in ruling out certain appeal options. In this chapter, I consider how these two factors—group size and social constraints—determine which groups are viable targets for candidates' appeals, and which are not. Building on this understanding, we can then identify the kinds of ethnic bonding, bridging, and bypassing appeals a given candidate is likely to make.

The chapter contains three parts. In Part I, I show that regional head candidates from viable ethnic groups are more likely to make ethnic bonding appeals, whereas those from nonviable groups usually prefer ethnic bridging and/or bypassing appeals. In Part II, I consider the multiple ethnic identities of candidates and predict the kinds of appeals they will make. To test these predictions, I draw on election poster data from 49 regional head elections and provide statistical analysis, a qualitative discussion of individual candidates, and two controlled comparisons. Next, I illustrate how ethnic diversity promotes bridging and bypassing appeals. In Part III, I show how ethnic bonding appeals can be suppressed by the three second-level factors introduced previously—a strong ethnic reputation, a crowded field of coethnic candidates, and an uncompetitive electoral contest.

7.1. Viable Ethnic Groups and Appeal Strategies

This chapter analyzes regional head elections held across 13 provinces between 2010 and 2012, including the election of provincial governors as well as district heads (mayors and regents) at the sub-provincial level. These elections, conducted every five years, involve pairs of candidates: a head and a deputy. Up until 2015, the leading candidate needed to secure at least 30% or more of the total vote to win the election in the first round of voting. If no candidate won 30%, the top two candidates competed in a runoff. Since 2015, candidates only needed a simple plurality to win. As described in Chapter 4, these regional head elections are highly candidate-centric, usually won by locally popular entrants with strong local networks and plenty of financial support. The competition can be quite stiff, as these are powerful and potentially very lucrative positions. Since Indonesia's extensive decentralization program was implemented after the transition to democracy, regional heads enjoy considerable control over local resources, revenues, and policymaking (Hofman and Kaiser 2004).

Although the candidates campaign as pairs, in my analysis I focus on the identity and actions of the head candidate, because this is the more important position and thus head candidates are scrutinized more carefully. In addition, head candidates select their running mate, and that choice is often part of their electoral strategy. They might choose a deputy from a different ethnic group to bridge across other groups, or a co-ethnic to signal an ethnic bonding strategy.

7.1.1. Viable Ethnic Groups

Since these elections are highly candidate-centric, I expected that the constituency rather than the party would affect candidate appeals. In Indonesia, ethnicity is an important part of social life and popular candidates have a good understanding of local ethnic demographics, identity attachments, social divisions, and social norms related to ethnic groups in their constituency. Candidates can draw on this information when deciding among ethnic bonding, bridging, and bypassing appeal strategies. Candidates who are members of a politically viable ethnic group will see distinct advantages in making ethnic bonding appeals directed at this group. For a candidate's group to be politically viable, it must satisfy two conditions: (1) the ethnic group must be large enough to win the election, and (2) there must be no social constraints discouraging candidates from appealing to this group. When candidates are members of politically nonviable ethnic groups, they are more likely to choose a bridging or a bypassing strategy— reaching out to other minority ethnic groups or avoiding the use of ethnicity in their campaign (as explained in Chapter 3).

Classifying Indonesian candidates as members of viable or nonviable indigenous groups is quite straightforward, since there are no broad constraints on any particular indigenous groups. If a candidate's indigenous group represented over 50% of the constituency's population, I classified that candidate as a member of a viable indigenous group, and I expected to see indigenous bonding appeals. If the candidate's indigenous group constituted less than 50% of the population, then I predicted indigenous bridging and/or bypassing, along with nationalist appeals (because nationalist appeals generally resonate with a larger group of voters). I chose 50% as the breakoff point because these were majoritarian elections and to be safe, a candidate would need to reach for 50% of the vote.[2]

Classifying viable and nonviable religious groups was more complicated. If the candidate's religious group was less than 50%, then I automatically identified it as a nonviable religious group and predicted a bridging or bypassing strategy. Alternatively, if the candidate was from a majority religious group within the constituency, then I considered whether there were any constraints on appealing to this religious group. Indeed, there are social constraints on appealing to non-Muslim groups in Indonesia, as I explained in Chapter 5 by reference to the historical development of Indonesian political parties and minority religions, along with other contemporary factors facing candidates and voters. Given this social constraint, non-Muslim candidates from winning religious groups have limited ability to appeal explicitly to their religious kin. As a result, they were classified as members of nonviable religious groups even if their group represented over 50% of the constituency's population. Accordingly, I expected all the non-Muslim candidates to make religious bridging and/or bypassing appeals, plus nationalist bridging appeals. Lacking similar constraints, Muslim candidates where Muslims represented a majority of the population were all classified as members of a viable religious group and were thus expected to make religious bonding appeals. These expectations are illustrated in Figure 7.1.

7.1.2. The Impact of Ethnic Group Viability on Appeals

To test the impact of being a member of a viable ethnic group on ethnic appeals, I first carried out a statistical analysis of all regional head candidate appeals. The dataset contains 1,501 uniquely designed posters from 246 candidates competing in 49 regional head constituencies. For the statistical analysis, I used seven dependent variables: three for indigenous bonding,

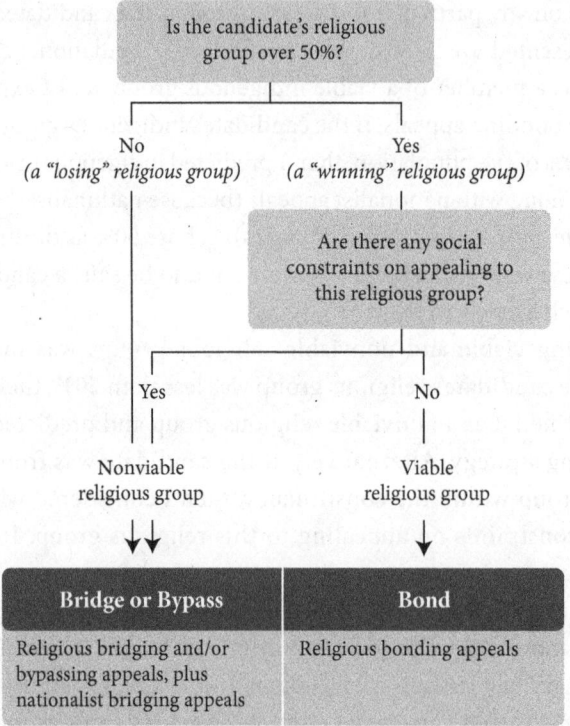

Figure 7.1 Classifying candidates as members of viable and nonviable religious groups.

bridging, and bypassing appeal variables; three for religious bonding, bridging, and bypassing appeal variables; and one nationalist bridging appeal variable. Each was measured as a percentage (from 0 to 100) of the candidate's total posters that contained the particular appeal. Essentially, these variables measure the degree to which every regional head candidate engaged in each type of appeal.

For the two key independent variables, as explained above, I determined whether each candidate was a member of a *viable indigenous group* and a *viable religious group*. These were binary variables, set to 1 if a candidate was a member of a viable group and 0 if not. I used the same set of covariates as in the previous chapters for ethnic attachment, modernization, gender, and population.[3] I also included a religious attachment variable specific to the candidate's religious group,[4] and I added another control variable, the number of candidates competing in the election. Potentially, when more candidates are competing, the expectation that ethnic groups would split their vote could lessen the utility of making ethnic bonding appeals.

Figure 7.2 illustrates the probabilities that candidates would make different kinds of appeals. The height of the bars represents the percentage of a candidate's poster campaign that contains bonding, bridging, or bypassing appeals. Appeals were measured separately for candidates from viable and nonviable indigenous and religious groups, and the other covariates and controls (e.g., levels of ethnic attachment, modernization) were held at their mean.[5] The differences between candidates were consistent with the prediction. Being a member of a viable ethnic group had a positive impact on

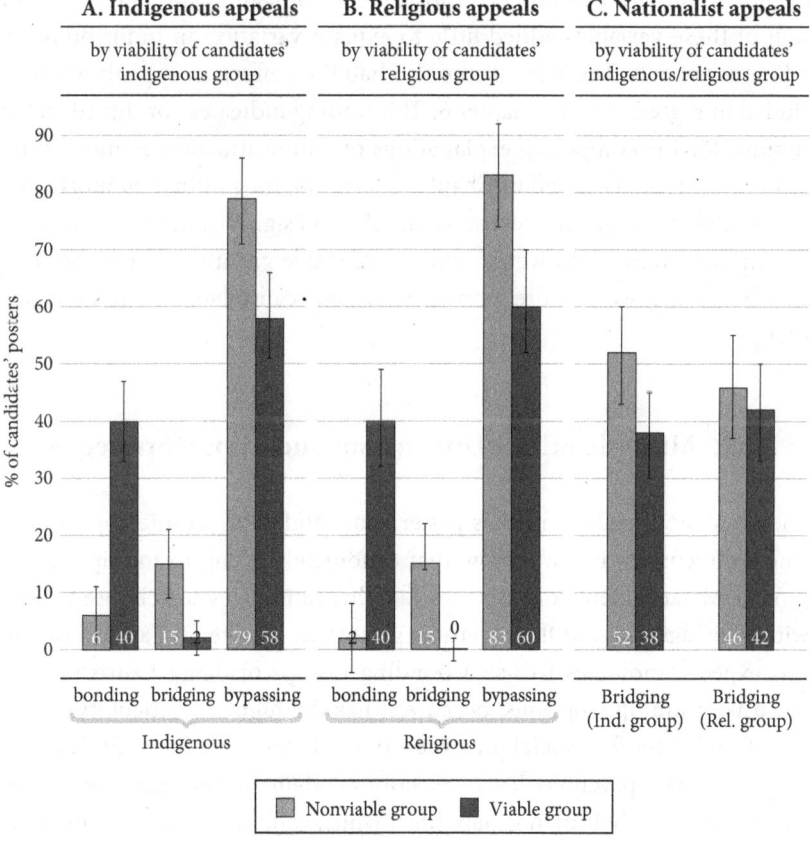

Figure 7.2 Ethnic appeals of candidates from viable and nonviable groups. Error bars represent 90% confidence intervals. See the "Figure 7.2" section in Appendix A for the regression table from which these data are drawn.

indigenous and religious bonding appeals, but a negative impact on bridging and bypassing appeals. The impact of viable indigenous and religious group membership was substantial, and also statistically significant in all cases except one—namely, viable religious group membership's impact on nationalist bridging appeals. For candidates belonging to a viable indigenous or religious group, approximately 40% of all campaign posters were bonding posters, as compared to only 2% to 5% for members of a nonviable group. Importantly, religious group size alone could not explain religious appeals; social constraints on non-Islamic religious appeals were also a factor. This point will become clearer when we look closer at candidate posters in Part II of this chapter.

Almost all the measures used for strength of indigenous and religious attachment and level of modernization were not significant, and the inclusion of these variables added little to explain variation in indigenous and religious appeals. These measures also had little effect on appeals when included in regressions in Chapter 6. This finding indicates continued lack of support for the competing explanations of ethnic attachment and cultural modernization, discussed in Chapter 3. Overall, the findings supported the theory. Bonding appeals were substantially and significantly more common among candidates who were members of viable groups, whereas bridging and bypassing were more prevalent among candidates from nonviable groups.

7.2. Multiple Ethnic Dimensions and Appeal Strategies

The regression analysis reveals patterns of candidates' ethnic appeals on a single dimension, but we know that candidates belong to multiple ethnic groups. My argument considers the fact that candidates can choose to bond with or bridge across different ethnic groups. In Chapter 3, I argued that we can expect candidates to use a bonding-trumps-bridging heuristic when faced with multiple options, because it has the highest probability of success. Candidates face social pressures to bond with their own ethnic group; co-ethnics have psychological dispositions and often experience social pressure to vote for their own group. Meanwhile, candidates face credibility issues in targeting non-co-ethnics, and bridging is undermined by intergroup rivalries and distrust. As a result, more time and effort will be spent bonding as it is a less risky strategy compared to bridging.

Table 7.1 Candidates with Two Ethnic Identities and Their Appeal Strategies

Viable Group	Candidate Type	Dominant Appeal	Secondary Appeal
Indigenous and religious	Viable dual-group candidate	Bond with indigenous and/or religious group	
Indigenous	Viable indigenous group candidate	Bond with indigenous group	Bridge across or bypass religious dimension
Religious	Viable religious group candidate	Bond with religious group	Bridge across or bypass indigenous dimension
None	Nonviable dual-group candidate	Bridge across or bypass indigenous and religious dimensions, plus nationalist bridging	

Table 7.1 presents a typology in which four types of Indonesian candidates are classified in terms of the viability of their indigenous and religious groups. Candidates from religious and indigenous groups that are both viable (top left quadrant) can make bonding appeals to both groups. Others have only one viable group, either religious or indigenous (top right and bottom left). I expect them to bond with the viable group, but to bridge across the other dimension of ethnicity. Based on the bonding-trumps-bridging heuristic, I expect the bonding option to be dominant, with the bridging approach secondary. Finally, the candidates with no viable group to appeal to (bottom right) are expected to make bridging and bypassing appeals and to have the highest level of nationalist bridging appeals, compared to the other candidate types. The following sections present evidence from statistical tests, qualitative examples, and controlled comparisons of candidates' election posters to demonstrate how these four types of candidates engage in these patterns of ethnic appeals.

7.2.1. Statistical Evidence

To visualize the kinds of appeals different candidate types made, I divided the dataset into the four types of candidates. Figure 7.3 presents the data for each type of appeal by candidate type. Each bar represents one type of ethnic

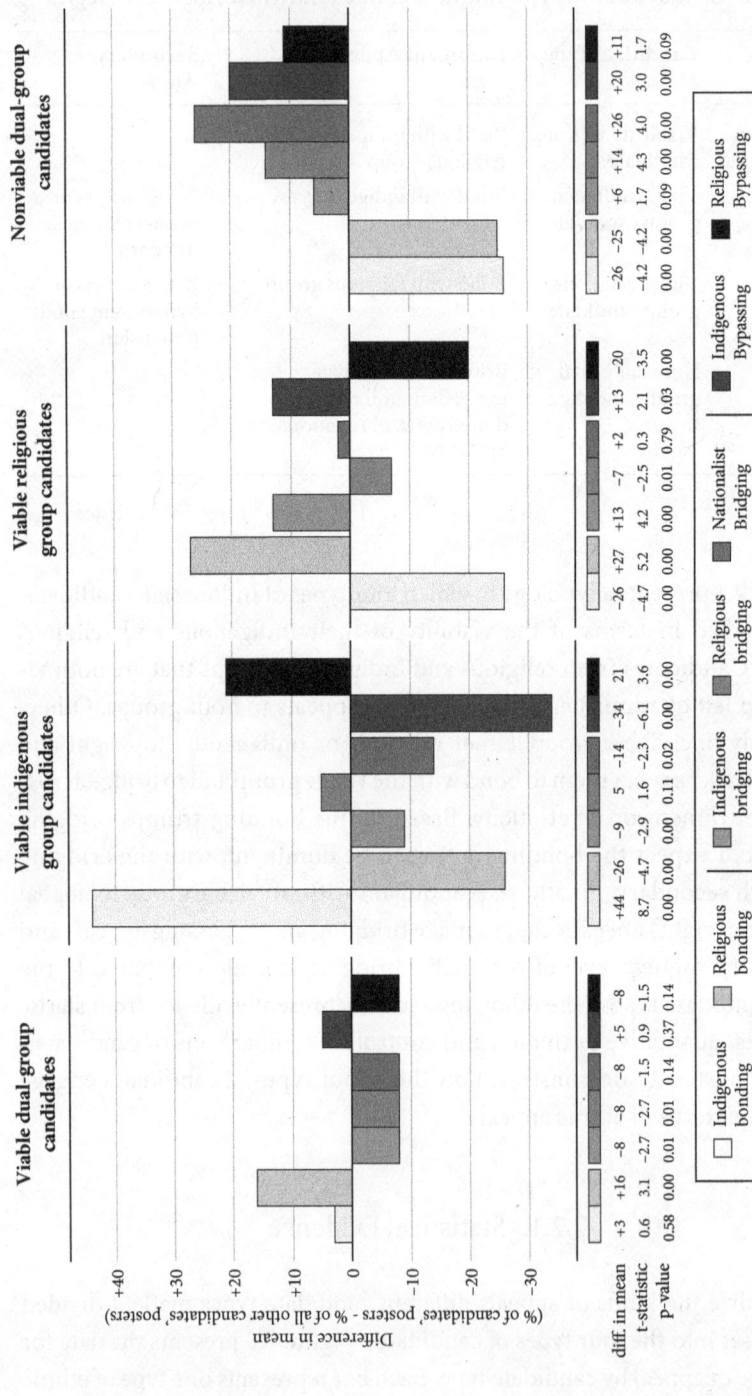

Figure 7.3 Frequency of ethnic appeals by candidate type. Statistical significance was computed by testing the equality of the means (*t*-statistic and *p*-value).

appeal for one type of candidate, and the height of the bar measures the degree to which the frequency of the ethnic appeal was above or below the average for all other candidates. This difference between the means ("diff. in mean") is also written under each bar. Below, I present the results for each of the four categories of candidates.

First, viable dual-group candidates were expected to use predominantly bonding appeals. The average level of bonding appeals for the 74 viable dual-group candidates, as compared to that for all other candidates, offers support for this prediction. The proportion of candidate posters with indigenous and religious bonding appeals was above average by 3% and 16%, respectively. These findings reflect the expected preference for bonding, but the difference for religious bonding appeals was much higher and also statistically significant. Meanwhile, in line with expectations, the other types of bridging appeals and religious bypassing appeals were below average in frequency. The only exception was indigenous bypassing, which was slightly above average.

These 74 viable dual-group candidates in the dataset also provided an opportunity to test the widely accepted "minimum winning size" concept. These candidates belonged to indigenous and religious groups that were large enough to ensure victory. If candidates wanted to choose the "minimum winning size" ethnic category, we would expect them to target their appeals toward the smaller of these two groups. The evidence, however, points in the opposite direction. On average, only 26% of their posters targeted the smaller group with ethnic bonding appeals and 36% targeted the larger group. (The remaining 38% of their posters had nonethnic appeals.) Thus, the "minimum winning size" concept fails to explain the behavior of candidates who were in a position to form a minimum winning coalition. Furthermore, the concept tells us nothing about the other 172 candidates (70% of the dataset) who were not in a position to choose between a minimum- and a maximum-size ethnic category. Notably, all the dual-group candidates were Muslim, many of which campaigned in the more homogeneous constituencies in Java. The empirical evidence here suggests that when given the option, they had a clear preference to make Islamic rather than indigenous appeals.

Second, we turn to the candidates who had only a viable indigenous group. The results for the 62 candidates who fit this criterion overwhelmingly supported the expectation that their dominant ethnic appeal would be to bond with their indigenous group. Indigenous bonding appeals were 44% above average, a statistically significant difference. Meanwhile, their secondary appeals were both above average as expected, with religious bridging

5% above average and religious bypassing 21% above average. All other appeals were above or below average as expected, and the differences were statistically significant. Most of these candidates were Christian candidates, and many were competing in Christian-majority constituencies. However, there were virtually no appeals to their religious group, a further indication of the strong social constraints on non-Islamic religious appeals.

Third, 64 candidates had only a viable religious group. As expected, these candidates' posters displayed above-average occurrences of their dominant appeal, religious bonding (+27%), and also their secondary appeal, indigenous bridging (+13%) and indigenous bypassing (+13%). All these results were statistically significant. Patterns of appeals among candidates who had only one viable group to appeal to presents evidence for the bonding-trumps-bridging heuristic. For these candidates, the expected bonding and bridging appeals were both above average, but bonding was markedly higher than bridging.

Finally, the 46 nonviable dual-group candidates constituted probably the most interesting set. Due to the small size of their ethnic groups and/or the presence of social constraints, they had strong incentives to make ethnic bridging or bypassing rather than bonding appeals. The data reflect this situation, with indigenous and religious bridging and bypassing all above average by statistically significant margins. These candidates were also the most likely to use nationalist bridging appeals. This result is also not surprising, since in the absence of any viable group to bond with, nationalism could be adopted as a broadly inclusive form of identity and used to bridge across indigenous and religious groups.[6]

7.2.2. Qualitative Evidence

I will now discuss qualitative evidence for the four types of candidates delineated in the preceding discussion. For each candidate type, I discuss general patterns of appeals in their posters as well as specific poster examples, which are presented as images in a series of figures.

Viable Dual-Group Candidates

Viable dual-group candidates had the option to bond with either their indigenous or religious group. Three examples of these candidates come from the 2011 district head elections in Salatiga, a small city in Central Java. Salatiga sits at the foot of Mount Merbabu, among the fruit- and vegetable-growing highlands, and has a cool climate. It is a center for trade in agricultural products, textile production, and crafts, such as batik, basket weaving, and wood carving. The majority of inhabitants are Javanese (94%) and Muslim (76%), but there is also a significant number of Christians.

In the 2011 election, two candidate teams mixed Javanese and Islamic symbolism to a great extent. Diah Sunarsasi, a Muslim woman and the incumbent deputy mayor, led one of the teams. To present a religiously mixed ticket, Diah chose a young Christian chairman of the local parliament as her running mate. Diah's posters had a youthful and bright feel to them and included the name *Dihati*, as a team name.[7] Rather than wearing traditional Javanese batik clothing, the pair dressed in bright red modern batik. Diah wore an Islamic headdress in all their posters, but in a loose style, allowing her Javanese hairstyle to show through (for an example, see Figure 7.4, top left). To shore up her Islamic affiliation, Diah also had posters that advertised her endorsement by Salatiga's Kyai forum—local experts in Islam and leaders in Salatiga's mosques and Islamic schools (*pesantren*). To affirm her Javanese connections, the Javanese language was used on their posters, with phrases such as "*Cedhak Karo Wong Cilik*" ("Close to the Little People") and "*Ora Iki Ora!*" ("This Is My Only Choice!"). In addition, most of Diah's posters made some nationalist bridging appeals by incorporating design elements that represented the red and white of the Indonesian flag. Red, the primary color of their posters and clothing, is also the main color of Diah's supporting party, the PDI-P. Overall, her posters primarily espoused Islam and Javanese indigeneity, but they also touched on themes of youth, class, partisanship, and nationalism.

Bambang Supriyanto led another candidate team and also used Islamic and Javanese imagery in his posters. Bambang was involved in the construction business, and his running mate was a local academic. Both were Muslim and Javanese. In his posters, Bambang Supriyanto wore a secular suit and a *songkok* (a traditional truncated, cone-shaped hat) while his running mate wore a conservative Islamic headdress that fully covered her hair. They also used phrases from the Javanese language such as "*Iki Sing Tak Pilih*" ("These Are My Choices") and Islamic calligraphy in some of their posters. Overall, Bambang Supriyanto's poster campaign coupled prominent Islamic appeals with moderately high levels of Javanese imagery and language.

Finally, in contrast to their two competing tickets, the candidate Bambang Soetopo's posters drew exclusively on Javanese identity and avoided Islamic

Figure 7.4 Viable dual-group and viable indigenous group candidate posters. Top left: Diah Sunarsasi and Teddy Sulistio (Dihati), Salatiga. Top right: Bambang Soetopo and Rosa Darwanti (Poros), Salatiga. Bottom left: Martua Sitanggang and Mangiring Tamba, Samosir. Bottom right: Sumbul Sembiring Depari and Paham Ginting (Erdilo), Karo.
Source: Author.

symbolism altogether. This was Bambang Soetopo's third run for the district head position. In previous attempts, Bambang used more Islamic appeals, but due to his lack of success he tried a different tactic this time, appealing to Javanese indigeneity and reaching out across religious divides. He chose a female Christian running mate, Rosa Darwanti. In their posters, she dressed in Javanese clothing, complete with a traditional Javanese hairstyle (*sanggul*). The background imagery gave the posters a feeling of mysticism and timelessness, with ancient Javanese patterns etched into a background of bright stars and contrasting shades of yellow (see Figure 7.4, top right). Religious and nationalist imagery were noticeably absent from all their posters. Overall, these three candidates, Diah Sunarsasi, Bambang Supriyanto, and Bambang Soetopo, are good examples of viable dual-group candidates, candidates who sought to bond with their religious and/or indigenous kin through their election posters.

Viable Indigenous Group Candidates
Samosir, the scenic island introduced at the beginning of this chapter, is overwhelmingly populated by Christian Batak Toba. Accordingly, all candidates, both heads and deputies, who competed in Samosir's election were Batak Toba with a Protestant or Catholic faith. They qualified as viable indigenous group candidates because they had incentives to appeal to their majority indigenous group, but they were constrained in making Christian appeals. As expected, these candidates bonded with their indigenous group primarily through the use of indigenous Batak symbolism, invariably dressing in suits with a traditional Batak Toba cloth (an *ulos*) slung over the shoulder. Background images displayed Samosir's scenic landscape and the distinctive Batak Toba traditional houses. Textual content on the posters was often written in the Batak Toba language, and the Batak greeting "*horas*" was a common feature. Martua Sitanggang's posters, presenting a strong indigenous image, were typical of this candidate type (see Figure 7.4, bottom left).

To the north of Samosir is the district of Karo, a rural highland district rich in agricultural produce and home to Mount Sinabung, a volcano that began erupting in 2010 after 400 years of dormancy. The district is mostly (75%) populated by the indigenous Batak Karo, who commonly speak their own Karo language. Christian missions were established in Karo during the 19th century, but not until after Indonesia's independence in 1945 did Christianity take hold. Today the district is predominantly Christian (75%), and there are numerous Protestant, Catholic, and (more recently) Charismatic churches scattered around the district.

In Karo's district head election, ten candidate tickets competed. Nine of the head candidates were Karo Christians and qualified as viable indigenous group candidates. All nine used some Karo symbolism, and six drew on Karo identity in almost all their posters. Karo identity was symbolized through the use of the red traditional Karo fabric draped over candidates' shoulders, slogans in the Karo language, imagery of traditional Karo houses, and traditional Karo patterns used as design elements (see Figure 7.4, bottom right). In addition, candidates used Karo's scenic imagery as a common visual element. Images included Mount Sinabung and agricultural fields lush with produce. One candidate took the idea of being indigenous to the region to a visual extreme by literally appearing to grow out of the land in one poster. Overall, the viable indigenous group candidates frequently used indigenous symbolism and regional imagery that reflected a tight connection to their indigenous identity and the region.

Viable Religious Group Candidates
A number of candidates who competed in the 2010 election in Medan are good examples of viable religious group candidates. A large urban city of over two million people and the capital of North Sumatra, Medan is located on the east coast of Sumatra, next to the Strait of Malacca. It is the region's center for retail, finance, and education, and an important city for the export of agricultural products, such as palm oil. Over the years, Medan has attracted many indigenous groups, including Batak (35%), significant numbers of Javanese (33%), and smaller proportions of Chinese, Minangkabau, Malays, and others. No single indigenous group represents a majority in the city. Approximately 68% of the population is Muslim, but there are significant numbers of Christians (22%) and Buddhists (9%).

Ten candidate tickets competed in Medan's election. Most head candidates were Muslim, but a number of tickets were religiously mixed, and even more were mixed indigenous tickets. Two good examples of viable religious group candidates from this election were Sigit Pramono Asri and Rahudman Harahap. At the time, Sigit Pramono Asri, a Javanese Muslim, was a high-ranking member of the Islamist party, PKS, and a member of North Sumatra's provincial government. In his posters, images of Medan's famous mosque (Mesjid Raya) frequently served as a backdrop for photos of Sigit and his running mate, both impeccably dressed in clean white Islamic clothing (see Figure 7.5, top left). Sigit also heavily promoted himself as the PKS candidate in his posters and included images of prominent PKS leaders. Occasionally, the logos of the three other Islamic parties supporting him

Figure 7.5 Viable religious group and dual-bridging candidates. Top left: Sigit Pramono Asri and Nurlisa Ginting (Bersinar), Medan. Top right: Rahudman Harahap and Dzulmi Eldin, Medan. Bottom left: Sofyan Tan and Nelly Armayanti, Medan. Bottom right: Barkat Shah and Boundeth Damanik (Akat), Pematangsiantar, North Sumatra.
Source: Author.

were displayed on the posters as well. Text written in Arabic, such as "*insya Allah*" ("God willing") and "*rajin sholat, jama'ah ke masjid dari kecil sampai sekarang*" ("Diligently praying, worshiping in the mosque from a young age until now") invoked Allah and depicted Sigit as a pious Muslim. With the exception of some posters with indigenous bridging appeals targeting the Karo population and women (discussed below), Sigit's poster strategy was what we would expect from a viable religious group candidate, composed largely of religious bonding appeals.

Rahudman Harahap was another Muslim candidate in the Medan election. A former bureaucrat, Rahudman lacked the Islamic party endorsements of Sigit, but he still portrayed a very strong Islamic image in his team's election posters, in which he and his running mate primarily wore Islamic garbs. They also incorporated images of the city's financial and government buildings, along with photos of political leaders from their supporting parties, Golkar and Partai Demokrat. Walking a line between the traditional and the modern, one of their slogans was "*Modern, madani, & religius*" ("Modern, civil, & religious"; see Figure 7.5, top right). Overall, the dominant strategy of both candidates was to bond with their religious group and occasionally bridge across indigenous groups.

Nonviable Dual-Group Candidates

The last group is the nonviable dual-group candidates, who have no ethnic bonding options and must use either ethnic bridging or bypassing appeals. One prominent example of a nonviable dual-group candidate was Sofyan Tan, who ran a very successful campaign in the first round of the Medan election. He is a Buddhist of Chinese descent—both very small minorities in Medan—but against the odds, he managed to qualify for the runoff. He entered the election late, having just secured support from the secular-nationalist PDI-P and the PDS—which had a Christian support-base. Competing in the Muslim-majority constituency of Medan, he chose a Muslim woman from the Minangkabau indigenous group, Nelly Armayanti, as his running mate. More than any other candidate, Sofyan made bridging appeals central to his campaign, which contrasted sharply with the extensive Islamic appeals of many other candidates. Eighty percent of Sofyan's posters contained nationalist bridging appeals, and he had the highest combined level of indigenous and religious bridging appeals among all 246 candidates in the dataset. His posters were among the few to display images of multiple religious places of worship side by side—a mosque, a church, and Hindu and Buddhist temples (see Figure 7.5, bottom left). He also drew on regionalist and nationalist images, along with indigenous Karo symbolism, in his campaign posters. Although Sofyan Tan performed impressively in the first round, Rahudman Harahap, focusing on an Islamic message, beat him soundly in the runoff, picking up many votes from other Muslim candidates such as Sigit Pramono.[8]

Another example of a nonviable dual-group candidate was Barkat Shah, who competed in the election in Pematangsiantar. Similar to Sofyan, Barkat used various kinds of bridging appeals, including the use of images of different houses of worship, in his posters (Figure 7.5, bottom right). In the next section, I provide more examples of appeals and posters from nonviable dual-group candidates in Pematangsiantar and Ambon.

7.2.3. Comparative Evidence

Overall, the statistical tests and my qualitative analysis of the individual posters offer compelling evidence for my argument on viable ethnic groups. To provide added support, I use comparative methods to show that ethnic group size and social constraints were the driving forces behind the candidates' ethnic appeal choices. First, I present a most different systems design by comparing campaigns between two very different cities, Pematangsiantar and Ambon. Second, I use a most similar systems design by comparing how members of the same ethnic group, the Batak Toba, campaigned across similar constituencies in North Sumatra.

Most Different Systems Design: Pematangsiantar and Ambon
A most different systems design involves picking cases that are very different in nature yet have the same outcome with regard to the variable one seeks to explain. The underlying logic is that it is easier to identify a causal factor common to all cases when the cases are very different. Using this method, I compared the mayoral elections in the cities of Pematangsiantar, North Sumatra, and Ambon, Maluku. I photographed election posters in these cities, gathered constituency and election data, read the local press reports, and conducted interviews. My key finding was that although the two cities differ in many ways, their campaigns were strikingly similar. I contend that the similarity is because they have similar demographics and social constraints.

The first election campaign I attended was in Pematangsiantar. Located in the center of North Sumatra, Pematangsiantar is the second-largest city in the province after Medan, with a population of approximately 250,000. Surrounded by plantations, it is a center for the trade and processing of rubber, palm oil, and other agricultural products. It is also known for wood carving, the production of traditional fabrics and foods, as well as for indigenous Batak culture, art, and music.

In the 2010 election, ten candidate teams competed, and all ten were ethnically mixed tickets. Nine head candidates chose a running mate from a different religion, and five selected a running mate from a different indigenous group. Consistent with this strategy, Islamic and indigenous bonding appeals were almost totally absent in the posters in Pematangsiantar. A few candidates engaged in a small amount of indigenous bridging, though religious bridging was more common. Some Christian candidates used Islamic symbolism occasionally, and a few Christian and Muslim candidates made very general references to improving the religiosity of the city and promoting indigenous and religious pluralism. Nationalism was also invoked, as the Indonesian flag was a very common visual element in candidates' posters. The eventual winner of the election, Hulman Sitorus, primarily used nationalist imagery, designing his posters (see Figure 7.6, left) in the red and white colors of Indonesia's flag. He made no references to religion or indigeneity.

Figure 7.6 Candidates in Pematangsiantar and Ambon. Left: Hulman Sitorus (Pematangsiantar). Right: Paulus Kastanya (Ambon).
Source: Author.

My observation of the dominant use of ethnic bridging and bypassing appeals provided a notable contrast to the prevalence of ethnic bonding in other campaigns I had experienced. Behind these atypical campaign appeals lies Pematangsiantar's unusual demographic structure, which includes a slim Christian majority group (at 51%) and no indigenous majority group. Batak Toba are the largest indigenous group at 45%, followed by the Javanese at 25% and then various other smaller groups. This demographic structure, coupled with constraints on Christian appeals, meant that all candidates were by default nonviable dual-group candidates and had to resort to ethnic bridging and bypassing appeals.

To help me confirm the importance of these factors, I then looked for another constituency that was very different to Pamatangsiantar, except in terms of its demographic structure and social constraints. Ambon, the capital of Maluku, proved to be the perfect case. It also had a slight Christian majority (at 60%) and no indigenous group majority. The largest indigenous group was the Ambonese at approximately 30%, followed by various other groups such as the Buton, Seram, Javanese, and Bugis.

Located in Maluku province, which consists of a group of islands known during the colonial era as the Spice Islands, Ambon has a history of rebellion and conflict. It experienced an uprising against colonial Dutch rule in 1817 and a revolt against rule by the newly established Republic of Indonesia in 1950, during which it proclaimed an independent South Moluccan Republic. Although the Indonesian military put down that rebellion, some low-level guerrilla warfare continued for the next decade. After the fall of Suharto, the ensuing political instability and economic crisis exacerbated political disputes in Maluku. Conflicts between Christian and Muslim communities broke out across the province, with Ambon experiencing a number of deadly riots. Religious communities had been quite mixed before the conflict, but religious segregation increased afterwards because the conflict prompted Muslims to flee Christian regions, including Ambon, while Christians likewise fled Muslim regions. Although some religious tensions still simmered when I arrived there in 2011, life in Ambon was generally peaceful.

In the election, eight mixed-ticket candidate teams competed. Seven Christian head candidates chose a Muslim running mate, and the one Muslim head candidate, Olivia Latuconsina, chose a popular local Christian singer, Andre Hehanussa, to run for deputy. Just as in Pematangsiantar, religious symbolism in campaign posters was very rare. Latuconsina, the only Muslim head candidate and the incumbent deputy mayor, used Islamic symbolism, but it consisted mainly of wearing standard Islamic clothing. A few other candidates had some general mentions of God or religion in their posters, and a few posters displayed inside Christian communities wished Christians a happy Easter. Similarly, indigenous bonding appeals were quite rare even though most of the candidates were Ambonese. Local newspapers reported on candidates visiting a range of different indigenous group meetings and events across the city, indicating their efforts to reach out broadly across Ambon's fragmented indigenous demographics. Candidates also appealed frequently to a broader regional Maluku identity, using regional scenic views of the island and historic monuments such as Maluku's regional symbol, Kapitan Pattimura, a Moluccan leader who was hanged for leading an armed rebellion against the Dutch in 1817. The Indonesian flag was probably the most common visual element among the posters and in newspaper campaign advertisements; I found its prevalence somewhat surprising given the region's history of rebellion and separatist aspirations.

Overall, candidates in Ambon's election acted and presented themselves in very similar ways to the candidates in Pematangsiantar. They formed multi-religious tickets, tended to dress in formal business attire, primarily used regionalist and nationalist imagery, and largely avoided overt religious or indigenous bonding appeals. Paulus Kastanya's poster (Figure 7.6, right) is a typical example from Ambon.

Conceivably, the dominance of these bridging strategies in both cities could be explained by noting that the candidates that year happened to be pluralistic in orientation. However, looking at elections in the past confirmed that mixed tickets have been the norm in both cities, and interviewees indicated that similar bridging tactics were commonly used in earlier elections. Moreover, Braeuchler (2011) noted how all candidates in Ambon's 2006 election carefully used religiously integrated election slogans on their posters.

In short, although Ambon has a different history and different indigenous groups and is more than 3,000 kilometers away from Pematangsiantar, the election campaigns in the two cities were remarkably similar. Of the 49 regional head elections in the dataset, Pematangsiantar and Ambon had the highest levels of bridging and bypassing appeals. The explanation is that these cities shared a similar demographic structure and the same social constraints. The lack of an indigenous majority and the inability to appeal openly to the Christian majority left all candidates without a viable group to appeal to. Consequently, they used ethnic bridging and bypassing appeals.

Most Similar Systems Design: Batak Toba Candidates

When applying a most similar systems design, one selects cases that seem very similar but have different outcomes. The logic here is that by comparing these cases, one can hope to identify the influential factor that exists in one case but not in the other. Using this method, I return to the example used in the introduction to this chapter. The dataset contains several Christian Batak Toba candidates who competed in a number of constituencies across North Sumatra, but made markedly different appeals in some constituencies compared to others.

12 Christian Batak Toba head candidates ran in Samosir and Toba Samosir, two constituencies where they were a majority. Aligning with expectations, these candidates used indigenous bonding appeals to target their Batak Toba group. They formed homogeneous pairs by selecting Christian Batak Toba running mates and almost exclusively used Batak Toba clothing, patterns, and imagery in their posters. Indigenous or religious bridging appeals were rare or completely absent. Meanwhile, five Christian Batak Toba candidates ran in neighboring Pematangsiantar. However, because Batak Toba are a minority in Pematangsiantar, these candidates eschewed appeals to their Batak Toba group. Instead, they formed mixed pairs by choosing Muslim running mates from other indigenous groups and used ethnic bridging strategies, occasionally appealing to other religious and indigenous groups and frequently incorporating the Indonesian flag in their posters. An example of a Batak Toba candidate poster in Samosir, complete with traditional Batak houses and the Batak *ulos* fabric, is shown in Figure 7.4, bottom left. This poster can be contrasted with the far more secular-nationalist poster created by Hulman Sitorus, a Batak Toba candidate who won the Pematangsiantar election (Figure 7.6, left).

Again, the evidence indicates that the difference in campaign appeals between candidates is due to differences in the electoral viability of the ethnic group. In Samosir and Toba Samosir, the Batak Toba were a majority group and could therefore be targeted with indigenous bonding appeals. In contrast, they were a minority in Pematangsiantar, so Batak Toba candidates had to resort to ethnic bridging and bypassing appeals.

7.2.4. Ethnic Diversity

Ultimately, the many individual campaign strategy decisions made by candidates on the microlevel should result in a predictable pattern of ethnic appeals across constituencies on the macrolevel. This is where the microfoundations of ethnic appeal strategy aggregate into broader patterns of ethnic politicization. Specifically, I expected to find ethnic bridging and bypassing appeals in ethnically diverse constituencies with small and fragmented ethnic groups. In these constituencies, no candidate is a member of a viable group, so there is little incentive to bond with their ethnic group. When an ethnic group is large enough to be politically viable, and when there are no social constraints on appealing to it, candidates from the group increasingly use bonding appeals to target this group. As a result, in the more homogeneous constituencies dominated by one viable ethnic group, we can expect more ethnic bonding appeals and fewer bridging and bypassing appeals.

To further explore the relationship between ethnic diversity and ethnic appeals and to examine the possibility that this relationship may be nonlinear, I constructed Figure 7.7, which presents levels of bonding and bridging appeals in comparison to group size, using fractional polynomial plots. In Figure 7.7(A), the percentage of candidates' posters using bonding,

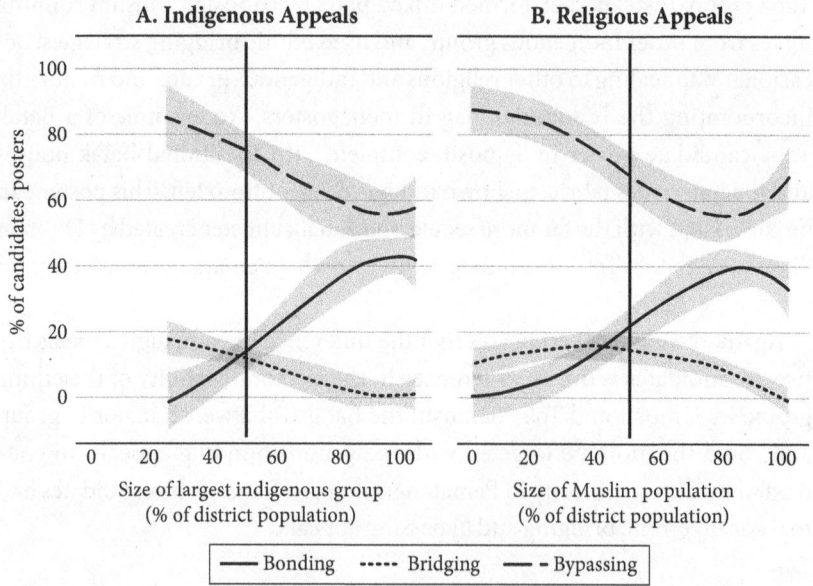

Figure 7.7 Levels of ethnic appeals based by ethnic group size for regional head candidates. These are fractional polynomial plots. Shading represents 90% confidence intervals. See the "Figure 7.7" section in Appendix A for the same figure for legislative candidates.

bridging, and bypassing appeals is calculated for different sizes of the largest indigenous group in the dataset. The size of the largest indigenous group can be used in each case, since there are no major social constraints on appealing to any indigenous group. In Figure 7.7(B), bonding, bridging, and bypassing appeals are calculated for different sizes of the Muslim population. The size of this religious group is the one that matters because practically all religious appeals were Islamic appeals.

The plots show that bridging and bypassing appeals were most frequent, and that bonding appeals were least common, when the largest indigenous group (or the Muslim population) was a minority. Ethnic diversity effectively promoted bridging and bypassing appeals and had a dampening impact on bonding appeals. As the size of the largest indigenous group (or the Muslim population) rose, bridging and bypassing appeals declined, and bonding appeals increased.[9]

7.3. Second-Level Factors

In Chapter 3, I argued that in some circumstances, candidates can be prompted to make fewer bonding appeals that target their viable ethnic group. This occurs when candidates are influenced by three second-level factors: (1) when they have a strong reputation for representing a particular ethnic group, (2) when they compete in a crowded field of co-ethnic candidates, or (3) when they compete in an uncompetitive electoral contest. These second-level factors can suppress candidates' use of ethnic bonding appeals. Instead, candidates have incentives to (1) deploy ethnic bonding appeals not to their viable ethnic group but targeting a smaller, nonviable ethnic group; (2) make bridging appeals to other ethnic groups; or (3) bypass ethnicity altogether. In an effort to attain sufficient support, candidates often use a mixture of these strategies. Below, I present some qualitative and quantitative evidence on the impact of these second-level factors.

7.3.1. A Strong Ethnic Reputation

In many of the Indonesian electoral contests, some candidates had an established reputation as champions of a particular respective ethnic group. We can expect these candidates to have a lesser need for ethnic bonding appeals, as their reputation among their ethnic kin precedes them. For them, shifting (at least to some degree) from ethnic bonding to ethnic bypassing strategies could allow them to craft a more inclusive campaign that would be less likely to scare off potential voters from other ethnic groups. They might also make bridging appeals, as long as they felt that doing so would not result in a backlash from co-ethnics.

The first tentative piece of supporting evidence comes from looking at the level of appeals in Figure 7.7. Overall, bypassing appeals were surprisingly prevalent among candidates. Even in constituencies with a majority indigenous or Muslim group, most campaign posters contained bypassing rather than bonding appeals. This finding may be partly due to the limited use of ethnic bonding appeals by some candidates who already had a strong ethnic reputation. I was struck by this phenomenon while observing the campaigns of a number of candidates who were well-known locally for their staunch ethnic credentials.

In the 2011 election campaign in Salatiga, the campaign strategy of the Yuliyanto-Haris ticket exemplified the deployment of bypassing and bridging strategies. While Yuliyanto was a businessman, he led what was widely seen as the Islamic ticket. This was largely due to his choice of running mate: Muhammad Haris, a long-time high-ranking member of the Islamist party PKS and the coordinator for Muslim youth in Central Java. They also received support from two large Islamist parties, PKS and PPP. Given this background and the fact that they were a viable dual-group ticket, it might have seemed surprising that their posters were almost totally devoid of any reference to Islam and only occasionally used Javanese symbolism. Instead, they primarily presented an image of businesslike professionalism and nationalism. The two wore smart suits and ties, and the main graphic element in almost all their posters was a large, realistic Indonesian flag, over which was emblazoned the slogan "*Nasionalis Merakyat*" ("Nationalist Populist"; see Figure 7.8, top left). In addition, they were also the only ticket in the Salatiga election that explicitly used pluralistic messages such as "*Menjaga Pluralisme di Kota Salatiga*" ("Preserve Pluralism in Salatiga") on their posters.

Whereas the book's main argument would have predicted far more religious and indigenous bonding appeals from the Yuliyanto-Haris ticket, their strategy makes sense when we consider the effect of their reputation as the Islamic ticket, which made religious bonding campaign appeals unnecessary for them. A more inclusive campaign that coupled bypassing and bridging strategies allowed them to assuage fears from Salatiga's sizable

Figure 7.8 Posters from candidates using alternative appeal strategies. Top left: Yuliyanto and Haris (Yaris), Salatiga, Central Java. Top right: Sjahrial R. Anas and Yahya Sumardi, Medan, North Sumatra. Bottom left: Nurlisa Ginting, Medan, North Sumatra. Bottom right: Siti Perangin-Angin and Salmon Sagala (Si-Sura), Karo, North Sumatra.
Source: Author.

Christian minority while retaining Muslim support. Although Salatiga has a Muslim-majority population (76%), it is the constituency in Java with the largest number of Christians. Promoting pluralism may have helped them gain support from the Christian minority and inspire confidence among the more moderate Muslims in Salatiga. Most likely, this strategy contributed to their success. They won the 2011 election in the first round and won again in 2017.

7.3.2. Crowded Field of Co-Ethnic Candidates

The next second-level factor that can prompt candidates to bond less strongly with their viable ethnic group and to pursue other strategies occurs when a number of candidates from the same ethnic group compete for votes from the same ethnic bloc. This scenario provides incentives for these candidates to pursue different appeal strategies in order to stand out.

The first piece of evidence that candidates in such a situation reduce their ethnic bonding appeals comes from looking at appeals across constituencies. In Figure 7.7, the frequency of ethnic bonding appeals rises until an ethnic group constitutes more than 80% of the population. At this point, bonding appeals plateau or begin to decline, but there is an uptick in ethnic bypassing appeals and even a slight rise in indigenous bridging appeals. Why might this be the case? In constituencies with such a high percentage of Muslims (or members of the largest indigenous group), most if not all of the candidates in the race are from the same group. When numerous candidates attempt to mobilize the same ethnic majority, the group will invariably split its vote across candidates. As a result, candidates are less certain that they can get enough votes from the majority ethnic group to win and consequently search for alternative strategies.

Medan's 2011 election serves as a good qualitative case study of appeal strategies in a crowded field. In this election, nine of the ten head candidates were Muslims and many of them made Islamic bonding appeals directed at the Muslim-majority population. Since the Muslim vote would be split, some candidates also used the three alternative appeal strategies.

First, some appealed to their indigenous group, even though all indigenous groups are minorities in Medan and thus nonviable. Sjahrial and his running mate adopted this approach with vigor. They appealed to their minority Minangkabau indigenous group by dressing in traditional, ornate

Minangkabau clothing and using images of Minangkabau buildings in most of their posters (see Figure 7.8, top right).

Second, given the uncertainty regarding how much of the Muslim vote a candidate could get, some Muslim candidates supplemented their Islamic posters with posters that appealed to other indigenous groups. For example, although most of Sigit Pramono Asri's posters predominantly featured Islamic themes (as discussed above), he did draw on his running mate's indigenous identity in some posters. Nurlisa Ginting, a Muslim bureaucrat from the indigenous Batak Karo group, enabled Sigit to make a bridging appeal to the Karo group. In most of their posters, she wore Islamic headdress and clothing (see Figure 7.5 top left). However, in the region of Medan that is predominantly inhabited by the Karo, Sigit displayed a whole new set of campaign posters, in which Nurlisa became the most prominent visual element and Sigit's image was reduced in size or absent. Against a backdrop of traditional Karo houses and cloth patterns, Nurlisa was dressed in ornate traditional Karo clothing[10] (see Figure 7.8 bottom left). This was a shrewd move as there was no Karo head candidates in the race.

The third strategy was to bypass ethnicity altogether and appeal to other identity categories. Sigit's choice of a female deputy can also be viewed as an effort to bypass ethnicity and appeal to female voters. His appeals to women became even more apparent when several Muslim leaders came out publicly against women running for political office. In response, Sigit put up posters to support female leaders. They featured Nurlisa with the message "*Perempuan Mampu. . . !!!*" ("Women Are Capable . . . !!!") and contained messages to celebrate International Women's Day and to stop the trafficking of women and children.

Siti Perangin-Angin, a candidate who ran in an election in the district of Karo, North Sumatra, fully engaged with a bypassing strategy. Facing a field crowded with candidates appealing to their indigenous Karo identity, Siti choose a different strategy: as a prominent local PDI-P leader, she drew on her party label. Her posters included images of PDI-P's leader, Megawati, and her late father and Indonesia's former president, Sukarno (see Figure 7.8, bottom right). Together with her running mate, they dressed in professional business attire rather than the indigenous clothing common among the other candidates. There was a good reason for this appeal strategy. With the other Karo candidates drawing on their indigenous identity in their campaigns, they all began to look the same. Promoting a party image could make a candidate stand out. Also, the PDI-P was the most popular party in Karo and had more seats in the local parliament than any other party. By mobilizing PDI-P supporters, Siti won the first round by a slim margin with 19% of the vote. However, although the PDI-P was popular in Karo, it was not so popular as to mobilize a majority of voters in the constituency. In the second round, Siti was beaten comfortably by Surbakti, who bonded with the Karo indigenous group in almost all his election posters.

Similarly, other candidates competing in a crowded field in the Medan election also bypassed ethnicity and appealed to other identity categories. For instance, Indra Harahap appealed to young people by emphasizing his own youth with phrases such as "young person," "new generation," and "energetic," and claimed that Medan needed young leaders ("*Medan Butuh Pemimpin Muda*") (see Figure 7.9, bottom left). Another candidate, Usman Siregar, appealed to the same age group through his youthful dress, hand gestures, and slang (see Figure 7.9, bottom right).[11]

Figure 7.9 More posters from candidates using alternative appeal strategies. Left: Indra Harahap and Delyuzar, Medan, North Sumatra. Right: Usman Siregar and Gunawan Ang, Medan, North Sumatra.
Source: Author.

7.3.3. Uncompetitive Electoral Contest

Finally, the competitiveness of an election might affect appeals. The intuitive expectation is that when elections become more competitive, candidates will more readily use ethnic bonding appeals to galvanize their ethnic base. Conversely, we can expect less ethnic bonding in uncompetitive electoral contests. To measure the competitiveness of regional head elections, I used the winning candidate's margin of victory over the second-place candidate, which ranged from 0.36% (very competitive) to 37% (very uncompetitive). The results illustrated in Figure 7.10 plot the level of indigenous and religious appeals across regional head elections from competitive to uncompetitive ones. They indicate that as elections became less competitive, indigenous and religious bonding appeals declined. There was also a rise in indigenous bridging appeals and in religious bypassing appeals.[12]

Overall, the evidence suggests ways in which these three second-level factors reduced candidates' efforts to bond with their viable ethnic group. Prominent alternative strategies by Indonesian candidates included efforts to bond with one of their nonviable ethnic groups, bridge across ethnic

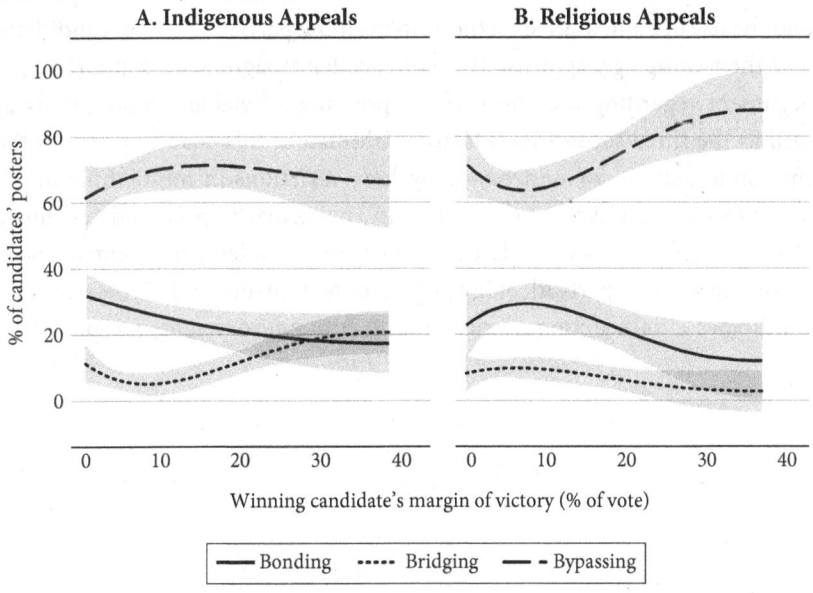

Figure 7.10 Frequency of ethnic bonding appeals based on how competitive the election was. These are fractional polynomial plots. Shading represents 90% confidence intervals.

groups, or bypass ethnicity entirely. Notably, these strategies actually help to keep electoral contests from becoming dominated by one ethnic cleavage. This runs against conventional expectations as to how the politicization of ethnicity is expected to polarize societies. More specifically, the ethnic outbidding model would expect candidates in these elections to become locked into increasing spirals of appeals along one dimension of ethnicity, with each candidate trying to outdo the others (Rabushka and Shepsle 1972). However, rather than simply trying to outbid each other for support from the majority group, candidates can sometimes be prompted to seek alternative ways to appeal for support.

7.4. Conclusion

This chapter has tested the argument that the viability of ethnic groups determines the kinds of ethnic appeals candidates make, and specifically whether they choose to bond with their indigenous or religious groups or engage in ethnic bridging or bypassing appeal strategies. The mixed methods used to test the argument included a statistical analysis of ethnic appeals from over 1,500 posters, a qualitative discussion of candidates' individual posters, and the use of comparative methods to examine particular sets of candidates and their campaign appeals. The evidence lends significant support to the argument regarding the effect of the presence of viable ethnic groups as well as the three second-level factors. Ultimately, this chapter provides the microfoundations for understanding how variations in multiethnic diversity affect the politicization of ethnicity, particularly in candidate-centric elections. Chapter 8 extends the investigation under party-centric rules. Under these rules, party ideology plays a more influential role in determining candidates' choice among ethnic bonding, bridging, or bypassing appeals.

8
Party Ideology

In the 1950s, Indonesian life was vibrant and largely revolved around a thick network of social organizations. Youth, women's, indigenous, religious, labor, and educational organizations were popular across the archipelago. Within this context, the 1955 election featured a broad array of political parties, each one associated formally or informally with its own social organizations. Political parties campaigned intensely in 1954 and 1955 and extended their reach down into the villages. They promoted their leaders and ideologies through speeches and posted party logos in large numbers across Indonesian villages, cities, and towns. Virtually every public event was an opportunity for campaigning. As Feith (1962: 353) explained, campaigners promoted their parties at national and Islamic holiday celebrations, protest rallies, scout parades, and meetings of unions, peasants, and students.

As politics and social life grew more tightly intertwined, all social organizations became rooted in the nationalist, communist, or Islamic ideology of their associated political party (Feith 1962: 361). Partai Nasional Indonesia (PNI) and Partai Komunis Indonesia (PKI) drew on their party platforms to make broad appeals to nationalism and class as they sought to reach out to all ethnic groups. Meanwhile, the Islamic party candidates drew on their party's religious ideology and more narrowly appealed to their religious communities by mobilizing religious networks.[1] These strategies bore some success, with the PNI, PKI, and two Islamic parties (Masyumi and Nahdlatul Ulama) emerging as the four big winners in the election. However, with no clear ideological winner, the ongoing contestation between political parties and the highly charged political environment would soon lead to the decline of democratic governance.

Compared to the heady 1950s, political party competition was far more constrained during the New Order, and elections were very predictable affairs. Since the reintroduction of democracy, however, Indonesia's party system and its political parties have evolved in some important ways. One early approach to understanding post-Suharto political party competition focused on how political parties began to act like cartels. Scholars observed how, after elections, Indonesian political parties formed collusive alliances to share the spoils of the state (Slater 2004, 2018; Ambardi 2008). The evidence of this process was the creation of post-transition "rainbow coalitions"—governing coalitions far larger than what would be required to rule and pass legislation. From this perspective, the ideological nature of parties, which had been such a strong force in the past, now seemed largely irrelevant. Moreover, the emergence of presidential parties, which functioned merely as electoral vehicles for presidential candidates, also appeared to indicate that ideology had become redundant in Indonesia's political party structure (Ufen 2008). In response to the "cartelization" literature on Indonesia, Mietzner (2013) highlighted that Indonesian parties were still closely intertwined with Islamic organizations, church associations, and pluralist groups, and he showed how Indonesian parties were quite vigorous in defending their ideological positions in major legislative debates. This scholarly debate on the role of ideology in Indonesian politics, and whether it is in decline or resurgent, continues today.

Although party ideology can also play a role in government formation, crafting of legislation, and state–society relations, this chapter focuses specifically on how ideology is used in election campaigns and how its impact is mediated by the electoral rules. It contains two parts. In Part I, I show that party ideology has a greater impact in party-centric elections. I do this by examining the extent to which candidate appeals align with the ideology of their political party in legislative elections as compared with the more candidate-centric regional head elections. In Part II, I turn to electoral competition in the province of Aceh, the only region in Indonesia where regional political parties are allowed to compete without being registered across the country. By comparing the election posters from Aceh with those used elsewhere, I show how the ethnic ideologies of these regional political parties are more prominently reflected in their candidates' ethnic appeals.

8.1. Appeals by Candidates Who Compete Nationally

8.1.1. Indonesian Parties

In terms of party ideology, Indonesian parties fit largely into two categories: nationalist and Islamic. In fact, Indonesian parties are primarily defined by how they view the role of Islam in the public domain, in contrast to Western nations where party differences are usually rooted in right–left splits along economic lines.[2]

Nationalist parties are based on the state's philosophical foundation and national ideology, Pancasila.[3] Drawing on the five principles of Pancasila (religiosity, internationalism, nationalism, representative democracy, social justice), these parties have a nationalist and multiethnic ideology. In 2009, the main nationalist parties were Golkar, PDI-P, Gerindra, Hanura, PDS and Partai Demokrat.[4] Beyond their national and multiethnic orientation, there is some variation among the nationalist parties. Both PDI-P and Gerindra have some leftist origins; PDI-P was influenced by Sukarno's Marhaenist thought (which stressed a commitment to the poor), while Gerindra, under the leadership of Subianto Prabowo, initially established itself as a representative of Indonesia's rural farming and fishing communities. Meanwhile, PDS was a small Christian party, though it had nationalist ideological commitments rooted in Pancasila. Finally, Partai Demokrat was founded in 2001 and was labeled "nationalist-religious" to set it apart from the more secular-oriented nature of the other nationalist political parties (Mietzner and Muhtadi 2018).

To achieve greater granularity, this chapter makes a distinction between two types of Islamic parties: Islamist and Muslim democratic. Although the two types are similar in many ways, the ideological distinction between them on the role of Islam matters greatly. The Islamist political parties believe that Islam has a critical role to play in politics, and they are guided by an Islamic ideology. In the 2009 election from which I gathered election posters, five Islamist parties campaigned nationally (PPP, PBR, PBB, PPNUI, PKS), while three more (PAAS, PBA, and PDA)[5] campaigned for the regional legislature in Aceh. Formed in 1973, PPP is the oldest Islamist party in Indonesia. Soon after the transition to democracy, a movement within the party split off and went on to form PBR. PBB, PPNUI, and PKS were all formed in 1998, from varied origins. PBB styled itself as the successor to the Islamist Masyumi party, which was banned by Sukarno in 1960; PPNUI was founded by a group of Islamist anti-Shia activists associated with the religious organization, Nahdlatul Ulama (NU); and PKS was created as the political vehicle of a campus proselytizing network modeled after the cadre-based Egyptian Muslim Brotherhood.[6]

The three Muslim democratic parties that competed in 2009 were PAN, PKB, and PKNU. Both PAN and PKB were formed in 1998, whereas PKNU was founded in 2006 by a splinter group from PKB. These three parties were largely supported by orthodox Muslims and had strong ties to Indonesia's two largest Islamic organizations. PAN was associated with Muhammadiyah, while PKB and PPNU had ties with Nahdlatul Ulama. However, although these parties viewed Islam as an important source of inspiration and guidance, unlike the Islamists, they did not believe that it should be the basis for public policy. Overall, they had a more neutral stance with regard to religion. They did not include Islam as part of their formal ideology; instead, they drew on the national ideology of Pancasila. As a result, in terms of their connection with Islam, they fit somewhere between the nationalist and the Islamist political parties. Of course, party ideologies can also shift over time. For example, Gerindra has shifted to the right and adopted a stronger emphasis on economic nationalism in recent years, while PAN has become more Islamic.

As I explained in Chapter 3, under party-centric rules, a candidate's campaign strategy is largely dictated by the political party. As a result, party ideology significantly influences the kinds of ethnic appeals candidates make. Party leaders have the power to sanction candidates or to reward them and advance their careers. As a result, candidates have incentives to appease party leaders. One way to do so is by toeing the party line and making campaign appeals that align with the party's ideological underpinnings. In the case of Indonesia's parties, this means that appeals will reflect the party's stance on religion.

By examining the appeals made by Indonesian candidates in nationalist, Muslim democratic, and Islamist parties, we can test the degree to which candidates align with their party's nationalist or Islamic orientation, as well as whether party ideology is more influential in party-centric elections. First, we can make comparisons across parties. If the argument is correct, we should find that Indonesian candidates from the nationalist parties make nationalist appeals that bridge across voters. They may also make religious bridging appeals that reach out across religious groups, or they may bypass religion altogether, as either strategy is consistent with a nationalist ideology in a religiously diverse country. In contrast, we expect Indonesia's Islamist party candidates to make more religious bonding appeals. These expectations are illustrated in Figure 8.1. Muslim democratic candidates should fit somewhere in between, making more religious bonding appeals than they nationalist party candidates, but less than the Islamist party candidates. Second, we can make comparisons across elections. Here we would expect parties' nationalist or Islamist ideological underpinnings to have a stronger impact on

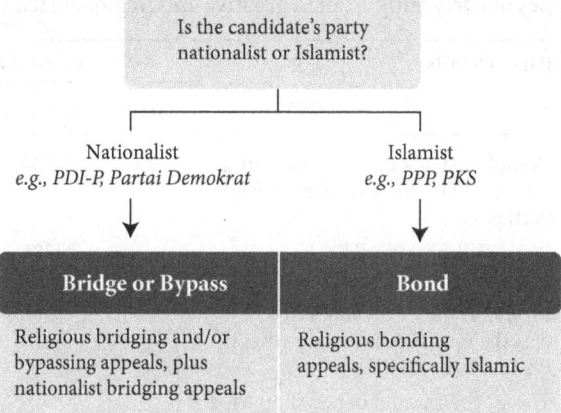

Figure 8.1 Impact of party ideology on Indonesian candidates' appeals.

appeals in Indonesia's legislative elections than in the more candidate-centric regional head elections.

To study the impact of party ideology, I conducted a statistical analysis of election poster appeal data, comparing candidates from nationalist, Muslim democratic, and Islamist parties who competed in both the legislative and regional head elections. Because Indonesian parties differ ideologically along an Islamic/nationalist cleavage, I focused on a limited set of four appeal measures: the three measures of religious bonding, bridging, and bypassing, plus the nationalist bridging measure. As before, these are continuous variables (0 to 100), representing the percentage of each candidate's poster campaign that contained the appeal.

The key independent variable is the ideology of the candidate's party. In the legislative elections, every candidate is supported by one political party. To investigate the impact of party ideology, I created three binary variables for *Islamist party*, *Muslim democratic party*, and *Nationalist party*. Each binary variable was set at 1 if the candidate was from one of the parties in that category or 0 otherwise. All parties that competed in the 2009 legislative election were represented in the dataset: the 38 parties that competed nationally and the six parties that only competed in Aceh. Of the 1,876 candidates represented, 1,304 were from nationalist parties, 288 were from Muslim democratic parties, and 284 were from Islamist parties (see Table 8.1).

In the regional head elections, I also created binary variables for *Islamist party*, *Muslim democratic party*, and *Nationalist party*. However, regional

Table 8.1 Types of Party Support in Legislative and Regional Head Elections

Party Type	Party Details	Candidates		
		Parties	Legislative	Reg. Head
Nationalist	Demokrat, Golkar, PDI-P, Gerindra Hanura, PDS, and all other national parties	33	1,304	67
Muslim Democratic	PAN, PKB, and PKNU	3	288	5
Islamist	PKS, PPP, PBB, PBR, and PPNUI, plus the Acehnese Islamist parties of PAAS, PBA, and PDA	8	284	6
Coalition of party types	This is when a candidate is supported by more than one party type, such as PKS (Islamist) and Golkar (Nationalist). Only candidates competing in regional head elections can receive support from multiple political parties.	–	–	86
	Total	44	1,876	164

Note. 1,304 legislative candidates were supported by a nationalist party, while 67 regional head candidates were supported by one or more nationalist parties (but no other party types). See the section entitled "Table 5.2" in Appendix A for a list of all parties and their categorization by type. These tables also include more detailed information on the numbers of posters and candidates from each party, as well as the number of constituencies in which they competed. I only include the three Islamist Acehnese parties, as the other Acehnese parties did not fit one of the three party types. I analyze all of the regional Acehnese parties later in this chapter.

head candidates can run as independents or be supported by multiple parties. To deal with these issues, I first excluded the 58 regional head candidates who ran as independents from the main analysis, resulting in 164 candidates with party support. Next, I assigned the value of 1 to each party variable if the candidate was supported by one or more party of that type; otherwise, it was set at 0. This means that candidates could be coded as supported by an Islamist party even if they were also supported by one or more nationalist and/or Muslim democratic parties. I included the same set of covariates as in Chapter 6 to control for ethnic demographics, ethnic attachment, modernization, candidate gender, and population size.

Finally, I separated legislative from regional head candidates to consider how much impact party ideology has in one type of election relative to another. The impact of party ideology was tested using a linear probability model (OLS) with robust standard errors. I also ran alternative models that excluded the control variables and used alternative measures for party support in regional head elections.[7]

8.1.2. The Impact of Party Ideology

To visualize the impact of party ideology, the probability that a candidate would make each kind of appeal was predicted for legislative candidates and then for regional head candidates, as shown in Figure 8.2. The bars show the percentage of a candidate's poster campaign that contains bonding, bridging, or bypassing appeals, depending on whether the candidate belongs to a nationalist, Muslim democratic, or Islamist party. I controlled for ethnic

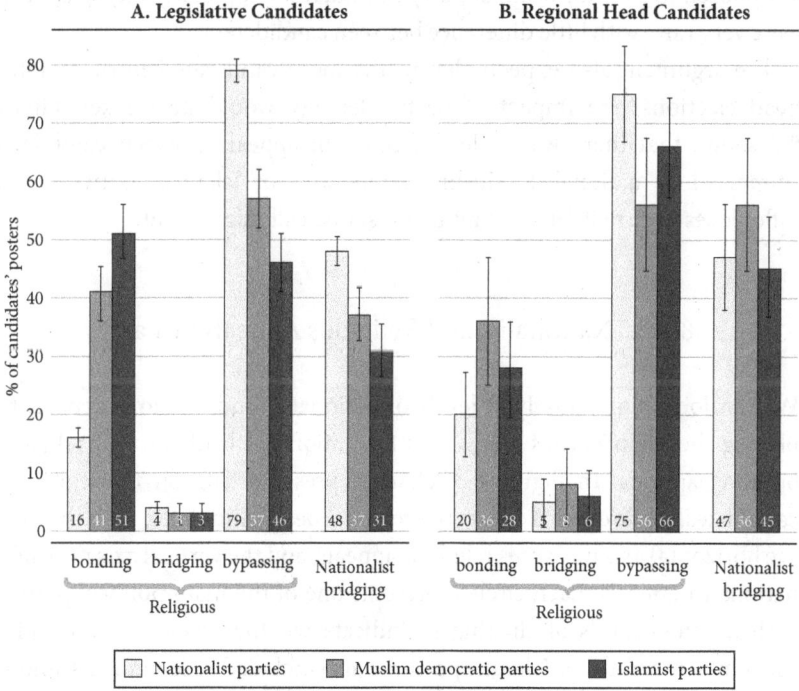

Figure 8.2 Predicted probabilities of appeals for candidates supported by nationalist, Muslim democratic, and Islamist parties. Probabilities are calculated for party ideology type while holding all other independent variables at their mean. Error bars represent 90% confidence intervals. See the section entitled "Figure 8.2" in Appendix A for the regression table from which these data are drawn.

demographics, ethnic attachment, modernization, gender, and population by holding them at their mean.

In the legislative elections, being a member of an Islamist party (compared to membership in a nationalist party) had a positive impact on religious bonding appeals. Fifty-one percent of poster campaigns by legislative Islamist party candidates contained Islamic bonding appeals, compared to only 16% of poster campaigns by nationalist party candidates. The figure for Muslim democratic candidates was in between these two results, as 41% of their poster campaigns contained Islamic bonding appeals. This is what we might expect from parties that have both a nationalist ideology and strong connections to Islamic organizations. Overall, nationalist party candidates tended to bypass religious appeals, placing greater emphasis on nationalist appeals; 48% of their candidates' poster campaigns had nationalist appeals, as opposed to 31% for Islamist party candidates. Religious bridging appeals were very rare, with little difference between candidates.

The argument also expects that in the more candidate-centric regional head elections, the impact of party ideology would be weaker. Figure 8.2 shows that there was little difference in appeals between candidates supported by nationalist, Muslim democratic, or Islamist parties. These differences were neither substantial nor statistically significant.[8]

8.1.3. Nationalist and Religious Appeals by Party

We can look more closely at levels of nationalist and religious appeals by placing the main parties along axes for nationalist bridging and religious bonding appeals. In Figure 8.3, chart A presents data on the legislative candidates, while chart B covers the regional head candidates. In each chart, the horizontal axis measures religious appeals, and the vertical axis measures nationalist appeals. Each circle represents one of the main political parties, with different levels of shading to indicate whether they are nationalist, Muslim democratic, or Islamist parties. I also included independents among the regional head candidates.

Looking at the legislative candidates, we see a clear split between the Islamist and nationalist party candidates. The latter group had higher levels of nationalist bridging appeals and lower levels of religious bonding appeals. Although they occasionally invoked Islam though their use of clothing, imagery, or messaging, their posters primarily contained nationalist and

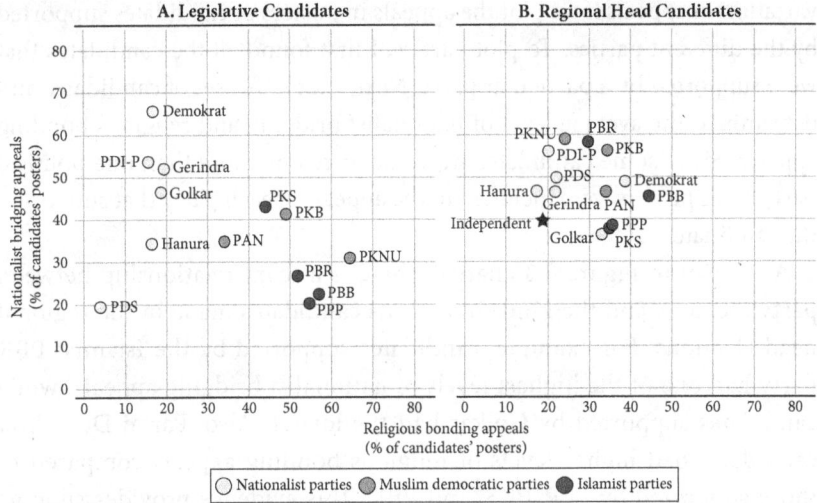

Figure 8.3 Nationalist and religious appeals in legislative and regional head elections by political party type.

populist imagery and rhetoric. Their party slogans in particular tended to be quite populist in nature, though Partai Demokrat was an exception, combining the two ideologies with the slogan *"Religius dan Nasionalis"* ("Religious and Nationalist").

The Muslim democratic parties PAN and PKB, along with PKS, occupy the middle of the chart. Their candidates made fewer religious bonding appeals and more nationalist bridging appeals in their posters. Although Islam is important for these parties, they display relative moderation in the use of Islamic rhetoric and symbolism in their campaigns. Finally, candidates from the three Islamist parties, plus the Muslim democratic PKNU, shown in the lower right of Figure 8.3(A) employed higher levels of religious bonding appeals and lower levels of nationalist bridging appeals than the other candidates.[9]

Overall, party ideology had an impact on candidates' religious bonding and nationalist bridging appeals in the legislative elections. There was a clear Islamic-nationalist divide among Indonesian political parties.[10] This was not the case in the regional head elections, however.

In regional head elections, placing the main parties along axes for nationalist and religious bonding appeals is a little more difficult because candidates are often supported by multiple parties. Still, we get some sense of the variation in appeals if we plot the appeals in posters of candidates supported by the different parties. To plot parties, I first found all the candidates that were supported by a particular party. Next, I took this set of candidates and determined the average level of nationalist bridging and religious bonding appeals. Since some candidates were supported by more than one political party, their posters were included in the appeals of each party that supported the candidate.

As shown in Figure 8.3 chart B, there is a scant relationship between party ideology and the kinds of appeals candidates made in the regional head elections. For example, candidates supported by the Islamist PBR party had one of the highest levels of nationalist bridging appeals, while candidates supported by Golkar had the lowest. Also, Partai Demokrat candidates had higher levels of religious bonding appeals compared to those supported by PPP, PKS, and PBR. This evidence provides support for the argument that party ideology did not have a predictable effect on ethnic appeals made by regional head candidates. Interestingly, the independent candidates had very low levels of nationalist and religious bonding appeals. More than other candidates, the independents were free to step outside Indonesia's defining nationalist/religious cleavage. Instead, they often appealed to indigenous, regional, or youth identity groups or played up their own image.

Overall, these findings indicate that under party-centric rules, the ideology of political parties has a major impact on candidates' appeals. However, there is evidence that under these rules, two other factors can affect appeals: a strong party label and a strong Islamic reputation. These factors might help explain one outlier, the Islamist PKS. Suprisingly, of all the Islamist parties, PKS had the highest frequency of nationalist appeals and the lowest level of religious appeals in the legislative elections.

Compared to other parties, PKS was known for having a strong party label. It originated from an Islamic social movement in Indonesian universities in the late 1970s, and since developing into a political party, it has selected its candidates through a rigorous recruitment system. As a result, candidates have already been socialized into the party and have strong loyalty and attachment to the party.[11] This was reflected in their posters. PKS candidates often used official poster templates which invariably contained plenty of party-oriented design elements (such as PKS logos and flags, and images of PKS rallies) and candidates rarely wore anything but PKS party clothing. As a result, of all the Islamic parties, PKS had the highest proportion of posters with partisan appeals—appeals that potentially displaced explicit Islamic appeals.

Beyond having a strong party label, PKS was also viewed as having a strong Islamic reputation. And it was because their support of Islam was so well known amongst voters, that candidates may not have needed to make explicit Islamic appeals. I should note that I also provide evidence supporting this logic in Chapter 7, where I show how regional head candidates with a strong Islamic reputation had lower than expected levels of religious appeals. Additionally, in Chapter 9, I show how candidates who *lack* an Islamic reputation are more likely to mobilize voters along religious lines.

Overall, the PKS example suggests that a strong party label and an Islamic reputation can reduce Islamic appeals to some degree. Certainly, there will be other factors that, in some contexts, have a marginal effect on ethnic appeals. For instance, in other work, myself and a colleague found that Indonesian Islamic party candidates made more Islamic appeals and fewer nationalist appeals in urban constituencies (relative to rural ones) and in regional legislative elections (relative to national elections) (Fox and Menchik 2022). Extending this line of inquiry, I examined the effect of urban and regional factors on the nationalist candidates studied in this book, but found that they had little or no effect.

While this section has studied the appeals of political parties that compete for votes across the country, possibly, political parties confined to a particular region will have different ethnic appeal strategies. To investigate, in Part II, I study the appeals of regionally based ethnic political party candidates in the province of Aceh and compare them to candidates from parties that compete nationally.

8.2. Appeals by Candidates in Regional Parties

The literature offers evidence that the ethnocentric nature of ethnic parties can vary depending on how regionally based they are. Federal and decentralized systems tend to foster regionally based ethnic parties. In these systems, the power gained by ethnic parties that control a regional government can be significant. Compared to ethnic parties that compete across the country, regionally based ethnic parties tend to be supported by smaller ethnic groups, compete in more ethnically homogeneous regions, craft a staunch ethnic image, and strongly favor ethnic appeals. Brancati (2006) reported that regionally based parties have a higher tendency to reinforce regional identities, mobilize ethnic groups, and produce legislation in favor of certain ethnic groups compared to parties that compete across the country.

In contrast, ethnic parties that compete nationally often represent an ethnic majority or a large ethnic minority. Because they may compete in regions where their group is a minority, their ethnic appeals vary more considerably across the country and, overall, tend to be more moderate than the regionally based parties. This helps them compete in regions where they are not the majority and offers more legitimacy as a nationally (as opposed to regionally) representative ethnic party.[12] Drawing on these insights, I argue that regional ethnic parties will make more ethnic bonding appeals, targeting the party's favored ethnic group. In contrast, ethnic parties that compete nationally should be more inclined to reach out to other groups, engaging in more bridging and bypassing strategies.

8.2.1. Regional Parties in Aceh

These expectations can be tested in Aceh, the only province in Indonesia where regional parties are allowed to compete in provincial and district legislative elections without being active in other provinces. This situation arose because, until 2004, the province of Aceh had an ongoing separatist insurgency led by Gerakan Aceh Merdeka (Free Aceh Movement, GAM). Following the 2004 tsunami that devastated parts of Aceh, GAM signed a peace deal with the Indonesian government. A key component of this agreement was that regional parties would be allowed to compete in Aceh's local legislative elections.

Six regional parties formed to compete in the local legislative elections in 2009. Partai Aceh composed primarily of former members of GAM, was the most prominent of these. As an ethno-nationalist group, GAM cultivated a strong indigenous Acehnese identity to differentiate itself from the Indonesian state.[13] This Acehnese identity has been inherited by Partai Aceh and is reflected in its support. In the 2009 election, the party was popular among the indigenous Acehnese but lacked support among other indigenous minorities in Aceh (Barter 2011). There were also three Acehnese Islamist parties: Partai Daulat Atjeh (PDA) was the main vehicle for non-GAM religious clerics (*ulama*) from Acehnese Islamic schools; Partai Aceh Aman

Sejahtera (PAAS) represented many of Aceh's ulama; and Partai Bersatu Atjeh (PBA) included many former members of PAN and was founded by a former Muhammadiyah activist.[14]

To test whether regional ethnic parties are more ethnocentric in their appeals, I compared the ethnic appeals made by Acehnese ethnic party candidates with those of candidates from Indonesian parties that compete across the country. I expected that party ideology would have a greater impact on the indigenous and religious bonding appeals made by candidates in the Acehnese parties. Specifically, I expected Aceh's indigenous party candidates (Partai Aceh) to use the most indigenous bonding appeals; Aceh's Islamist party candidates to use the most Islamic bonding appeals; and Indonesian's nationalist party candidates to use the most nationalist appeals.

To analyze campaign appeals, I used a subset of the election posters from candidates who competed in Aceh's district and provincial legislative elections. These posters were photographed in Aceh's capital, Banda Aceh, located on the northern tip of Sumatra. The city is homogeneously Islamic (96%), and 86% of its residents are indigenously Acehnese. The posters came from 128 candidates who competed in Banda Aceh's DPRD elections. The candidates represent five different types of parties: nationalist, Muslim democratic and Islamist parties that competed nationally, as well as the regional Islamist and indigenous parties that competed only in Aceh. Table 8.2 shows

Table 8.2 Types of Parties Competing in the Legislative Elections in Aceh

Party Type	Party Details	Parties	Candidates
National Nationalist	PKPI, PPD, PPI, PPPI, Gerindra, Hanura, PAN, Demokrat, PDI-P, PDK, PIS, PKB, PKNU, PKPB, PNBK, Patriot, PPRN, Republikan, Golkar	19	50
National Muslim Democratic	PAN, PKB, and PKNU	3	15
National Islamist	PBB, PBR, PKS, PPP	4	26
Regional Islamist	PDA, PAAS, PBA	3	16
Regional indigenous	Partai Aceh	1	21
	Total	30	128

Note. See the section entitled "Table 5.2" in Appendix A for a list of all parties and their categorization by type.

a breakdown by type of the parties used in the analysis, including the number of posters and candidates for each.

Three dependent variables were used in the analysis: religious bonding appeals, indigenous bonding appeals, and nationalist bridging appeals. Indigenous and religious bridging appeals are rare in Banda Aceh, primarily because the region is ethnically homogeneous, so they were not included. The key independent variables were the five types of parties: nationalist, Muslim democratic, and Islamist parties at the national level and Aceh's regional Islamist and indigenous parties—each coded as binary data. I included one control, a binary variable for candidate gender, and used OLS regression analysis with clustered robust standard errors.[15]

8.2.2. Ethnocentric Appeals in Aceh

Figure 8.4 shows the predicted probabilities for each party. The findings support the expectation that regional parties would be more ethnocentric in their campaigns, compared to ethnic parties that competed nationally.

First, Aceh's indigenous party, Partai Aceh, clearly had the highest level of indigenous bonding appeals, at 86% of all candidates' poster campaigns, compared to 11% or less for the other parties. It was very common for candidates from Partai Aceh to appeal to indigenous identity by wearing traditional Acehnese clothing (see Figure 8.5, top left). Second, candidates in the Acehnese Islamist parties had the highest levels of Islamic bonding appeals in their poster campaigns, at almost 70%. See Figure 8.5 (bottom) for an example of an Acehnese Islamist party poster. It uses Islamic symbolism, including Banda Aceh's mosque (Masjid Raya Baiturrahman) and references to the Islamic clerics (*ulama*). As we would expect, the Acehnese Islamist parties were followed in order by the Islamist, Muslim democratic, and nationalist parties that competed nationally, and then by Partai Aceh. Finally, Indonesian's nationalist party candidates made the most nationalist appeals. Figure 8.5 (top right) offers an example from the nationalist Partai Demokrat, invoking nationalism though the use of a large Indonesian flag in the background.[16]

We can also compare the appeal data from Aceh with the national data. This comparison highlights how candidate appeals are influenced by regional

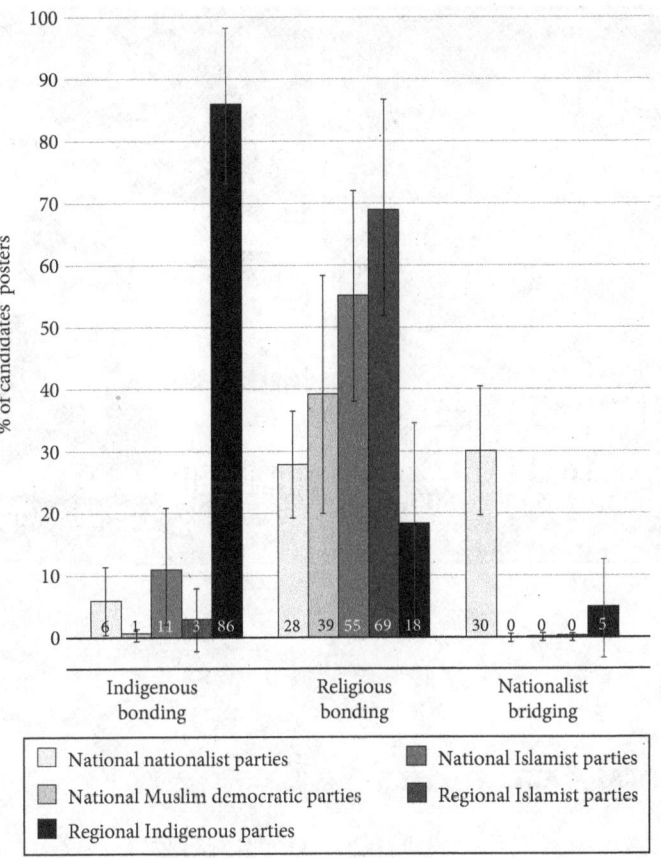

Figure 8.4 Predicted probabilities of candidates' appeals in regional legislative elections in Banda Aceh. Probabilities were calculated for each of the five types of parties while holding all other independent variables at their mean. Error bars represent 90% confidence intervals. For the regression table from which these data are drawn, see the section entitled "Figure 8.4" in Appendix A.

forces, specifically Aceh's relatively homogeneous demographics and the province's history of separatism. Table 8.3 uses data from Figure 8.2 and Figure 8.4. It shows that the nationalist party candidates nearly doubled their religious appeals in Aceh, compared to the rest of the country, while reducing their nationalist appeals. Meanwhile, both the Islamist and Muslim democratic party candidates maintained a relatively high level of religious bonding

Figure 8.5 Posters from Banda Aceh. Top left: Acehnese indigenous party poster (Partai Aceh). Top right: Indonesian nationalist party poster (Partai Demokrat). Bottom: Acehnese Islamist party poster (PDA).
Source: Author.

appeals in Aceh but eliminated nationalist appeals. Overall, the poster analysis in Aceh offers evidence that regional parties are more ethnocentric and engage in higher levels of ethnic bonding appeals. As expected, candidates in Partai Aceh promoted a strong Acehnese indigenous identity, while the Islamist Acehnese parties primarily made Islamic appeals.

Table 8.3 Comparing Appeals Across Indonesia with Appeals in Aceh by Party Type

	Religious Bonding Appeals (%)		Nationalist Bridging Appeals (%)	
	Indonesia	Aceh Only	Indonesia	Aceh Only
National Nationalist parties	16	28	48	30
National Muslim Democratic parties	41	39	37	0
National Islamist parties	51	55	31	0

Note. The percentages are drawn from the data illustrated in Figure 8.2 and Figure 8.4.

8.3. Conclusion

The findings presented in Part I of this chapter show that in legislative elections, the party's ideology influences candidates' choice between religious bonding and nationalist bridging appeals. In regional head elections, however, there was little or no connection between party ideology and candidates' appeals. These findings indicate that party ideology affects candidate appeals, but that its influence declines as elections become more candidate-centric. Part II of this chapter showed that a party's ideology was particularly influential among candidates in Aceh's regional ethnic parties, thereby supporting the idea that regional parties tend to be more ethnocentric than parties that compete nationally.

This chapter began with insights on Indonesian political parties and their historical importance in shaping the country's politics. Although the study of parties remains important, the importance of individual candidates in Indonesia has clearly increased. With a shift to a more candidate-centric system in both legislative and executive elections, the importance and influence of political parties have waned. Today, to understand Indonesian politics, the study of candidates and their constituencies is critical. I will elaborate on this idea and on broader implications of the argument in the final chapter (Chapter 10).

IV
IMPLICATIONS

9
Religious Polarization in Indonesia

On 27 September 2016, the governor of Jakarta, Basuki "Ahok" Tjahaja Purnama, delivered a speech at a community center on an island near Jakarta. Behind him, two neat rows of government officials sat in front of a poster presentation with images depicting the islands' shores and marine life. All were dressed in their government-issued, short-sleeve beige uniforms or muted batik shirts. In front, a small audience of locals listened as Ahok spoke about the struggles of the local fishermen and his program to develop the region's economy. Jakarta's gubernatorial election would be held in less than five months and Ahok, who had been elevated from deputy to governor after Joko Widodo won the presidency in 2014, was leading in almost every opinion poll. If successful, he would become the first Indonesian Chinese and the first Christian to be elected to the governorship in the capital, a historic and symbolic achievement for minorities in Indonesia.[1]

Exuding a quiet confidence, Ahok made a casual, almost offhand remark, which would eventually lead to his political downfall and would raise serious questions concerning the tolerance of minorities in Indonesia. Ahok told the audience that they should not be fooled by his adversaries who were using a verse from the Qur'an to urge people not to vote for him. The verse in question, Maidah 51, is often interpreted as forbidding Muslims from taking Christians or Jews as allies, and it has been reinterpreted by some conservative Islamic groups to mean that Muslims must not vote for a non-Muslim. At the time, the locals and officials in attendance didn't take much notice of the remark, and Ahok wrapped up the speech to smiles and polite applause. After the event, the provincial government of Jakarta uploaded a video of Ahok's speech to its YouTube channel.

The next day, a doctored 30-second clip taken from Ahok's hour-long speech was posted on YouTube by a university lecturer, Buni Yani. The out-of-context video gave the impression that Ahok was saying the Qur'an was tricking Muslims into not voting for him. The video went viral, and conservative Muslim groups subsequently charged that Ahok had insulted the

Qur'an and committed blasphemy. These accusations were followed by massive demonstrations, a contentious election campaign, and a criminal trial. Seven and a half months after the ill-judged remark, Ahok sat in a high-security detention facility in West Java; he had lost his reelection bid, been found guilty of blasphemy and inciting violence, and received a harsh sentence of two years in prison.

Many observers viewed the Islamist mobilization against Ahok as evidence of a conservative turn, a rise in religious intolerance, and a dangerous precedent for the use of Islam in election campaigns.[2] International reports echoed these concerns and often framed the episode as a reflection of weakening democracy and rising religious intolerance in Indonesia (Lamb 2017; Cochrane 2017). After the election, there were concerns that the "Ahok effect" could inspire religiously divisive campaigns in upcoming regional head elections in 2018 (Gaul 2017; Siswoyo et al. 2017). The rise of a powerful Islamic movement in politics was all the more surprising, considering that just a few years earlier, voting for Indonesian Islamic parties had hit historic lows and scholars had begun to question whether Islam was still relevant at all in Indonesian politics (Hamayotsu 2011b; Mujani and Liddle 2009).

Given this context, how do we explain the events surrounding the election in Jakarta? Do they represent a fundamental upward shift in the polarization of Indonesian politics, or were they simply a unique outcome of unusual events? The Ahok incident poses a broader issue for this book: under what conditions does the politicization of religion (or ethnicity more broadly) result in highly contentious, polarized campaigns? To understand polarization in election campaigns, in this chapter I examine the religious appeals and polarization that occurred during gubernatorial elections from 2017 to 2020. In this way, I extend my argument beyond why candidates make ethnic appeals and what kinds of appeals they make to explain why campaigns can become so polarized along the religious dimension.

I start with the intuitive expectation that when the key factors presented in the main argument encourage high levels of religious bonding appeals, then the potential for religious polarization is highest. More specifically, the potential for polarization occurs when (1) the constituency has a Muslim majority and an indigenous minority, (2) a non-Muslim head candidate competes against an all-Muslim ticket, (3) the non-Muslim candidate is a competitive challenger, (4) only two candidates are running, and (5) the Muslim candidate lacks a strong religious reputation. These elements give the

Muslim candidate the greatest incentives to make Islamic bonding appeals, while the non-Muslim candidate can only make bridging appeals or try to bypass religion altogether. In this situation, underlying normative views that object to non-Muslims governing Muslim-majority constituencies emerge. Importantly, both the campaign dynamics and these normative views create opportunities for hard-line leaders to mobilize behind the Muslim ticket and inflame societal religious tensions through protests and provocative activities. In extreme cases, the result is widespread divisive polarization along religious lines.

My analysis shows that the two gubernatorial constituencies most prone to religious polarization in the future are West Kalimantan and North Sumatra. Although Ahok's misfortunes unfolded in Jakarta, I conclude that they occurred due to rare circumstances that are unlikely to occur again in the capital.

This chapter contains four parts. In Part I, I review scholars' and observers' explanations of polarization in the Jakarta governor race as well as their analyses of polarization in the 2018 gubernatorial elections. I then present my alternative argument as to the specific conditions that can heighten the chances of religious polarization. In Part II, I provide initial evidence for the argument by showing that competitive elections in certain types of constituencies are particularly prone to high levels of ethnic bonding appeals, a condition that makes them more susceptible to ethnic polarization. In Part III, I analyze the complete set of Indonesian gubernatorial elections from 2017 to 2020 to see if the argument can explain where religious polarization did and did not occur. Finally, in Part IV, I return to the Jakarta case to assess the repercussions of Jakarta's contested election and suggest which constituencies may be most prone to religious polarization in future elections.

9.1. Explaining Religiously Polarized Campaigns in Indonesia

9.1.1. Jakarta's 2017 Gubernatorial Campaign

Three tickets competed in Jakarta's gubernatorial election. Ahok teamed up with a Muslim Javanese running mate, Djarot Saiful Hidayat; they were supported by the PDI-P. The other two tickets were composed of Muslims.

One was led by former president Susilo Bambang Yudhoyono's son, Agus Yudhoyono, and the other by an academic and former education and culture minister, Anies Baswedan.

Ahok's attempt to be the first Christian Chinese to win the Jakarta governorship was bound to be controversial. Islamic groups had protested against him, but their objections got little public traction until his remark on the Quran went viral in September 2016. In October, the Indonesian Ulama Council (Majelis Ulama Indonesia, MUI) issued a fatwa stating that Muslims could be ruled only by a Muslim leader. The statement effectively barred any Muslims who respected the council's authority from voting for Ahok. Meanwhile, the militant Front Pembela Islam (Islamic Defenders' Front, FPI) and other hard-line Muslim groups and leaders increasingly spread anti-Ahok and anti-religious minority rhetoric online, and organized street demonstrations to demand that Ahok should be disqualified from the election and imprisoned. Two massive demonstrations called "Action to Defend Islam" ("Aksi Bela Islam"), held in Jakarta in November and December 2016, attracted hundreds of thousands of protesters—a number unprecedented in the post-Suharto era.[3] The Jokowi administration concluded that the only way to defuse the crisis and limit negative impacts on Jokowi's leadership was to arrest Ahok and put him on trial for blasphemy (IPAC 2018a; Fealy 2016).

The contentious environment polarized the electorate and shifted the focus from programmatic reforms to religion. It also provided plenty of media attention for hard-line Islamists such as FPI leader Habib Rizieq, weakened Ahok's poll numbers considerably, and increased the support for his challengers. Despite the blasphemy charge, mass demonstrations, and the relentless anti-Ahok campaign, Ahok won the first round. However, he failed to win an absolute majority and thus had to face his nearest challenger, Anies Baswedan, in a runoff the following month. Although two Islamic parties, PKB and PPP, threw their support behind Ahok in the second round, he was still convincingly beaten by Anies, who was supported by Gerindra, PKS, and PAN, as well as by hard-line Islamist factions. Ahok had lost the election despite consistently high approval ratings as incumbent. Less than three weeks later, Ahok stood in a South Jakarta courtroom where the judge sentenced him to two years in prison.[4]

Observers and scholars largely interpreted the events surrounding the election and Ahok's defeat in either economic or religious terms. Those with an economic lens argued that the election campaign and in particular the mobilization against Ahok had been driven by underlying economic insecurity, stereotypes of Indonesian Chinese economic dominance, and manipulation by oligarchs. Wilson (2016, 2017) focused on rising inequality in Jakarta, its detrimental impact on the poor, and the resulting fears of job insecurity and rising costs of living among the middle class. He argued that the campaigns exploited these anxieties in different ways. On one hand, Ahok's campaign appealed to the middle class—those who aspire to live in a city like Singapore or Seoul—with his no-nonsense approach to pursuing urban redevelopment, infrastructure improvements, and forced eradication of slums. In addition, his campaign embraced his double minority status, presenting progressive pluralist views on diversity and tolerance. On the other hand, groups supporting Anies Baswedan's campaign, including hard-line Islamic clerics, used critiques of neoliberalism and xenophobic statements to appeal to voter anxieties. They opposed Ahok's developmentalist approach and liberal pluralism, framing him as an agent of Chinese crony capitalism—a narrative that fed into deeply rooted stereotypes of Chinese Indonesian economic dominance. Indeed, there is some evidence for the salience of these anti-Chinese views. In a survey experiment during the election, Sumaktoyo (2021) found that Muslims' opposition to Ahok was driven by his Chinese rather than his Christian identity.[5] These interpretations suggest that underlying economic interests made the religious-based movement against Ahok effective on a large scale.[6]

Other scholars, meanwhile, have interpreted the election more directly in terms of voters' views on Islam and the mobilization of Islamic groups. In opinion surveys, Mietzner and Muhtadi (2017) found that a large majority were actually satisfied with Ahok's performance in office, including his economic policies. However, 30% of the voters who ultimately voted against Ahok were also satisfied with his tenure in office. Looking more closely at this critical group of voters, Mietzner and Muhtadi found that almost all of them were Muslim, 74% of them were persuaded by the allegations that Ahok was guilty of blasphemy, and over half of them indicated that a common religious identity drove their voting decision. In line with this argument, others have highlighted the lack of class-based stratification in voting patterns, noting that Muslims voted against Ahok in roughly equal numbers regardless of their income and educational levels (Warburton and Gammon 2017).

9.1.2. The 2018 Gubernatorial Election Campaigns

Having successfully mobilized against Ahok and elected Anies Baswedan, Gerindra, PKS, and PAN announced that they would form a coalition to support candidates in the upcoming regional head elections. It was expected that their candidates would be more sympathetic to the Islamist movement. In addition, Islamist groups like the FPI, having raised their profile considerably through their leadership of the massive demonstrations and online agitation, appeared to be in a strong position to mobilize votes for the more staunch Islamist candidates. As a result, there were real concerns that the politicization of Islam observed in the 2017 Jakarta governor election would become a strategic template to defeat moderate and non-Muslim candidates in the 2018 elections.[7]

On June 27, 2018, a new round of regional head elections took place, comprising 17 gubernatorial and 154 district head elections. Those concerned with a repeat of Jakarta's polarized contest focused largely on five of the gubernatorial elections: three in the large and populous provinces of West, Central, and East Java and two in the ethnically diverse provinces of North Sumatra and West Kalimantan. Studies and commentary on these five elections tended to frame them as competitions between an Islamic and a more moderate Muslim or non-Muslim candidate. Although appeals to Islam were prevalent in all these elections, only in West Kalimantan did the divisiveness rival that in Jakarta, in terms of a deep, religiously inspired cleavage that polarized the province.

Explanations as to why the other four elections avoided becoming so religiously polarized revolved around the behavior of the candidates and their supporting political parties and groups. Some argued that moderate Muslim candidates with more pluralist views protected themselves from attack from conservative factions by enhancing their Islamic image. They did so by strategically choosing deputies with firmer Islamic credentials and connections to Islamic networks and by seeking support from a mix of nationalist and Islamic parties—a strategy reportedly encouraged by Jokowi's administration and the PDI-P. For instance, two moderates, Ridwan Kamil in West Java and Ganjar Pranowo in Central Java, engaged in this strategy. They thus gained access to local Islamic networks and their elections lacked a divisive religious cleavage between competing candidates.[8] However, the moderate candidates in East Java and North Sumatra did not embrace this approach, yet their elections were also relatively tame affairs.[9] More broadly, the percentage of gubernatorial candidates supported by Islamic–nationalist coalitions in 2018 was much the same as in 2017.[10] Consequently, it is hard to see how efforts by moderates to enhance their Islamic image dampened polarization in 2018,

Other explanations for the lack of polarization in 2018 focused on the more Islamic candidate in each race, suggesting that if the Islamic candidate was uncharismatic and unpopular, he could not mobilize support for an Islamic agenda, mitigating any polarization. Sudrajat in West Java and Sudirman in Central Java were described as examples of such unpopular candidates, failing to energize voters and languishing in the polls for most of the campaign (Power 2018; Warburton 2018). However, there were also cases of popular Islamic candidates whose campaigns did not foster divisive polarization. In these instances, the candidates themselves appeared to be more restrained. For instance, Edy Rahmayadi in North Sumatra led a strong Islamic ticket and eventually won the election, but during much of his campaign he emphasized his and his running mate's connections to the region instead of their religion (Simandjuntak 2018).

Finally, some explanations considered the role of Islamic factions in supporting candidates. Polarization had been anticipated in provinces where hard-line factions, such as the FPI, had strong roots or where a candidate was supported by the Gerindra–PKS–PAN coalition. In terms of hard-line support, FPI proved to be largely ineffective in polarizing campaigns even where it had a strong local presence, such as in West Java. And in terms of party support, none of the six gubernatorial elections where a candidate received support from Gerindra, PKS, and PAN were particularly polarized.[11] Their candidates were also not very successful, winning only in North Sumatra and East Kalimantan.

In the one religiously polarized election in 2018, West Kalimantan, various factors, which are difficult to verify, were cited to explain the divisiveness. They included: high levels of ethnic diversity, a history of conflict, a lack of restraint by candidates and their supporting factions, and tactics learned from the mobilization against Ahok.[12] In the run up to the 2020 regional head elections, the memory of Jakarta's election had begun to fade, as did concerns of religiously polarizing campaigns. And when the elections passed without signs of heightened religious contestation, it was attributed to the ongoing Covid-19 pandemic (Wilson and Hui 2020). Studies of the 2018 gubernatorial elections offer invaluable insights and details on how the campaigns unfolded, but ultimately, they fail to provide us with a clear argument on why some Indonesian elections became religiously polarized while others did not.

9.1.3. The Religious Polarization Argument

My explanation for religious polarization starts with an intuitive expectation that when more of the factors that foster religious bonding appeals are present, religious polarization becomes more likely. The cumulative effect of these factors can tip an election campaign from one with relatively benign religious bonding appeals into a more religiously divisive, intolerant, and ultimately polarizing one.

Since the regional head elections studied in this chapter use candidate-centric electoral rules, candidates already have incentives to target ethnic groups in their constituency with a relatively high level of ethnic appeals. However, this factor alone cannot predict religiously polarized campaigns. The following five key factors help to predict when polarization occurs in Indonesia's regional head elections.

First, I consider the viability of ethnic groups. The key question is whether the constituency has a Muslim majority. When it does, we can expect higher religious bonding appeals.[13] Importantly, we also need to consider the size of indigenous groups, as that can affect candidate appeal strategies. When Muslim-majority candidates are also from an indigenous majority, they can appeal to voters based on indigeneity instead of religion. This reduces the potential for religious bonding appeals. In contrast, when there is no indigenous majority, all Muslim candidates will be from an indigenous minority and will more exclusively appeal to their religious group. In sum, we can expect Muslim candidates to mobilize support largely through religious appeals in the Muslim-majority, indigenous-minority constituencies. However, if only Muslim candidates compete in these constituencies, these religious bonding appeals will likely stay relatively benign.

A second important factor is the presence of a non-Muslim head candidate in the race. This phenomenon, as I discuss further below, is more likely to occur in constituencies with a narrow but firm Muslim majority. In these Muslim-majority, indigenous-minority constituencies, we can get starkly contrasting campaigns when a non-Muslim runs. In these constituencies, the non-Muslim candidate is also an indigenous (or Chinese) minority, so their only appeal strategies are to bridge across religious and indigenous groups or to bypass ethnicity entirely. In contrast, Muslim candidates in these constituencies, and particularly tickets composed of two Muslims, are expected to adopt a religious bonding approach. As a result, we will likely see some religious polarization, but if a Muslim candidate is positioned to win easily, divisive polarization is unlikely.

Accordingly, as the third factor, widespread divisive religious polarization becomes a very real possibility when the non-Muslim candidate is a competitive challenger. Amidst the possibility that a non-Muslim candidate could win, underlying normative views that object to non-Muslims governing Muslim-majority constituencies are likely to emerge in public discussion regarding the election. Surveys have found that this view is prevalent among Muslim leaders and the broader population,[14] subjecting non-Muslim candidates to considerable social constraints when they try to compete in Muslim-majority constituencies.

Fourth, these polarizing campaign dynamics are exacerbated even further when there are only two candidates in the race. Without the potential for a split in the Muslim vote, the Muslim candidate has no incentives to pursue alternatives to a religious bonding strategy.

Finally, a fifth and somewhat counterintuitive contributing factor concerns reputation. Muslim candidates who lack a strong religious reputation have a stronger reason to be more strident in their religious appeals, or at least more permissive of religiously polarizing agitation within society, because they have a stronger need to shore up their religious credentials.

These five factors are illustrated in Figure 9.1, with religious polarization placed on a spectrum from lower to higher potential. While the combination of the first three factors is critical for widespread polarization to occur in regional head elections, the fourth and fifth factors can exacerbate polarization even further.

Although the argument above focuses on the conditions that make campaigns more religiously polarized, widely divisive contestation also requires mobilization from within society, often led by hard-liners. This is an important part of how polarization spreads, but I do not include it on the list of key factors, because I view the factors discussed above as creating the permissive conditions for hard-line leaders to mobilize support for their ideological agenda. Given this opening, opportunistic hard-liners organizing street rallies, protests, and online campaigns in support of the Muslim ticket that can inflame societal religious tensions. This agitation and provocation, coupled with the religious campaign rhetoric, make it difficult for the broader

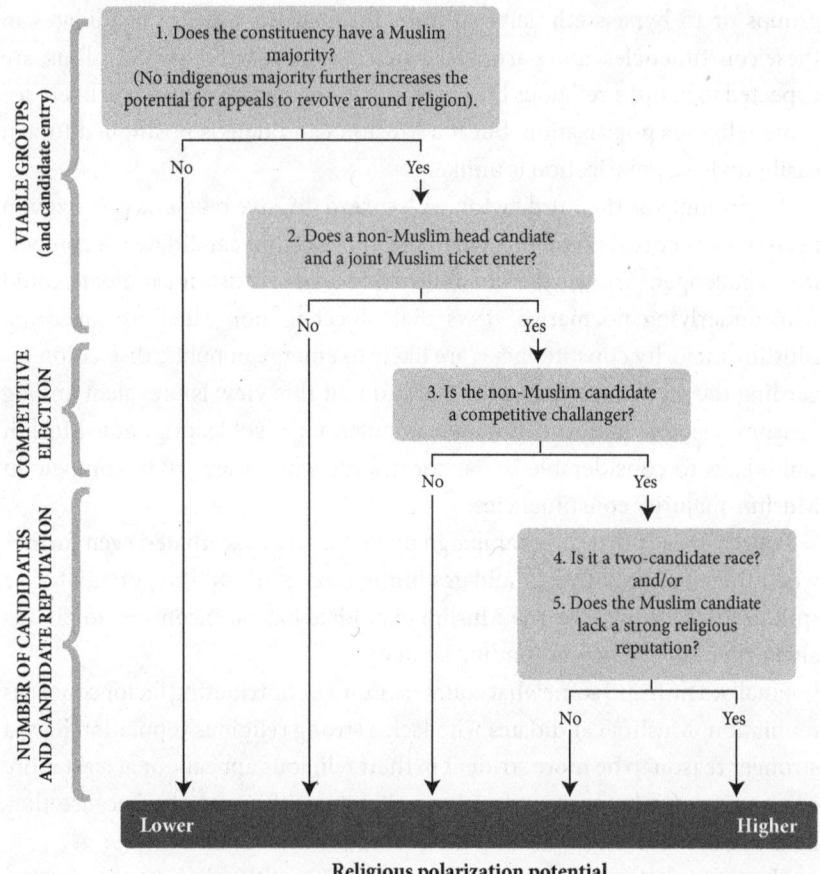

Figure 9.1 Factors that affect the potential for religious polarization in regional head election campaigns.

electorate not to prioritize religion when choosing a candidate. The ultimate outcomes are divisive polarization along religious lines and an overall rise in intolerance. In Part II and Part III, I explore the empirical evidence for this argument.

9.2. Heightened Ethnic Bonding Appeals in Regional Head Elections

As an initial first step, I examine ethnic appeal data from regional head elections to see where religious bonding appeals are most prevalent. These

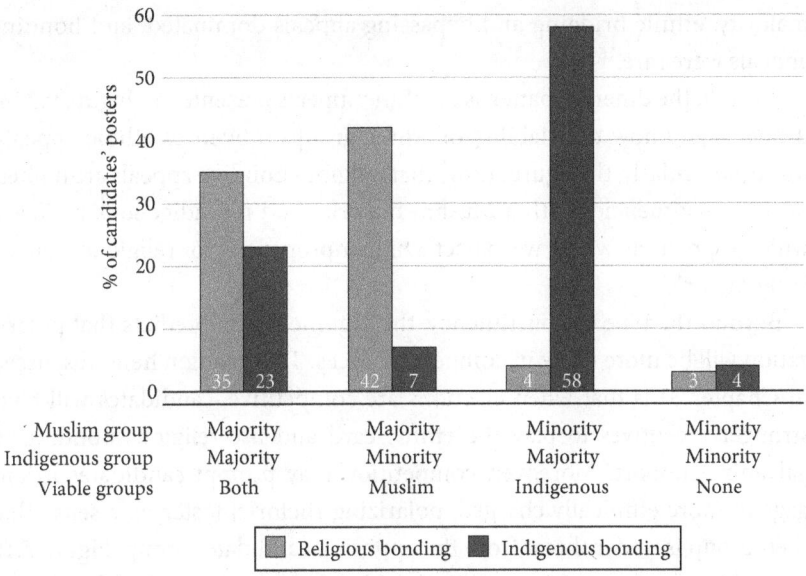

Figure 9.2 Frequency of ethnic bonding appeals based on whether the Muslim and indigenous groups are viable (majority) or nonviable (minority).

data (already analyzed in Chapter 7) contain election posters of 246 regional head candidates competing in 49 constituencies. Figure 9.2 presents the percentage of poster campaigns with bonding appeals based on the size of viable groups within constituencies—specifically, whether the Muslim and indigenous groups represent a viable (majority) or nonviable (minority) group. The bar heights represent the average percentage of candidates' poster campaigns with religious and indigenous bonding appeals.

We would expect religious bonding appeals to be more prevalent in Muslim-majority constituencies, and they were. Constituencies with a double majority, many of which are in Java, had high levels of both religious and indigenous bonding appeals. However, the highest level of religious bonding appeals was found in Muslim-majority constituencies where the largest indigenous group was a minority. Most of these candidates were Muslims, and due to the bonding-trumps-bridging heuristic outlined in previous chapters, they had incentives to prioritize bonding appeals to their religious kin. Many Indonesian cities fit this type, as well as some rural districts outside Java. In constituencies with an indigenous majority and a Muslim minority, candidates almost exclusively engaged in indigenous bonding appeals.[15] In constituencies with no Muslim or indigenous majority, ethnic bridging and bypassing appeals dominated, and bonding appeals were rare.[16]

Overall, the different patterns of ethnic appeals presented in Figure 9.2 indicate clearly how the viability of ethnic groups influences ethnic appeals. More particularly, the figure shows that religious bonding appeals are highest in the constituencies with a Muslim majority and no indigenous majority, which is precisely where we expect a higher propensity for religiously polarizing rhetoric.

Beyond the type of constituency, the argument also predicts that polarization will be more likely in competitive races. The intuition here (discussed in Chapter 3) is that when elections are competitive, candidates will have stronger incentives to play the ethnic card and use religious bonding to galvanize support. Moreover, competition may prompt candidates to engage in more ethnically charged, polarizing rhetoric, fostering a sense that their group is under threat from the opposing candidate's group. Figure 7.10 plotted levels of appeals across regional head elections, ranging from competitive to uncompetitive ones. It showed that as elections become more competitive there is a substantive and statistically significant rise in religious bonding appeals. This relationship provides evidence that the competitiveness of elections is associated with more religious bonding appeals, which in turn increase the chances of religious polarization in campaigns.

9.3. Polarization in Gubernatorial Elections (2017–2020)

To gain a better understanding of the kinds of elections where polarizing rhetoric occurs, I analyzed all 34 of Indonesia's gubernatorial elections in the round from 2017 to 2020. On the same day as the first round of Jakarta's February 2017 gubernatorial election, seven other governor elections also took place.[17] In June 2018, seventeen more gubernatorial elections occurred,[18] and the remaining nine gubernatorial elections were held in December 2020,[19] during the COVID-19 pandemic.[20]

In Table 9.1, I divide Indonesia's gubernatorial constituencies into four categories based on the viability of religious and indigenous groups in each constituency. Drawing on the main argument in this book, I predict the most prevalent appeals within each type of constituency and whether they should contribute to a higher, medium, or lower potential for polarization

Table 9.1 Appeals and Polarization in Provincial Constituencies

Constituency Type	Appeals	Polarization Potential (Based on Demographics)		Provinces	Pop.
		Religious	Indigenous		
1. Muslim majority, indigenous majority	Bonding	Medium	Medium	Aceh; West Sumatra; Lampung; Bangka Belitung Islands; West, Central, and East Java; Yogyakarta; West Nusa Tenggara; South Kalimantan; Gorontalo	161 million (59%)
2. Muslim majority, indigenous minority	Religious bonding	Higher	Lower	North and South Sumatra; Riau and the Riau Islands; Jambi; Bengkulu; Jakarta, Banten; West, Central, East, and North Kalimantan; Central, South, Southeast, and West Sulawesi, Maluku, North Maluku	95.9 million (35%)
3. Muslim minority, indigenous majority	Indigenous bonding	Lower	Higher	Bali	4.3 million (2%)
4. Muslim minority, indigenous minority	Bridging and bypassing	Lower	Lower	East Nusa Tenggara; North Sulawesi; West Papua; Papua	13.4 million (5%)

along religious and indigenous lines. Notably, only in the Muslim-majority, indigenous-minority constituencies (type 2) do I expect elevated levels of religious bonding appeals and the highest chance of religiously polarized campaigns. Turning to the gubernatorial head and deputy candidates who ran, Table 9.2 indicates their religious identities and political party endorsements from nationalist parties, Islamic parties, or both, as well as tallies for independent candidates.

Table 9.2 Governor Candidates Running in Provincial Constituencies

Constituency Type	Head and Deputy Religion					Party Support			Ind.
	M-M	M-C	C-M	C-C	H-H	Nat. only	Isl. Only	Both	
1. Muslim majority, indigenous majority	37					5	1	27	4
2. Muslim majority, indigenous minority	46	5	3	1		11	1	41	2
3. Muslim minority, indigenous majority				2		1		1	
4. Muslim minority, indigenous minority			4	8		4		8	
Number of tickets	83	5	7	9	2	21	2	77	6
Percent of tickets	78%	5%	7%	8%	2%	20%	2%	73%	6%

Note. Under "Head and Deputy Religion," M represents Muslim, C is Christian, and H is Hindu. So, M-C means that the head candidates was Muslim and the deputy candidate was Christian. Nat. = Nationalist party; Isl. = Islamic party; Both = Both nationalist and Islamic party; Ind. = Independent.

In the following discussion, I examine each of the four types of provincial constituencies qualitatively. For each type, I discuss whether Muslim and non-Muslim candidates ran, the kinds of appeals and strategies that were prevalent, and why religious polarization did or did not occur. Various specific cases of pertinent regional head elections are discussed.

9.3.1. Muslim- and Indigenous-Majority Provinces

The first category of provinces is those with both a Muslim and an indigenous majority. My argument predicts that in general, double-majority candidates (Muslim candidates from the largest indigenous group) would enter these races and that they would use either religious or indigenous bonding appeals. There is some potential for religious polarization involving double-majority candidates. However, the presence of an indigenous majority makes it more likely that candidates will be from this indigenous group. Being part of an indigenous majority gives candidates the opportunity to appeal to voters based on indigeneity instead of religion and thus reduces the likelihood that religion will become the main ethnic cleavage.

Most of Indonesia's population resides in these 11 provinces. In these provinces, both the Muslim and indigenous majorities are very large, averaging 96% and 77%, respectively. Given these demographics, it is not surprising that all 37 candidate pairs entering these races were Muslim. With no minority candidate or group to mobilize against, the potential for polarization was minimal.

In terms of appeals, both the moderate and the more Islamic candidates often emphasized their Islamic credentials. They sought support from and organized events with Islamic leaders, and they advised constituents on the benefits of an Islamic education and living a pious Islamic life. In West Java, for instance, the moderate Ridwan emphasized his more orthodox Islamic (*santri*) roots and promoted his travels while doing the hajj pilgrimage through social media. Although some Islamic-inspired smear campaigns showed up online in the final days of the West Java campaign, they did not come directly from the candidates and had little effect on the outcome. Meanwhile, there were also some indigenous appeals. For instance, Dedi Mulyadi, a deputy candidate in the race, appealed to West Java's largest indigenous group, the Sundanese (Warburton 2018). Given the religious and indigenous homogeneity of these provinces, such appeals are neither surprising nor new.

Figure 9.2 shows similarly high levels of indigenous and religious appeals in regional head election posters for this type of constituency. Although it was not a governor election, a mayoral election in 2015 in Surakarta, commonly known as Solo, offers some insight here. The constituency of Solo is a double majority, with a Muslim population of 79% and a Javanese population of 95%. In 2012, F. X. Hadi Rudyatmo, known as Rudy, was elevated from deputy to mayor when Solo's mayor, Jokowi, became governor of Jakarta. Rudy served until 2015 and then entered Solo's mayoral election. His candidacy bore uncanny similarities to Ahok's. Like Ahok, Rudy had served as a deputy for Jokowi, had had great success continuing Jokowi's reforms, and was praised for his performance. Moreover, he was supported by the PDI-P and was a non-Muslim (a Catholic) competing against a joint-Muslim ticket in a Muslim-majority constituency. Surprisingly, however, Solo's election lacked the divisive religious politics of Jakarta. Why might that be the case? The key difference was that Rudy belonged to an indigenous majority group—he was a Javanese competing in a homogeneously Javanese constituency. As a result, he could make indigenous bonding appeals. In his election posters, for instance, he frequently appeared in traditional Javanese garb, connecting with the majority of constituents based on Javanese indigenous identity rather than religious identity. In contrast, Ahok, a double minority in Jakarta, did not have that option.

Overall, the electoral rules and small size of non-Muslim groups made it highly unlikely that these gubernatorial elections would ever become religiously polarized. These underlying factors help explain why there were no minority candidates and why they made Islamic and indigenous appeals, though in a largely benign and obligatory fashion.

9.3.2. Muslim-Majority, Indigenous-Minority Provinces

The second category includes 18 constituencies with a Muslim majority and an indigenous minority. I would expect mostly Muslim candidates with a variety of indigenous backgrounds to enter these races and to make primarily religious bonding appeals during their campaigns. Because the argument expects polarization to be most likely in this set of constituencies, I provide more detail on them in Table 9.3. It shows how the dominance by the Muslim population ranges widely among these provinces, from 51% in Maluku to 98% in Bengkulu.[21] This range is critical in determining which gubernatorial campaigns are prone to religious polarization. Joint-Muslim tickets were most common (there were 46), and nine other tickets were mixed. Importantly, most of these mixed pairings ran in the four provinces with the lowest percentages of Muslims. These regions have relatively large Christian populations and potential opportunities for minority Christians to run. But non-Muslim candidates become very rare when the Muslim population exceeds 70%. One Christian deputy candidate in North Kalimantan and another in Central Sulawesi competed in uneventful campaigns. Placed in this context, the fact that a non-Muslim like Ahok could enter the race in Jakarta—a province with a Muslim population of 86%— as the head candidate is a very rare event, one brought on by unusual circumstances.

As I discuss below, the two elections that became highly polarized along religious lines were in West Kalimantan and Jakarta. Taking a closer look, we find that these two elections (highlighted in gray in Table 9.3) had a key factor in common: *a popular ticket headed by a minority Christian candidate*

Table 9.3 Governor Elections for Muslim-Majority, Indigenous-Minority Provinces (2017–2020)

Year	Province	Muslim Population	Head and Deputy Religion				Party Support			Ind.
			M-M	M-C	C-M	C-C	Nat. Only	Isl. Only	Both	
2018	Maluku	51%		2	1				2	1
2018	West Kalimantan	59%	1		1	1	1		2	
2018	North Sumatra	66%	1	1					2	
2020	North Kalimantan	71%	2	1					3	
2020	Central Kalimantan	74%	2				1		1	
2018	North Maluku	74%	4				1		3	
2020	Central Sulawesi	78%	1	1			1		1	
2020	Riau Islands	80%	3						3	
2017	West Sulawesi	83%	3				1		2	
2017	Jakarta	86%	2		1		1		2	
2018	East Kalimantan	86%	4				2		2	
2018	Riau	88%	4				1		3	
2018	South Sulawesi	90%	4						3	1
2017	Banten	95%	2				1		2	
2018	Southeast Sulawesi	95%	3				1		2	
2020	Jambi	96%	3				1	1	1	
2018	South Sumatra	97%	4						4	
2020	Bengkulu	98%	3						3	
	Number of tickets		46	5	3	1	11	1	41	2
	Percent of tickets		84%	9%	5%	2%	20%	2%	75%	4%

Note. Under "Head and Deputy Religion," M represents Muslim and C is for Christian.

competed in a race with at least one all-Muslim ticket. This kind of matchup is uncommon, as it did not occur in any other gubernatorial election studied.

Of all the provinces, three provinces—Maluku, West Kalimantan, and North Sumatra—deserve a closer look. Because they all fit into the band of provinces with a narrow Muslim majority, they appear to be especially prone to having this kind of matchup in their future gubernatorial elections. Below, I discuss the gubernatorial election in each case, explaining why there was religious polarization in West Kalimantan and why it could happen in the future in North Sumatra. I also discuss the curious case of Maluku, a province that may have insulated itself from polarization due to more tolerant social norms that prevent volatile matchups from occurring.

West Kalimantan

West Kalimantan is an ethnically diverse province rich in natural resources and with a history of ethnic conflict. The most recent major incidents occurred in the late 1990s and were directed against Madurese transmigrants by Dayaks and Malays (Davidson 2008a; Peluso 2008). The Muslim population (59%) is composed of Malays, Javanese, Madurese, and some Dayaks. The Christian population (39%) is mostly Dayak, while Buddhists constitute 5% of the population and are predominantly Indonesian Chinese. Given the Muslim majority, we can expect Muslim candidates to run, but in view of the large size of the minority Christian group, the presence of Christian candidates should not be surprising. Indeed, this has been the pattern in the past, and it occurred again in 2018.

One prominent Muslim Malay candidate was Sutarmidji,[22] a popular mayor of Pontianak, widely viewed as an honest and competent technocrat. Although he had some Islamic lineage, with his father formerly having been a member of Masyumi,[23] he was not known for supporting hard-line Islamic groups. However, before entering the race for governor, he began cultivating a more Islamic image. In 2016, he attended a protest by the FPI in Pontianak to demand the jailing of Ahok and promised to lead the next protest if Ahok was not charged with blasphemy (Setijadi 2018). In doing so, he aligned himself publicly with the anti-Ahok movement, which was broadly supported by the Muslim mainstream in West Kalimantan (IPAC 2018a). Having cemented his image as the Islamic candidate, he would go on to host another FPI protest in Pontianak in 2017. Then, rather than picking a Christian running mate, Sutarmidji formed a joint-Muslim ticket, choosing a Malay Muslim, and sought support from PKS and PKB, as well as Golkar,

Partai NasDem (National Democratic Party), and Hanura. Securing support though Islamic networks and pursuing a religious bonding strategy was a strategic move. It allowed Sutarmidji to cast himself as the Muslim candidate rather than a Malay candidate. In this way, he appealed to the majority—the Malays, Javanese and Madurese, as well as some Muslim Dayaks. Overall, we would expect that Sutarmidji's strategy of appealing to his viable Muslim group rather than just his nonviable Malay group would offer him the best chance of electoral success.

Karolin Margret Natasa, a Christian Dayak, also entered the race. A district head of Landak, Karolin was a hugely popular former national parliamentarian[24] and the daughter of the outgoing PDI-P governor, Cornelis, who had served two terms. While Sutarmidji pursued a bonding strategy, Karolin, as a Christian from a minority indigenous group, had to engage in a bridging strategy. Her father had successfully pursued a similar bridging strategy in the past by appealing to both Dayak and Chinese identity groups in a religiously polarizing 2007 election.[25] Karolin's campaign was open about mobilizing Dayak identities, as she had appeared in campaign posters dressed in Dayak clothing and headdress. Moreover, Cornelis, who was managing her campaign, made explicit appeals to all Dayak subgroups and their leaders to unite behind the Dayak candidate, his daughter (IPAC 2018a). In addition, Karolin reached out to the Javanese population through her husband, a prominent member of the Javanese community (Rafsadie et al. 2020). Overall, she played down religion and instead bridged across indigenous Dayaks, Javanese, and Indonesian Chinese groups. Again, this bridging appeal strategy is what we would expect from a candidate in her position.

Although the ethnic appeal strategies of Sutarmidji and Karolin were predictable, volatility resulted because hard-line groups perceived their appeals to disparate groups as offering an opportunity to politicize religious cleavages and polarize communities. Even when candidates themselves remain relatively positive, their more hard-line supporters can make incendiary appeals and derogatory statements concerning the opposition candidate.

In Sutarmidji's campaign, hard-line supporters, such as the FPI, explicitly politicized religion before and during the campaign. The FPI has had a local presence in West Kalimantan since it brought FPI founder Habib Rizieq to the province in 2000, and over time it has cultivated links to some members of the revived Sultanate of Pontianak (IPAC 2018a; Sebastian and Arifianto 2021). During 2017, it brought in conservative speakers and organized various protests with staunch Islamic themes—protesting to jail Ahok, defending the Ulama, and opposing Cornelis's promise to expel Habib Rizieq if he came to West Kalimantan. These hard-line Islamic activities were publicly challenged. In one instance, conservative clerics who flew into West Kalimantan were held up on the tarmac by members of the Dayak Customary Council (Dewan Adat Dayak, DAD) dressed in traditional war clothing (IPAC 2018a).

During the campaign, anti-Karolin attacks were common. Through social media and messaging apps, and in mosque sermons, Muslims were urged not to vote for a Christian candidate because Islam forbids Muslims to choose non-Muslim leaders. As a final reminder, Muslims were invited via social media to take part in a mass morning prayer on the day of the election (Setijadi 2018; IPAC 2018b).

Ultimately, the election was defined by the issue of religion. In the end, Sutarmidji's religious bonding strategy beat Karolin's bridging strategy. The province voted along religious rather than indigenous lines, and Sutarmidji received 52%, winning the Muslim vote including most of the Muslim Dayak voters. Despite her bridging efforts, Karolin failed to gain much of the Muslim Dayak or Javanese vote.[26] Tensions were high as the results were released, with a few minor incidents of property damage and intimidation by angry Dayaks, but no major violence occurred. One reason why the situation did not deteriorate further was the efforts of local media and civil society groups, who set up a system to monitor social media messaging apps and expose untruths, particularly when they concerned religion or indigeneity.[27]

In the end, this election had almost all the factors that we expect to result in more religious bonding appeals and a higher chance of religious polarization. It was in a Muslim-majority, indigenous-minority constituency; a non-Muslim head candidate was a competitive challenger facing a joint-Muslim ticket; and the Muslim head candidate lacked a strong religious reputation. The only key element technically missing was that it was not a two-candidate race, but the third candidate was never a real contender.[28]

Another election in Singkawang, West Kalimantan also fits all the argument's criteria, and it too became polarized along religious lines. The city of Singkawang has a small Muslim majority (54%) and no indigenous majority. In the 2012 election, the two main candidate teams were an all-Muslim ticket and a non-Muslim Chinese ticket with strong links to the Dayak population. The election quickly became religiously polarized as the Malay organization (Majelis Adat Budaya Melayu) mobilized support behind the Muslim ticket and called on Muslims to vote for Muslim candidates. Meanwhile, the Chinese ticket mobilized non-Muslim Chinese and Dayak voters.[29] Overall, the evidence from these elections adds support to the argument.

North Sumatra

North Sumatra is another province where we might expect polarization. It has a demographic very similar to West Kalimantan: 66% Muslim (mostly Javanese, Malay, and Minangkabau along with some Batak) and 31% Christian (predominantly Batak). Although Islam certainly figured in the election, it did not become as hotly contested an issue as in West Kalimantan or Jakarta, mainly because both candidates for regional head were Muslims. However, as the campaign unfolded, some similarities with the more polarized cases of West Kalimantan and Jakarta appeared.

The more moderate candidate was Djarot Syaiful Hidayat, a Muslim Javanese who had been Ahok's running mate the previous year in the Jakarta election. Djarot was put forward by the PDI-P and, like Karolin in West Kalimantan, he pursued an ethnic bridging strategy. In an effort to appeal to the large Batak population, he chose a Christian Batak as his running mate. In addition, to connect with the Javanese, Djarot drew on his Javanese identity, securing support from Pujakesuma, North Sumatra's Javanese organization (Simandjuntak 2018).

Djarot's opponent, Edy Rahmayadi, projected a stronger Islamic image and pursued a religious bonding strategy. He formed an all-Muslim ticket, got support from most Islamic clerics, and benefited from some sermons in mosques that encouraged voters to choose the Muslim candidates. His campaign called for Muslims to join in a mass morning prayer on election day. However, it also used regional appeals, presenting Edy and his running mate as genuine sons of the soil. Since Edy was a former military commander in North Sumatra and his running mate was a local businessman, these appeals may have resonated. Meanwhile, Djarot didn't have much connection with the Javanese in North Sumatra. Additionally, his Batak running mate was somewhat disconnected from the province, having spent much of his life and career in Jakarta.

In the end, Edy's religious bonding strategy and regional appeals appeared to work. As the vote split largely along religious lines, Edy received 58% of the vote. Djarot's efforts to bridge across indigenous groups were less successful, though he did quite well with Javanese and Muslim Batak voters in Simalungun and Pematangsiantar.

As the argument would predict, the absence of a critical factor—a non-Muslim challenger—made religious polarization very unlikely. However, contentious polarization along religious lines is quite possible in a future North Sumatran race if a popular Christian candidate faces an all-Muslim ticket. Indeed, this almost occurred in the 2008 gubernatorial election when a popular Christian Batak candidate, Rudolf Pardede, put his name forward. Rudolf had been elevated from deputy to governor after the elected governor died in a plane crash in 2005. During his time in office, Rudolf faced resistance from the PKS and protests from hard-line Islamic groups such as the FPI—actions very reminiscent of what Ahok experienced after his succession to governor of Jakarta. His opponents drew on a scandal involving Rudolf's inability to produce a verified authentic high school diploma—a requirement for all politicians holding elected office.[30] This became an obstacle for Rudolf when he wanted to run in the 2008 gubernatorial election, and his party, the PDI-P, ended up supporting another candidate for governor.

Another case of a religiously polarized campaign occurred in North Sumatra's capital, Medan, which has much the same demographics as the province. In the 2010 mayoral race, a popular Christian Chinese candidate, Sofyan Tan, ran against an all-Muslim ticket led by Rahudman Harahap in the second round of the election. I discussed the bridging strategies of Sofyan and the religious bonding strategies of Rahudman in Chapter 7. This case adds support for the polarization argument as it fits all the criteria; it took place in a Muslim-majority, indigenous-minority constituency and pitted a competitive non-Muslim candidate against a joint-Muslim ticket led by a candidate, Rahudman, who lacked a strong religious reputation.

Maluku

Finally, Maluku is another province where we might have expected polarization. It is divided along religious lines, and 20 years earlier it experienced a devastating conflict between Christians and Muslims that left at least 2,000 dead (van Klinken 2007). Puzzlingly, given its demographics and history of conflict, the 2018 campaign was remarkably amicable. Maluku's razor-thin Muslim majority of just 51% may have actually contributed to this outcome. This demographic is actually similar to constituencies with a slight Christian majority, where ethnic bridging and bypassing strategies prevail—constituencies such as Maluku's capital city of Ambon, Pematangsiantar in Sumatra, or the province of West Papua (discussed below). In Maluku, without a solid Muslim majority and needing a large share of the votes, candidates have some incentives to avoid religious bonding appeals and to choose bridging strategies instead. There is just too much uncertainty for any candidate to believe he or she can secure all the Muslim vote.

In the 2018 governor election, all three tickets were mixed pairs of Muslim and Christian candidates, reducing the religious volatility. In fact, a joint-Muslim or joint-Christian pair has never run in a gubernatorial election in Maluku. This pattern suggests that a consensus in favor of bridging strategies has emerged in Maluku because Muslims do not have a firm majority. As a result, gubernatorial campaigns have been remarkably peaceful affairs, with candidates largely reaching out across groups with bridging appeals.[31] Although there is some tendency for voters to back their religious kin, candidates play down religion, and hard-line groups, lacking opportunities for agitation, are not visible in campaigns.

Maluku presents us with a curious case where a genuine normative consensus appears to have developed among candidates and the general community that candidates should bridge, forming mixed tickets and reaching across communities for support. It is an example of the ways in which social constraints can affect—in this case dampen—ethnic bonding appeals. In light of the sensational reporting on Jakarta's election, the stories of candidates bridging across religious divides in provinces that have experienced such violent conflict in the past deserve far more attention.

9.3.3. Muslim-Minority Provinces

In contrast to the prevalence of religious bonding appeals in elections in the provinces where Muslims are a majority, I didn't expect to find religious bonding appeals or polarization in the elections in the Muslim-minority provinces. Bali is the only province with a Muslim minority and an indigenous majority. It is relatively homogeneous—85% Hindu and Balinese; not surprisingly, the two candidates were Hindu Balinese and there was no religious polarization. The campaign largely revolved around balancing the protection and promotion of Balinese culture with development and tourism.

Four provinces have a Muslim minority and an indigenous minority: East Nusa Tenggara, North Sulawesi, West Papua, and Papua. As expected, due to the fragmented indigenous demographics, the 12 candidates who ran in these provinces came from a variety of indigenous groups. All head candidates were Christians, again not surprising since all the provinces had a Christian majority. Also in line with expectations, candidates often made bridging appeals to reach out across indigenous and religious groups or bypassed ethnicity altogether. One way in which they did so was through their choice of running mate. Focusing on religious bridging, West Papua is illustrative. Among all of the Muslim-minority provinces, West Papua had the largest Muslim population (39%) and consequently, all three head candidates chose Muslim deputies. As another indication of religious bridging, most candidates in the Muslim-minority provinces secured support from a mix of nationalist and Islamic political parties.

Islamic parties, such as PAN and PKS, were very willing to support non-Muslim candidates in these provinces even while they mobilized against Ahok in Jakarta. In 2017, PAN supported the winning candidate in West Papua; another candidate, Irene Manibuy, was supported by three Islamic parties—PKS, PKB, and PPP. Moreover, Irene made bridging appeals to reach out to the Muslim community, promising to build a grand mosque in the province. In response to Irene's Islamic party support, PKS and PPP party leaders in West Papua commented that they did not look at religion when nominating regional heads, adding that a political party must face political realities in elections (Lestari 2017). This fact further indicates that normative views against non-Muslim leaders are largely confined to Muslim-majority constituencies. In the end, Islamic party backing didn't seem to hinder candidates' success, as three of the four winning candidates in these provinces were supported by Islamic parties.[32]

Indeed, it is quite common for Islamic parties to support Christian candidates in district head and legislate elections across these provinces. Given the need for a large proportion of votes, candidates and supporting parties must achieve broad appeal within a constituency to be successful. That imperative might result in PKS supporting a female Christian candidate in West Papua, or in a more moderate candidate choosing an Islamic running mate elsewhere, as we saw in the cases of Ridwan in West Java or Ganjar in Central Java. Though the strategies are different, the end goal of candidates and parties is the same: to win.

9.4. Returning to Jakarta

Jakarta's 2017 election fits all the criteria laid out in the polarization argument. In a Muslim-majority, indigenous-minority constituency, Ahok, a competitive non-Muslim candidate, faced Anies, a Muslim candidate who needed to shore up his Islamic credentials. This matchup created opportunities for Ahok's political opponents and for hard-line Islamic factions. They seized on his outspoken nature to politicize religion effectively and skillfully, thereby muting more moderate Islamic voices. Ultimately, the electoral result and Ahok's decision to go to prison rather than appealing his sentence brought the crisis to an end.

This chapter has highlighted how religious polarization, though not on the same scale as in the contentious race in Jakarta, occurred in gubernatorial elections in West Kalimantan in 2018 (and 2007), as well as in mayoral elections in Medan in 2010, and Singkawang in 2012. What separated these regional head elections from others is that they shared, almost without exception, the key factors contained in the polarization argument. Since these factors were also present in Jakarta, the religiously polarized campaign there should not have been a surprise. What is surprising, though, is how a non-Muslim candidate could enter a race in an 86% Muslim constituency as the frontrunner. From this perspective, it is difficult to overstate the unusual nature of Jakarta's election. Among the thousands of regional head elections that have taken place in Indonesia, it is extremely rare for a non-Muslim candidate from a dual minority to run in a constituency with such a large Muslim population.[33] Ahok's competitive candidacy was thus not representative of the vast majority of regional head elections.

Looking to the future, I have argued that of all the 34 Indonesian provinces, the two that are most prone to polarization in gubernatorial elections are West Kalimantan and North Sumatra, due to their demographic makeup. Additionally, only 15 of Indonesia's 508 regional head districts fit the demographic criteria, at the time of writing.[34] Overall, only a very small number of electoral constituencies are prone to religious polarization.

As noted in the introduction, a number of observers viewed Jakarta's contentious election as a major conservative turn in Indonesian society and politics. I do not share that view. As I have argued, the polarization in Jakarta was largely due to a constellation of particular factors rather than a sudden conservative shift in society or politics, despite how it might have appeared in the Indonesian or foreign press. As I have shown throughout this book, the politicization of religion in Indonesian elections is not new. Post-*Reformasi*, it became an increasingly common feature of elections well before the 2016 protests—specifically with the introduction of direct regional head elections and PR open-list legislative elections. Additionally, normative intolerant views within society that place restraints on non-Muslim candidates are very real and have existed for a long time.

Nevertheless, the politicization of religion has its limits. Islamic groups who organized the Jakarta protests had a primary goal of prosecuting Ahok, but they also had a larger, aggressive Islamic agenda, including constitutional changes to compel Muslims to follow Islamic law and the banning of non-Muslims from holding executive office in Muslim-majority constituencies. Although the massive turnouts at their protests might have given the impression that the vast majority of mainstream Indonesian Muslims supported the organizers' very conservative Islamic agenda, that does not appear to have been the case. Fealy (2016) reported that only a minority of those who attended the protests were affiliated with hard-line Islamic groups, and most of those interviewed at the protests rejected any efforts to change the constitution or place restrictions on non-Muslims. Moreover, most attendees saw the protests as largely a social rather than a political event—a once-in-a-lifetime opportunity to pray with hundreds of thousands of other Muslims in a celebration of Islam.

On that note, my argument should not be seen as overly deterministic. Candidates and the broader public can restrain the politicization of religion in any specific context through their choices and actions. For instance, in North Sumatra, Edy's campaign exhibited restraint by not focusing only on religion and also by using regional appeals. Even in West Kalimantan, the polarized campaign could have spiraled out of control and become violent if not for the proactive actions of local groups that monitored digital media for provocative messages. Additionally, after the official result, Karolin conceded defeat and congratulated the winner. Even under polarizing conditions, candidates and societal actors who abide by democratic rules, exhibiting tolerance and restraint, can prevent societal polarization from escalating into violence.

9.5. Conclusion

Jakarta's unprecedented election and the protests surrounding it made for an incredibly sensational event that captured the attention of the whole country as well as the international media. It demonstrated how elites can use religion to polarize an election for both political and ideological ends. It also gave the impression, at least for a time, that hard-line Islamists represented a large portion of Indonesia's Muslim community. More broadly, it undermined Indonesia's self-proclaimed image as a tolerant society and signaled to minorities that they cannot always rely on the government for protection. However, even though hard-line groups seized the opportunity to mobilize support on a large scale, the chances that another spectacularly visible, religiously polarizing event will occur in the near future are relatively low.

10
Conclusion

Writing on the power dynamics of the U.S. city of New Haven, Connecticut in the 1950s and early 1960s, Robert Dahl predicted a decline in ethnic politics. Dahl (1971: 62) argued that the pressures of modernization and the problems of urban life would encourage the emergence of "politicians with capacities for building durable coalitions out of traditionally noncooperative and even mutually suspicious social strata." As a result, he expected that ethnic groups in the United States would assimilate over time, concluding that "the strength of ethnic ties as a factor in local politics surely must recede."[1]

While many scholars echoed Dahl's sentiment on ethnic politics, Bill Liddle's insights and predictions from Indonesia differed. While Dahl studied New Haven, Liddle was living in and studying ethnic politics in the Indonesian provincial city of Pematang Siantar, one of the key sites of investigation for this book. During this contentious era of competitive ethnic politics in Indonesia, Liddle (1970: 227–230) took a more nuanced view of the interaction of ethnicity and politics. He observed that while ethnic loyalties remained strong, they were not necessarily destructive of national integration, democratic development, or effective government. As a result, he argued that instead of ignoring ethnicity or wishing it to recede, we should incorporate multiple overlapping ethnic, supraethnic, and nonethnic identities within the arena of political competition. Looking to the future, Liddle believed that ethnicity would remain prevalent in Indonesian politics despite modernization.

Since the 1950s, a wealth of research has shown that ethnic group identities have indeed remained influential in politics, affecting voters' political behavior and the mobilization strategies of political parties and candidates. In Indonesia, the long authoritarian years of Suharto's regime saw coercive attempts to suppress ethnic politics, but a new era of democracy has reinvigorated it. And in recent elections, the mobilization of overlapping indigenous, religious, regional, and nationalist identities has become an increasingly important means of engaging in political competition.

In this concluding chapter, I reflect on some broader implications of the book's argument in relation to contemporary Indonesia and the study of ethnic politics. In Part I, I consider the importance of candidates in recent Indonesian elections and the microfoundations underlying their behavior. In Part II, I provide insights on the rising importance of ethnicity in Indonesian politics and assess the country's shift to a more candidate-centric system. Finally, in Part III, I consider how to curb ethnic politics, focusing on two strategies: politicizing multiple dimensions of ethnicity and changing the boundaries of electoral constituencies.

10.1. The Microfoundations of Candidate Behavior

Much existing work on the politicization of ethnicity in Indonesian elections has used surveys and election returns to study voters and voting behavior. In recent years, there has been particular interest in using this approach to understand the impact of religion. Surveys have found that religion informs Indonesians' views of democracy and can influence their choice of candidates and political parties.[2] Meanwhile, the analysis of election returns has identified religious cleavages in Indonesian society.[3] In contrast to this accumulation of systematic knowledge on voters, much of our understanding of Indonesian candidates' behavior is anecdotal and specific to individual elections.[4] Additionally, candidate's campaigns are often understood in a narrow sense, in terms of whether they mobilized support or not. Less attention has been given to why candidates choose certain strategies and whether there are patterns in their campaigns.

Ethnic political strategies are an important area of research because the ways candidates politicize ethnicity can have profound effects on the opinions and behaviors of constituents. Take attitudes toward interreligious tolerance as an example. Surveys of Indonesian Muslims showed that levels of intolerance and radical attitudes had declined between 2010 and 2016.[5] However, surveys conducted after Jakarta's 2017 contentious election campaign revealed a dramatic rise in intolerant and exclusivist attitudes among Muslims. Moreover, the percentage of Muslims nationwide who rejected the idea that non-Muslims could hold office had increased by 7.3% to 49.6%. The effect was even stronger in Jakarta, where 47% of residents rejected the idea of a non-Muslim governor before the anti-Ahok campaign, 62% during the campaign, and 59% afterward.[6] These data indicate the dramatic impact that the politicization of ethnicity can have on voters.

Clearly, it is not enough just to understand changing patterns of voter attitudes; we also need to understand why candidates foster particular kinds of ethnic politics that have the potential to polarize communities. This book has sought to explain what shapes candidates' ethnic appeals and to argue that there are particular constituencies where candidates are more likely to carry out polarizing campaigns.

Using novel approaches to measure campaign appeals from newspaper reports and election posters, I demonstrated that three key factors have a substantial effect on candidates' decisions to politicize ethnicity: the degree to which the rules are candidate-centric, the viability of ethnic groups, and the ideologies of political parties. Using quantitative and qualitative evidence, I showed that the degree to which rules are candidate-centric functions like a dial, reducing the influence of the party while raising the importance of connecting with local and often with ethnic groups.

The results indicated that candidates, particularly those competing in highly candidate-centric regional head elections, are very sensitive to the ethnic makeup of their constituency. To come up with a strategy, these candidates search through their repertoire of ethnic categories to which they belong. If they identify a viable group, they have incentives to bond with it; if not, they tend to engage in ethnic bridging or to bypass ethnic appeals altogether. In contrast, the analysis determined that candidates competing in party-centric legislative elections made more partisan appeals, and that their choice of ethnic bonding or bridging appeals was influenced by their party's ideology to a greater extent.

Testing the argument on Indonesian elections provides an understanding of ethnic politics in the world's third-largest democracy and largest Muslim-majority country. The findings explain how Indonesian candidates formulate ethnic appeal strategies and provide insights into how the three most prominent forms of ethnic identification in Indonesia—religion, indigeneity, and nationalism—are used in campaigns. They also help to explain why and where religious polarization emerges in Indonesian elections.

10.2. The Politicization of Ethnicity

10.2.1. Increasing Ethnic Appeals

One of the enduring debates in Indonesian politics concerns the role of Islam and its effect on political behavior. As of 2011, many scholars and commentators believed that Islam had become less politically relevant since the transition to democracy. Evidence for this contention came from voter surveys[7] and the fact that votes for Islamic parties had declined since 1999.[8]

In contrast, two key pieces of evidence presented in this book indicate that since 2005, Islam has become more prominent in Indonesian politics. First, the evidence showed that use of Islam in elections increased after the introduction of regional head elections in 2005. The analysis of election posters demonstrated that Islamic appeals were more frequent in district head elections than in legislative elections, contributing to an overall increase in the prominence of Islam in Indonesian electoral competitions. Second, the analysis of newspaper reports indicated a rise in Islamic religious appeals after PR open lists were introduced in 2009. The data showed that candidates increasingly met with Islamic groups, sought support from Islamic elites and organizations, invoked their Islamic identity, and promoted their work experience with Islamic organizations.

Beyond the rise in Islamic appeals, evidence from the newspaper analysis suggests that in the legislative elections, nationalist party candidates have intensified their religious rhetoric and increasingly reached out to Islamic groups, elites, and associations in their campaigns. In regional head elections, most candidates are supported by both nationalist and Islamic parties and make similar kinds of ethnic appeals; as a result, it is often difficult to differentiate between the nationalist and Islamic orientations of candidates.

These findings are in line with the observations of other scholars, who have suggested in 2009 and thereafter that a mainstreaming of Islam has taken place, with nationalist parties and candidates increasingly supporting Islamic organizations, backing religiously inspired legislation, and using Islamic teachings to inform public policy decisions (Evans 2009; Platzdasch 2009; Sukma 2010; Tanuwidjaja 2010). Although I agree with this interpretation, this book goes further, arguing that the mainstreaming of Islam is driven in large part by the introduction of candidate-centric elections and candidates' efforts to reach out to their constituents using religion.

While Islamic politics have received considerable attention from scholars and commentators, indigenous ethnic politics have received far less.[9] This is partly because there are no indigenous political parties, so indigeneity is not as prominent on the national stage. Additionally, because there are so many indigenous groups across Indonesia, they constitute viable ethnic groups for politicians much less often than Muslims do. Nevertheless, I found an increasing politicization of indigeneity in election campaigns across the country, particularly in non-Muslim-majority constituencies. Again, this phenomenon is driven by the introduction of candidate-centric regional head elections and open-list PR.

10.2.2. Assessing Indonesia's Candidate-Centric System

Candidate-centric rules have been the primary factor driving increases in the politicization of ethnicity. Beyond resulting in a more prominent role for ethnicity, the candidate-centric system has had various costs and benefits. One key benefit is that it has helped to hold candidates accountable (Horowitz 2013: 185). Voters now play a direct role in choosing their political representatives, and they possess (although they do not always use it) the power to replace them for underperforming. The introduction of candidate-centric rules brought to an end the era during which party leaders could act as gatekeepers, appointing regional heads or putting their favorite candidates in safe places on a list. This change has prompted candidates to focus more attention on their constituents rather than on party leaders.

Second, with this change, candidates and political parties have realized that they need to understand their constituents more fully. This realization has resulted in a rise of consultancy firms that use surveys to identify how electable candidates are and their strengths and weaknesses. The consultants then help them overcome those weaknesses and develop campaign platforms that will resonate with constituents (Qodari 2010; Ufen 2011; Warburton 2016: 357–358). Using consultants and surveys in this way helps to identify important issues, desires, and needs of constituents and to relay this information to candidates and political parties.

Third, candidate-centric election campaigns create tighter connections between candidates and constituents. To win enough personal votes, candidates must go to great efforts building territorially organized campaign teams who will canvass for support from constituents. Candidates also frequently attend small ethnic and community campaign events, where they seek support from influential leaders of villages, neighborhoods, religious or indigenous associations, and sports clubs.[10] These events provide them with the opportunity to interact with voters from their own and from other ethnic groups. Notably, although candidates often use ethnic and religious appeals to foster support at these events, the ethnic appeals I observed in my research were invariably positive, and candidates avoided messaging that could slight or denigrate other ethnic groups.

Finally, candidate-centric elections have prompted more candidates who were born and bred in the region to compete—and to win. By drawing on their local networks, popular local candidates have proved to be very good at attracting personal votes, and many prominent local bureaucrats and business leaders have been elected.[11] It seems reasonable to hope that these candidates will have a stronger connection with and understanding of their constituency and its people.

On the other hand, Indonesia's candidate-centric system certainly has some downsides. First, it has weakened the connection between candidates and parties and fostered fierce competition between candidates within the same party. Under the new system, many candidates running for election do not have strong ideological connections with or loyalty to the political parties that nominate them. In regional head elections, candidates often receive party nominations not because they have been long-term party members but because they paid money in exchange for support (Hendrawan et al. 2021). Parties have come to expect this pattern, as they know it helps candidates avoid the very expensive process of gathering constituent signatures to run as independents (Mietzner 2013: 195). Moreover, when regional head candidates are supported by multiple parties (as most are), the influence and investment of any one party in a candidate is diluted, and their involvement in the candidate's campaign tends to be minimal.

In legislative elections, open-list PR has fostered intense intraparty competition, to the extent that when candidates in the 2014 legislative elections were asked who their main competitors were, the vast majority named other candidates from their own party (Aspinall and Sukmajati 2016: 13). Occasionally, candidates from the same party campaign together, but only when they are competing for seats in different constituencies or in legislatures at different levels (i.e., national, provincial, or district).[12]

Second, with more competition between candidates, the cost of campaigns has increased considerably (Mietzner 2015: 588). In large part, this is due to the extensive patronage distribution in which many candidates engage during campaign season, seeking support from organizations in exchange for financial support and deploying their campaign teams to mobilize voters through bribes. Voters, local leaders, and their organizations demand this kind of patronage, as they have come to expect some kind of payment in exchange for their support at the polls. The payments have become such an epidemic that Aspinall and Sukmajati (2016: 5) wrote in a volume on the 2014 elections, "Our findings demonstrate that patronage distribution is the central mode of political campaigning in Indonesian legislative elections." Obviously, patronage in elections is not new, but by all accounts its extent and sophistication have accelerated with the shift to candidate-centric elections.

The money needed to finance campaigns must come from somewhere, and political parties receive limited financial support from the state (Mietzner 2011). As a result, candidates rely on personal funds or their personal backers (Ufen 2011). The successful candidates are thus beholden to their financial supporters, who can exert undue influence over the elected official. For those who lose, candidates' personal investment in their campaigns can lead to financial ruin and, in some cases, even to suicide—a phenomenon that appears, sadly, to be more common among young, inexperienced female candidates (Buehler 2009).

Finally, candidate-centric systems have undermined Indonesians' identification with political parties. Just before the 1999 elections, 86% of voters identified themselves with a particular political party. This enthusiasm for parties was partly attributable to a general sense of euphoria over the introduction of a multiparty system that gave voters some choice at the polls. Party identification fell to 55% by the 2004 legislative election, but that figure was still reasonably high compared to other countries. It then declined sharply after the introduction of the first direct presidential election in July 2004 and regional head elections in 2005. In these elections, candidates ran personal campaigns that focused largely on their own character, and voters considered candidates rather than parties when making their selections. By the 2009 election, party identification stood at 20%, and in 2014 it was just 14%.[13] Whereas Mujani et al. (2018: 189) attribute this fall in party identification to a declining degree of trust in political parties among Indonesians, Mietzner (2013: 43–44) views the shift to a candidate-centric system as the driving factor, arguing that comparably low levels of party identification can be found in other Latin American countries, such as Brazil, that have similar candidate-centric elections.

Overall, the move to a candidate-centric system has certainly had some detrimental effects on politics, which have been well documented in the literature. But this type of election is very popular among Indonesians, who want to be able to choose their political representatives directly. This was demonstrated in 2014, when a law was passed to move from direct to indirect regional head elections, whereby local legislatures would appoint the regional heads. In reaction, regular Indonesians and civil society came out to strongly resist this return to the previous appointment system. In the end, President Yudhoyono made a popular decision to intervene and override the bill.

10.3. Curbing Contentious Ethnic Politics

Although candidates can use ethnicity to connect with constituents, on some occasions the politicization of ethnicity polarizes communities along identity lines, to the point at which an election becomes virtually a mere ethnic census. In these more extreme cases, efforts to curb ethnic politics are warranted.

The most prominent proposal to create stable democratic governance in societies with deep ethnic cleavages is Lijphart's consociational democracy. It recommends a parliamentary system with closed-list PR to enable small, ethnically oriented parties to represent their ethnic groups in a power-sharing government—an arrangement that ultimately results in these parties becoming invested in the political system.[14] In contrast, Horowitz (1991, 2002) recommends majoritarian electoral systems, which he claims will depoliticize ethnicity because they force candidates and parties to seek broader support, resulting in the formation of nationally oriented, multiethnic parties. The merits of consociational democracy have been debated for many years, and the empirical evidence as to whether PR or majoritarian systems produce more stable governance and less ethnic conflict in ethnically diverse societies has been decidedly mixed.[15]

After Indonesia's transition to democracy, one of the reformers' main goals was to curb ethnic politics. But they rejected Lijphart's consociational approach, preferring instead to encourage the growth of nationally oriented political parties. Ultimately, their proposal for a largely majoritarian electoral system was rejected, and closed-list PR was retained. Importantly, the reformers' rule requiring parties to establish branches across the country was implemented, and this provision has indeed prevented the formation of regionally based indigenous political parties. However, despite the lack of indigenous parties, ethnicity still plays an important role in Indonesian politics, as this book has shown. In light of the conflicting evidence regarding consociationalism, I wish to propose two other potential approaches to curbing ethnic politics that have emerged from my research.

10.3.1. Politicizing Multiple Dimensions of Ethnicity

One, somewhat counterintuitive, way to curb contentious ethnic politics is to promote it. The key distinction here is that I do not propose promoting ethnic parties per se, but instead encourage the politicization of *multiple* dimensions of ethnicity. In India, Chandra (2005) described how institutions that fostered politicizing multiple dimensions of ethnic identity (rather than a single dimension) helped to foster democratic stability. My book has detailed how a change in the electoral institutions—specifically, the introduction of candidate-centric rules—results in the politicization of different dimensions of ethnicity. My data from Indonesia suggest three ways in which the politicization of multiple dimensions of ethnicity can help to curb contentious ethnic politics.

First and most broadly, politicizing different dimensions of ethnicity creates cross-cutting and competing ethnic cleavages, which helps to prevent a master ethnic cleavage from developing. In Indonesia, some candidates bond with their religious group, others bond with their indigenous group, and still others engage in various bridging strategies—reaching out to other ethnic groups and drawing on the more encompassing regional and national identities. Furthermore, the potential for polarization along a master ethnic cleavage is reduced when multiple candidates in an election are using a wide variety of ethnic appeal strategies. Adding a further layer of complexity, individual candidates can and do politicize multiple dimensions of ethnicity in their campaigns. For instance, in the governor election in North Sumatra in 2018, Edy Rahmayadi engaged in a religious bonding strategy, but he also made regional appeals, emphasizing his connection to the region. In this case, politicizing regional identities helped dampen religious cleavages.

Second, with multiple politicized dimensions of ethnicity, opposing candidates in an election can be less confrontational because each one may politicize a different dimension of ethnicity. We find this tendency when we compare the appeals of Muslim and non-Muslim candidates. Indonesian Muslims tend to emphasize their religious identity over their indigenous identity in daily life, and their candidates also tend to show a preference for Islamic appeals above indigenous ones. Meanwhile, non-Muslim candidates are constrained from publicly politicizing their religion; as a result, they make indigenous appeals. When Muslim and non-Muslim candidates compete in an election, the use of Islamic versus indigenous mobilization strategies is less confrontational, and this variety of strategies helps to avoid reducing the election to a battle over which religion is superior.[16] Brewer (1999) found that when a group feels superior on dimensions that are important to the group's identity (such as indigeneity for non-Muslims), it can more readily tolerate the other group's superiority on another dimensions (i.e., religion for Muslims).

Third, with multiple, overlapping politicized dimensions of ethnicity in a constituency (e.g., an indigenous group with Muslim and Christian members), candidates often have the option to reach out to the broader, more inclusive ethnic category. For example, in the mayoral election in Solo, which has a large Javanese Muslim majority, a Christian Javanese candidate, Rudy, faced a joint Muslim ticket. Religion was not a major issue in the election, however, in part because Rudy could appeal to voters based on his Javanese as well as his regional identity, having been born in Solo.

10.3.2. Redrawing Constituency Boundaries

Another way to curb ethnic politics is to redraw the boundaries of constituencies. Candidate-centric elections are particularly sensitive to constituency boundary changes because they reshape the demographics, changing the viability of ethnic groups. Consequently, redrawing districts affects the kinds of candidates who run and the ethnic appeals they make. For instance, Sulaiman (2016) recounts a boundary change in one of Aceh's provincial legislative constituencies before the 2014 election. Previously, the constituency was dominated by Acehnese candidates who mobilized their majority indigenous kin while marginalizing the minority indigenous Gayo population. But after a boundary change, the indigenous Gayo formed a majority in a new breakaway constituency, prompting more Gayo candidates to run for office. These candidates used indigenous Gayo appeals to mobilize support—often successfully, as many of them went on to serve in the provincial legislature.

At a broad level, most electoral constituencies across Indonesia are quite homogeneous, some are very diverse, and a few are somewhere in between. In Chapter 9, I discussed how this last kind of constituency was most prone to ethnically contentious elections. In these constituencies, a viable ethnic group forms a small majority, but a sizable ethnic minority has sufficient strength to challenge the majority group. Drawing on the case of West Kalimantan's gubernatorial election, I illustrated how constituencies with a small Muslim majority can experience religiously contentious matchups between a Muslim and a non-Muslim candidate. Redrawing constituency boundaries is one way to defuse this kind of contestation in future elections. There are two options: redraw boundaries so that the new constituency is either more homogeneous or more diverse.

If boundaries are redrawn to make a constituency relatively homogeneous, the findings in this book indicate that candidates in the new constituency will invariably be from the same religious and indigenous group. They will make similar ethnic appeals—but in relatively benign ways. Due to the homogeneity of the constituency, ethnic polarization in elections is unlikely if not impossible. Over the years, constituencies in Indonesia have become increasingly homogeneous. In the legislative elections, this development has happened because the number of constituencies has increased while the number of seats per constituency has declined. In the regional head elections, increasingly homogeneous constituencies have formed due to the fact that districts and provinces have been allowed to lobby the government to split into new districts since 2001. Ethnically diverse districts have tended to split into more homogeneous districts. Positively, this process has contributed to a reduction in communal conflict (Pierskalla 2016), but a 2017 report by Indonesia's Setara Institute found that the religiously homogeneous districts are also the most religiously intolerant ones in the country.

Alternatively, if boundaries can be redrawn to make districts so ethnically diverse that no viable ethnic groups exist, all electoral candidates will be double minorities with a variety of religious and indigenous identities. As described in this book, ethnicity becomes largely depoliticized in these constituencies, as candidates generally make ethnic bridging and bypassing appeals. There is some evidence that norms of tolerance develop in such diverse constituencies. For example, constituents of the diverse city of Pematangsiantar largely rejected the identity politics of North Sumatra's governor election in 2018 (Tiola and Primarizki 2021:166–167). Also, the Setara Institute found that districts with more religious diversity were most tolerant. Indeed, this might be a broader phenomenon not limited to Indonesia. In Kenya, Kasara (2013) found higher levels of interethnic trust among people living in ethnically diverse communities than among those in more homogeneous communities. Such highly diverse constituencies can function as a bulwark against divisive, unidimensional forms of ethnic competition.

Overall, to curb ethnic politics, the politicization of multiple dimensions of ethnicity can help. However, in cases that are highly prone to ethnically polarized competition, changing the boundaries of constituencies to make them more homogeneous or, if possible, very diverse is an option worth considering.

The politicization of ethnicity has wide-ranging and long-term effects. It can affect voting behavior, party formation, ethnic cleavages, democratic stability, and communal violence. But to understand how ethnicity becomes politicized, we must first know why politicians choose to mobilize groups along particular ethnic lines. I hope that this study of Indonesia, one of the largest and most ethnically diverse countries in the world, will contribute to our understanding of ethnic politics and will encourage more effective interventions to reduce ethnic strife.

APPENDIX A

Statistical Analysis

In this section of the Appendix, I present notes on the variables used in the analyses as well as the accompanying tables and figures. I also include descriptions of the robustness checks and alternative regression models that I ran. The full regression output for these models can be found in the online supplementary materials on the author's website, colmfox.com. My website also contains all the replication data for the book.

A1.1. Chapter 5

A1.1.1. Table 5.2

Table 5.2 provided information on the number of election posters by province. To supplement this data, Table A5.1 and Table A5.2 provides information on the numbers of election posters across political parties in legislative and regional head elections.

Table A5.1 Distribution of Posters, Candidates, and Constituencies for Legislative Candidates by Political Party

Party	Ideology	Posters	Can.	Constituencies for Each Legislature			
				Dis.	Prov.	Nat.	All
Regional Acehnese Parties							
PA	Indigenous	24	21	1	1	0	2
PAAS	Islamist	5	5	1	1	0	2
PBA	Islamist	8	7	1	1	0	2
PDA	Islamist	7	4	1	0	0	1
PRA	Other	5	2	0	1	0	1
SIRA	Other	10	7	1	1	0	2
National Parties							
Barnas	Nationalist	26	23	9	6	2	17
Demokrat	Nationalist	232	179	16	19	14	49
Gerindra	Nationalist	87	69	16	11	9	36
Golkar	Nationalist	308	221	21	21	17	59
Hanura	Nationalist	105	81	12	13	12	37
PAN	Muslim democratic	241	178	20	19	18	57

(*continued*)

Table A5.1 Continued

Party	Ideology	Posters	Can.	Constituencies for Each Legislature			
				Dis.	Prov.	Nat.	All
Patriot	Nationalist	25	20	8	3	2	13
PBB	Islamist	70	57	12	7	10	29
PBN	Nationalist	14	13	4	3	1	8
PBR	Islamist	36	27	6	7	4	17
PDI-P	Nationalist	323	224	21	21	20	62
PDK	Nationalist	41	35	9	10	6	25
PDP	Nationalist	68	54	12	9	9	30
PDS	Nationalist	43	36	11	8	6	25
Pelopor	Nationalist	22	20	9	3	1	13
PIS	Nationalist	26	24	6	5	5	16
PK	Nationalist	17	13	5	3	0	8
PKB	Muslim democratic	89	75	16	12	8	36
PKDI	Nationalist	28	26	8	4	6	18
PKNU	Muslim democratic	51	35	9	9	7	25
PKP	Nationalist	25	23	8	6	4	18
PKPB	Nationalist	37	30	10	6	5	21
PKPI	Nationalist	14	12	3	5	2	10
PKS	Islamist	124	95	15	13	11	39
PM	Nationalist	13	11	6	2	0	8
PMB	Islamist	23	18	8	3	4	15
PNBKI	Nationalist	26	21	9	5	3	17
PNIM	Nationalist	12	11	5	2	2	9
PPD	Nationalist	11	11	4	1	3	8
PPDI	Nationalist	4	3	1	1	0	2
PPI	Nationalist	24	21	7	5	2	14
PPIB	Nationalist	14	13	5	5	1	11
PPNUI	Islamist	3	3	2	1	0	3
PPP	Islamist	121	86	13	12	9	34
PPPI	Nationalist	14	12	4	4	2	10
PPRN	Nationalist	47	43	10	12	5	27
PSI	Nationalist	4	4	1	1	0	2
RepublikaN	Nationalist	38	33	8	8	5	21
	Total	2,465	1,906				

APPENDIX A 239

Table A5.2 Distribution of Posters, Candidates, and Constituencies for Regional Head Candidates by Political Party

Party Type	Posters	Candidates	Constituencies for Each Level of Regional Head Elections		
			District	Province	All
Nationalist	410	67	32	2	34
Muslim democrat	24	5	3	1	4
Islamist	21	6	4	0	4
Coalition	758	86	38	3	41
Independent	242	58	27	0	27
Missing	46	24	10	2	12
Total	1,501	246			

Note. Regional head candidates could run as independents or with support from one or more political parties. The party type represents whether a candidate was supported by one or more nationalist parties, one or more Muslim democrat parties, one or more Islamist parties, or a coalition of two or three types of parties. I was unable to attain party information for 24 of the candidates in the dataset.

A1.2. Chapter 6

A1.2.1. Table 6.1

Supplementary materials. To provide more information for Table 6.1, I include further data on the types of events, endorsements, and group appeals in the online supplementary materials in Table SN6.1 and Table SN6.2, This information comprises summary statistics, the numbers of reports per year, and the percentage change in reports for all events, endorsements, and appeals from 1997 to 1999. Furthermore, in the supplementary materials, Table SN6.3 to Table SN6.12. include the full logit and logit odds ratio regression results for events, endorsements, appeals, and candidate attributes.

A1.2.2. Confounding Factors

To consider whether confounding factors affected the changes in religious and indigenous aspects of campaign events, appeals, and candidate attributes since 2009, I ran regressions which included a number of counfounding factors. In Table A6.1, the key independent variable is *legislative elections 2009–2014*. This variable is 1 if the report was on the 2009–2014 semi-candidate-centric election, or 0 if on the 1997–2004 party-centric elections. To account for confounding factors, I included decentralization, the number of parties, and the Islamic or nationalist orientation of parties as controls. I set the *decentralization* variable at 1 for all election reports after the introduction of decentralization (the 2004, 2009, and 2014 elections) and 0 otherwise (the 1997 and 1999 elections). *Number of parties* represents how many parties competed in each election. The *Islamist party* variable was coded as 1 for each report from an Islamist party and 0 for those from the Muslim democratic and nationalist parties. The four main parties coded as Islamist were PPP,

Table A6.1 The Impact of Semi-Candidate-Centric Rules on Campaigns

	Events			Endorsements			Group Appeals			Candidate Attributes		
	Rel.	Ind.	Comb.	Rel.	Ind.	Comb.	Rel.	Ind.	Comb.	Rel.	Ind.	Comb.
Legislative elections 2009–2014 (semi-candidate-centric)	2.08*	1.81*	2.73**	1.10^	1.91*	1.54*	1.31**	2.07*	1.44**	1.04	0.98	1.28*
	1.04	0.77	1.03	0.64	0.79	0.63	0.35	1.04	0.34	0.69	0.80	0.58
Decentralization	−1.55	—	−1.77^	−0.30	—	−0.54	−1.26**	−1.28	−1.24**	1.82	1.41	1.42
	1.07		1.06	0.69		0.68	0.37	1.08	0.36	1.20	1.22	0.89
Number of parties	−0.01	−0.01	−0.01	−0.01	0.00	−0.01	0.00	−0.01	0.00	0.00	−0.01	−0.01
	0.01	0.02	0.01	0.01	0.02	0.01	0.01	0.01	0.01	0.02	0.02	0.01
Islamist party	−1.16	−1.20	−1.21^	−0.19	−0.48	−0.34	1.70**	−1.81^	1.54**	1.52**	0.15	1.03*
	0.74	1.05	0.62	0.51	0.78	0.47	0.30	1.04	0.30	0.50	0.68	0.43
Constant	−2.32**	−3.88**	−2.12**	−2.45**	−4.07**	−2.22**	−0.87**	−2.57**	−0.82**	−5.50**	−4.72**	−4.37**
	0.43	1.04	0.42	0.48	1.08	0.46	0.30	0.54	0.29	1.41	1.30	0.97
Log likelihood	−93.21	−57.12	−119.93	−102.79	−60.20	−123.50	−206.07	−86.62	−217.91	−66.04	−57.59	−95.75
Pseudo-R_2	0.06	0.08	0.10	0.03	0.08	0.05	0.10	0.08	0.09	0.15	0.08	0.14
Observations	367	299	367	367	299	367	367	367	367	367	367	367

Note. Rel. = religion; Ind. = indigenous; Reg = regional; Comb. = combined. Candidate attributes refer to the data on candidate identity and work experience. Values are logit coefficients with standard errors listed below the coefficients. The absence of indigenous events and endorsements in the 2004 reports posed some convergence problems for those logit models. Those observations were dropped ($N = 299$), and the decentralization variable was subsequently omitted due to collinearity. Robust standard errors are below the coefficients. ^$p < 0.10$; *$p < 0.05$; **$p < 0.01$.

PKS, PBB, and PBR. The smaller parties coded as Islamist were PKNU, PMB, PPNUI, Partai Kebangkitan Umat, Partai Persatuan, Partai Masyumi Baru, Partai Politik Islam Indonesia Masyumi, Partai Syarikat Islam Indonesia, Partai Syarikat Islam Indonesia—1905, and Partai Ummat Islam. The Muslim democratic parties were PAN, PKB, Party Islam Democrat, and Party Umat Muslimin Indonesia. The rest of the parties were nationalist. For events, I created a "combined" dependent variable that encompassed reports with religious or indigenous events. I did the same for endorsements, group appeals, and candidate attributes. This facilitated testing the impact of the semi-candidate-centric rules on the politicization of ethnicity.

Supplementary materials. To supplement Table A6.1, Table SN6.13 to Table SN6.15 contain summary statistics, while Table SN6.16 contains regressions for all events, endorsements, group appeals, and candidate attributes, rerun using OLS instead of logit.

A1.2.3. Table 6.3

Supplementary materials. To supplement Table 6.3 on the change in religious and indigenous aspects of campaigns during Indonesia's transitional period, Table SN6.17 contains all events, endorsements, appeals, and candidates' attribute categories and their percentage of change in reports from the 1997 to the 1999 election.

A1.2.4. Figure 6.1

Table A6.2 presents the underlying table of regression results for Figure 6.1. There were some limitations on demographic data used to control for the size of the indigenous and Muslim populations. The data came from the 2010 national census and were acquired from the national statistics office (Badan Pusat Statistik) in Jakarta. For the district (Kabupaten/Kota) legislative elections, each administrative district contains multiple constituencies at the sub-district (Kecamatan) level. Unfortunately, demographic data were not available at this level at the time of writing. For these constituencies, indigenous and Muslim group sizes from the district level (one level up) were used as an approximation.

Supplementary materials. See Table SP6.1 to Table SP6.3 for summary statistics for the variables used in Table A6.2. A number of alternative models for Table A6.2 were run. They are included in the supplementary materials.

1. Models that exclude independent and control variables: Models with only the regional head and demographic variables. See Table SP6.4.
2. Models with alternative measures for the group size variables: Although *largest indigenous grp.* and *Muslim pop.* were used in these regressions, for robustness I ran all the regressions with alternative demographic measures. I used the ethnic fractionalization index (Herfindahl concentration formula) in Table SP6.5 and a polarization index (Reynal-Querol 2002) in Table SP6.6 for both indigenous and religious groups. The results were similar and had little effect on the key variable of interest, *regional head election*. Ultimately, measures of the largest indigenous group were used in the final analysis because they relate more directly to the book's argument, which stresses ethnic group size.

Table A6.2 The Impact of Candidate-Centric Electoral Rules on Candidate Appeals

	Indigenous Appeals			Religious Appeals			Nationalist appeals	Partisan Appeals
	Bond	Bridge	Bypass	Bond	Bridge	Bypass	Bridge	
	1	2	3	4	5	6	7	8
Regional head election (candidate-centric)	13.13** (2.62)	3.51* (1.67)	-16.64** (2.96)	9.65** (2.88)	2.11 (1.60)	-11.76** (3.12)	9.53** (3.36)	-67.79** (2.22)
Largest indigenous group	35.61** (3.13)	-5.97** (1.99)	-29.64** (3.56)	2.19 (3.59)	2.24 (1.78)	-4.43 (3.91)	-18.63** (4.61)	-5.71 (3.71)
Muslim population	-13.58** (3.45)	0.70 (2.10)	12.88** (3.89)	37.86** (3.41)	-8.03** (2.08)	-29.83** (3.97)	-12.04^ (4.79)	-7.10^ (4.01)
Indigenous law	2.78 (3.64)	-2.79 (1.70)	0.01 (3.91)	5.38 (4.30)	-4.62** (1.54)	-0.76 (4.50)	-15.15** (4.60)	-10.59* (4.45)
Mosques	-2.56* (1.24)	0.66 (0.48)	1.9 (1.21)	-0.61 (0.74)	0.64 (0.84)	-0.03 (1.08)	2.11 (1.36)	-0.58 (0.79)
Poverty	7.94 (9.29)	4.24 (6.85)	-12.18 (11.09)	-5.28 (10.19)	11.54 (7.24)	-6.26 (11.90)	47.08** (14.82)	4.19 (12.02)
Fishing/farming GRDP	-0.08 (6.59)	1.40 (4.34)	-1.32 (7.46)	-2.77 (7.21)	-3.64 (4.09)	6.42 (7.91)	-14.28 (8.96)	2.96 (7.31)
Female candidate	1.40 (1.69)	-2.05* (0.87)	0.65 (1.86)	35.27** (2.31)	-2.69** (0.82)	-32.58** (2.36)	2.99 (2.49)	4.89* (2.12)
Population (log)	1.02 (0.84)	-0.08 (0.47)	-0.94 (0.93)	-1.85^ (1.04)	0.31 (0.45)	1.54 (1.10)	6.79** (1.21)	-1.46 (1.08)
Constant	-14.87 (11.72)	7.96 (6.81)	106.92** (13.06)	11.86 (14.27)	4.24 (6.72)	83.90** (15.39)	-33.42^ (17.65)	105.27** (15.00)
Observations	2,152	2,152	2,152	2,152	2,152	2,152	2,152	2,152
R-squared	0.08	0.01	0.06	0.18	0.02	0.13	0.04	0.23

Note. The table presents the results of regression analyses for independent variables (rows) and dependent variables (columns). Entries are coefficients from the OLS regression model. Robust standard errors are below the coefficients. ^p <.10; *p <.05; **p <.01.

3. Models that cluster on the constituency: One issue concerning the data relates to how the posters were gathered from constituencies spread across the country. If candidates in the same constituency shared a predisposition to appeal to voters in particular ways, the standard errors might have a downward bias. In an alternative specification, I corrected the standard errors by clustering on the constituency. See Table SP6.7.
4. Models that include dummy variables for indigenous groups: Another issue was that candidates from particular indigenous or religious groups may have a predisposition to appeal to their group. Although I already controlled for ethnic attachment in the district, as a further check I also controlled for indigenous groups by including dummy variables for each of the 23 different indigenous groups that candidates came from. Unfortunately, I could not do the same for religious groups due to the high correlation between being a Muslim candidate and being from a viable religious group. See Table SP6.8.
5. Models that control for the legislature's level: Another issue was the relatively low number of personal votes needed for candidates to win a legislative election (although they do have competition from many other candidates). Candidates competing in district and potentially in provincial legislative elections may, on average, need fewer votes to win than those in regional head elections. However, candidates competing for a national legislative seat would need a similar number of votes, or even more. To ensure that the difference between appeals in legislative and regional head elections was not driven purely by the lower number of votes needed, I subdivided the dataset, running regressions with regional head candidates and with district legislative candidates only. This set of regressions produced similar results to those presented in the main text. Overall, these findings ruled out the possibility that the differences in campaign appeals in the semi-candidate-centric legislative elections, relative to the regional head elections, were due to the number of votes needed for victory. See Table SP6.9.
6. Models that use logit, ordered logit, and tobit: A final potential problem with the data was that many candidates had values of 0% or 100% for the different types of ethnic appeals, resulting in a non-normal distribution of the dependent variables. To address these concerns, I first ran logit and ordered models using different approaches to dichotomize the dependent variables. See Table SP6.10 to Table SP6.12. Second, I used tobit models to take into account the limited nature of the dependent variable, with a floor of 0 and a ceiling of 100. See Table SP6.13.
7. Models with the poster as the unit of analysis: Using the poster as the unit of analysis, I produced summary statistics for the dependent and independent variables, as well as a correlation matrix for the independent variables. Next, all regressions were rerun using OLS, with the poster as the unit of analysis ($N = 3,962$). See Table SP6.14.

A1.3. Chapter 7

A1.3.1. Figure 7.2

Table A7.1 presents the underlying table of regression results for Figure 7.2. This analysis uses regional head candidate data. Fortunately, I could gather religious identity data

Table A7.1 Impact of Politically Viable Groups on Candidate Appeals

	Indigenous Appeals			Religious Appeals			Nat. Appeals
	Bond	Bridge	Bypass	Bond	Bridge	Bypass	Bridge
	1	2	3	4	5	6	7
Viable indigenous group	34.17** (4.53)	-13.21** (3.06)	-20.96** (5.27)	-5.32 (5.46)	-3.69 (2.31)	9.01 (5.82)	-13.97* (5.70)
Viable religious group	-13.33** (5.11)	0.46 (3.77)	12.86* (6.16)	38.52** (5.91)	-15.86** (4.05)	-22.66** (7.07)	-4.09 (7.30)
Indigenous law	6.75 (10.75)	-2.7 (4.93)	-4.05 (11.71)	1.18 (12.03)	-3.40 (4.31)	2.22 (12.61)	1.93 (12.99)
Places of worship	1.69 (1.59)	-0.98 (0.89)	-0.70 (1.86)	0.03 (1.10)	0.34 (1.22)	-0.37 (1.63)	3.31^ (1.89)
Poverty	-7.20 (45.45)	-32.60* (14.70)	39.80 (48.03)	38.66 (28.81)	7.96 (15.96)	-46.62 (33.05)	-53.18 (43.85)
Fishing/farming GRDP	8.27 (13.91)	12.09 (8.05)	-20.37 (15.48)	-7.46 (11.91)	-2.66 (8.16)	10.12 (14.09)	-14.85 (15.41)
Female candidate	8.24 (8.25)	-7.09* (3.26)	-1.15 (9.64)	14.53 (9.37)	-2.04 (4.19)	-12.49 (9.64)	0.95 (11.06)
Population (log)	1.89 (2.27)	0.68 (1.57)	-2.57 (2.72)	-2.58 (2.94)	3.41* (1.56)	-0.83 (3.29)	-3.08 (2.93)
Constant	-18.84 (30.43)	10.51 (19.17)	108.33** (35.84)	33.30 (39.39)	-25.67 (17.44)	92.37* (42.57)	98.04* (39.23)
Observations	246	246	246	246	246	246	246
R-squared	0.26	0.12	0.11	0.23	0.12	0.10	0.08

Note. Results of regression analyses for independent variables (rows) and dependent variables (columns). Entries are coefficients from the OLS regression model. Robust standard errors are below the coefficients. ^$p < 0.10$; *$p < 0.05$; **$p < 0.01$.

APPENDIX A   245

on all the regional head candidates, as well as data on houses of worship for all religions. As a result, I could create a religious attachment variable (Places of worship) specific to each candidate's religious group. However, there was a lack of religious identity data on all legislative candidate. So, for any analysis in the book that involved legislative candiates, I measured religious attachment based on mosques. Specifically, the number of mosques per 1,000 Muslims in the constituency. This makes sense, as Islam is the dominant religion for religious appeals. Furthermore, while the number of places of worship is a more appropriate measure of religious attachment relevant to each candidate, the use of the mosques variable ultimately produced similar results in the main and supplementary models in this book.

Supplementary materials. See Table SP7.1 to Table SP7.3 for summary statistics for the variables used in Table A7.1 A number of alternative models for Table A7.1 were run. They are included in the supplementary materials.

1. Models that exclude the independent and control variables: These models used as variables only viable indigenous and viable religious group. See Table SP7.4.
2. Models that cluster on the constituency: Clustering on the constituency helped to control for any particular predisposition to appeal to voters in particular ways within a constituency. There were 49 constituencies. See Table SP7.5.
3. Models that include dummy variables for indigenous groups: These models helped to control for any predisposition candidates might have to appeal to a particular group. There were 34 different indigenous groups in the dataset. See Table SP7.6.
4. Models that use logit, ordered logit, and tobit: Many candidates had values of 0% or 100% for their measures of ethnic appeals, resulting in a non-normal distribution. To address this issue, I ran logit models with the ethnic appeal variable equal to 1 if the ethnic appeal was 50% or more of a candidate's posters, or 0 otherwise. I then ran other logit models with the ethnic appeal variable equal to 1 if any of the candidate's posters contained the ethnic appeal. I also ran ordered logit. See Table SP7.7 to Table SP7.9. Finally, I ran tobit models to take into account the limited nature of the dependent variable, with a floor of 0 and a ceiling of 100. See Table SP7.10.
5. Models with the poster as the unit of analysis: This analysis has more observations ($N = 1,501$), and was used as an alternative to using candidate's poster campaign as the unit of analysis. See Table SP7.11.
6. Models using mixed-effects: Models use the election poster as the unit of analysis, with random intercepts for candidates. See Table SP7.12.

A1.3.2. Figure 7.3

Figure 7.3 illustrated the frequency of different appeals by candidate type. In an alternative illustration, Figure A7. uses the same data to show how particular candidate types prefer different kinds of ethnic appeals. The results support the findings from Figure 7.3.

A1.3.3. Figure 7.7

Figure 7.7 illustrated the level of ethnic appeals based on ethnic group size for regional head elections. Figure A7.2 presents the same figure for legislative candidates.

APPENDIX A

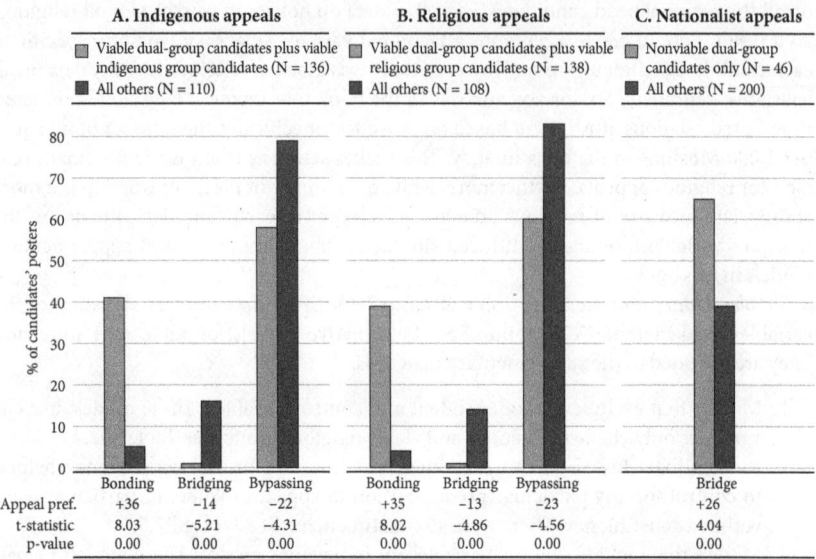

Figure A7.1 Ethnic appeal preference by type of candidate. Appeal preference is the average percent of candidates' poster campaigns that contain the appeal, above or below the average for all other candidates. *t*-statistics come from a test of the equality of the means for each type of appeal by candidate type. *p*-values are for two-sided tests.

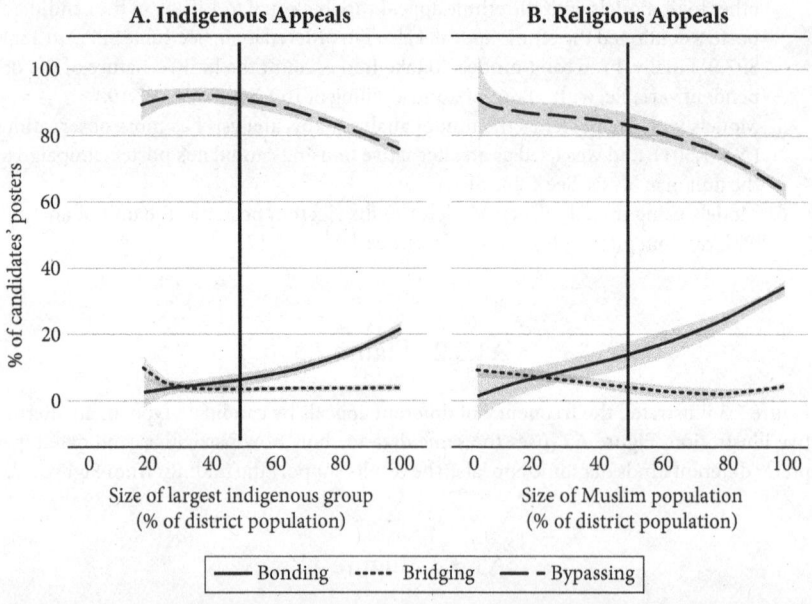

Figure A7.2 Level of ethnic appeals by legislative candidates based on the size of ethnic groups in their constituency. These are fractional polynomial plots. Shading represents 90% confidence intervals.

APPENDIX A   247

Supplementary materials. Supplementary fractional polynomial plots were made for regional head candidates' appeals using alternative measures. Specifically, ethnic fractionalization and ethnic polarization indexes replaced the size of indigenous groups and the size of the Muslim population. See Figure SP7.1 and Figure SP7.2.

A1.3.4. Figure 7.10

The one second-level factor that I could test using regression analysis was the competitiveness of an election. It was measured by taking the winning candidate's margin of victory over the second-place candidate, so lower figures meant that the election was more competitive. I acknowledge that it is problematic to measure competition from election results, as the voting occurs after campaign appeals have been made. Conceivably, the more frequent use of bonding appeals could result in more competitive races rather than the reverse. Ideally, it would have been better to measure the level of competition from pre-election public opinion surveys or previous electoral results. Unfortunately, such data were either not available or past results could not be used to measure competition because many new and untested candidates were competing. Another potential second-level factor, incumbency, could also decrease ethnic bonding and increase bridging appeals. Some evidence comes from the United States, where Collingwood (2020) found that incumbent white Democrats who have become reliant on Latino votes were more likely to make bridging appeals to Latinos. To test this possibility, I included a binary variable for regional head candidates who were incumbents in the regression models, but it had no effect. For the regression results for the competitiveness of an election and incumbency see Table A7.2.

A1.4. Chapter 8

A1.4.1. Figure 8.2

Table A8.1 presents the underlying table of regression results for Figure 8.2.

Supplementary materials. See Table SP8.1 to Table SP8.3 for summary statistics for the variables used in Table A8.1. A number of alternative models for Table A8.1 were run. They are included in the supplementary materials.

1. Models that exclude the control variables: Islamist, Muslim democratic, nationalist party, and demographic variables were included. See Table SP8.4.
2. Models with alternative binary party variables for the regional head elections: For the regional head candidates, I created four binary measures of candidate support by various combinations of parties—Islamic party (or parties) only, Muslim democratic party(ies) only, nationalist party(ies) only, and a coalition of party types. In the regression, I left out the nationalist party category. See Table SP8.5.

A1.4.2. Figure 8.4

Table A8.2 presents the underlying table of regression results for Figure 8.4.

Supplementary materials. See Table SP8.6 to Table SP8.8 for summary statistics for the variables used in Table A8.2.

Table A7.2 OLS: Impact of incumbency and competitiveness (UOA = Candidate)

	Indigenous Appeals			Religious Appeals			Nationalist Appeals
	Bond	Bridge	Bypass	Bond	Bridge	Bypass	Bridge
	1	2	3	4	5	6	7
Viable indigenous group	35.23**	−13.86**	−21.37**	−4.74	−3.84	8.57^	−17.27**
	(4.11)	(2.89)	(4.93)	(4.32)	(2.63)	(4.98)	(5.19)
Viable religious group	−17.09**	1.68	15.41**	38.08**	−15.13**	−22.94**	−4.61
	(4.40)	(3.04)	(5.26)	(4.46)	(3.43)	(5.53)	(5.73)
Incumbent	7.61	−5.58^	−2.04	7.99	−1.91	−6.07	−0.82
	(6.46)	(2.85)	(7.14)	(6.06)	(3.49)	(6.73)	(6.64)
Competitive election	0.18	−0.21	0.04	0.56**	0.18^	−0.73**	−0.13
	(0.21)	(0.16)	(0.26)	(0.19)	(0.10)	(0.20)	(0.26)
Female candidate	8.47	−6.76*	−1.71	13.65	−1.98	−11.67	2.92
	(8.44)	(3.11)	(9.49)	(9.49)	(4.08)	(10.00)	(10.66)
Population (log)	1.67	0.95	−2.62	−2.64	3.61*	−0.97	−2.65
	(2.22)	(1.62)	(2.70)	(2.84)	(1.63)	(3.26)	(2.96)
Intercept	−6.11	1.11	105.00**	42.84	−26.84	84.01*	88.49*
	(28.50)	(19.56)	(34.06)	(35.84)	(18.63)	(40.12)	(37.53)
N	246	246	246	246	246	246	246
R Squared	0.26	0.13	0.10	0.25	0.12	0.13	0.06

Note. Results of regression analyses for independent variables (rows) and dependent variables (columns). Entries are coefficients from the OLS regression model. Robust standard errors are in parentheses. ^$p < 0.10$; *$p < 0.05$; **$p < 0.01$.

Table A8.1 The Impact of Party Ideology on Candidate Appeals

	Legislative Elections				Regional Head Elections			
	Religious Appeals			Nat. Appeals		Religious Appeals		Nat. Appeals
	Bond	Bridge	Bypass	Bridge	Bond	Bridge	Bypass	Bridge
	1	2	3	4	5	6	7	8
Islamist party	34.93**	-1.32	-33.62**	-17.47**	0.03	0.49	-0.52	-4.56
	(2.78)	(1.09)	(2.84)	(2.94)	(6.68)	(3.67)	(7.26)	(6.84)
Muslim democratic party	24.42**	-1.60	-22.83**	-11.12**	5.76	1.49	-7.26	4.52
	(2.65)	(1.16)	(2.77)	(3.06)	(6.39)	(3.12)	(6.64)	(6.45)
Nationalist party					-13.72	2.93	10.79	7.49
					(12.37)	(1.96)	(12.06)	(11.80)
Largest indigenous group	4.46	3.51^	-7.98^	-12.39*	-9.18	-7.66	16.83	-33.07**
	(4.00)	(2.00)	(4.38)	(5.54)	(11.98)	(5.85)	(12.66)	(12.55)
Muslim population	22.91**	-7.12**	-15.79**	-11.05^	44.53**	-9.68*	-34.84**	17.88
	(3.92)	(2.65)	(4.69)	(6.09)	(10.36)	(4.74)	(11.47)	(11.47)
Indigenous law	3.06	-5.62**	2.56	-13.08*	2.32	0.94	-3.25	11.90
	(4.64)	(1.79)	(4.88)	(5.23)	(13.94)	(4.66)	(13.86)	(13.50)
Mosques	-0.93	0.21	0.72	-0.41	0.21	-0.92**	0.72	5.98**
	(1.25)	(0.85)	(1.35)	(1.82)	(1.21)	(0.29)	(1.21)	(1.17)

(continued)

Table A8.1 Continued

	Legislative Elections				Regional Head Elections			
	Religious Appeals			Nat. Appeals	Religious Appeals			Nat. Appeals
	Bond	Bridge	Bypass	Bridge	Bond	Bridge	Bypass	Bridge
	1	2	3	4	5	6	7	8
Poverty	−6.97	14.37^	−7.40	64.69**	73.52^	25.77	−99.29*	2.01
	(10.94)	(8.20)	(12.95)	(16.44)	(39.83)	(26.21)	(45.39)	(63.23)
Fishing/farming GRDP	−1.67	−4.30	5.96	−15.99	−9.95	4.55	5.40	−30.40
	(8.59)	(4.50)	(9.34)	(10.90)	(15.74)	(11.05)	(17.54)	(19.72)
Female candidate	37.42**	−2.94**	−34.49**	2.27	17.88	−2.02	−15.86	−1.66
	(2.14)	(0.86)	(2.23)	(2.58)	(11.23)	(3.40)	(10.82)	(13.80)
Population (log)	−0.40	−0.13	0.53	7.23**	0.34	1.72	−2.07	−4.50
	(1.07)	(0.47)	(1.15)	(1.34)	(3.72)	(1.59)	(3.85)	(3.29)
Constant	−6.38	9.73	96.65**	−39.46*	1.34	−11.98	110.63*	103.88*
	(14.83)	(7.20)	(16.06)	(19.70)	(49.16)	(17.86)	(50.35)	(45.67)
Observations	1,876	1,876	1,876	1,876	164	164	164	164
R-squared	0.29	0.02	0.23	0.06	0.22	0.07	0.16	0.12

Note. For legislative elections, all candidates are supported by an Islamist, or Muslim democratic, or nationalist political party. The nationalist party binary variable is excluded from the legislative election models. Therefore, the Islamist party coefficient indicates the impact of being supported by an Islamist party compared to being supported by a nationalist party. The same logic applies to the Muslim democratic party coefficient. For the regional head elections candidates can be supported by one or more parties, The Islamist party coefficient indicates the impact of being supported by an Islamist party (and potentially in conjunction with support from other types of parties) compared to not having the support of an Islamist party. Robust standard errors are below the coefficients. ^$p < 0.10$; *$p < 0.05$; **$p < 0.01$.

Table A8.2 The Impact of Party Ideology on Appeals in Aceh

	Indigenous Bonding Appeals	Religious Bonding Appeals	Nationalist Bridging Appeals
National Muslim democratic party	−5.49 (3.35)	11.23 (12.69)	−31.15** (6.61)
National Islamist party	5.48 (6.75)	27.13** (10.21)	−29.87** (6.42)
Regional Islamist party	−3.19 (4.80)	41.27** (11.73)	−29.29** (6.40)
Regional Indigenous party	79.67** (8.50)	−9.50 (10.89)	−25.13** (7.96)
Female candidate	4.46 (5.56)	52.07** (8.38)	−10.17^ (5.59)
Constant	5.20 (3.34)	18.63** (5.37)	31.83** (6.70)
Observations	128	128	128
R-squared	0.59	0.31	0.20

Note. Models are for legislative candidates competing in the provincial and district legislative elections in Aceh only. National nationalist party is the category excluded. Entries are coefficients from the OLS regression model. Robust standard errors are below the coefficients. ^$p < 0.10$; *$p < 0.05$; **$p < 0.01$.

APPENDIX B
Newspaper Data

To understand how Indonesian election campaigns have changed over time, I coded campaign appeals that appeared in the Indonesian newspaper reports. Here I provide some methodological notes on finding newspaper reports, codebook development, and a list of the coded variables. The complete codebook for the newspaper reports can be found on my website.

A2.1. Newspaper Archives

The codebook used to code the reports was developed during the course of eight months of field research in Medan in 2010. Another field trip took place in 2014 to gather reports from the 2014 election. In 2010, I initially reviewed archives of several Medan-based newspapers before settling on *Waspada*. Newspaper archives were obtained from the Library of Congress in Washington, DC, the Indonesian National Library in Jakarta, and the National Library of Australia in Canberra. More contemporary newspaper archives were reviewed at KIPPAS (Kajian Informasi, Pendidikan dan Penerbitan Sumatera), a media NGO in Medan. The regional papers reviewed included *Mestika*, *Mimbar Umum*, *Sinar Baru*, *Waspada*, *Sinar Indonesia Baru*, *Analisa*, and *Sumut Pos*. This review, plus interviews with journalists and constituents in North Sumatra, helped me select *Waspada* for detailed content analysis. *Waspada* was chosen because it is a long-running daily paper, is widely read by different ethnic groups, contains extensive coverage of politics, and has accessible archives that go back to the New Order period. I chose to code the printed version of *Waspada* because, as with most regional papers, *Waspada*'s online version did not stretch back to 1997. In addition, it was hard to verify that the online versions were not shortened, modified, or incomplete. Overall, it seemed more appropriate to use the printed version for each election year, as that was the version that campaign members distributed and constituents more frequently read.

A2.2. Codebook Overview

As I coded the newspaper reports, I worked diligently to minimize the risks of inconsistent coding and misinterpretation. To reduce inconsistencies, I spent months devising various coding fields and testing them on sample reports. The final codebook was based on a meaningful set of coding fields that captured candidates' ethnic campaign appeals over time. I then created a graphical user interface for consistent data entry. It contained an image of the report, predefined drop-down coding options, and space for a summary, transcriptions of verbal appeals, and any coder comments. This method allowed me to easily review previously coded reports and ensure consistency throughout the coding period.

I also adopted two approaches to minimize the potential for misinterpretation. First, I read and summarized key information in each report during the coding process. These summaries enabled me to present an informed interpretation of the narratives that candidates used to frame their appeals. Second, because I worked on the codebook and coding while in Medan, I had the opportunity to consult with my research assistants, as well as constituents, campaign managers, and journalists, on issues related to interpretation of the reports and the use of ethnic campaign appeals. These conversations also enhanced my overall understanding of election campaigns in North Sumatra. Below is a list of what I coded for each election report.

1. Index Information
    1.1. Report ID: Unique number automatically assigned.
    1.2. Coded: Whether report was coded. (Every second report was not coded)
    1.3. Title: Title of the report.
    1.4. Page: Page on which the report appeared.
    1.5. Day: Day on which the report was published.
    1.6. Month: Month in which the report was published.
    1.7. Year: Year in which the report was published.
    1.8. Report from: Any district (*kabupaten* or *kota*) name stated before the beginning of the report content.
    1.9. Political party: Name of party the report concerns (selected from a list of options).

2. Campaign Events
    2.1. Event ID: Unique number automatically assigned.
    2.2. Event comment: Any comments relating to the event.
    2.3. Event type: Selected from a list of options. The options included various types of political party, religious, indigenous, community, and occupational events, among others.
    2.4. Identity religion: Any religious group identity associated with the event, selected from a list of options.
    2.5. Identity indigeneity: Any indigenous group identity associated with the event, selected from a list of options.
    2.6. Identity occupation: Any occupational group identity associated with the event, selected from a list of options.
    2.7. Identity other: Any other group identity associated with the event, selected from a list of options.

3. Elite Endorsements
    3.1. Endorsement ID: Unique number automatically assigned.
    3.2. Endorsement comment: Any comments relating to the endorsement.
    3.3. Endorsement type: Type of endorsement, selected from a list of options including various types of political party, religious, indigenous, community, and occupational events, among others.
    3.4. Identity religion: Any religious group identity associated with the endorsement, selected from a list of options.
    3.5. Identity indigeneity: Any indigenous group identity associated with the endorsement, selected from a list of options.
    3.6. Identity occupation: Any occupational group identity associated with the endorsement, selected from a list of options.
    3.7. Identity other: Any other group identity associated with the endorsement, selected from a list of options.

4. Verbal Appeals
   4.1. Verbal appeal ID: Unique number automatically assigned.
   4.2. Verbal appeal comment: Any comments relating to the verbal group appeal.
   4.3. Verbal group appeal: Any appeal to an ethnic or non-ethnic social group. The options included various religious, indigenous, and occupational groups, as well as the poor and other groups, such as women and youth.
   4.4. Verbal issue/policy appeal: Any appeal related to an issue or policy. The options included policies related to various aspects of agriculture, business, consumer issues, corruption, economy, government services, infrastructure, jobs and welfare, reform and democracy, security and social order, and ethnic group issues.

Note: Verbal appeals came in two basic forms—a group appeal (V4.3) or an issue/policy appeal (V4.4). A verbal appeal could be coded as one or the other, or both. For example, an appeal to increase teachers' salaries so as to improve the quality of education was coded as a verbal group appeal to teachers in V4.3 and as an issue/policy appeal on government services in V4.4. Verbal appeals coded only as issue/policy appeals were not considered as ethnic appeals in the analysis.

5. Candidate Attributes
   5.1. Candidate identity ID: Unique number automatically assigned.
   5.2. Candidate identity comment: Any comments relating to the candidate's identity.
   5.3. Candidate identity: The candidate's identity that was referred to in the report. The options included religion, indigeneity, and other identities such as regional, national, sex, and youth.
   5.4. Candidate experience ID: Unique number automatically assigned.
   5.5. Candidate experience comment: Any comments relating to the candidate's work experience.
   5.6. Candidate experience: The candidate's work experience that was referred to in the report. The options included occupational experience, as well as organizational experience at religious, indigenous, and regional organizations.
   5.7. Candidate trait ID: Unique number automatically assigned.
   5.8. Candidate trait comment: Any comments relating to the candidate's personal traits.
   5.9. Candidate trait: The candidate's personal traits that were referred to in the report. The options included "strong leader," "compassionate," "honest," "intelligent," "moral," as well as others.

APPENDIX C
Election Poster Data

This appendix provides some methodological notes on my gathering of election posters, the criteria for poster eligibility for the study, and coding challenges, along with a list of the coded variables and the classifications of posters. The complete codebook for the election poster data can be found on my website.

A3.1. Gathering Election Posters

2009 Legislative Elections. Posters from candidates competing in Indonesia's legislative elections were photographed in 2009. In April of that year, elections were held for national and local legislatures, including the national upper house, the national lower house, the provincial legislature, and the district legislatures. To obtain a geographically diverse sample of posters, researchers working for an Indonesian survey company, SurveyMETER, were recruited. At the time, SurveyMETER was an Indonesian NGO research institution that provided data collection, analysis, and research services. It was responsible for gathering data for several iterations of Rand's longitudinal household surveys, known as the Indonesian Family Life Survey (IFLS). SurveyMETER researchers were spread out across Indonesia, in both urban and rural areas, so that the NGO could gather data for nationally representative samples. In the weeks before the election, a colleague of mine and I emailed these researchers, inviting them to photograph as many election posters as they could in the areas where they lived. They were instructed to photograph the entire poster and were paid on a per-poster basis. These poster photographs were then gathered and stored in a database.

2010–2012 Regional Head Elections. By 2010, the first five-year term for many regional heads was expiring; new elections, held on a rolling basis, began in various provinces and districts. In 2010, the same email was again sent to SurveyMETER researchers, inviting them to photograph election posters in regional head elections if one was occurring in their region. I also drew on a personal network of researchers to photograph regional head election posters in the areas where they lived. Furthermore, between 2010 and 2012, I traveled around the country photographing posters during numerous regional head elections in North Sumatra, Central Java, and Maluku. All these photographs were added to the dataset.

A3.2. Poster Eligibility

After the posters were photographed, they were processed in professional photography archiving software (Adobe Lightroom). First, they were sorted by party and candidate. Each photograph was cropped to contain a single election poster, and the set of posters was digitally enhanced for readability. Next, five types of posters were excluded before coding:

1. *Irrelevant posters.* Some photos were taken by mistake, either because they were left over from a previous election or advertised a product (such as a cell phone or noodles), not a candidate.
2. *Poster or flag with no information.* Some posters or flags had no picture, no imagery, and no written appeal. To qualify for coding, they needed to have a name (and a party logo if for the legislative election).
3. *Party poster.* Some posters promoted only their party as a whole and did not mention any local candidate. These posters are not helpful in understanding the individual campaign behavior of candidates. They are also very rare in contemporary Indonesian elections.
4. *Group posters for legislative elections.* Posters promoting groups of candidates from a single political party competing in different legislative elections were also removed from the dataset, so as to maintain a tighter connection between the appeals on each poster and a particular candidate competing in a specific legislative election constituency. This was particularly important for the analysis, because the constituencies for district, provincial, and national legislatures are of different sizes. As a result, they have different ethnic demographics. Thus, for example, a candidate competing for a district legislative seat might have a small and ethnically homogeneous constituency, whereas another candidate in the same town but competing for a national legislative seat could be appealing to a larger and more ethnically diverse constituency. Group election posters were very rare, so their removal had little impact on the size of the dataset. Where they did appear, it was usually among arguably the most disciplined of Indonesia's political parties—the Islamic PKS and the Acehnese regional party Partai Aceh.
5. *Duplicate posters.* By this term, I refer to posters with the same design, used by the same candidate in different geographic areas. Some researchers included duplicate posters among their photographs, but others did not. To avoid possible bias, I retained just one unique design of each election poster in the dataset.

A3.3. Codebook Overview

The development of the codebook and the interpretation of the election posters were undertaken during my fieldwork in Indonesia. There were some challenges in initial attempts to code the posters. Early in the process, it became apparent that no individual Indonesian research assistant had all the knowledge necessary to code all the posters. This was because many posters contained elements specific to particular identity groups and regions—types of clothing, regional buildings, symbols, etc. Previous scholars also found that content analysis of campaign materials often requires a certain level of expertise to interpret identity-related content. For example, Chandra (2005) relied on expert decisions to code whether a party was ethnic based on their campaign materials. Also, McIlwain and Caliendo (2011) used their expertise to code racial appeals in television advertisements. In both cases, the scholars were careful to provide details on their definitions of ethnic or racial appeals. Given these challenges, I largely coded the posters myself, the bulk of which was done during fieldwork in Indonesia.

To store and organize the posters, I used photography archiving software. I then coded each poster, by hand, for index information (e.g., Political party, Candidate number) and visual elements (Candidate Clothing and Imagery) I also transcribed all the text from each poster and created word counts from this text. Next, I analyzed these word counts and created multiple custom dictionaries of words related to ethnic and partisan identities. I could then machine-code the text using these dictionaries. This process allowed me to code each poster's visual and textual elements in a comprehensive and consistent manner.

Although my codebook added consistency to the coding process, I sought outside help in interpreting poster appeals. Specifically, during my fieldwork, I consulted with research assistants, local residents, and campaign team members from different parts of the country and various ethnic groups, to identify unknown elements in the posters. Online resources, encyclopedias, and scholarly works on ethnic and religious clothing and architecture supplemented the identification of poster elements. In addition, the coding protocol, interpretation issues, and some preliminary results were presented on two occasions in Jakarta—to a general audience at the Freedom Institute and to a panel of experts at the Center for Strategic and International Studies. The feedback received there contributed to coding and interpretation revisions.

Below is a list of variables coded for each election poster. Any variables that refer to a second candidate (e.g., Second candidate name, Clothing 2 etc.) apply only to the deputy head candidate in regional head candidate posters. Also, there are some mentions of BPS code numbers. Each Indonesian province or district is assigned a code number by the government's statistics department (BPS), and these codes are updated every few years.

1. Index Information
    1.1. BPS year: The year in which the BPS released the applicable code numbers for provinces and districts.
    1.2. Candidate number: A unique number for each legislative or regional head candidate in a constituency. It is on the ballot and on each legislative candidate's poster, and usually on each regional head candidate's poster.
    1.3. Sub-constituency number: The sub-constituency number (*dapil*) for candidates competing for a seat in a district legislature. The number can represent one or more subdistricts (*kecamatan*).
    1.4. District code: The district code for regional head election constituencies. It is the BPS code for the province or district.
    1.5. Constituency number: Specific constituency numbers are assigned in the legislative elections. For the regional head elections, this number is the same as variable 1.4.
    1.6. Election: The type of election in which the candidate shown in the poster was competing—e.g., lower house national legislature election or provincial governor election.
    1.7. Province code: The provincial code assigned by the BPS.
    1.8. Poster image name: The name of the poster image file in the software.
    1.9. First candidate name: The name of the legislative candidate on the poster. In the case of regional head elections, if there were two candidates on the poster, the name of the head candidate was placed here. However, if the deputy head candidate was the only candidate on the poster, the deputy head candidate's name was entered here.
    1.10. Second candidate name: In regional head election posters, if the names and/or pictures of two candidates appeared, the deputy candidate's name was entered here.
    1.11. Number of candidates: The number of candidates on the poster, either 1 or 2.
    1.12. Poster set: A variable to indicate if the poster came from one of nine districts that were photographed intensively using GPS coordinates.

1.12. Poster number: A number for a unique poster design of a candidate. (Most candidates had more than one poster design in the dataset.)
1.13. Gender 1: Gender of the first candidate on the poster.
1.14. Gender 2: Gender of the second candidate on the poster.
1.15. Item Id: A unique identification number for each poster, generated in the coding software.
1.16. Political party: A unique number for each political party (selected from a list).

2. Candidate Clothing
    2.1. Clothing 1: The style or type of clothing for the first candidate on the poster (e.g., ethnic Acehnese, Islamic, government, suit and tie).
    2.2. Clothing 2: The style of clothing for the second candidate on the poster.
    2.4. Headdress 1: The style of headdress for the first candidate (e.g., jilbab, turban).
    2.5. Headdress 2: The style of headdress for the second candidate.
    2.6. Cloth accessory 1: Any cloth accessory held by the first candidate (e.g., Batak cloth (*ulos*), turban cloth (*sorban*)).
    2.7. Cloth accessory 2: Any cloth accessory used by the second candidate.
    2.8. Party clothing 1: Whether the first candidate wore official party clothing or used the party logo or color prominently in his or her clothing (e.g., a red suit when the party color was red).
    2.9. Party clothing 2: Whether the second candidate wore party colors or party logos.

3. Imagery
    3.1. Supporting institution: Name of the institution or individual supporting or endorsing the candidate on the poster.
    3.2. Supporter identity: Identity category of the institution or individual supporting or endorsing the candidate (e.g., ethnic Acehnese, Islamic, nationalist).
    3.3. Party support: Presence and prominence of support for regional heads by their nominating parties.
    3.4. Party logo or flag: Presence of a party logo or a party flag in the background of the poster.
    3.5. Elite image: Presence and type of any elite image in the poster (e.g., Megawati, Islamic leader, Christian leader, Javanese leader).
    3.6. Indonesian flag: Presence of an Indonesian flag in the background or on a candidate's clothing.
    3.7. Imagery: Any other images, signs, or symbols on the poster (e.g., buildings, monuments, symbols, patterns, landscapes, events, maps).

4. Textual Content
    4.1. Common text messages: Any of the common messages that often appear on posters (e.g., website address).
    4.2. Non-Indonesian language: Any language, other than Indonesian, used on the poster (e.g., Arabic, Javanese).
    4.3. Non-Indonesian transcription: All the non-Indonesian language text on the poster.
    4.4. Non-Indonesian translation: Translation into English of the non-Indonesian text.
    4.5. Indonesian transcription: All the Indonesian-language text on the poster.

A3.4. Classifying Individual Posters

After coding the poster content, I classified each poster in terms of the kinds of appeals it contained. Posters were classified for religious and indigenous appeals separately. With regard to religious appeals, the logic behind the classification of each poster is displayed in Figure A4.1. This logic draws on the method presented in Chapter 2 and allows us to classify each poster into one of the following four mutually exclusive categories shown in the figure. In the book's analysis, broad religious bridging and cross-religious bridging were combined. Using the same logic, the posters were then classified according to the four categories of indigenous bonding and bridging functions: indigenous bypassing, broad indigenous bridging, cross-indigenous bridging, and indigenous bonding.

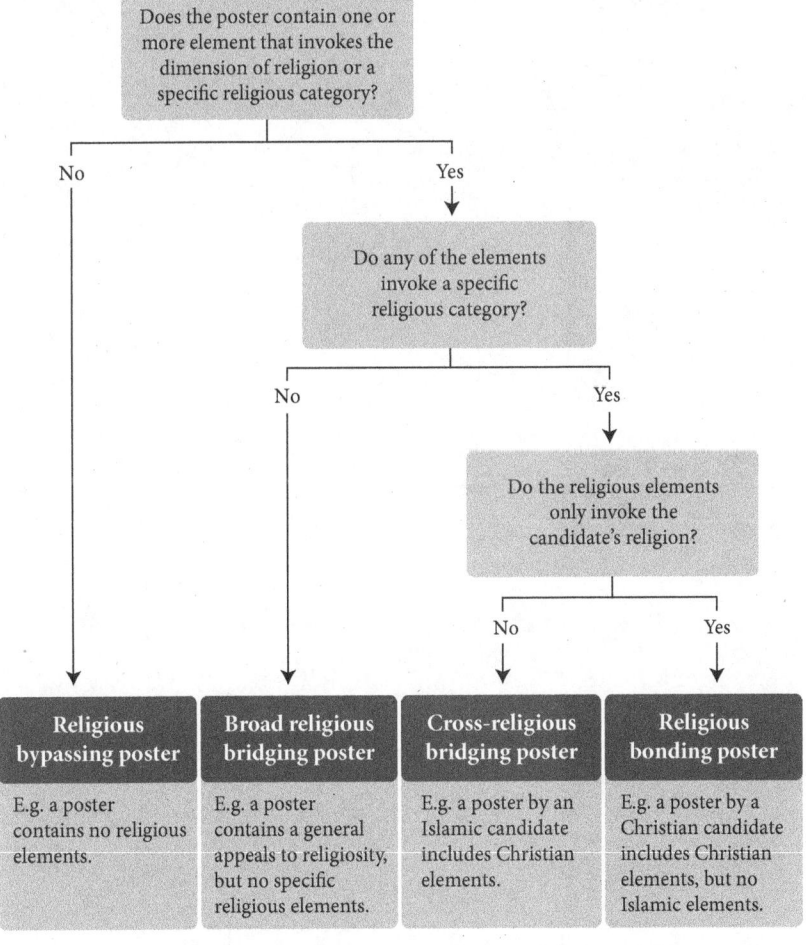

Figure A4.1 Classifying posters in terms of religious bonding, bridging, or bypassing functions.

Notes

Chapter 1

1. See Kaplan (1993, 1994) for the best-known journalistic accounts on the adverse effects of ethnicity and tribalism. Connor (1993) and Kaufman (2001), among others, have also emphasized the power of ethnic bonds and how politicians can instrumentally manipulate ethnic attachment for their own ends. More broadly, for a review of the scholarship on the divisive nature of ethnicity, see Hale (2008: 16–25).
2. See Chandra (2012); Posner (2004, 2005); Wilkinson (2004); Huber (2017); Dickson and Scheve (2006); Reilly (2000).
3. The concept of "minimum winning coalitions" originates with Riker's (1962) studies on government formation. It was initially applied to ethnic politics by Bates (1974) and later by Posner (2005).
4. The study of microfoundations is often used in economics to understand how individual behavior underpins macroeconomic theory, but it has also been used in political science. For example, studies by Laitin (1998), Kalyvas (2006), and Hale (2008) use a microfoundations approach to study conflict and ethnic politics.
5. The use of these terms has been inspired by and adapted from works by Putnam (2002) and Norris (2004).
6. Research on local politicians in India is a key exception, with seminal works by Wilkinson (2004), Chandra (2004), Varshney (2002), and Brass (2003). Similarly, more recent comparative publications on India and Indonesia have explored how local candidates can gain strategic benefit through fomenting violence by religious vigilante groups (Jaffrey 2021) and patronage networks organized along religious lines (Berenschot 2020).
7. Evidence in support of the theory comes from Sisk and Reynolds (1998) and from Reilly (2001), whereas evidence against comes from Suberu and Diamond (2002) and from Huber (2012).
8. For a seminal article on this topic, see Carey and Shugart (1995), who presented an ordinal scoring system of electoral systems based on the degree of incentive to cultivate a personal reputation. Also see Samuels (1999).
9. A large part of the research on personal vote-seeking strategies comes from American politics (Cain et al. 1987; Fenno 1978; Mayhew 1974). Applications to other countries include Anagnoson (1983) on New Zealand, Lancaster and Patterson (1990) on West Germany, and Shugart et al. (2005) on six European countries.
10. Later in the book I will also show how ethnic bonding appeals increase when these second-level factors take on their inverse values, i.e., when there is a lack of a strong ethnic reputation, a two-candidate race, and a competitive election.

11. Legislative elections are held at the national, provincial, and district (i.e., sub-provincial) levels. There are also executive elections for the positions of president, governor, and district head.
12. On the transformation of transitional society in North Sumatra, see Liddle (1970: 19–66). He also described the class-based identities among plantation workers and squatters living in rural regions of Simalungun, North Sumatra.
13. See Bowen (2003), Henley and Davidson (2007), Fealy and White (2008), and Menchik (2016).
14. See Bertrand (2004), van Klinken (2007), Sidel (2006), Davidson (2008a) Tajima (2014), Barron (2019) and Toha (2021) for various analyses of violent conflict during this period.
15. See Barron (2019) on postconflict violence in Maluku, North Maluku, and Aceh.
16. 2010 National Census, Central Agency on Statistics (Badan Pusat Statistik).
17. Ananta et al. (2015); see also Suryadinata et al. (2003) on the 2000 census.
18. There are few examples. For instance, McIlwain and Caliendo (2011) gathered racial appeals in political advertisements during the 2008 U.S. presidential election; and Gadjanova (2021) gathered ethnic appeals from various sources during African presidential campaigns that took place between 2006 and 2008.
19. For an example of using ethnic voting to study ethnic politicization, see Huber (2012). The Manifesto Project's dataset of party manifestos measures party positions on ethnocultural issues (Klingemann et al. 2006). It is the main source for studies of ethnic appeals. For an example, see Gadjanova (2015). The Manifesto Project's dataset mainly covers Western countries but has recently expanded its coverage to some countries in Asia and Latin America. Its coding of ethnic issues has received some criticism, however (Protsyk and Garaz 2013).
20. In one of the largest studies, Holtz-Bacha Novelli and Rafter (2017) with their team of researchers collected and coded 1,445 election posters from 28 EU member states during the 2014 European Parliament election campaign. Also, Holtz-Bacha and Johansson (2017) provide a number of country studies using smaller numbers of election posters. Dumitrescu (2009, 2010, 2012) gathered and analyzed a few hundred election posters from elections in France and Belgium. In a separate study on campaigns in Thailand, I gathered and analyzed over 12,000 Thai election posters posted across the country, almost 600 of these had a unique design (see Fox 2018).

Chapter 2

1. Some of prominent works include Bates (1983); Horowitz (1985); Posner (2004); Wilkinson (2004); Chandra (2004).
2. Mendelberg (2001) sparked a debate on implicit racial appeals. This debate includes valuable contributions by Valentino et al. (2002) as well as by Huber and Lapinski (2006). Also see Haney López (2015) for an updated contribution on this topic. On

the changing norms of racial appeals in recent years see Reny et al. (2019); Stephens-Dougan (2020); Valentino et al. (2018).

3. On the rise of right-wing parties see Blee and Creasap (2010); Mudde (2007). For examples of how these parties use anti-immigrant appeals, see Hogan and Haltinner (2015); Schmuck and Matthes (2017).

4. McIlwain and Caliendo (2011: 12). Supreme Court Justice Potter Stewart became famous for using this phrase in reference to pornography.

5. Chandra defines an ethnic group as "a subset of categories in which descent-based attributes are necessary for membership" (Chandra 2011: 154).

6. In the vast majority of cases, members of the group will not all know each other. In a few instances, an ethnic group may dwindle in size to the point at which all members personally know each other. But even in such instances, at some previous point members of the ethnic group did not all know each other personally.

7. For example, Fearon (2003) included such features as a shared group consciousness, cultural features valued by members, a real or imagined homeland, and a shared history. See Chandra and Wilkinson (2008) for more detail on debates over how to define an ethnic group.

8. Chandra restricts her definition to a subset of a country's population. In this way, Chandra avoids, for example, using the term "American" as an ethnic category within the United States. As she explains, American is not an ethnic category in the United States, but it is in other countries. Although this restriction is useful for the purposes of Chandra's paper, which focuses on the coding of parties based on national boundaries, it is somewhat arbitrary for other studies. There is no special reason to consider national boundaries more relevant to ethnic definitions than continental, regional, or electoral district boundaries. As a result, I have dropped this restriction and use the term "identity category" in my definition rather than "subset of categories," which Chandra uses in her definition.

9. For instance, see Ruane and Todd's (2010) introduction to a special issue of *Ethnopolitics*, entitled "Ethnicity and Religion: Intersections and Comparisons."

10. Religion, for instance, is a more worldly identity concerned with sacred and personal confessional practices, whereas indigenous identities are more associated with territoriality and a shared history.

11. For examples see Horowitz (1985); Posner (2005); Chandra (2004).

12. See Posner (2005), Chandra (2006), as well as Chandra and Wilkinson (2008). The approach is also in line with recent scholarship in sociology that argues against "groupism" (Brubaker 2004).

13. See Chandra's (2012) edited volume for a more detailed discussion of ethnic structure.

14. Prominent works include Mendelberg (1997, 2001, 2008); Huber and Lapinski (2006); Peffley and Hurwitz (2002); Peffley et al. (1997); Entman (2004).

15. See Reny et al. (2019); Valentino et al. (2018).

16. Cross-cultural research and laboratory experiments on intergroup prejudice have found that individuals' positive ingroup identification does not automatically lead to outgroup negativity (Brewer 1999).

17. Examples include Rabushka and Shepsle (1972); de Figueiredo and Weingast (1999); Dickson and Scheve (2006); Chandra (2004); Horowitz (1985); Posner (2005); Haney López (2015); Mendelberg (2001).
18. Horowitz (2016) showed how presidential candidates in Kenya appealed to swing voters (i.e., members of groups that did not have a co-ethnic leader in the race) by holding rallies in regions where swing voters lived.
19. Several studies have considered how candidates target core supporters or swing voters in advanced democracies (Cox and McCubbins 1986; Dixit and Londregan 1996; Stokes 2005). However, they do not specifically identify ethnicity as an important defining feature of a core or swing group. One rare exception is Horowitz (2016), who examined how candidates campaign for support from outside their ethnic kin.
20. Even in the United States, a consensus around a shared national identity is regularly contested. Lieven (2016) argued that in the United States, the prevailing civic nationalist consensus has been undermined by an alternative vision during Donald Trump's presidency. According to a Jacksonian vision, American national identity is more exclusive and largely confined to being white and Christian. Trump has espoused this view far more explicitly than previous Republicans. Given his interpretation of American national identity, patriotic appeals by Trump's election campaign do not have the expected positive connotations or represent broad bridging appeals for many Americans.
21. Six religions are officially recognized: Islam, Protestantism, Catholicism, Hinduism, Buddhism, and Confucianism.
22. In some of the separatist regions, such as Aceh and Papua, national identity is, unsurprisingly, lower.
23. See studies by Transue (2007: 79–80) and by Charnysh et al. (2015).
24. See Varshney (2002: 21). Though he critiqued the use of quantitative methods, Varshney went on to quantify ethnic riots and combined quantitative measures with rich description.
25. Brass (1997) and Kaufman (2001) are two excellent examples of more qualitative approaches.
26. For example, Chandra (2005); Chandra and Wilkinson (2008).
27. Sulkin (2009) and Druckman (2004) measured issue-based appeals, whereas McIlwain and Caliendo (2011) and DeFrancesco Soto and Merolla (2006) quantified racial and ethnic appeals.
28. In studying ethnic politics in Zambia, Posner (2005: 181) found that evidence on candidate's ethnic appeals was scattered and incomplete.
29. Even more broadly, there is skepticism about studying electoral behavior at all. When I was a graduate student, one of my professors remarked, "Studying electoral behavior is like counting pimples on the bottom of the body politic!"
30. On the impact of imagery and music see Brader (2005); on the effect of repetitive messaging see Grimmer et al. (2012).
31. See Valentino et al. (2002). For more recent contributions see Reny et al. (2019); Schmuck and Matthes (2017).

Chapter 3

1. For example, the use of ethnic and nationalist rhetoric to mobilize ethnic groups has been shown to affect economic growth (Easterly and Levine 1997), political stability and competition (Rabushka and Shepsle 1972), interethnic relations (Horowitz 1985: 326–332), ethnic violence (Kaufman 2001; Cederman et al. 2010), as well as international and civil wars in emerging democracies (Mansfield and Snyder 2005; Snyder 2000; Cederman et al. 2013).
2. Some classic examples include Almond (1956), Dahl (1971), Lijphart (1977), and Powell (1982).
3. One critique claims an overemphasis on policy differences between ethnic groups (Fearon 2008: 859). Another argues that the multidimensional nature of ethnicity can actually mitigate against ethnic outbidding (Chandra 2005). See Reilly (2000: 164–166) for a brief review of this literature on the detrimental effects of ethnic diversity.
4. The logic is that proportional representation and multiseat districts produce a more proportional outcome. This enables small, ethnically oriented parties to form because they can win seats by appealing only to their ethnic kin. In contrast, under majoritarian rules, parties need broader support to win elections. As a result, more nationally oriented parties form. To reach a broad cross-section of voters, they appeal to voters as either a multiethnic or a nonethnic party.
5. Evidence in support comes from Sisk and Reynolds (1998) and from Reilly (2001); contrary evidence comes from Suberu and Diamond (2002) and from Huber (2012).
6. Lijphart (1977) argued that proportional representation is beneficial because it offers ethnic representation in government and promotes general support for the system. However, Horowitz (1985) argued that majoritarian systems that encourage vote-pooling are superior because they help diffuse ethnic tensions.
7. Bates (2000) found evidence of a switch from protest to violent action in Africa when the size of the largest ethnic group reached 50% or more of the population. Collier (2001: 150) showed that countries with an ethnically dominant group (i.e., 45–90% of the population) are twice as likely to experience civil war. Wilkinson (2004) demonstrated how ethnic minorities are vulnerable to violence when they are not an important part of a governing party or coalition's current (or future) support base. Hale (2004) illustrated how ethno-federal states are more prone to collapse if they contain a core ethnic region (i.e., a single-ethnic region that is dominant in terms of its population size).
8. Important works include Chandra (2012), Posner (2004, 2005), Wilkinson (2004), and Huber (2017).
9. See Chandra (2012), Posner (2004, 2005), Wilkinson (2004), Huber (2017), and Reilly (2000). Also, Dickson and Scheve (2006) use a formal model of political speech.
10. Chandra and Boulet (2012: 234) observe that the term "minimum winning size" has been widely accepted. It was used by Bates (1974), Chandra (2004), and Posner (2005).
11. For example, see Rabushka and Shepsle (1972), Chandra (2004), and Posner (2005).

12. Other scholars have built on Riker's (1962) emphasis on size, presenting more complex arguments on how parties want to keep coalitions ideologically coherent but also face institutional constraints in the process of coalition formation. See Tavits (2008: 495–496) for a review of this literature.
13. Similarly, Barreto and Bozonelos (2009) found that U.S. Democratic and Republican politicians encourage religiosity among Protestants, Jews, and Catholics, but are constrained from promoting religiosity among Muslims. As a result, Muslim Americans with high levels of religiosity and perceptions of discrimination against Muslims have difficulty identifying with either political party.
14. Carey and Shugart (1995) also add that an increase in district magnitude (i.e., the number of seats in a district) has an unusual effect in that it makes candidate-centric electoral rules more candidate-centric and party-centric rules more party-centric. As the authors explain, in candidate-centric systems, as the number of fellow party candidates in a district increases, more pressure is placed on candidates to establish a unique reputation in order to stand out from the crowd. In contrast, under party-centric systems, as the number of fellow party candidates increases, the importance of individual candidates and their personal ability to secure votes for the party decline. For empirical support, see Shugart et al. (2005).
15. For studies of American politics, see Cain et al. (1987). For other countries, see Anagnoson (1983), Lancaster and Patterson (1990), and Shugart et al. (2005).
16. Some studies have looked at the impact of candidate-centric rules on gender politics and women's representation. In a study of 57 countries between 1980 and 2005, Thames and Williams (2010) found that candidate-centric systems decreased women's representation in parliament.
17. See Caselli and Coleman (2013), Fearon (1999), as well as Laitin and Van Der Veen (2012); also, Aspinall and Berenschot (2019: 131–132) observed this phenomenon in Indonesia.
18. The number of candidates competing in an election may either increase or decrease the estimated size of a winning group. On one hand, it can increase the size of a winning group if multiple candidates are appealing to the same ethnic group, thus splitting their vote. On the other hand, it can decrease the size of the winning group as votes become spread among more candidates, making heavy support from a smaller ethnic group enough to secure a seat.
19. Work in recent years has focused on factors that may decrease co-ethnic support, such as when co-ethnics voters reside in areas dominated by another ethnic group (Ichino and Nathan 2013), when cross-cutting cleavages are present (Dunning and Harrison 2010); or when co-ethnic candidates have engaged in corrupt or shirking behavior in the past (Carlson 2015).
20. Collingwood (2020) as well as Devasher and Gadjanova (2021) make this argument. Notably, broad ethnic bridging (e.g., appeals to a superordinate identity such as nationalism) likely poses less risk for candidates because it softens ethnic group boundaries and focuses attention on the broader group (Transue 2007: 79–80; Charnysh et al. 2015).
21. Recent work in this area includes Transue (2017: 79–80) and Charnysh et al. (2015).

22. Scholars who have promoted the positive aspects of national parties include Riker (1964), Stepan (2001), and Filippov et al. (2004).
23. Chandra (2011) highlights a range of indicators that can be used to classify a party as ethnic. They include the party's name, campaign messages that explicitly and implicitly advocate for an ethnic group, ethnic voting patterns, ethnic representation within the party, and venues where the party seeks votes.
24. I do not include social constraints as affecting the appeals made by ethnic parties. This is because social constraints will tend to affect the formation of ethnic parties, inhibiting the growth of parties who champion an ethnic group. In other words, if an ethnic party can form at all, then there are probably no social constraints severe enough to limit its public appeals.
25. There is some evidence for this logic. In public opinion surveys in Africa, Eifert et al. (2010) found that Africans are more likely to identify themselves in ethnic terms during election campaigns, particularly when the elections are competitive. In addition, Kuenzi and Lambright (2013) found that in competitive elections, candidates try to distinguish themselves by making more ethnic appeals.
26. This strategy is more likely when there are other salient dimensions of ethnicity. Chandra (2005) argued that when institutions foster multiple dimensions of ethnic identity, ethnic parties emerge that can mobilize groups along alternative ethnic identity dimensions.
27. As noted above, Collingwood (2020) as well as Devasher and Gadjanova (2021) argued that candidates weigh up the potential of a backlash by co-ethnics when considering cross-ethnic appeals.
28. Both Horowitz (2017, 2022) and Gadjanova (2017) found that presidents in Kenya and Zambia spent considerable time and resources campaigning for votes from other ethnic groups who did not have a candidate in the race.
29. In relation to having a strong ethnic reputation and ethnic support, Taylor (2017) found that African political parties who drew support from a large ethnic group were feared by other ethnic groups because these groups believed they would not benefit from these parties. To assuage these fears and reach out to these ethnic groups, the political parties promoted inclusive programmatic policy appeals.
30. In a similar sense, Chandra and Wilkinson (2008) identified ethnic parties by their public use of ethnic appeals that were both explicit and central to their campaigns.
31. Hale (2004: 461–462) has argued that divisions between primordialists, who see ethnic groups as fixed, and constructivists, who view ethnic groups as more malleable are inaccurate, and often unhelpful. He finds plenty of agreement among so-called primordial and constructivist scholars. Davidson (2008b), in a review of research on ethnicity in Southeast Asia, draws on primordial, situational, constructivist, and more recent approaches.
32. For the most notable journalistic example of the detrimental aspects of ethnic attachments and past hostilities, see Kaplan (1993, 1994) on the Balkans and West Africa.
33. For example, according to Geertz (1957: 51), the polarized politics in Indonesia during the 1950s was more than just a political competition over which party would

rule; it was a direct consequence of a battle over basic cultural values and symbols of meaning. See Laitin (1986) for a review of Weber and Geertz on the politicization of ethnicity. There has also been some debate over Geertz's view of ethnicity. Whereas Laitin (1986) casts Geertz as a primordialist, Davidson (2008b) has argued that Geertz's writing on ethnicity reflects its constructed nature.

34. Some of the earliest work on modernization came from Karl Marx, Max Weber, and Émile Durkheim. However, in the 1950s and 1960s, authors such as Deutsch (1953, 1964), Lipset (1959, 1981), and Rostow (1960) revived the theory of modernization and wrote extensively about it. These ideas were subsequently extended by Gellner (1983), Hobsbawm (1990), and Anderson (1983).

35. Some authors, such as Daniel Bell (1999), have focused on a new, postindustrial stage of modernization, which occurs with a shift from manufacturing to the service sector and is accompanied by increases in education, geographic mobility, and technological advancement. In Western postindustrial societies, Inglehart (1990, 1997) has argued, social identities have weakened, while society and politics have become more fragmented and individualized. As a result, political party support, once rooted in religion and class, has become more contingent on particular leaders, issues, and events.

36. This observation was made as early as the 1970s; see Melson and Wolpe (1970), Young (1976), Bates (1983), or (more recently) Eifert et al. (2010). Collingwood (2020) has highlighted how white Democrats are particularly prone to making cross-ethnic appeals in urban areas where larger numbers of Latino immigrants live.

37. Works relating critical junctures to the rise of ethnic politics include Beissinger (2009) on the Soviet Union, Petersen (2002) on Eastern Europe, and Bertrand (2004) on Indonesia.

38. Mansfield and Snyder (1995, 2002, 2005) use these domestic factors to explain why democratizing countries are prone to international war. Snyder (2000) applies the same argument to explain the detrimental effect of democratization on internal ethnic conflict.

39. Good examples of this scholarship include Mousseau (2001), Saideman et al. (2002), and Cederman et al. (2013).

Chapter 4

1. Carey and Shugart (1995) referred to these three features using the terms *ballot*, *vote*, and *pool*, respectively.
2. See Eklöf (1997: 1183). Golkar's full name, Golongan Karya, literally means "functional groups."
3. See Ward's (1974) study of Golkar and its ideological underpinnings during the 1971 election campaign. Ward also provided an analysis of the other major political parties that competed.
4. See Schiller (1999: 4) on Golkar's power over ordinary individuals. Antlöv (2004: 115) recounted how Pemuda Pancasila members accompanied the Golkar cadre during visits to hesitant households.

5. Antlöv (2004: 114) told of one of the poorest hamlets in the village of Sariendah, West Java, that was promised a new mosque if Golkar obtained more than 90% of the votes in the hamlet. Falling short of the 90%, no Mosque was built.
6. See Eklöf (1997: 1183), King (2003: 26), and Crouch (2010: 44). Candidates could not be members of the long-banned Indonesian Communist Party, nor could they have been directly or indirectly involved in the 1965 coup attempt (National Democratic Institute 1997: 15).
7. East Timor became the 27th province when it was annexed in 1976.
8. See Gaffar (1992: 70), as cited in King (2003: 29). For more on the electoral rules and summaries of voting during the New Order elections, see King (2003: 15–45).
9. Accounts of the fall of Suharto's regime claim that it was a corrupt system that collapsed due to multiple factors, including inherent internal pressures, an external push from a democracy movement led by students and professionals, as well as the abandonment of the regime by Chinese-Indonesians and their substantial capital. For three prominent accounts, see Hadiz and Robinson (2004), Aspinall (2005), and Pepinsky (2009).
10. See Crouch (2010: 47). Also, see Liddle (2021). He provides an account of Habibie that gives him more agency, arguing that Habibie was a transforming and inspiring president who effectively stretched the constraints he was working under to enable Indonesia's democratic transition.
11. For details on this system of allocating seats to candidates, see Ellis (2000: 242–244); Horowitz (2013: 83–84); Allen (2018: 929).
12. Pancasila, the philosophical foundation for the state of Indonesia, is based on five principles and was first presented by Sukarno in a speech in June 1945. The principles are belief in the one and only God, just and civilized humanity, the unity of Indonesia, democracy guided by the inner wisdom of deliberations of representatives, and social justice for all Indonesian people. Courses on Pancasila were compulsory for students and public servants.
13. Approximately 10,000 civil servants held leadership positions in Golkar, but many of them left the party after the other parties and the public successfully pressed for reform under which civil servants were no longer allowed to be members of political parties. On these reforms of the party system, see King (2003: 50–55); Antlöv (2004: 10); Crouch (2010: 49).
14. On the restriction of political parties, see Reilly (2007: 1362–1363); Crouch (2010: 47–48); Aspinall (2011: 296); Horowitz (2013: 68–70).
15. On party branch requirements and thresholds see King (2004: 51), Crouch (2010: 47–48), and Mietzner (2013: 62-65). I should note that while King and Crouch state that party branches needed to be established in a third of all provinces. Mietzner's study of the Party and Election Laws show that party branches needed to be established in half of the provinces and half of the districts within those provinces.
16. The election was administered by a semi-independent election commission and supervised by domestic and international independent election monitors (Antlöv 2004: 10; King 2003: 53).

17. The PKB won 12.6%, PPP 10.7%, and PAN 7.1%. Sixteen smaller parties also won some seats.
18. For more detail on the "open lists" in 2004 see Horowitz (2013: 143); Crouch (2010: 63–65); Sherlock (2009).
19. The national legislature was increased to 550, and after several of the larger provinces were divided up, there were a total of 69 constituencies (Allen 2018: 926–927).
20. See Reilly (2007: 1362). It should be noted that a whopping 152 political parties formed before the 1999 election but failed to qualify (King 2003: 51).
21. On branch requirements and thresholds for the 2004 election see Crouch (2010: 65) and Mietzner (2013: 63-65).
22. The upper house is called the House of Regional Representatives (Dewan Perwakilan Daerah or DPD), and its members have been elected every five years at the same time as the lower house. Candidates stand as independents in each province, and voters are presented with a list of candidates from whom they select one. In each province, four seats are allocated to the candidates with the highest votes. See Sherlock (2005) for more on the creation, role, and election of the DPD.
23. See Sherlock (2009). A technical rule that required voters who chose a candidate to also select the candidate's party resulted in many disallowed votes.
24. For more detail on the issue of the open list-reforms, see Horowitz (2013: 184–186); Sherlock (2009); Crouch (2010: 73–75).
25. See Butt (2015) on the Constitutional Court and its active involvement in elections since Indonesia's transition.
26. Parties could still win and retain seats in regional legislatures even if they fell below the threshold.
27. On the issue of gender quotas after the transition, see Siregar (2005); Sherlock (2009); Shair-Rosenfield (2012).
28. On the regional autonomy reforms, see Turner et al. (2003); Hofman and Kaiser (2004); Smith (2008); Crouch (2010: 92–95).
29. The first direct presidential election was held a few months after the 2004 legislative elections. Nominating parties were required to have won 5% of the vote or 3% of the seats in the preceding 2004 legislative elections. This was raised to 25% of the vote or 20% of the seats in 2009, making it likely that there would only be two candidates, each supported by multiple parties. In 2019, presidential and legislative elections were held concurrently; the 2014 legislative results were used to assess the vote and seat percentages of nominating parties.
30. The term *pilkada* is derived from *pemilihan kepala daerah langsung* (direct elections for regional heads).
31. On the regional head electoral reforms, see Crouch (2010: 108–109); Aspinall and Berenschot (2019: 77). See Erb and Sulistiyanto (2009), particularly Chapter 1 to Chapter 5, for details on the electoral rules and the weakness of political parties in the initial round of regional head elections. Also, see Hidayat (2009) on corrupt practices during this round.
32. See Allen (2018: 923); Aspinall and Berenschot (2019: 77).

Chapter 5

1. I am greatly indebted to Jeremy Menchik for suggesting the study of election posters and for working with me to gather posters from across the country.
2. On ethnic vote share measures, see Chandra (2011: 162–164), Huber (2012), and Horowitz (1985: 293).
3. For example see Wimmer et al. (2009) and Cederman et al. (2010).
4. Over the years, other measures have been added to the ERP dataset, such as settlement patterns of ethnic groups, links to rebel organizations, and regional autonomy. For details on the 2014 version, see Vogt et al. (2015). The website for the most up-to-date dataset was https://icr.ethz.ch/data/epr/. See Wucherpfennig et al. (2011) for information on a geocoded version of the dataset.
5. I do not mean to underestimate the considerable time and skill required to acquire and compile these data. Particularly in developing countries, researchers must often spend a significant amount of time interviewing local informants and in-country experts to gather data on the ethnic composition of parties and governments. Also, to understand ethnic voting patterns, complex methods of ecological inference are invariably needed.
6. The project was established in 1979 as the Manifesto Research Group. Since 2009, it has been called Manifesto Research on Political Representation (MARPOR). Over time, various scholars have built on the Manifesto Project approach by adding more granularity and tackling potential undercounting; see Protsyk and Garaz (2013). For more detail on the project, see Klingemann et al. (2006). The project website is https://manifesto-project.wzb.eu/. For critiques, see Gemenis (2013).
7. See Chandra (2009) as well as Chandra and Wilkinson (2008). The size of the vote for each party is incorporated into the measure, and an EVOTE index is developed to represent the aggregate vote obtained by ethnic parties across countries.
8. Even at the time of this book's completion, except for some of the wealthier candidates competing on the national stage or in the presidential election, online media were still not an important part of campaigning in Indonesian elections.
9. On campaign events, see Horowitz (2016); on candidate endorsements, see Kahn and Kenney (2002); on candidate attributes, see Balmas and Sheafer (2010), Druckman (2004), as well as Stevens and Karp (2012); and on issues, see Druckman (2004), Jerit (2004), Sulkin (2009), as well as Bleck and Van de Walle (2013). Finally, Taylor (2017) coded policy, patronage, and attribute appeals.
10. Herrera (2007) coded local newspapers to understand Russian regional separatist movements; Laitin (1998) studied newspapers to track changes in the terms used to describe Russian speakers in the former Soviet republics.
11. Kuenzi and Lambright (2015) coded ethnic appeals from newspaper coverage of a gubernatorial election in Nigeria. Additionally, Collingwood (2020) coded U.S. candidate websites for cross-racial appeals to Latinos.

12. According to government statistics, in 2009, 90% percentage of Indonesians watched television during a given week whereas only 19% read a newspaper or a magazine (Badan Pusat Statistik 2009: 31).
13. On political party coverage, see Tomsa (2007); on war and diplomacy, see Flournoy (1992); on news, see Steele (2003); on development, see Hermant and Gati (1994); on ethnic conflict, see Barron et al. (2009), Varshney et al. (2008), and Ariyanto et al. (2008); and for a discourse analysis of election campaign rhetoric in Indonesian election-related reports, see Voionmaa (2004).
14. Candidates' ability to influence their campaign reports was highlighted in a number of my interviews with campaign managers and journalists in Indonesia.
15. North Sumatra was also the province where Bill Liddle conducted fieldwork on ethnic politics in the 1960s. See Liddle (1970). West Kalimantan was also considered, but it had one-third of North Sumatra's population, a lower population density, a less developed regional press, and recent communal violence.
16. For some local history of North Sumatra, particularly the capital of Medan, see Anderson (2013). For an analysis of local ethnic politics in the North Sumatran districts of Simalungun and Pematangsiantar in the 1950s and 1960s, see Liddle (1970).
17. All population data in this paragraph come from the 2010 national census.
18. See Purdey (2006). On ethnic riots during the transition in other ethnically diverse districts, see Toha (2017).
19. Personal interview with Ali Murthado, editor of *Analisa*, December 7, 2009. Information on the exact number of publications was unavailable.
20. Personal interview with Ali Murthado, December 7, 2009.
21. The acronym SARA stands for ethnicity, religion, race, and other social divisions. The other social division implied was class, since it was a major source of division up until 1965. During the New Order, discussions or reporting on topics related to ethnicity, religion, race, and other social divisions were banned. The government's justification was that these identity issues had the potential to disturb social order.
22. The two weeks of *Waspada* after each election were photographed to study reactions to the elections, but they were not used in the quantitative content analysis. I accessed the newspaper archives at the Library of Congress in Washington, DC, at *Waspada*'s office in Medan, and through the media NGO KIPPAS. See Appendix B (Newspaper Data) for more detail.
23. I excluded all reports on national politicians and party heads, reports on the organization and implementation of elections, opinion pieces, and editorials. These reports were not a significant source of information about how local candidates campaigned.
24. See Appendix B (Newspaper Data) for more detail on procedures used to minimize inconsistent coding as well as for a list of all the variables coded for each report. Also, the complete newspaper report codebook is available at the author's website (https://www.colmfox.com).
25. With a large number of Protestants, North Sumatra is one of the few provinces where *Parkindo*, the Indnesian Christian Party, performed relatively well in the 1955 election.

26. Doing so would have been somewhat problematic, since some reports were on political parties broadly, whereas others focused more specifically on individual candidates. Applying the concept of ethnic bonding or bridging to a party is somewhat different from applying it to a candidate, as discussed in Chapter 2.
27. See Kirkpatrick and Sheikh (2012). The candidate, Hazem Salah Abu Ismail, was later disqualified. His supporters made even more posters (Cairo 2012).
28. Norris (2000) described election posters as from the premodern era of campaigning. Brader (2005), Huddy and Gunnthorsdottir (2000), Masters and Sullivan (1983), and Roseman et al. (1986) have shown that visual cues, images, and emotive words can trigger emotions and affect voting behavior.
29. Both scholars and consultants have noted these advantages of nonverbal communication in election posters. See Willnat et al. (2017); D'Aprile and Jacobs (2010).
30. See Holtz-Bacha and Johansson's (2017) edited volume for a number of studies on election posters from around the world. For a large study of election posters and TV commercials used during the 2014 European Parliament election campaign, see Holtz-Bacha Novelli and Rafter (2017).
31. See Suwondo et al. (1987) for an analysis of 300 election posters displayed during the 1982 legislative elections in Central Java.
32. For more detail on the use of posters in Indonesia since the 1955 election, see Fox (2022).
33. One contributor was Hari Prast, a designer who became famous after he produced comic-book renderings of Jokowi in the style of Tintin during the 2014 presidential election campaign. See Lukman (2019).
34. Personal correspondence with Kuskridho Ambardi, July 25, 2013.
35. Two studies in Indonesian cities highlighted how election posters evoked identity themes of Islam, nationalism, and "the people." Duile and Bens (2017) studied 215 posters from Pontianak, West Kalimantan during the 2014 legislative election campaign; Duile and Tamma (2021) examined 124 posters from South Jakarta during the 2019 legislative election campaign.
36. See Appendix C (Election Poster Data) for more detail on the gathering and selection of posters for coding.
37. These six parties were allowed to compete only in Aceh's provincial and district legislative elections. Allowing regional parties in Aceh was a key component of a peace deal signed in 2005 that ended a separatist insurgency. Chapter 8 provides more detail on the Acehnese parties and regional elections.
38. Of these 2,152 candidates, 1,906 competed in the legislative elections and 246 in the regional head elections. The number of regional head candidates is smaller because these are single-seat elections in which, generally, only two to 10 candidates compete. They do, however, tend to produce more uniquely designed posters. In contrast, many more seats are available in legislative elections with proportional representation and multiseat constituencies. However, legislative candidates often operate on tighter budgets and produce fewer unique poster designs.
39. See Table A5.1 and Table A5.2 in Appendix A (Statistical Analysis) for the distribution of election posters across political parties in legislative and regional head elections.

40. See Appendix C for more detail on coding and on challenges in coding the posters. Also, the complete election poster codebook is available at the author's website (https://www.colmfox.com).
41. Posters also contained appeals to women, youth, particular social classes, and specific policy interests. I classified each poster along these lines as well, but I did not use this information in the analysis.
42. See Appendix C for more detail.
43. Examples of predominantly indigenous-based Christian churches that resulted from these practices include the Batak Christian Church in Sumatra, the Protestant Church of Maluku, the Javanese Christian Church, the Toraja Church in Sulawesi, and the Protestant Church in Papua (Hoon 2013: 460). See Aritonang and Steenbrink (2008: 533–552) on the development of the Batak Christian Churches in North Sumatra and how they largely accommodated indigenous Batak beliefs.
44. These traditional religions were officially called *aliran kepercayaan* or cultural belief systems.

Chapter 6

1. *Waspada* reported on this event. See "Jurkam Golkar Sumut H. Marzuki-Kita Butuh Pemimpin Yang Beriman Dan Rasional," *Waspada*, 16 May 1997.
2. *Waspada* reported on this event and included a picture of Serta receiving the *ulos*. See "Orang Karo Dukung Serta Ginting," *Waspada*, 5 April 2009.
3. Ali Wongso Halomoan Sinaga and Anthon Sihombing were the two candidates.
4. See the section entitled "Table 6.1" in Appendix A for more detail on the supplementary data.
5. If the ethnic or religious affiliation of participants was not explicitly mentioned in an article, I coded the report as "community." For this reason, I may have underestimated the ethnic nature of some events.
6. A logit regression model was used with binary variables to control for the presence or absence of decentralization and for whether the report concerned one of the Islamic parties. The number of parties competing in the election year was also added. These control variables did not have a systematic impact and were largely insignificant. See the "Confounidng Factors" section in Appendix A, for the regression output and for more detail on the variables and alternative models.
7. The demographic data for indigenous groups and the Muslim population come from the 2010 national census.
8. In analyzing the role of the Islamic headscarf in the 2019 legislative elections, Ni'mah (2021) found that it was used largely as a religious appeal, with some nuance. She argued that different styles of headscarves were worn depending on the appeal: Islamist party candidates used the headscarf to convey piety, Muslim democratic candidates sought to convey the moderate nature of Islam, and nationalist party candidates used it more selectively when targeting the Muslim vote.

9. Poverty data are from Data and Poverty Information of Regency/Municipalities 2009. The fishing and farming GRDP data are from Financial Statistics of Regency/Municipality Governance 2008–2009. Measures of indigenous ethnic law (Adat) come from Village Potential Statistics (Potensi Desa 2003 (PODES), Badan Pusat Statistik). Data for the number of houses of worship come from Village Potential Statistics 2008 (Potensi Desa 2008 (PODES), Badan Pusat Statistik). Population data come from the 2010 national census.
10. See the section entitled "Figure 6.1" in Appendix A for the regression results, a discussion on alternative models, and details on the use of alternative measures of demographics and religious attachment.. The alternative regression models produced results very similar to those of the OLS models. Since the OLS model offered more conservative estimates for the coefficients and is more easily interpreted, I report only the OLS results.
11. As types of regional appeals, I coded regional elements such as images of the city, coast, forests, and jungles; regional maps; regional monuments; and references to the region. I found that regional appeals were more than twice as frequent in candidate-centric regional head elections than in legislative elections.
12. Specifically, I dropped the candidates who competed for the national and provincial legislative seats from the regression models, and this change had little effect on the significance of the key independent variables. For more detail, see point five in the "Figure 6.1" section in Appendix A.
13. See the section entitled "Figure 6.1" in Appendix A.
14. See the section entitled "Figure 6.1" in Appendix A.
15. Aliran originates from Clifford Geertz's writings on the three cultural streams of the Javanese people. See Ufen (2008) on aliran and how it relates to the Indonesian party system before and after the fall of Suharto.

Chapter 7

1. The other Batak groups are Pakpak/Dairi, Simalungun, Karo, Angkola, and Mandailing.
2. Figure 7.8 shows how appeals change across groups of different sizes.
3. In brief, these covariates were the percentage of villages in the district that use traditional indigenous law; the percentage of people living below the poverty line; the percentage of gross regional domestic product derived from farming or fishing; a binary variable for candidate gender; and the constituency's population. See Chapter 6 for more details on these variables.
4. See the "Figure 7.2" section in Appendix A for more detail on the religious attachment variable.
5. Underlying the predicted probabilities is a linear probability model (OLS) with robust standard errors for each of the dependent variables. A battery of robustness checks and alternative models was also used. Results were similar to those with the

OLS model. For the main OLS model and details on the robustness checks and alternative models see the "Figure 7.2" section in Appendix A.
6. In another statistical test, I calculated the mean of each type of ethnic appeal made by candidates who I predicted would make those kinds of appeals. I then compared them with all the other candidates. For instance, I calculated the mean level of indigenous bonding appeals made by viable dual-group and indigenous group candidates and compared them with the average for all the other candidates. T-tests confirmed that certain kinds of appeals were preferred by particular groups of candidates, as expected. See the section entitled "Figure 7.3" in Appendix A for the results.
7. Often, one of the most prominent elements on campaign posters is the team name. This is usually a simple word, typically combining letters from the names of the head and deputy candidates. Invariably, the letters either function as an acronym or spell out a term that has positive connotations. Team names help voters to easily remember and differentiate between the candidates.
8. See Aspinall et al. (2011) for more on the role of indigenous and religious identities in this election.
9. The same analysis was done for the legislative candidates. See the section entitled "Figure 7.7" in Appendix A, for the fractional polynomial plots for legislative candidates. While the overall patterns in the plots were similar, the levels of bridging, bonding, and bypassing appeals were flatter across various group sizes. This indicates that ethnic group size had less of an impact on the legislative candidates compared to the regional head candidates. This difference aligns with the overall argument, which predicts that ethnic group size will have a greater impact on candidates competing in candidate-centric elections than in party-centric elections.
10. In the first round of this election, Aspinall et al. (2011) found that candidates engaged in broad patterns of indigenous bridging, or what they called cross-ethnic alliance building.
11. Usman never obtained enough signatures to get on the ballot, but he did produce many entertaining posters.
12. In statistical tests (using linear models), the competitiveness of an election had a statistically significant impact only on religious bonding and bypassing appeals. In these models, I also included another potential second-level factor, incumbency. It had no effect on candidates' appeals. See the section entitled "Figure 7.10" in Appendix A for more details on these variables and the regression output.

Chapter 8

1. See Liddle (1970: 67–97) for more detail on these campaign strategies.
2. For views of the ideologies of various Indonesian political parties and, more generally, what they stand for, see Mietzner (2013), Sherlock (2004), Evans (2009), Hwang (2011: 77–79), Ufen (2008: 28–29), and Suryakusuma (1999: 592).

3. Before Indonesia's democratic transition, Pancasila was a required philosophical basis for every party. After the transition, the new laws permitted parties with any ideology to form, provided that the ideology did not conflict with Pancasila (King 2003: 51). As a result, none of the current Islamist parties oppose Pancasila.
4. Scholars have also defined a number of the nationalist parties as "presidentialist parties" and argued that these parties serve primarily as vehicles for their founding leaders' presidential ambitions (Ufen 2008; Mietzner 2013: 54–56). At the time of this study, the main three parties that fell into this category were Partai Demokrat, Hanura, and Gerindra.
5. The three other Aceh parties were the Aceh Party, SIRA, and PRA.
6. PKS was initially the "Justice Party" (Partai Keadilan) but was renamed the Prosperous Justice Party before the 2004 election.
7. For the alternative models, see the section entitled "Figure 8.2" in Appendix A.
8. See the "Figure 8.2" section in Appendix A for the full regression output.
9. The Islamist party PPNUI was excluded because the number of posters was too small for any meaningful interpretation.
10. Incidentally, the positioning of the parties on these axes was associated with vote shares in the legislative elections. Those parties with more nationalist appeals and fewer religious appeals performed better than the parties that used more Islam and less nationalism.
11. See Buehler (2013). On recruitment, see Hamayotsu (2011a); on the PKS's development as a party, see Bubalo et al. (2008: 49–74).
12. Scholars disagree on the effect of ethnic parties on political stability. Brancati (2006) presented evidence that regionally based ethnic parties contribute to conflict and instability. In contrast, Birnir (2007) found that ethnic parties help to stabilize elections in emerging democracies. Finally, Chandra (2005) argued that ethnic party competition does not have to descend into conflict (via ethnic outbidding) when numerous identity cleavages are institutionalized.
13. Aspinall (2009) explains how GAM emerged from the remnants of an Islamic movement (Darul Islam) and grew into an ethno-nationalist movement, not an Islamic movement. He argues that as the Acehnese sought independent statehood, "the justification for the struggle became a claim of distinct Acehnese national identity and history" (Aspinall 2009: 218).
14. I excluded two other parties that competed in Aceh from the analysis because they could not be considered either Islamist or indigenous parties. They were Suara Independen Rakyat Aceh (SIRA) and Partai Rakyat Aceh (PRA). SIRA had former connections with GAM, and PRA was a party of left-leaning intellectuals and activists who criticized how Islamic law was applied in Aceh. See Barter (2011: 8) and International Crisis Group (2008: 2) for brief descriptions of the parties.
15. The other control variables were not needed because there was only slight variation in ethnic demographics and economic development across the district and provincial constituencies in Banda Aceh.
16. Regressions on partisan appeals (not shown) revealed that there was no statistical difference in levels of partisan appeals between the parties.

Chapter 9

1. There was one other Christian governor of Jakarta in 1964–1965: artist Henk Ngantung, who had been appointed as deputy governor by President Sukarno in 1960 and then succeeded to the governorship when Soemarno Sosroatmodjo was named Minister of the Interior.
2. For some examples of these views at the time of the election and after, see Fauzi (2016), Lindsey (2016), Chaplin (2017), and Arifianto (2020).
3. The demonstrations were organized by the National Movement to Guard the MUI Fatwa (GNPF-MUI), a coalition of Islamist groups led by FPI founder Habib Rizieq. The main participating groups alongside the FPI were Hizbut Tahrir Indonesia (HTI), the Council for Young Islamic Scholars and Intellectuals (MIUMI), and Wahdah Islamiyah (Fealy 2016).
4. Later, a court sentenced Buni Yani, the lecturer who posted the doctored 30-second clip, to one and a half years in prison for spreading hate speech.
5. Surveys also revealed that voters disliked Ahok's mannerisms and personality (Setijadi 2017). However, this aversion to Ahok's blunt remarks, coarse language, and overall straight-talking approach are often rooted in anti-Chinese stereotypes.
6. Hadiz (2017: 267) extends the economic arguments by arguing that the three candidates were essentially proxies for competing coalitions of powerful entrenched elites, and that the mobilization of Islam during the election merely reflected "the ability of oligarchic elites to deploy the social agents of Islamic politics in their own interests."
7. These concerns are raised and explored in studies of the 2018 regional head elections by Power (2018), Setijadi (2017), Simandjuntak (2018), Warburton (2018), and Warburton et al. (2018).
8. See Warburton (2018) on West Java. Also, see Power (2018), who looked more broadly at the 2018 gubernatorial elections.
9. In the case of the unremarkable campaign in East Java, the moderate Islamic organization, Nahdlatul Ulama, may have helped to dampen any potential for polarization (Arifianto 2021).
10. In 2018, 79% of gubernatorial candidates had Islamic and nationalist party support, while in 2017 the figure was 78%.
11. The six gubernatorial elections were in West Java, East Kalimantan, North Maluku, Central Java, North Sumatra, and Southeast Sulawesi. The candidate backed by this coalition was also supported by other parties in the latter three cases. The Gerindra–PKS–PAN coalition did not support any candidates in the 2020 gubernatorial elections.
12. For a report on West Kalimantan, see Setijadi (2017). See also Power (2018); Warburton et al. (2018).
13. Social constraints on religious bonding appeals by non-Muslim candidates, as I have argued in this book, mean that religious bonding appeals will be very low in non-Muslim majority constituencies.

14. Prior to the 2017 election in Jakarta, 40% of Muslims were opposed to a non-Muslim governor of Jakarta (Mietzner and Muhtadi 2020). Meanwhile, 48% of NU and Muhammadiyah leaders held the same opinion. In contrast, 17% of these religious leaders objected to Christian political leaders in Christian majority constituencies, such as Manado in North Sulawesi (Menchik 2019).
15. These are mostly Christian-majority districts in the heartland of a particular indigenous group, such as Samosir and Toba Samosir in North Sumatra.
16. These are often urban constituencies outside Java with Christian majorities and many indigenous groups. Examples include Pematangsiantar in North Sumatra and Ambon in Maluku.
17. The 2017 gubernatorial elections were held in Aceh, Bangka Belitung Islands, Jakarta, Banten, West Sulawesi, Gorontalo, and West Papua. I also include the mayoral election in Yogyakarta. While the official governor of Yogyakarta is the unelected Hamengkubuwono X, the sultan of Yogyakarta, the city's mayor is the one who handles the day-to-day management of the province.
18. In 2018, 152 million constituents were eligible to vote in gubernatorial elections held in North Sumatra, Riau, South Sumatra, Lampung, West Java, Central Java, East Java, Bali, West Nusa Tenggara, East Nusa Tenggara, West Kalimantan, East Kalimantan, South Sulawesi, Southeast Sulawesi, Maluku, North Maluku, and Papua.
19. The 2020 gubernatorial elections were held in Riau Islands, West Sumatra, Jambi, Bengkulu, Central Kalimantan, South Kalimantan, North Kalimantan, Central Sulawesi, North Sulawesi. On the same days as the governor elections, there were 100 district head elections in 2018, 154 in 2019, and 261 in 2020.
20. Various interest groups called for a delay due to public health risks, but the government ignored their concerns and held the elections on schedule. Despite social-distancing regulations, 43% of campaign activities were face-to-face and 71 candidates tested positive for Covid-19, along with thousands of election officials. Four candidates died from the virus before the election (Wilson and Hui 2020).
21. Among these provinces, the size of the largest indigenous group ranges from 11% to 45%.
22. Although Sutarmidji identified with and was characterized as Malay, he was actually of Indian Tamil and Chinese–Javanese descent (IPAC 2018a).
23. Masyumi was the Muslim modernist party banned by Sukarno in 1960.
24. With no political experience, but with her father's support, Karolin ran for the national legislature for the first time in 2009 and was the third-leading candidate in the entire country. In the 2014 elections, she was the top vote-getter (IPAC 2018a).
25. Specifically, Cornelis's 2007 campaign described Dayaks as marginalized and argued that it was time for a Dayak governor. He also chose a Chinese running mate, the only one in the race, to appeal to the Chinese vote. The election became quite polarized along religious lines, with Muslim groups scrambling unsuccessfully to rally support behind one of the three Muslim candidates (Tanasaldy 2015), ultimately resulting in a split Muslim vote.

26. A third mixed-pair ticket was not competitive in the campaign, receiving just 7% of the vote.
27. The NGO Masyarakat Anti-Fitnah Indonesia led this campaign from a Hoax Crisis Center that it set up before the election (IPAC 2018b).
28. Third candidate, Milton Crosby, won only 6.65% of the vote.
29. See Tanasaldy (2015) and Aspinall (2017) for more detail. In Singkawang, the Muslims are mostly Malay, Javanese, and Madurese, whereas the Dayaks and Chinese are mostly Christian or Buddhist.
30. The scandal became known as "Ijazah-gate" (*Ijazah* is the word for diploma). A police investigation ensued, though it did not result in criminal charges.
31. Tomsa (2009) described the 2008 campaign as a rather muted affair with friendly competition between candidates. Karel Ralahalu won by a large margin, partly because he had built strong connections with indigenous Adat leaders across the province.
32. The elections in these provinces were not completely without incident. In Papua, there were a number of sporadic attacks on military and police personnel involved in organizing the elections, though these attacks were linked to the independence movement and not to any candidates or supporters (IPAC 2018b).
33. The only other such instances of which I am aware are Ahok's own previous candidacies—in the district head election in East Belitung in 2005 (96% Muslim) and then in the 2007 governor's race in Belitung (89% Muslim).
34. Four of these districts are in West Kalimantan (Ketapang, Kapuas Hulu, Singkawang, Melawi), three in Maluku (Seram Bagian Barat, Maluku Tengah, Buru Selatan), three in North Sumatra (Simalungun, Kota Medan, Kota Sibolga), two in Central Kalimantan (Barito Timur, Lamandau), two in West Papua (Fakfak, Sorong), and one in North Maluku (Halmahera Timur).

Chapter 10

1. Dahl did acknowledge one exception: African Americans.
2. For example, Fossati (2019) found through surveys that voter opinions on the role of Islam in politics inform Indonesians' views of democracy and policy and shape their voting behavior. Sumaktoyo et al. (2016) showed that Muslim voters are more likely to vote for religious candidates. Pepinsky et al. (2012) found that Muslims choose Islamic parties when they are uncertain about parties' economic policies.
3. Gueorguiev et al. (2018) analyzed voting patterns in the 2014 presidential elections, finding that conservative Muslims overwhelmingly supported Prabowo over Jokowi. Similarly, in their 2019 rematch, Pepinsky's (2019) analysis indicated that non-Muslims and Javanese Muslims voted for Jokowi, whereas non-Javanese Muslims favored Prabowo.
4. There are some exceptions. For instance, Hendrawan et al. (2021) gathered data on the coalition behavior of thousands of regional head candidates across Indonesia, showing that they often paid political parties for their endorsements. Also, Aspinall

et al. (2020) surveyed over 500 members of provincial legislatures, finding that they were very supportive of democracy and had a stronger commitment to liberal norms compared to general voters.
5. See Mietzner and Muhtadi (2018). To measure tolerance, respondents were asked questions on their attitudes toward such things as the holding of non-Muslim religious events or the construction of non-Muslim places of worship in their neighborhood, as well as the election of non-Muslims. Measures of radicalism drew on questions pertaining to radical behavior, such as whether respondents had donated to an organization committed to the implementation of Islamic law.
6. See Mietzner et al. (2018) for more detail. The Jakarta surveys were conducted by Saiful Mujani Research and Consulting.
7. Using surveys, Liddle and Mujani (2007) as well as Mujani and Liddle (2010) found that religious orientation was not a significant factor influencing the 1999, 2004, and 2009 legislative and presidential choices of voters. The data indicated that economic issues and party leaders were more important factors influencing voter choice.
8. Votes for the Islamic parties (including PAN and PKB) in the national legislature declined from 34% in 1999 and 35% in 2004 to 26% in 2009. See Hamayotsu (2011b) for an explanation of why some Islamic parties have floundered while others advanced in the 2009 election. Results from the 2014 election indicate that the vote for Islamic parties increased somewhat, but it declined again in 2019.
9. Exceptions include works by Edward Aspinall and his co-authors (Aspinall 2011; Aspinall et al. 2011); Van Klinken (2003, 2008); and Davidson and Henley (2007). In addition, Purdey (2006) and Setijadi (2016) have written specifically on the Indonesian Chinese.
10. See Aspinall and Sukmajati (2016), who documented candidates' campaigns across the country during the 2014 legislative election.
11. Buehler (2010), Buehler and Tan (2007), Mietzner (2006), and Ufen (2008) noted this trend in the first round of regional head elections. Rinakit's (2005) survey of 90 regional head elections found that bureaucrats and businessmen were frequent winners.
12. For instance, in 2014, the PDI-P candidate Sofyan Tan campaigned in North Sumatra for a seat in the national legislature. Many members of his campaign team also campaigned for three other Chinese candidates. These candidates coordinated their campaigns because they were all targeting a similar voter base, but they were not in direct competition with each other. One of the other three candidates was competing for a seat in the provincial legislature and two for seats in different constituencies in Medan's legislature (Damanik 2016: 79).
13. The surveys were conducted by Lembaga Survei Indonesia (LSI). For more details, see Mujani et al. (2018: 186–189) and Mietzner (2013: 43–44).
14. Other components of consociational democracy include power sharing in the executive branch and in other parts of the government (such as the civil service, judiciary, and police), a ceremonial head of state, and the option of federalism. See Lijphart (1977, 1999) as well as Grofman and Lijphart (1986).

15. Sisk and Reynolds (1998) as well as Reynolds (1998) found evidence supporting Lijphart's contention that PR politicizes ethnicity, facilitates the inclusion of ethnic minorities in the legislature, and helps to reduce ethnic conflict. However, Barkan (1998), Suberu and Diamond (2002), as well as Huber (2012) undermined Lijphart's argument by showing that majoritarian systems foster ethnic parties and politicize ethnicity above and beyond PR.
16. This is more difficult when each indigenous group is largely of a particular religion. For example, in West Kalimantan, Dayaks and Chinese are mostly non-Muslim. In the 2018 gubernatorial election, Karolin Natasa's indigenous appeals to Dayaks and Chinese were essentially appeals to non-Muslims. With her opponent Sutarmidji appealing to the Muslim majority, the election became polarized along religious lines.

References

Abdelal, Rawi, Rose McDermott, Alastair Iain Johnston, and Yoshiko M. Herrera, eds. 2009. *Measuring Identity: A Guide for Social Scientists.* New York: Cambridge University Press.

Allen, Nathan. 2018. "Electoral Systems in Context: Indonesia." In *The Oxford Handbook of Electoral Systems*, ed. Erik S. Herron, Robert J. Pekkanen, and Matthew S. Shugart. New York: Oxford University Press, 921–42.

Almond, Gabriel. 1956. "Comparative Political Systems." *Journal of Politics* 18:391–409.

Ambardi, Kuskridho. 2008. *The Making of the Indonesian Multiparty System: A Cartelized Party System and Its Origin.* The Ohio State University. https://etd.ohiolink.edu/acprod/odb_etd/etd/r/1501/10?clear=10&p10_accession_num=osu1211901025.

Anagnoson, J. Theodore. 1983. "Home Style in New Zealand." *Legislative Studies Quarterly* 8:157–75.

Ananta, Aris, Evi Nurvidya Arifin, and M. Sairi Hasbullah. 2015. *Demography of Indonesia's Ethnicity.* Singapore: ISEAS Publishing.

Anderson, Benedict R.O'G. 1972. *Java in a Time of Revolution: Occupation and Resistance, 1944-1946.* Ithaca, NY: Cornell University Press.

Anderson, Benedict R.O'G. 1983. *Imagined Communities: Reflections on the Origins and Spread of Nationalism.* London: Verso.

Anderson, Benedict R.O'G. 1990. *Language and Power: Exploring Political Cultures in Indonesia.* Ithaca, NY: Cornell University Press.

Anderson, Benedict R.O'G. 1996. "Elections and Participation in Three Southeast Asian Countries." In *The Politics of Elections in Southeast Asia*, ed. Robert H. Taylor. New York: Woodrow Wilson Center Press with Cambridge University Press, 12–33.

Anderson, Benedict R.O'G. 2013. "Impunity and Reenactment: Reflections on the 1965 Massacre in Indonesia and Its Legacy." *Asia Pacific Journal* 11:1–16.

Ankario, Kris. 2011. "A Digital Comeback for Outdoor Advertising?" *Campaigns & Elections.* https://campaignsandelections.com/campaigntech/a-digital-comeback-for-outdoor-advertising/.

Antlöv, Hans. 2004. "National Elections, Local Issues: The 1997 and 1999 National Elections in a Village on Java." In *Elections in Indonesia: The New Order and Beyond*, ed. Hans Antlöv, and Sven Cederroth. London; New York: RoutledgeCurzon, 111–37.

Arifianto, Alexander R. 2020. "Rising Islamism and the Struggle for Islamic Authority in Post-Reformasi Indonesia." *TRaNS: Trans-Regional and-National Studies of Southeast Asia* 8:37–50.

Arifianto, Alexander R. 2021. "The 2018 Simultaneous Regional Elections and 2019 Simultaneous National Elections in East Java." In *The 2018 and 2019 Indonesian Elections: Identity Politics and Regional Perspectives*, ed. Leonard C. Sebastian, and Alexander R. Arifianto. London; New York: Routledge, 100–26.

Aritonang, Jan Sihar, and Karel Adriaan Steenbrink. 2008. *A History of Christianity in Indonesia.* Leiden; Boston: Brill.

Ariyanto, Amarina, Matthew J. Hornsey, Thomas A. Morton, and Cindy Gallois. 2008. "Media Bias During Extreme Intergroup Conflict: The Naming Bias in Reports of Religious Violence in Indonesia." *Asian Journal of Communication* 18:16–31.

Aspinall, Edward. 2017. "Interpreting the Jakarta Election." *New Mandala*. https://www.newmandala.org/interpreting-jakarta-election/.

Aspinall, Edward. 2005. *Opposing Suharto: Compromise, Resistance, and Regime Change in Indonesia*. Stanford, CA: Stanford University Press.

Aspinall, Edward. 2009. *Nation and Islam: Separatist Rebellion in Aceh, Indonesia*. Stanford, CA: Stanford University Press.

Aspinall, Edward. 2010. "Indonesia in 2009: Democratic Triumphs and Trials." *Southeast Asian Affairs* 2010:102–25.

Aspinall, Edward. 2011. "Democratization and Ethnic Politics in Indonesia: Nine Theses." *Journal of East Asian Studies* 11:289–319.

Aspinall, Edward, and Ward Berenschot. 2019. *Democracy for Sale: Elections, Clientelism, and the State in Indonesia*. Ithaca, NY: Cornell University Press.

Aspinall, Edward, Sebastian Dettman, and Eve Warburton. 2011. "When Religion Trumps Ethnicity: A Regional Election Case Study From Indonesia." *Southeast Asia Research* 19:27–58.

Aspinall, Edward, Diego Fossati, Burhanuddin Muhtadi, and Eve Warburton. 2020. "Elites, Masses, and Democratic Decline in Indonesia." *Democratization* 27:505–26.

Aspinall, Edward, and Mada Sukmajati. 2016. "Patronage and Clientelism in Indonesian Electoral Politics." In *Electoral Dynamics in Indonesia: Money Politics, Patronage and Clientelism at the Grassroots*. ed. Edward Aspinall, and Mada Sukmajati Singapore: NUS Press, 1–38.

Badan Pusat Statistik. 2009. "Statistik Sosial Budaya 2009: Survei Sosial Ekonomi Nasional."

Balmas, Meital, and Tamir Sheafer. 2010. "Candidate Image in Election Campaigns: Attribute Agenda Setting, Affective Priming, and Voting Intentions." *International Journal of Public Opinion Research* 22:204–29.

Barkan, Joel D. 1998. "Rethinking the Applicability of Proportional Representation for Africa." In *Elections and Conflict Management in Africa*, ed. Timothy D. Sisk, and Andrew Reynolds. Washington, DC: US Institute of Peace Press, 57–70.

Barreto, Matt A. 2007. "Isí Se Puede! Latino Candidates and the Mobilization of Latino Voters." *American Political Science Review* 101:425–41.

Barreto, Matt A. 2010. *Ethnic Cues: The Role of Shared Ethnicity in Latino Political Participation*. Ann Arbor: University of Michigan Press.

Barreto, Matt A., and Dino N. Bozonelos. 2009. "Democrat, Republican, or None of the Above? The Role of Religiosity in Muslim American Party Identification." *Politics and Religion* 2:200–29.

Barron, Patrick. 2019. *When Violence Works: Postconflict Violence and Peace in Indonesia*. Ithaca, NY: Cornell University Press.

Barron, Patrick, Sana Jaffrey, and Ashutosh Varshney. 2016. "When Large Conflicts Subside: The Ebbs and Flows of Violence in Post-Suharto Indonesia." *Journal of East Asian Studies* 16:191–217.

Barter, Shane Joshua. 2011. "The Free Aceh Elections? The 2009 Legislative Contests in Aceh." *Indonesia* 91:113–30.

Bates, Robert H. 1974. "Ethnic Competition and Modernization in Contemporary Africa." *Comparative Political Studies* 6:457–84.

Bates, Robert H. 1983. "Modernization, Ethnic Competition and the Rationality of Politics in Contemporary Africa." In *State versus Ethnic Claims: African Policy Dilemmas*, ed. Donald Rothchild, and Victor A. Olorunsola. Boulder, CO: Westview Press, 152–71.
Bates, Robert H. 2000. "Ethnicity and Development in Africa: A Reappraisal." *AEA Papers and Proceedings* 90:131–4.
Beissinger, Mark R. 2009. "Nationalism and the Collapse of Soviet Communism." *Contemporary European History* 18:331–47.
Bell, Daniel. 1999. *The Coming of Post-Industrial Society: A Venture in Social Forecasting*. New York: Basic Books.
Berenschot, Ward. 2020. "Patterned Pogroms: Patronage Networks as Infrastructure for Electoral Violence in India and Indonesia." *Journal of Peace Research* 57:171–84.
Bertrand, Jacques. 2004. *Nationalism and Ethnic Conflict in Indonesia*. Cambridge, UK; New York: Cambridge University Press.
Birnir, Johanna Kristin. 2007. *Ethnicity and Electoral Politics*. New York: Cambridge University Press.
Bleck, Jamie, and Nicolas van de Walle. 2013. "Valence Issues in African Elections: Navigating Uncertainty and the Weight of the Past." *Comparative Political Studies* 46:1394–421.
Blee, Kathleen M., and Kimberly A. Creasap. 2010. "Conservative and Right-Wing Movements." *Annual Review of Sociology* 36:269–86.
Bowen, John R. 2003. *Islam, Law, and Equality in Indonesia: An Anthropology of Public Reasoning*. London: Cambridge University Press.
Brader, Ted. 2005. "Striking a Responsive Chord: How Political Ads Motivate and Persuade Voters By Appealing to Emotions." *American Journal of Political Science* 49:388–405.
Braeuchler, Birgit. 2011. "The Transformation of the Media Scene: From War to Peace in the Moluccas, Eastern Indonesia." In *Politics and the Media in Twenty-First Century Indonesia*, ed. Krishna Sen, and David T. Hill. London; New York: Routledge, 119–40.
Brancati, Dawn. 2006. "Decentralization: Fueling the Fire or Dampening the Flames of Ethnic Conflict and Secessionism?" *International Organization* 60:651–85.
Brass, Paul R. 1997. *Theft of an Idol: Text and Context in the Representation of Collective Violence*. Princeton, NJ: Princeton University Press.
Brass, Paul R. 2003. *The Production of Hindu-Muslim Violence in Contemporary India*. Seattle: University of Washington Press.
Brennan, Geoffrey, and Alan Hamlin. 1998. "Expressive Voting and Electoral Equilibrium." *Public choice* 95:149–75.
Brewer, Marilynn. 1999. "The Psychology of Prejudice: Ingroup Love or Outgroup Hate?" *Journal of Social Issues* 55:429–44.
Brubaker, Rogers. 2004. *Ethnicity Without Groups*. Cambridge, MA: Harvard University Press.
Bruner, Edward M. 1961. "Urbanization and Ethnic Identity in North Sumatra." *American Anthropologist* 63:508–21.
Bubalo, Anthony, Greg Fealy, and Whit Mason. 2008. *Zealous Democrats: Islamism and Democracy in Egypt, Indonesia and Turkey*. Lowy Institute Paper 25. New South Wales: Lowry Institute.
Buehler, Michael. 2009. "Suicide and Progress in Modern Nusantara." *Inside Indonesia* 97. https://www.insideindonesia.org/editions/edition-9710/suicide-and-progress-in-modern-nusantara

Buehler, Michael. 2010. "Decentralisation and Local Democracy in Indonesia: The Marginalisation of the Public Sphere." In *Problems of Democratisation in Indonesia: Elections, Institutions and Society*, ed. Edward Aspinall, and Marcus Mietzner. Singapore: ISEAS Publishing, 267–85.

Buehler, Michael. 2013. "Revisiting the Inclusion-Moderation Thesis in the Context of Decentralized Institutions." *Party Politics* 19:210–29.

Buehler, Michael, and Paige Tan. 2007. "Party-Candidate Relationships in Indonesian Local Politics: A Case Study of the 2005 Regional Election in Gowa, South Sulawesi Province." *Indonesia* 84:41–69.

Butt, Simon. 2015. *The Constitutional Court and Democracy in Indonesia*. Leiden, Boston: Brill Nijhoff.

Cain, Bruce, John Ferejohn, and Morris Fiorina. 1987. *The Personal Vote: Constituency Service and Electoral Independence*. Cambridge, MA: Harvard University Press.

Cairo, Al Arabiya. 2012. "Egypt's Presidential Campaigns to Cost Billions: Analysts." *Al Arabiya News*.

Carey, John M., and Matthew Soberg Shugart. 1995. "Incentives to Cultivate a Personal Vote: A Rank Ordering of Electoral Formulas." *Electoral Studies* 14:417–39.

Carlson, Elizabeth. 2015. "Ethnic Voting and Accountability in Africa: A Choice Experiment in Uganda." *World Politics* 67:353–85.

Caselli, Francesco, and Wilbur John Coleman. 2013. "On the Theory of Ethnic Conflict." *Journal of the European Economic Association* 11:161–92.

Cederman, Lars-Erik, Skrede Kristian Gleditsch, and Simon Hug. 2013. "Elections and Ethnic Civil War." *Comparative Political Studies* 46:387–417.

Cederman, Lars-Erik, Andreas Wimmer, and Brian Min. 2010. "Why Do Ethnic Groups Rebel? New Data and Analysis." *World Politics* 62:87–119.

Chandra, Kanchan. 2004. *Why Ethnic Parties Succeed: Patronage and Ethnic Head Counts in India*. New York: Cambridge University Press.

Chandra, Kanchan. 2005. "Ethnic Parties and Democratic Stability." *Perspectives on Politics* 3:235–52.

Chandra, Kanchan. 2006. "What is Ethnic Identity and Does it Matter?" *Annual Review of Political Science* 9:397–424.

Chandra, Kanchan. 2009. "A Constructivist Dataset on Ethnicity and Institutions." In *Measuring Identity: A Guide for Social Scientists*, ed. Rawi Abdelal, Yoshiko Herrera, Alastair Ian Johnston, and Rose McDermott. New York: Cambridge University Press, 250–77.

Chandra, Kanchan. 2011. "What Is an Ethnic Party?" *Party Politics* 17:151–69.

Chandra, Kanchan, ed. 2012. *Constructivist Theories of Ethnic Politics*. New York: Oxford University Press.

Chandra, Kanchan, and Cilanne Boulet. 2012. "A Combinatorial Language for Thinking About Ethnic Identity Change." In *Constructivist Theories of Ethnic Politics*, ed. Kanchan Chandra. New York: Oxford University Press, 179–226.

Chandra, Kanchan, and Steven Wilkinson. 2008. "Measuring the Effect of Ethnicity." *Comparative Political Studies* 41:515–63.

Chaplin, J. Chris. 2017. "Mobilising Islam for Political Gains." *New Mandala*. https://www.newmandala.org/mobilising-islam-political-gains/

Charnysh, Volha, Christopher Lucas, and Prerna Singh. 2015. "The Ties That Bind." *Comparative Political Studies* 48:267–300.

Cochrane, Joe. 2017. "Did Sectarian Politics Win in Jakarta? Only the Runoff Will Tell." *New York Times*. https://www.nytimes.com/2017/02/16/world/asia/jakarta-governor-election.html
Collier, Paul. 2001. "Implications of Ethnic Diversity." *Economic Policy* 16:129–66.
Collier, Paul, and Anke Hoeffler. 1998. "On Economic Causes of Civil War." *Oxford Economic Papers* 50:563–73.
Collingwood, L. 2020. *Campaigning in a Racially Diversifying America: When and How Cross-Racial Electoral Mobilization Works*. New York: Oxford University Press.
Connor, Walker. 1993. "Beyond Reason: The Nature of the Ethnonational Bond." *Ethnic and Racial Studies* 16:373–89.
Cox, Gary W., and Mathew D. McCubbins. 1986. "Electoral Politics as a Redistributive Game." *Journal of Politics* 48:370–89.
Crouch, Harold. 2010. *Political Reform in Indonesia After Soeharto*. Singapore: ISEAS Publishing.
D'Aprile, Shane, and Jeremy P. Jacobs. 2010. "You Ain't From Around Here." *Campaigns & Elections*, March 2010.
Dahl, Robert Alan. 1971. *Polyarchy: Participation and Opposition*. New Haven, CT: Yale University Press.
Damanik, Ahmad Taufan. 2016. "Medan, North Sumatra: Between Ethnic Politics and Money Politics." In *Electoral Dynamics in Indonesia: Money Politics, Patronage and Clientelism at the Grassroots*, ed. Edward Aspinall, and Mada Sukmajati. Singapore: NUS Press, 70–85.
Davidson, Jamie S. 2018. *Indonesia: Twenty Years of Democracy*. Cambridge, UK: Cambridge University Press.
Davidson, Jamie S. 2008a. *From Rebellion to Riots: Collective Violence on Indonesian Borneo*. Madison: University of Wisconsin Press.
Davidson, Jamie S. 2008b. "The Political Study of Ethnicity in Southeast Asia." In ed. Erik Kuhonta, Toung Vu, and Dan Slater. Stanford: Stanford University Press.
DeFrancesco Soto, Victoria M., and Jennifer L. Merolla. 2006. "Vota Por Tu Futuro: Partisan Mobilization of Latino Voters in the 2000 Presidential Election." *Political Behavior* 28:285–304.
Deutsch, Karl W. 1953. *Nationalism and Social Communication: An Inquiry Into the Foundations of Nationality*. Cambridge, MA: MIT Press.
Deutsch, Karl W. 1964. "Social Mobilization and Political Development." *American Political Science Review* 55:493–514.
Devasher, Madhavi, and Elena Gadjanova. 2021. "Cross-ethnic Appeals in Plural Democracies." *Nations and Nationalism* 27:673–89.
Dickson, Eric S., and Kenneth Scheve. 2006. "Social Identity, Political Speech, and Electoral Competition." *Journal of Theoretical Politics* 18:5–39.
Dixit, Avinash, and John Londregan. 1996. "The Determinants of Success of Special Interests in Redistributive Politics." *Journal of Politics* 58:1132–55.
Druckman, James N. 2004. "Priming the Vote: Campaign Effects in a U.S. Senate Election." *Political Psychology* 25:577–94.
Duile, Timo, and Jonas Bens. 2017. "Indonesia and the 'Conflictual Consensus': A Discursive Perspective on Indonesian Democracy." *Critical Asian Studies* 49:139–62.
Duile, Timo, and Sukri Tamma. 2021. "Political Language and Fake News: Some Considerations From the 2019 Election in Indonesia." *Indonesia and the Malay World* 49:82–105.

Dumitrescu, Delia. 2009. *Spatial Visual Communications in Election Campaigns: Political Posters Strategies in Two Democracies*. Ohio State University.

Dumitrescu, Delia. 2010. "Know Me, Love Me, Fear Me: The Anatomy of Candidate Poster Designs in the 2007 French Legislative Elections." *Political Communication* 27:20–43.

Dumitrescu, Delia. 2012. "The Importance of Being Present: Election Posters as Signals of Electoral Strength, Evidence From France and Belgium." *Party Politics* 18:941–60.

Dunning, Thad, and Lauren Harrison. 2010. "Cross-Cutting Cleavages and Ethnic Voting: An Experimental Study of Cousinage in Mali." *American Political Science Review* 104:21–39.

Easterly, William, and Ross Levine. 1997. "Africa's Growth Tragedy: Policies and Ethnic Divisions." *Quarterly Journal of Economics* 112:1203–5.

Eifert, Benn, Edward Miguel, and Daniel N. Posner. 2010. "Political Competition and Ethnic Identification in Africa." *American Journal of Political Science* 54:494–510.

Eklöf, Stefan. 1997. "The 1997 General Election in Indonesia." *Asian Survey* 37:1181–96.

Elliott, Williiam Allan. 1986. *Us and Them: A Study of Group Consciousness*. Aberdeen: Aberdeen University Press.

Ellis, Andrew. 2000. "The Politics of Electoral Systems in Transition: The 1999 Elections in Indonesia and Beyond." *Representation* 37:241–8.

Entman, Robert. 2004. *Projections of Power: Framing News, Public Opinion, and U.S. Foreign Policy*. Chicago: University of Chicago Press.

Erb, Maribeth, and Priyambudi Sulistiyanto. 2009. *Deepening Democracy in Indonesia? Direct Elections for Local Leaders (Pilkada)*. Singapore: ISEAS Publishing.

Evans, Kevin. 2009. "Political Streams in Indonesia." *Tempo*.

Fauzi, Ihsan Ali. 2016. "Mobocracy? Counting the Cost of the Rallies to 'Defend Islam.'" *Indonesia at Melbourne*.

Fealy, Greg. 2016. "Bigger Than Ahok: Explaining the 2 December Mass Rally." *Indonesia at Melbourne*.

Fealy, Greg, and Sally White. 2008. "Introduction." In *Expressing Islam: Religious Life and Politics in Indonesia*, ed. Greg Fealy, and Sally White. Singapore: ISEAS Publishing, 1–12.

Fearon, James D. 1999. "Why Ethnic Politics and 'Pork' Tend to Go Together." *Ethnic Politics and Democratic Stability Conference*. Wilder House, University of Chicago, May 21–23, 1999.

Fearon, James D. 2003. "Ethnic and Cultural Diversity By Country." *Journal of Economic Growth* 8:195.

Fearon, James D. 2008. "Ethnic Mobilization and Ethnic Violence." In *The Oxford Handbook of Political Economy*, ed. Donald Wittman, and Barry R Weingast. New York: Oxford University Press, 852–68.

Feith, Herbert. 1954. "Toward Elections in Indonesia." *Pacific Affairs* 27:236–54.

Feith, Herbert. 1957. *The Indonesian Elections of 1955*. Ithaca, NY: SEAP Publications.

Feith, Herbert. 1962. *The Decline of Constitutional Democracy*. Ithaca, NY: Cornell University Press.

Fenno, Richard F. 1978. *Home Style: House Members in Their Districts*. Boston; Toronto: Little, Brown and Company.

de Figueiredo, Rui J. P., and Barry R. Weingast. 1999. "Rationality of Fear: Political Opportunism and Ethnic Conflict." In *Military Intervention in Civil Wars*, ed. Barbara Walter, and Jack Snyder. Columbia University Press, 260–300.

Filippov, Mikhail, Peter C. Ordeshook, and Olga Shvetsova. 2004. *Designing Federalism: A Theory of Self-Sustainable Federal Institutions*. Cambridge, UK: Cambridge University Press.

Flournoy, Don Michael, ed. 1992. *Content Analysis of Indonesian Newspapers*. Yogyakarta, Indonesia: Gadjah Mada University Press.

Fossati, Diego. 2019. "The Resurgence of Ideology in Indonesia: Political Islam, Aliran and Political Behaviour." *Journal of Current Southeast Asian Affairs* 38:119–48.

Fossati, Diego. 2022. *Unity through Division: Political Islam, Representation and Democracy in Indonesia*. Cambridge, UK: Cambridge University Press.

Fox, Colm A. 2022. "Visualizing Politics in Indonesia: The Design and Distribution of Election Posters." *International Journal of Communication* 16:4187–209.

Fox, Colm A, and Jeremy Menchik. 2022. "Islamic Political Parties and Election Campaigns in Indonesia." *Party Politics* 29:608–24.

Fox, Colm A. 2018. "Is All Politics Local? Determinants of Local and National Election Campaigns." *Comparative Political Studies* 51:1899–934.

Gadjanova, E. 2017. "Ethnic Wedge Issues in Electoral Campaigns in Africa's Presidential Regimes." *African Affairs* 116:484–507.

Gadjanova, Elena. 2013. "What is an Ethnic Appeal? Policies as Metonymies for Ethnicity in the Political Rhetoric of Group Identity." *Ethnopolitics* 12:307–30.

Gadjanova, Elena. 2015. "Measuring Parties' Ethnic Appeals in Democracies." *Party Politics* 21:309–27.

Gadjanova, Elena. 2021. "Status-Quo or Grievance Coalitions: The Logic of Cross-Ethnic Campaign Appeals in Africa's Highly Diverse States." *Comparative Political Studies* 54:652–85.

Gaffar, Afan. 1992. *Javanese Voters: A Case Study of Election Under a Hegemonic Party System*. Yogyakarta, Indonesia: Gadjah Mada University Press.

Gaul, Marselinus. 2017. "Korban Persekusi 'the Ahok Effect' Tercatat Mencapai 59 Orang." *CNN Asia*.

Geertz, Clifford. 1957. "Ritual and Social Change: A Javanese Example." *American Anthropologist* 59:32–54.

Gellner, Ernest. 1983. *Nations and Nationalism*. Ithaca, NY: Cornell University Press.

Gemenis, Kostas. 2013. "What to Do (and Not to Do) With the Comparative Manifestos Project Data." *Political Studies* 16:3–23.

Gerber, Alan S., Donald P. Green, and Christopher W. Larimer. 2008. "Social Pressure and Voter Turnout: Evidence From a Large-Scale Field Experiment." *American Political Science Review* 102:33–48.

Grimmer, Justin, Solomon Messing, and Sean J. Westwood. 2012. "How Words and Money Cultivate a Personal Vote: The Effect of Legislator Credit Claiming on Constituent Credit Allocation." *American Political Science Review* 106:703–19.

Grofman, Bernard, and Arend Lijphart. 1986. "Introduction." In *Electoral Laws and Their Political Consequences*, ed. Bernard Grofman, and Arend Lijphart. New York: Agathon Press Inc., 1–15.

Gueorguiev, Dimitar, Kai Ostwald, and Paul Schuler. 2018. "Rematch: Islamic Politics, Mobilisation, and the Indonesian Presidential Election." *Political Science* 70:240–52.

Hadiz, Vedi R. 2017. "Indonesia's Year of Democratic Setbacks: Towards a New Phase of Deepening Illiberalism." *Bulletin of Indonesian Economic Studies* 53:261–78.

Hadiz, Vedi R., and Richard Robison. 2004. *Reorganising Power in Indonesia: The Politics of Oligarchy in an Age of Markets*. London; New York: Routledge.

Hale, Henry. 2004. "Explaining Ethnicity." *Comparative Political Studies* 37:458–85.

Hale, Henry E. 2008. *The Foundations of Ethnic Politics: Separatism of States and Nations in Eurasia and the World*. New York: Cambridge University Press.

Hamayotsu, Kikue. 2011a. "The Political Rise of the Prosperous Justice Party in Post-Authoritarian Indonesia: Examining the Political Economy of Islamist Mobilization in a Muslim Democracy." *Asian Survey* 51:971–92.

Hamayotsu, Kikue. 2011b. "The End of Political Islam? A Comparative Analysis of Religious Parties in the Muslim Democracy of Indonesia." *Journal of Current Southeast Asian Affairs* 30:133–59.

Haney López, Ian. 2015. *Dog Whistle Politics: How Coded Racial Appeals Have Reinvented Racism and Wrecked the Middle Class*. New York: Oxford University Press.

Hardgrave, Robert Jr. 1994. "India: The Dilemmas of Diversity." In *Nationalism, Ethnic Conflict and Democracy*, ed. Larry Diamond, and Marc F. Plattner. Baltimore: Johns Hopkins University Press, 71–85.

Hefner, Robert W. 1993. "Of Faith and Commitment: Christian Conversion in Muslim Java." In *Conversion to Christianity: Historical and Anthropological Perspectives on a Great Transformation*, ed. Robert W. Hefner. Berkeley: University of California Press, 99–125.

Hefner, Robert W. 1997. "Islamization and Democratization in Indonesia." In *Islam in an Era of Nation-States*, ed. Robert W. Hefner, and Patricia Horvatich. Honolulu: University of Hawaii Press, 75–128.

Hefner, Robert W. 2004. "Hindu Reform in an Islamizing Java: Pluralism and Peril." In *Hinduism in Modern Indonesia*, ed. Martin Ramstedt. London: Routledge, 93–108.

Helbling, Marc, Tim Reeskens, and Dietlind Stolle. 2013. "Political Mobilisation, Ethnic Diversity and Social Cohesion: The Conditional Effect of Political Parties." *Political Studies* 63:101–22.

Hendrawan, Adrianus, Ward Berenschot, and Edward Aspinall. 2021. "Parties as Pay-Off Seekers: Pre-Electoral Coalitions in a Patronage Democracy." *Electoral Studies* 69:1–10.

Henley, David, and Jamie S. Davidson. 2007. *The Revival of Tradition in Indonesian Politics: The Deployment of Adat From Colonialism to Indigenism*. London; New York: Routledge.

Hermant, Shah, and Gayatri Gati. 1994. "Development News in Elite and Non-Elite Newspapers in Indonesia." *Journalism Quarterly* 71:411–20.

Herrera, Yoshiko M. 2007. *Imagined Economies: The Sources of Russian Regionalism*. New York: Cambridge University Press.

Hill, David T. 2006. *The Press in New Order Indonesia*. Jakarta: Equinox Publishing.

Hill, David T. 2009. "Assessing Media Impact on Local Elections in Indonesia." In *Deepening Democracy in Indonesia? Direct Elections for Local Leaders (Pilkada)*, ed. Maribeth Erb, and Priyambudi Sulistiyanto. Singapore: ISEAS Publishing, 229–55.

Hobsbawm, Eric John. 1990. *Nations and Nationalism Since 1780: Programme, Myth, Reality*. Cambridge, UK: Cambridge University Press.

Hofman, Bert, and Kai Kaiser. 2004. "The Making of the 'Big Bang' and Its Aftermath: A Political Economy Perspective." In *Reforming Intergovernmental Fiscal Relations and the Rebuilding of Indonesia*, ed. Alm James, Jorge Martinez-Vazquez, and Sri Mulyani Indrawati. Edward Elgar Publishing, 15–46.

Hogan, Jackie, and Kristin Haltinner. 2015. "Floods, Invaders, and Parasites: Immigration Threat Narratives and Right-Wing Populism in the U.S.A., U.K. and Australia." *Journal of Intercultural Studies* 36:520–43.

Holtz-Bacha, Christina, and Bengt Johansson, eds. 2017. *Election Posters Around the Globe: Political Campaigning in the Public Space*. Cham, Switzerland: Springer.
Holtz-Bacha, Christina, Edoardo Novelli, and Kevin Rafter. 2017. *Political Advertising in the 2014 European Parliament Elections*. London: Palgrave Macmillan.
Hoon, Chang-Yau. 2013. "Between Evangelism and Multiculturalism: The Dynamics of Protestant Christianity in Indonesia." *Social Compass* 60:457–70.
Horowitz, Donald L. 2002. "Constitutional Design: Proposals Versus Processes." In *The Architecture of Democracy: Constitutional Design, Conflict Management, and Democracy*, ed. Andrew Reynolds. Oxford: Oxford University Press, 15–36.
Horowitz, Donald L. 1985. *Ethnic Groups in Conflict*. Berkeley: University of California Press.
Horowitz, Donald L. 1991. *A Democratic South Africa? Constitutional Engineering in a Divided Society*. Berkeley: University of California Press.
Horowitz, Donald L. 2013. *Constitutional Change and Democracy in Indonesia*. New York: Cambridge University Press.
Horowitz, Jeremy. 2016. "The Ethnic Logic of Campaign Strategy in Diverse Societies Theory and Evidence From Kenya." *Comparative Political Studies* 49:324–56.
Horowitz, Jeremy. 2022. *Multiethnic Democracy: The Logic of Elections and Policymaking in Kenya*. Oxford: Oxford University Press.
Houle, Christian. 2017. "Does Ethnic Voting Harm Democracy?" *Democratization* 25:824–42.
Howell, Julia Day. 2001. "Sufism and the Indonesian Islamic Revival." *Journal of Asian Studies* 60:701–29.
Huber, Gregory A., and John S. Lapinski. 2006. "The 'Race Card' Revisited: Assessing Racial Priming in Policy Contests." *American Journal of Political Science* 50:421–40.
Huber, John D. 2012. "Measuring Ethnic Voting: Do Proportional Electoral Laws Politicize Ethnicity?" *American Journal of Political Science* 56:986–1001.
Huber, John D. 2017. *Exclusion By Elections: Inequality, Ethnic Identity, and Democracy*. Cambridge, UK; New York: Cambridge University Press.
Huddy, Leonie, and Anna H. Gunnthorsdottir. 2000. "The Persuasive Effects of Emotive Visual Imagery." *Political Psychology* 21:745–78.
Hwang, Julie Chernov. 2011. *Peaceful Islamist Mobilization in the Muslim World: What Went Right*. New York: Palgrave Macmillan.
Ichino, Nahomi, and Noah L. Nathan. 2013. "Crossing the Line: Local Ethnic Geography and Voting in Ghana." *American Political Science Review* 107:344–61.
Inglehart, Ronald. 1990. *Culture Shift in Advanced Industrial Society*. Princeton, NJ: Princeton University Press.
Inglehart, Ronald. 1997. *Modernization and Postmodernization: Cultural, Economic and Political Change in 43 Societies*. Princeton, NJ: Princeton University Press.
International Crisis Group. 2008. "Indonesia: Pre-Election Anxieties in Aceh." *Asia Briefing* 81:1–16.
IPAC. 2018a. "The West Kalimantan Election and the Impact of the Anti-Ahok Campaign." Report No. 43:1–13.
IPAC. 2018b. "Update From IPAC on West Kalimantan and Papua." Report No. 50:1–15.
Jaffrey, Sana. 2021. "Right-Wing Populism and Vigilante Violence in Asia." *Studies in Comparative International Development* 56:223–49.
Jerit, Jennifer. 2004. "Survival of the Fittest: Rhetoric During the Course of an Election Campaign." *Political Psychology* 25:563–75.

Johnson Tan, Paige. 2002. "Anti-Party Reaction in Indonesia: Cause and Implications." *Contemporary Southeast Asia* 24:484–508.

Kahn, Kim Fridkin, and Patrick J. Kenney. 2002. "The Slant of the News: How Editorial Endorsements Influence Campaign Coverage and Citizens' Views of Candidates." *American Political Science Review* 96:381–94.

Kalyvas, Stathis N. 2006. *The Logic of Violence in Civil War*. New York: Cambridge University Press.

Kam, Cindy D., and Elizabeth J. Zechmeister. 2013. "Name Recognition and Candidate Support." *American Journal of Political Science* 57:971–86.

Kaplan, Robert D. 1993. *Balkan Ghosts: A Journey Through History*. New York: St. Martin's Press.

Kaplan, Robert D. 1994. "The Coming Anarchy." *Atlantic Monthly* 273:44–76.

Kasara, Kimuli. 2013. "Separate and Suspicious: Local Social and Political Context and Ethnic Tolerance in Kenya." *Journal of Politics* 75:921–36.

Kaufman, Stuart J. 2001. *Modern Hatreds: The Symbolic Politics of Ethnic War*. Ithaca, NY: Cornell University Press.

Kimura, Ehito. 2013. *Political Change and Territoriality in Indonesia: Provincial Proliferation*. London; New York: Routledge.

King, Dwight Y. 2003. *Half-Hearted Reform: Electoral Institutions and the Struggle for Democracy in Indonesia*. New York: Praeger.

Kirkpatrick, David D., and Mayy El Sheikh. 2012. "In Streets and Online, Campaign Fever in Egypt." *The New York Times*.

Klingemann, Hans-Dieter, Andrea Volkens, Judith Bara, and Ian Budge. 2006. *Mapping Policy Preferences Ii: Estimates for Parties, Electors and Governments in Central and Eastern Europe, European Union and Oecd, 1990–2003*. Oxford: Oxford University Press.

Kramon, Eric. 2017. *Money for Votes: The Causes and Consequences of Electoral Clientelism in Africa*. Cambridge, UK: Cambridge University Press.

Kuenzi, Michelle, and Gina Lambright. 2015. "Campaign Appeals in Nigeria's 2007 Gubernatorial Elections." *Democratization* 22:134–56.

Laitin, David D. 1986. *Hegemony and Culture: Politics and Religious Change Among the Yoruba*. Chicago: University of Chicago Press.

Laitin, David D. 1998. *Identity in Formation: The Russian-Speaking Populations in the Near Abroad*. Ithaca, NY: Cornell University Press.

Laitin, David D., and Maurits Van Der Veen. 2012. "Ethnicity and Pork: A Virtual Test of Causal Mechanisms." In *Constructivist Theories of Ethnic Politics*, ed. Kanchan Chandra. New York: Oxford University Press, 341–58.

Lamb, Kate. 2017. "Jakarta Governor Election a 'Litmus Test' of Indonesian Islam." *The Guardian*.

Lancaster, Thomas D., and W. David Patterson. 1990. "Comparative Pork Barrel Politics: Perceptions From the West German Bundestag." *Comparative Political Studies* 22:458–77.

Langer, Ana Ines. 2010. "The Politicization of Private Persona: Exceptional Leaders or the New Rule? The Case of the United Kingdom and the Blair Effect." *International Journal of Press/Politics* 15:60–76.

Lestari, Sri. 2017. "Mengapa Partai Islam Dukung Calon Non-Muslim Di Pilkada 2017 Di Papua Barat?" *BBC Indonesia*.

Lev, Daniel S. 1966. *The Transition to Guided Democracy: Indonesian Politics, 1957–1959.* Ithaca, NY: Cornell University Press.

Liddle, R. William. 1970. *Ethnicity, Party, and National Integration: An Indonesian Case Study.* New Haven; London: Yale University Press.

Liddle, R. William. 1996. "A Useful Fiction: Democratic Legitimation in New Order Indonesia." In *The Politics of Elections in Southeast Asia*, ed. Robert H. Taylor. New York: Woodrow Wilson Center Press with Cambridge University Press, 34–60.

Liddle, R. William, and Saiful Mujani. 2007. "Leadership, Party, and Religion: Explaining Voting Behavior in Indonesia." *Comparative Political Studies* 40:832–57.

Lieven, Anatol. 2016. "Clinton and Trump: Two Faces of American Nationalism." *Survival* 58:7–22.

Lijphart, Arend. 1977. *Democracy in Plural Societies: A Comparative Exploration.* New Haven, CT: Yale University Press.

Lijphart, Arend. 1999. *Patterns of Democracy: Government Forms and Performance in Thirty-Six Countries.* New Haven, CT: Yale University Press.

Lindberg, Staffan I. 2010. "What Accountability Pressures Do MPs in Africa Face and How Do They Respond? Evidence From Ghana." *Journal of Modern African Studies* 48:117–27.

Lindsey, Tim. 2016. "Blasphemy Charge Reveals Real Fault Lines in Indonesian Democracy." *Indonesia at Melbourne.* https://indonesiaatmelbourne.unimelb.edu.au/blasphemy-charge-reveals-real-fault-lines-in-indonesian-democracy/

Lipset, Seymour Martin. 1959. "Some Social Requisites of Democracy." *American Political Science Review* 53:69–105.

Lipset, Seymour Martin. 1981. *Political Man: The Social Bases of Politics.* Baltimore, MD: The Johns Hopkins University Press.

Lukman, Josa. 2019. "Poster Exhibition Celebrates Jokowi's Victory." *The Jakarta Post.*

Mansfield, Edward D., and Jack L. Snyder. 1995. "Democratization and the Danger of War." *International Security* 20:5–38.

Mansfield, Edward D., and Jack L. Snyder. 2002. "Democratic Transitions, Institutional Strength, and War." *International Organization* 56:297–337.

Mansfield, Edward D., and Jack L. Snyder. 2005. *Electing to Fight: Why Emerging Democracies Go to War.* Cambridge, MA: MIT Press.

Marsh, Michael. 2004. "None of That Post-Modern Stuff Around Here: Grassroots Campaigning in the 2002 Irish General Election." *British Elections & Parties Review* 14:245–67.

Masters, Roger D., and Denis G. Sullivan. 1983. "Nonverbal Behavior and Leadership: Emotion and Cognition in Political Information Processing." In *Explorations in Political Psychology*, ed. Shanto Iyengar, and William McGuire. Durham, NC: Duke University Press, 150–82.

Matthes, Jorg, and Desiree Schmuck. 2017. "The Effects of Anti-Immigrant Right-Wing Populist Ads on Implicit and Explicit Attitudes: A Moderated Mediation Model." *Communication Research* 44:556–81.

Mayhew, David R. 1974. *Congress: The Electoral Connection.* New Haven, CT: Yale University Press.

McCauley, John F. 2014. "The Political Mobilization of Ethnic and Religious Identities in Africa." *American Political Science Review* 108:801–16.

McIlwain, Charlton D., and Stephen M. Caliendo. 2011. *Race Appeal: How Candidates Invoke Race in U.S. Political Campaign.* Philadelphia: Temple University Press.

Melson, Robert, and Howard Wolpe. 1970. "Modernization and the Politics of Communalism: A Theoretical Perspective." *American Political Science Review* 64: 1112–30.

Menchik, Jeremy. 2016. *Islam and Democracy in Indonesia: Tolerance Without Liberalism*. New York: Cambridge University Press.

Menchik, Jeremy. 2019. "Moderate Muslims and Democratic Breakdown in Indonesia." *Asian Studies Review* 43:415–33.

Mendelberg, Tali. 1997. "Executing Hortons: Racial Crime in the 1988 Presidential Campaign." *Public Opinion Quarterly* 61:134–57.

Mendelberg, Tali. 2001. *The Race Card: Campaign Strategy, Implicit Messages, and the Norm of Equality*. Princeton, NJ: Princeton University Press.

Mendelberg, Tali. 2008. "Racial Priming Revived." *Perspectives on Politics* 6:109–23.

Mietzner, Marcus. 2006. "Local Democracy." *Inside Indonesia* 85 https://www.insideindonesia.org/archive/articles/local-democracy

Mietzner, Marcus. 2011. "Funding Pilkada: Illegal Campaign Financing in Indonesia's Local Elections." In *The State and Illegality in Indonesia*, ed. Edward Aspinall, and Gerry Van Klinken. Leiden: KITLV Press, 123–38.

Mietzner, Marcus. 2013. *Money, Power and Ideology: Political Parties in Post-Authoritarian Indonesia*. Singapore: NUS Press.

Mietzner, Marcus. 2015. "Dysfunction By Design: Political Finance and Corruption in Indonesia." *Critical Asian studies* 47:587–610.

Mietzner, Marcus, and Burhanuddin Muhtadi. 2018. "Explaining the 2016 Islamist Mobilisation in Indonesia." *Asian Studies Review* 42:479–97.

Mietzner, Marcus, and Burhanuddin Muhtadi. 2020. "The Myth of Pluralism." *Contemporary Southeast Asia* 42:58–84.

Mietzner, Marcus, and Burhanuddin Muhtadi. 2017. "Ahok's Satisfied Non-Voters: An Anatomy." *New Mandala*. https://www.newmandala.org/ahoks-satisfied-non-voters-anatomy/

Mietzner, Marcus, Burhanuddin Muhtadi, and Rizka Halida. 2018. "Entrepreneurs of Grievance: Drivers and Effects of Indonesia's Islamist Mobilization." *Journal of the Humanities and Social Sciences of Southeast Asia* 74:159–87.

Mousseau, Demet Yalcin. 2001. "Democratizing With Ethnic Divisions: A Source of Conflict?" *Journal of Peace Research* 38:547–67.

Mudde, Cas. 2007. *Populist Radical Right Parties in Europe*. Cambridge, UK: Cambridge University Press.

Mujani, Saiful, R. William Liddle, and Kuskridho Ambardi. 2018. *Voting Behaviour in Indonesia Since Democratization*. New York: Cambridge University Press.

Mujani, Saiful, and R. William Liddle. 2009. "Muslim Indonesia's Secular Democracy." *Asian Survey* 49:575–90.

Mujani, Saiful, and R. William Liddle. 2010. "Personalities, Parties, and Voters." *Journal of Democracy* 21:35–49.

National Democratic Institute. 1997. "The May 29, 1997 Parliamentary Elections in Indonesia: A Background Paper." 1–17. https://www.ndi.org/node/21591.

Ni'mah, Z. 2021. "The Political Meaning of the Hijab Style of Women Candidates." *Journal of Current Southeast Asian Affairs* 40:174–97.

Nickerson, David W. 2008. "Is Voting Contagious? Evidence From Two Field Experiments." *American political Science review* 102:49–57.

Norris, Pippa. 2000. *A Virtuous Circle: Political Communications in Post-Industrial Societies*. New York: Cambridge University Press.

Norris, Pippa. 2004. *Electoral Engineering: Voting Rules and Political Behavior*. Cambridge, UK; New York: Cambridge University Press.

Nteta, Tatishe, and Brian Schaffner. 2013. "Substance and Symbolism: Race, Ethnicity, and Campaign Appeals in the United States." *Political Communication* 30:232–53.

Nyczepir, Dave. 2012. "Digital Billboards Thrive on Campaign Trail." *Campaigns & Elections*. https://campaignsandelections.com/creative/digital-billboards-thrive-on-campaign-trail/

Nyczepir, Dave. 2013. "Digital Billboards Spawn Lawsuit." *Campaigns & Elections*. https://campaignsandelections.com/industry-news/digital-billboards-spawn-lawsuit/

Oey, Hong Lee. 1971. *Indonesian Government and Press During Guided Democracy*. Zug, Switzerland: Inter Documentation Company.

Panagopoulos, Costas. 2009. "Street Fight: The Impact of a Street Sign Campaign on Voter Turnout." *Electoral Studies* 28:309–13.

Peffley, Mark, and Jon Hurwitz. 2002. "The Racial Components of 'Race-Neutral' Crime Policy Attitudes." *Political Psychology* 23:59–75.

Peffley, Mark, Jon Hurwitz, and Paul M. Sniderman. 1997. "Racial Stereotypes and Whites' Political Views of Blacks in the Context of Welfare and Crime." *American Journal of Political Science* 41:30–60.

Peluso, Nancy Lee. 2008. "A Political Ecology of Violence and Territory in West Kalimantan." *Asia Pacific Viewpoint* 49:48–67.

Pepinsky, Thomas B. 2009. *Economic Crises and the Breakdown of Authoritarian Regimes: Indonesia and Malaysia in Comparative Perspective*. New York: Cambridge University Press.

Pepinsky, Thomas B. 2019. "Islam and Indonesia's 2019 Presidential Election." *Asia Policy* 26:54–62.

Pepinsky, Thomas B., R. William Liddle, and Saiful Mujani. 2012. "Testing Islam's Political Advantage: Evidence From Indonesia." *American Journal of Political Science* 56:584–600.

Petersen, Roger Dale. 2002. *Understanding Ethnic Violence: Fear, Hatred, and Resentment in Twentieth-Century Eastern Europe*. New York: Cambridge University Press.

Petersen, Roger Dale. 2012. "Identity, Rationality, and Emotion in the Processes of State Disintegration and Reconstruction." In *Constructivist Theories of Ethnic Politics*, ed. Kanchan Chandra. New York: Oxford University Press, 387–421.

Pierskalla, Jan H. 2016. "Splitting the Difference? The Politics of District Creation in Indonesia." *Comparative politics* 48:249–68.

Platzdasch, Bernhard. 2009. "Down But Not Out: Islamic Parties Did Not Do Well, But Islamic Politics Are Going Mainstream." *Inside Indonesia* 97. https://www.insideindonesia.org/editions/edition-9710/down-but-not-out

Pomper, Gerald. 1966. "Ethnic and Group Voting in Nonpartisan Municipal Elections." *Public Opinion Quarterly* 30:79–97.

Posner, Daniel N. 2004. "The Political Salience of Cultural Difference: Why Chewas and Tumbukas Are Allies in Zambia and Adversaries in Malawi." *American Political Science Review* 98:1–17.

Posner, Daniel N. 2005. *Institutions and Ethnic Politics in Africa*. New York: Cambridge University Press.

Powell, G. Bingham. 1982. *Contemporary Democracies: Participation, Stability, and Violence*. Cambridge, MA: Harvard University Press.

Power, Thomas, and Eve Warburton, eds. 2020. *Democracy in Indonesia: From Stagnation to Regression?* Singapore: ISEAS Publishing.

Power, Thomas P. 2018. "Jokowi's Authoritarian Turn and Indonesia's Democratic Decline." *Bulletin of Indonesian Economic Studies* 54:307–38.

Protsyk, Oleh, and Stela Garaz. 2013. "Politicization of Ethnicity in Party Manifestos." *Party Politics* 19:296–318.

Purdey, Jemma. 2006. *Anti-Chinese Violence in Indonesia: 1996–1999*. Singapore: NUS Press.

Putnam, Robert D., ed. 2002. *Democracies in Flux: The Evolution of Social Capital in Contemporary Society*. New York: Oxford University Press.

Qodari, Muhammad. 2010. "The Professionalisation of Politics: The Growing Role of Polling Organisations and Political Consultants." In *Problems of Democrtisation in Indonesia: Elections, Institutions and Society*, ed. Edward Aspinall, and Marcus Mietzner. Singapore: ISEAS Publishing, 122–39.

Rabushka, Alvin, and Kenneth Shepsle. 1972. *Politics in Plural Societies: A Theory of Democratic Instability*. Columbus, OH: Merrill.

Rafsadie, Irsyad, Dyah Ayu Kartika, and Siswo Mulyartono. 2020. "16. Rumour, Identity and Violence in Contemporary Indonesia: Evidence from Elections in West Kalimantan." In *Democracy in Indonesia: From Stagnation to Regression?*, ed. Thomas Power, and Eve Warburton. Singapore: ISEAS Publishing, 326–45.

Reilly, Benjamin. 2000. "Democracy, Ethnic Fragmentation, and Internal Conflict: Confused Theories, Faulty Data, and the 'Crucial Case' of Papua New Guinea." *International Security* 25:162–85.

Reilly, Benjamin. 2001. *Democracy in Divided Societies: Electoral Engineering for Conflict Management*. New York: Cambridge University Press.

Reilly, Benjamin. 2006a. *Democracy and Diversity: Political Engineering in the Asia-Pacific*. New York: Oxford University Press.

Reilly, Benjamin. 2006b. "Political Engineering and Party Politics in Conflict-Prone Societies." *Democratization* 13:811–27.

Reilly, Benjamin. 2007. "Democratization and Electoral Reform in the Asia-Pacific Region is There an 'Asian Model' of Democracy?" *Comparative Political Studies* 40:1350–71.

Reny, Tyler T., Loren Collingwood, and Ali A. Valenzuela. 2019. "Vote Switching in the 2016 Election: How Racial and Immigration Attitudes, Not Economics, Explain Shifts in White Voting." *Public Opinion Quarterly* 83:91–113.

Reynal-Querol, Marta. 2002. "Ethnicity, Political Systems, and Civil Wars." *Journal of Conflict Resolution* 46:29–54.

Reynolds, Andrew. 1998. "Elections in Southern Africa: The Case for Proportionality, a Rebuttal." In *Elections and Conflict Management in Africa*, ed. Timothy D. Sisk, and Andrew Reynolds. Washington DC: US Institute of Peace Press, 71–80.

Ricks, Jacob. 2020. "The Effect of Language on Political Appeal: Results From a Survey Experiment in Thailand." *Political Behavior* 42:83–104.

Riker, William. 1962. *The Theory of Political Coalitions*. New Haven, CT: Yale University Press.

Riker, William. 1964. *Federalism: Origin, Operation, Significance*. Boston: Little, Brown and Company.

Riker, William. 1990. "Heresthetic and Rhetoric in Spatial Models." In *Advances in the spatial theory of voting*, ed. James M. Enelow, and Melvin J. Hinich. New York: Cambridge University Press, 46–65.

Rinakit, Sukardi. 2005. "Indonesian Regional Elections in Praxis." *RSIS Commentaries* 65:1–4.

Robert, A Dahl. 1961. *Who Governs? Democracy and Power in an American City*. New Haven; London: Yale University Press.

Roseman, Ira, Robert P. Abelson, and Michael F. Ewing. 1986. "Emotion and Political Cognition: Emotional Appeals in Political Communication." In *Political Cognition: The 19th Annual Carnegie Mellon Symposium on Cognition*, ed. Richard R. Lau, and David O. Sears. Hillsdale, NJ: Lawrence Erlbaum, 279–94.

Rostow, Walt W. 1960. *The Stages of Economic Growth: A Non-Communist Manifesto*. Cambridge, UK: Cambridge University Press.

Ruane, Joseph, and Jennifer Todd. 2010. "Ethnicity and Religion: Redefining the Research Agenda." *Ethnopolitics* 9:1–8.

Saideman, Stephen M., David J. Lanoue, Michael Campenni, and Samuel Stanton. 2002. "Democratization, Political Institutions, and Ethnic Conflict: A Pooled Time-Series Analysis,1985–1998." *Comparative Political Studies* 35:103–29.

Samuels, David J. 1999. "Incentives to Cultivate a Party Vote in Candidate-Centric Electoral Systems: Evidence From Brazil." *Comparative Political Studies* 32:478–518.

Schiller, Jim. 1999. "The 1997 Indonesian Elections: 'Festival of Democracy' or Costly 'Fiction'?" *Centre for Asia Pacific Initiatives* #22:1–27.

Sebastian, Leonard C., and Alexander R. Arifianto. 2021. "Conclusion: What Have We Learned?" In *The 2018 and 2019 Indonesian Elections: Identity Politics and Regional Perspectives*, ed. Leonard C. Sebastian, and Alexander R. Arifianto. London; New York: Routledge, 299–300.

Sen, Krishna, and David Hill. 2000. *Media, Culture, and Politics in Indonesia*. Melbourne, New York: Oxford University Press.

Setijadi, Charlotte. 2016. "'A Beautiful Bridge': Chinese Indonesian Associations, Social Capital and Strategic Identification in a New Era of China–Indonesia Relations." *Journal of Contemporary China* 25:822–35.

Setijadi, Charlotte. 2018. "West Kalimantan Gubernatorial Election 2018: Identity Politics Proves Decisive." *ISEAS* 58:1–10.

Setijadi, Charlotte. 2017. "Ahok's Downfall and the Rise of Islamist Populism in Indonesia." *ISEAS* 38:1–9.

Shair-Rosenfield, Sarah. 2019. *Electoral Reform and the Fate of New Democracies: Lessons From the Indonesian Case*. Ann Arbor: University of Michigan Press.

Shair-Rosenfield, Sarah. 2012. "The Alternative Incumbency Effect: Electing Women Legislators in Indonesia." *Electoral Studies* 31:576–87.

Shams, Hafiz Noor. 2010. "Why Do We Have Poster Wars?" *The Malaysian Insider*.

Sherlock, Stephen. 2004. "The 2004 Indonesian Elections: How the System Works and What the Parties Stand for." *Center for Democratic Institutions* 1–44. Canberra: Australian National University.

Sherlock, Stephen. 2005. "Indonesia's Regional Representative Assembly: Democracy, Representation and the Regions." *Centre for Democratic Institutions* 1:1–48.

Sherlock, Stephen. 2009. "Indonesia's 2009 Elections: The New Electoral System and the Competing Parties." *Centre for Democratic Institutions* 1:1–44.

Shugart, Matthew Soberg, Melody Ellis Valdini, and Kati Suominen. 2005. "Looking for Locals: Voter Information Demands and Personal Vote-Earning Attributes of Legislators Under Proportional Representation." *American Journal of Political Science* 49:437–49.

Sidel, John Thayer. 2006. *Riots, Pogroms, Jihad: Religious Violence in Indonesia*. Ithaca, NY: Cornell University Press.

Simandjuntak, Deasy. 2018. "North Sumatra's 2018 Election: Identity Politics Ruled the Day." *ISEAS* 60:1–11.

Siregar, Wahida Zein Br. 2005. "Parliamentary Representation of Women in Indonesia: The Struggle for a Quota." *Asian Journal of Women's Studies* 11:36–72.

Sisk, Timothy D., and Andrew Reynolds. 1998. *Elections and Conflict Management in Africa*. Washington, DC: US Institute of Peace Press.

Siswoyo, Harry, Anwar Sadat, Dwi Royanto, Nur Faishal, and Adi Suparman. 2017. "Efek Ahok Mungkinkah Menyebar Ke Tanah Jawa?" *Viva.co.id*.

Slater, Dan. 2004. "Indonesia's Accountability Trap: Party Cartels and Presidential Power After Democratic Transition." *Indonesia* 78:61–92.

Slater, Dan. 2018. "Party Cartelization, Indonesian-Style: Presidential Power-Sharing and the Contingency of Democratic Opposition." *Journal of East Asian Studies* 18:23–46.

Smith, Benjamin. 2008. "The Origins of Regional Autonomy in Indonesia: Experts and the Marketing of Political Interests." *Journal of East Asian Studies* 8:211–34.

Snyder, Jack L. 2000. *From Voting to Violence: Democratization and Nationalist Conflict*. New York: W. W. Norton.

Sokhey, Anand Edward, and Scott D McClurg. 2012. "Social Networks and Correct Voting." *Journal of Politics* 74:751–64.

Steele, Janet. 2003. "Representations of 'the Nation' in Tempo Magazine." *Indonesia* 76:127–45.

Stepan, Alfred. 2001. *Arguing Comparative Politics*. Oxford: Oxford University Press.

Stephens-Dougan, LaFleur. 2020. *Race to the Bottom: How Racial Appeals Work in American Politics*. Chicago: University of Chicago Press.

Stevens, Daniel, and Jeffrey A. Karp. 2012. "Leadership Traits and Media Influence in Britain." *Political Studies* 60:787–808.

Stokes, Susan. 2005. "Perverse Accountability: A Formal Model of Machine Politics With Evidence From Argentina." *American Political Science Review* 99:315–25.

Suberu, Rotimi T., and Larry Diamond. 2002. "Institutional Design, Ethnic Conflict Management, and Democracy in Nigeria." In *The Architecture of Democracy: Constitutional Design, Conflict Management, and Democracy*, ed. Andrew Reynolds. Oxford: Oxford University Press, 400–28.

Sukma, Rizal. 2010. "Indonesia's 2009 Elections: Defective System, Resilient Democracy." In *Problems of Democratisation in Indonesia*, ed. Edward Aspinall, and Marcus Mietzner. Singapore: ISEAS Publishing, 53–74.

Sulaiman, Teuku Muhammad Jafar. 2016. "Bener Meriah, Aceh: Money Politics and Ethnicity in a New Electoral District." In *Electoral Dynamics in Indonesia: Money Politics, Patronage and Clientelism at the Grassroots*, ed. Edward Aspinall, and Mada Sukmajati. Singapore: NUS Press, 54–69.

Sulkin, Tracy. 2009. "Campaign Appeals and Legislative Action." *Journal of Politics* 71:1093–108.

Sumaktoyo, Nathanael Gratias. 2021. "Ethnic and Religious Sentiments in Indonesian Politics: Evidence From the 2017 Jakarta Gubernatorial Election." *Journal of East Asian Studies* 21:141–64.

Sumaktoyo, Nathanael Gratias, Victor Ottati, and Vinaya Untoro. 2016. "The Paradoxical Religiosity Effect: Religion and Politics in Indonesia and the United States." *Politics and Religion* 9:481–507.

Suryadinata, Leo, Evi Nurvidya Arifin, and Aris Ananta. 2003. *Indonesia's Population: Ethnicity and Religion in a Changing Political Landscape*. Singapore: ISEAS Publishing.

Suryakusuma, Julia. 1999. *Almanak Parpol Indonesia: Pemilu'99*. Bogor: SMK Grafika Mardi Yuana.

Suwondo, Kutut, Arief Budiman, and Pradjarta Dirdjonsanjoto. 1987. *Pemilu Dalam Poster: Jawa Tengah 1982*. Jakarta: Pustaka Sinar Harapan.

Tajfel, Henri. 1982. *Social Identity and Intergroup Relations*. New York: Cambridge University Press.

Tajima, Yuhki. 2014. *The Institutional Origins of Communal Violence: Indonesia's Transition From Authoritarian Rule*. New York: Cambridge University Press.

Tanasaldy, Taufiq. 2015. "A Decade After the Reform: Political Activism of the Chinese of West Kalimantan, Indonesia." *Asian Ethnicity* 16:446–79.

Tanuwidjaja, Sunny. 2010. "Political Islam and Islamic Parties in Indonesia: Critically Assessing the Evidence of Islam's Political Decline." *Contemporary Southeast Asia* 32:29–49.

Tavits, Margit. 2008. "The Role of Parties' Past Behavior in Coalition Formation." *American Political Science Review* 102:495–507.

Taylor, Charles Fernandes. 2017. "Ethnic Politics and Election Campaigns in Contemporary Africa: Evidence From Ghana and Kenya." *Democratization* 24:951–69.

Thames, Frank C., and Margaret S. Williams. 2010. "Incentives for Personal Votes and Women's Representation in Legislatures." *Comparative Political Studies* 43:1575–600.

Tiola Primarizki, Adhi. 2021. "The 2018 Simultaneous Regional Elections and 2019 Simultaneous National Elections in North Sumatra." In *The 2018 and 2019 Indonesian Elections: Identity Politics and Regional Perspectives*, ed. Leonard C. Sebastian, and Alexander R. Arifianto. London, New York: Routledge, 152–78.

Toha, Risa. 2017. "Political Competition and Ethnic Riots in Democratic Transition: A Lesson From Indonesia." *British Journal of Political Science* 47:631–51.

Toha, Risa. 2021. *Rioting for Representation: Local Ethnic Mobilization in Democratizing Countries*. Cambridge, UK: Cambridge University Press.

Tomsa, Dirk. 2007. "Party Politics and the Media in Indonesia: Creating a New Dual Identity for Golkar." *Contemporary Southeast Asia* 29:77–96.

Tomsa, Dirk. 2009. "Electoral Democracy in a Divided Society: The 2008 Gubernatorial Election in Maluku, Indonesia." *South East Asia Research* 17:229–59.

Transue, John E. 2007. "Identity Salience, Identity Acceptance, and Racial Policy Attitudes: American National Identity as a Uniting Force." *American Journal of Political Science* 51:78–91.

Turner, Mark, Owen Podger, Maria Sumardjono, and Wayan Tirthayasa. 2003. *Decentralisation in Indonesia: Redesigning the State*. Canberra: Asia Pacific Press.

Ufen, Andreas. 2008. "From Aliran to Dealignment: Political Parties in Post-Suharto Indonesia." *South East Asia Research* 16:5–41.

Ufen, Andreas. 2011. "Direct Local Elections and the Fragmentation of Party Organization in Indonesia." *Annual Meeting of the American Political Science Association*. Seattle.

Valentino, Nicholas A., Ted Brader, and Ashley E. Jardina. 2013. "Immigration Opposition Among Us Whites: General Ethnocentrism or Media Priming of Attitudes About Latinos." *Political Psychology* 34:149–66.

Valentino, Nicholas A., Vincent L. Hutchings, and Ismail K. While. 2002. "Cues That Matter: How Political Ads Prime Racial Attitudes During Campaigns." *American Political Science Review* 96:75–90.

Valentino, Nicholas A., Fabian G. Neuner, and L. Matthew Vandenbroek. 2018. "The Changing Norms of Racial Political Rhetoric and the End of Racial Priming." *Journal of Politics* 80:757–71.

Valenzuela, Alia, and Melissa R. Michelson. 2016. "Turnout, Status, and Identity: Mobilizing Latinos to Vote With Group Appeals." *American Political Science Review* 110:615–30.

van Klinken, Gerry. 2003. "Ethnicity in Indonesia." In *Ethnicity in Asia*, ed. Colin Mackerras. London, New York: RoutledgeCurzon, 64–87.

van Klinken, Gerry. 2007. *Communal Violence and Democratization in Indonesia: Small Town Wars*. London, New York: Routledge.

van Klinken, Gerry. 2008. "The Limits of Ethnic Clientelism in Indonesia." *Review of Indonesian and Malaysian Affairs* 42:35–65.

Varshney, Ashutosh. 2002. *Ethnic Conflict and Civic Life: Hindus and Muslims in India*. New Haven, CT: Yale University Press.

Varshney, Ashutosh. 2008. "Analyzing Collective Violence in Indonesia: An Overview." *Journal of East Asian Studies* 8:341–59.

Vogt, Manuel, Nils-Christian Bormann, Seraina Rüegger, Lars-Erik Cederman, Philipp Hunziker, and Luc Girardin. 2015. "Integrating Data on Ethnicity, Geography, and Conflict: The Ethnic Power Relations Data Set Family." *Journal of Conflict Resolution* 59:1327–42.

Voionmaa, Kaarlo. 2004. "Elections and the Media: A Discourse Analysis of the 1997 and 1999 Elections in Indonesia." In *Elections in Indonesia: The New Order and Beyond*, ed. Hans Antlöv, and Sven Cederroth. London; New York: RoutledgeCurzon, 138–61.

Volkan, Vamik D. 1988. *The Need to Have Enemies and Allies: From Clinical Practice to International Relationships*. Northvale, NJ: Jason Aronson.

Wantchekon, Leonard. 2003. "Clientelism and Voting Behavior: Evidence From a Field Experiment in Benin." *World Politics* 55:399–422.

Warburton, Eve. 2016. "Southeast Sulawesi: Money Politics in Indonesia's Nickel Belt." In *Electoral Dynamics in Indonesia: Money Politics, Patronage and Clientelism at the Grassroots*, ed. Edward Aspinall, and Mada Sukmajati. Singapore: NUS Press, 341–63.

Warburton, Eve. 2018. "West Java's 2018 Regional Elections: Reform, Religion, and the Rise of Ridwan Kamil." *ISEAS* 42:1–11.

Warburton, Eve, and Liam Gammon. 2017. "Class Dismissed? Economic Fairness and Identity Politics in Indonesia." *New Mandala*. https://www.newmandala.org/economic-injustice-identity-politics-indonesia/

Warburton, Eve, Deasy Simandjuntak, and Charlotte Setijadi. 2018. "Indonesia's 2018 Regional Elections: Between Local and National Politics." *ISEAS* 31:1–9.

Ward, Ken. 1974. *The 1971 Election in Indonesia*. Monash University Publishing.

Wilkinson, Steven. 2004. *Votes and Violence: Electoral Competition and Ethnic Riots in India*. New York: Cambridge University Press.

Willnat, Lars, Roshni Verghese, and Rashad Mammadov. 2017. "Symbols, Slogans, and Charisma: Political Posters in India's 2014 National Election." In *Election Posters Around the Globe*, Springer, 187–209.

Wilson, Ian. 2010. "The Rise and Fall of Political Gangsters in Indonesian Democracy." In *Problems of Democratisation in Indonesia: Elections, Institutions and Society*, ed. Edward Aspinall, and Marcus Mietzner. Singapore: ISEAS Publishing, 199–218.

Wilson, Ian. 2017. "Jakarta: Inequality and the Poverty of Elite Pluralism." *New Mandala*. https://www.newmandala.org/jakarta-inequality-poverty-elite-pluralism/

Wilson, Ian. 2016. "Making Enemies Out of Friends." *New Mandala*. https://www.newmandala.org/making-enemies-friends/

Wilson, Ian, and Yew-Foong Hui. 2020. "Signs of Democratic Contraction and Recentralisation of Power in Indonesia's 2020 Regional Elections." *ISEAS* 140:1–12.

Wimmer, Andreas. 2013. *Ethnic Boundary Making: Institutions, Power, Networks*. New York: Oxford University Press.

Wimmer, Andreas, Lars-Erik Cederman, and Brian Min. 2009. "Ethnic Politics and Armed Conflict. A Configurational Analysis of a New Global Dataset." *American Sociological Review* 74:316–37.

Wucherpfennig, Julian, Nils B. Weidmann, Luc Girardin, Lars-Erik Cederman, and Andreas Wimmer. 2011. "Politically Relevant Ethnic Groups Across Space and Time: Introducing the Geoepr Dataset." *Conflict Management and Peace Science* 28:423–37.

Young, Crawford. 1976. *The Politics of Cultural Pluralism*. Madison: University of Wisconsin Press.

Index

For the benefit of digital users, indexed terms that span two pages (e.g., 52–53) may, on occasion, appear on only one of those pages.

Tables and figures are indicated by *t* and following the page number

Aceh
  constituency boundaries in, 233
  ethnic bonding appeals in, 20, 193*t*, 209*t*
  legislative elections of 2009 in, 181, 188–90, 191*f*
  posters from the 2009 legislative elections in, 192*f*
  regional parties' importance in, 178
  separatist movement in, 14, 78, 86, 188
Aceh Sovereignty Party (PDA), 179, 182*t*, 188–89, 189*t*, 190, 192*f*
Aceh Unity Party (PBA), 179, 182*f*, 188–89, 189*t*
Adat (indigenous law), 135–36, 141
Ahok (Basuki "Ahok" Purnama)
  Chinese ethnic background of, 197, 200, 212
  economic development emphasis of, 200–1
  election loss (2017) of, 200–1
  imprisonment for blasphemy of, 200
  Islamist mobilization against, 197–98, 200–1, 214–16
  Qur'an speech controversy (2016) and, 197–98, 200
  religious polarization in the campaign (2017) against, 20
  running mate of, 199–200
Ambardi, Kuskridho, 107–8
Ambon (Indonesia), 163, 165–66, 218–19
Amin, Ma'ruf, 107
Anies Baswedan, 199–202
Arab Americans, 23, 28
Argentina, 69–70

Asian financial crisis (1997–98), 144–45, 76
Aspinall, Edward, 83–84, 229–30
Australia, 105

Bali, 112*t*, 117, 209*t*, 219
Bambang Soetopo, 157–59, 158*f*
Bambang Supriyanto, 157–59
Banda Aceh (Indonesia), 189–90, 191*f*, 192*f*
Barkat Shah, 161*f*, 163
Batak
  Batak Karo and, 99, 129–30, 159–63, 173–74
  Batak Mandailing and, 98, 129–30
  Batak Pakpak and, 129–30
  Batak Toba and, 146–47, 159, 163, 165, 167
  indigenous electoral appeals and, 129, 167
  in Medan, 160–63
  nationalist bonding appeals by, 167
  North Sumatra province and, 98
  in Pematangsiantar, 165
Belgium, 105–6
Belitung Islands, 209*t*
Bengkulu, 112*t*, 209*t*, 212–14, 213*t*
Boundeth Damanik, 161*f*
Brazil, 47, 70, 230
Buddhists in Indonesia, 15, 160, 162–63, 214
Buni Yani, 197–98, 280n.4
Bush, George H. W., 27–28

candidate-centric elections
    candidate nomination processes
        and, 47, 69
    connections between candidates and
        constituents in, 228
    consultancy firms and, 228
    costs of campaigns in, 229–30
    decline in Indonesians' party
        identification and, 230
    in developing countries, 48
    ethnic appeals and, 8, 8f, 9–10, 19–20,
        34, 49, 50, 50f, 51f, 125–26, 127t,
        128–32, 133
    ethnic politicization and, 11, 15–16, 20, 48
    indigenous appeals and, 130–31, 137–
        38, 137f
    Indonesia's movement toward, 68, 80,
        145, 193
    open-list systems and, 7, 69
    personal vote strategies and, 7, 46, 47–48
    pork-barrel politics and, 7, 8, 47–48
    regional head elections and, 136–
        37, 147–48
    religious appeals and, 227
Carey, John M., 47, 68–69, 268n.14
Catholics in Indonesia, 15, 116, 146, 159
Central Java, 112t, 202–3, 209, 209t, 220.
    See also Salatiga (Indonesia)
Central Kalimantan, 117
Central Sulawesi, 212, 213t
Chandra, Kanchan, 24, 28–29, 57–58, 94–95
Chinese Indonesians
    Ahok's campaign for governor of Jakarta
        and, 197, 200, 212
    Chinese language publications and, 99
    ethnic-based violence against, 14, 98
    in Medan, 98, 160, 162–63
Christians in Indonesia
    in Ambon, 165
    in Karo, 159–60
    in Maluku, 115, 117
    overall numbers of, 15
    in Pematangsiantar, 165
    in Salatiga, 170–72
    as viable indigenous candidates, 155–56
    in West Kalimantan, 115, 214
    in West Papua, 115, 117
closed lists
    ethnic politics and, 231

Indonesian Constitution Court's
    invalidation (2008) of, 82
Indonesian legislative elections and, 85t
Indonesian legislative elections of 1955
    and, 72
Indonesian legislative elections of 1999
    and, 78
Indonesian legislative elections of 2004
    and, 79, 80–81
New Order era legislative elections
    and, 75–76
party-centric elections and, 7
proportional representation systems
    and, 69–70, 73, 75, 80–81
Confucians in Indonesia, 15, 116–17
Connor, Walker, 1, 61
Constitutional Court (Indonesia),
    82, 88, 90
Constructivist Dataset on Ethnicity and
    Institutions (CDEI), 94–95
Cornelis, 215–16
critical junctures
    democratic transitions as, 63–64, 142–44
    as potential explanation for ethnic
        appeals, 63–64, 142–45
crowded fields of co-ethnic candidates,
    10–11, 59, 147, 169, 172–74
cultural modernization, 60, 62–63, 135–
    36, 141–42

Dahl, Robert, 224
Darwanti, Rosa, 157–59, 158f
Dayak Customary Council (DAD), 215–16
Dayaks, 14, 214–16, 281n.25, 284n.16
Delyuzar, 174f
Democratic Party (United States), 29, 46
Depari, Sumbul Sembiring, 158f
Diah Sunarsasi, 157–59, 158f
digital billboards, 104
Djarot Syaiful Hidayat, 199–200, 217
"dog whistles," 23, 27–28
Dukakis, Michael, 27–28
Dzulmi Eldin, 161f

East Java, 112t, 202–3, 209t
East Kalimantan, 112t, 203, 213t
East Nusa Tenggara, 112t, 117,
    209t, 219–20
East Timor, 14, 78, 86

INDEX 307

Edy Rahmayadi, 203, 217, 222, 232
Egypt, 105
election posters in Indonesia
    design of, 107, 108
    endorsements and, 139–40, 139t
    formats of, 104
    indigenous imagery in, 113
    legislative elections of 1955 and, 106–7
    legislative elections of 2009 and, 16–17, 109, 112t, 134–40, 141–42
    low cost of producing, 108
    nationalist imagery in, 113
    New Order era (1965–98) and, 106–7
    partisan appeals and imagery in, 113, 114–15, 115f
    public opinion regarding, 107–8
    regional head elections (2010–12) and, 16–17, 109–10, 134–40
    regional head elections of 2010 and, 112t
    visual nature of, 17, 19, 104–5, 108–9, 111–13
ethnic appeals
    candidate attributes and, 131–32
    candidate-centric elections and, 8, 8f, 9–10, 19–20, 34, 49, 50, 50f, 51f, 125–26, 127t, 128–32, 133
    critical junctures as potential explanation for, 63–64, 142–45
    crowded fields of co-ethnic candidates and, 10–11, 59, 147, 169, 172–74
    cultural modernization as potential explanation for, 62–63
    definition of, 5–6, 30–32
    discursive analysis of, 39
    election posters and, 95
    electorally viable ethnic groups and, 44, 51f, 149–52
    endorsement of candidates and, 49, 129–30, 139–40
    ethnic attachment as potential explanation for, 60–62, 135–36, 140–41
    ethnic group size's impact on, 167–69, 168f
    events and, 128–29
    explicit versus implicit forms of, 27–29, 30, 30t
    goals of, 30t, 31
    group appeals and, 130–31
    to groups someone does not belong to, 44
    Indonesia's increasing levels of, 226–28
    majoritarian electoral systems and, 6–7, 51–52
    means of expressing, 30–31, 30t
    Medan mayoral campaign (2010) and, 1–2
    minimum winning size logic and, 3–4, 32, 44, 45, 146, 155
    multiple ethnic dimensions and, 152–69, 153t
    newspaper coverage of elections in Indonesia and, 95, 96–100
    online forums and, 95–96
    party-centric elections and, 8–9, 8f, 10, 34, 51f, 56, 125–26, 127t, 128–32
    political parties as a potential factor constraining, 4, 46
    populist politicians and, 23
    pork-barrel politics and, 8, 48
    press coverage of, 100–4, 103f
    proportional representation systems and, 6–7, 51–52, 126–32
    quantitative measurement of, 38–40
    racial intolerance as factor constraining, 46
    regional parties and, 188–90
    at religious meetings, 129
    social constraints on, 116–18, 135, 147, 219
    stigmas as factor constraining, 4, 9–10, 45
    tone of, 30t, 31
    typology of, 100–4, 103f
    uncompetitive elections and, 10–11, 59, 147, 169, 175–76
ethnic attachment, 60–62, 135–36, 140–41
ethnic bonding
    Aceh province and, 20, 193t, 209t
    bonding-trumps-bridging heuristic and, 9–10, 52–54, 54t, 64, 152–53, 156
    candidate-centric electoral systems and, 136–37
    candidates with strong ethnic reputations and, 59, 169–72
    definition of, 5–6, 32, 34, 35f
    election posters and, 17, 118–19
    in elections with crowded field of co-ethinc candidates, 172–74
    electoral viability of ethnic groups and, 9–10, 19–20, 51f, 52, 55–56, 55f, 148
    ethnic ideology and, 58

ethnic bonding (*cont.*)
　ethnic parties and, 58
　ingroup solidarity and, 38
　negativity toward outgroups and, 5–6
　to nonviable ethnic groups, 59
　polarization and, 12
　regional head elections and, 147, 206–8
　regional parties and, 188, 190–92
　stigmas as obstacle to, 52
　uncompetitive elections and, 59
　viable dual-group candidates scenarios and, 53–54, 54*t*
ethnic bridging
　bonding-trumps-bridging heuristic and, 9–10, 52–54, 54*t*, 64, 152–53, 156
　broad ethnic bridging appeals and, 36–37, 38–39
　candidate-centric electoral systems and, 136, 137–38
　cross-ethnic bridging appeals, 38, 53, 57
　definition of, 6, 32, 34, 35*f*
　desertion risk and, 6
　election posters and, 17, 118–19
　electoral viability of ethnic groups and, 52, 55–56, 55*f*
　in ethnically diverse countries, 57
　intergroup rivalries as obstacle to, 53
　nationalism and, 6, 37
　national parties and, 20, 57, 58
　party-centric elections and, 10, 57
　pork-barrel politics and, 53
　psychological factors as potential obstacle to, 53
　reasons for engaging in, 53–54, 54*t*
　regional head elections and, 147
　regionalist appeals and, 37, 138
　social capital and, 32–33
ethnic bypassing
　candidate-centric electoral systems and, 136
　definition of, 6, 32, 34, 35*f*
　election posters and, 17, 118–19
　in elections with crowded field of co-ethnic candidates, 174
　electoral viability of ethnic groups and, 52, 55–56, 55*f*
　national parties and, 20, 58
　party-centric electoral rules and, 10

　reasons for engaging in, 36, 53–54, 54*t*
　regional head elections and, 147
ethnicity
　definition of, 5, 13, 24–25
　dimensions of, 26–27, 26*f*, 38–39, 52–54
　socialization and, 61
　structure *versus* activation of, 25–27, 26*f*
ethnic parties
　definition of, 57–58
　ethnic bonding and, 58
　ethnic ideologies and, 10, 58
　as nationalist parties, 57
　party-centric elections and, 58
　platforms of, 94
　regionally based ethnic parties and, 58
　restrictions on the establishment of, 11
ethnic politicization
　candidate-centric elections and, 11, 15–16, 20, 48
　in ethnically diverse *versus* ethnic majority countries, 43
　ethnic composition of government as measure of, 93–94
　ethnic vote share as measure of, 93–94
　multidimensional nature of ethnicity and, 43–44
　polarization and, 11
　proportional representation systems and, 42
Ethnic Power Relations (EPR) dataset, 93

Fossati, Diego, 67
France, 105–6
Free Aceh Movement (GAM), 188–89, 279n.13

Gadjanova, Elena, 29–31, 44, 94
Gayo, 129–30, 233
Geertz, Clifford, 60–61, 67–68, 269–70n.33
Gerindra
　economic nationalism and, 179–80
　Jakarta gubernatorial election (2017) and, 200
　nationalist party ideology of, 179, 182*t*
　regional head election coalition (2018) and, 202, 203
　regional press coverage in North Sumatra of, 100*t*

rural farming and fishing communities and, 179
Ghana, 1, 24
Ginting, Nurlisa, 161*f*, 171*f*, 173
Ginting, Paham, 158*f*
Golkar
   ant-corruption campaign messaging and, 123–24
   anti-communist emphasis of, 124–25
   economic development emphasis of, 124–25
   election posters for, 106–7
   as "the electoral face of civilian bureaucracy" during New Order era, 74
   electoral reforms of 1999 and, 77
   electoral reforms of 2004 and, 79
   establishment (1964) of, 73–74
   as hegemonic political party in New Order era of Indonesia, 13, 73–75, 76
   legislative elections of 1971 and, 73–74, 123
   legislative elections of 1997 and, 123–24
   legislative elections of 1999 and, 78–79, 124, 144
   legislative elections of 2004 and, 81, 124
   Medan mayoral election (2010) and, 162
   nationalist bridging appeals by, 186
   nationalist party ideology of, 179, 182*t*
   party-centric era of legislative elections in Indonesia (1955–2004) and, 69–70, 73
   patronage politics in New Order era by, 74
   regional autonomy reforms (1999) and, 86
   regional press coverage in North Sumatra of, 100*t*
   West Kalimantan gubernatorial election (2018) and, 214–15
Guided Democracy (Indonesia), 72–73
Gunawan Ang, 174*f*

Habibie, B. J., 76, 86–87
Habib Rizieq, 200, 215–16
Haney López, Ian, 27–28
Hanura
   legislative elections of 2014 and, 124
   nationalist party ideology of, 179, 182*t*
   Prosperous Peace Party absorbed into, 117–18
   regional press coverage in North Sumatra of, 100*t*
   West Kalimantan gubernatorial election (2018) and, 215
Haris, Muhammad, 170–72, 171*f*
Hatta, Mohammad, 71
Hehanussa, Andre, 165–66
Hindus in Indonesia, 15, 116–17, 219
Horowitz, Donald
   ethnicity defined by, 5, 24, 61
   on ethnic parties in multiethnic societies, 93
   on Indonesia's Constitutional Court and election law, 82
   on Indonesia's elite consensus-building approach to constitutional design, 67
   majoritarian electoral systems recommended by, 231
Horowitz, Jeremy, 29
Horton, Willie, 27–28
Hulman Sitorus, 164*f*, 164, 167

incumbency, 278n.12
Idrus, H. Ani, 99
India, 1, 37, 43, 232
indigenous bonding
   candidate-centric elections and, 136–37
   election posters and, 114–15, 115*f*
   electoral viability of ethnic groups and, 149–52, 151*f*
   in indigenous majority constituencies, 209*t*, 210–11
   Islamist parties and, 191*f*
   Muslim Democratic parties and, 191*f*
   nationalist parties and, 191*f*
   nonviable dual-group candidates and, 154*f*
   regional parties and, 190, 191*f*
   in uncompetitive elections, 175*f*, 175–76
   viable dual-group candidates and, 154*f*, 155, 156–59, 158*f*
   viable indigenous group candidates, 154*f*, 155–56, 159
   viable religious group candidates and, 154*f*

indigenous bridging
  candidate-centric electoral systems
    and, 137–38
  election posters and, 114, 115*f*
  electoral viability of ethnic groups and,
    151*f*, 149–52
  in Medan elections (2011), 173
  nonviable dual-group candidates and,
    154*f*, 156, 162–63
  Pematangsiantar mayoral election
    (2010) and, 164
  viable dual-group candidates and, 154*f*
  viable indigenous group candidates
    and, 154*f*
  viable religious group candidates and,
    154*f*, 156
indigenous bypassing
  election posters and, 114, 115*f*
  electoral viability of ethnic groups and,
    151*f*, 149–52
  nonviable dual-group candidates and,
    154*f*, 156, 162–63
  viable dual-group candidates and, 154*f*
  viable indigenous group candidates
    and, 154*f*
  viable religious group candidates and,
    154*f*, 156
Indonesia. *See also specific cities, elections,
    and provinces*
  Asian financial crisis (1997–98) and,
    76, 144–45
  candidate-centric elections in, 68, 80,
    145, 193
  colonial era in, 14, 70–71, 116
  democratic regression in, 67
  ethnic and religious diversity of
    population in, 13, 15
  ethnic ideology of political parties in, 13
  independence (1949) of, 12, 71
  Japanese occupation (1942–45) of, 106
  legislative seat allocations (1971) in, 73
  martial law (1957) in, 72–73
  national identity in, 14–15, 24, 37
  official religion requirements in, 116
  party-centric era of legislative elections
    (1955–2004) in, 69*f*, 69–70, 76, 81,
    84, 125–26
  polarization in, 67
  regional autonomy reforms (1999) in,
    86–87, 132–33
  regional identities in, 13–14
  regional press coverage of elections in, 92
  semi-candidate centric elections
    (2009–19) in, 69*f*, 70
Indonesian Communist Party (PKI), 71,
  72–73, 116–17, 123, 177
Indonesian Democratic Party (PDI), 74–
  75, 77, 100*t*, 106–7
Indonesian Democratic Party of Struggle
  (PDI-P)
  electoral reforms of 2004 and, 79
  Jakarta gubernatorial election (2017)
    and, 199–200
  legislative elections of 1999 and, 78–79
  legislative elections of 2004 and, 81
  legislative elections of 2009 and, 84
  Medan elections (2010–11) and, 162–
    63, 173–74
  nationalist party ideology of, 179, 182*t*
  North Sumatra gubernatorial election
    (2018) and, 217
  regional press coverage in North
    Sumatra of, 100*t*
  Salatiga district head elections and, 157
  Solo mayoral election (2015)
    and, 211–12
Indonesian Justice and Unity Party
  (PKPI), 100*t*, 189*t*
Indonesian legislative elections of 1955
  election posters and, 106–7
  electoral reforms prior to, 71–72
  electoral rules for, 72–73, 85*t*
  parties competing in, 117, 177
  Sukarno and, 12
Indonesian legislative elections of 1971,
  73–74, 117
Indonesian legislative elections of 1997,
  75, 143*t*
Indonesian legislative elections of 1999
  closed lists for, 78
  electoral reforms prior to, 77–78
  electoral rules for, 78–79, 85*t*, 124–26
  indigenous appeals and, 143, 143*t*
  party-centric elements of, 12–13
  religious appeals and, 143, 143*t*
  results of, 78–79

Indonesian legislative elections of 2004
  electoral reforms preceding, 79–80
  electoral rules for, 12–13, 80–81, 85*t*
  results of, 81
  women candidates and, 83
Indonesian legislative elections of 2009
  cultural modernization arguments regarding, 141–42
  electoral posters from, 16–17, 109, 112*t*, 134–40, 141–42
  electoral reforms prior to, 81–83, 127*t*
  electoral rules for, 13, 83, 85*t*
  endorsements for candidates in, 140
  open-list system for, 134, 145
  women candidates and, 83
  "zipper system" of party lists and, 83
Indonesian legislative elections of 2014, 82–84, 124
Indonesian legislative elections of 2019, 83–84
Indonesian Nahdlatul Community Party (PPNUI), 179, 182*t*
Indonesian Nationalist Party (PNI), 71, 177, 189, 190
Indonesian Ulama Council (MUI), 200
Indra Harahap, 174*f*, 174
Iraq, 1, 70
Ireland, ix, 104–6
Irian Jaya separatist conflict, 14
Islamic Defenders' Front (FPI), 200, 202, 203, 214–15, 218
Islamic electoral appeals
  in Ambon mayoral election (2010), 165–66
  candidate-centric electoral systems and, 130–31
  election posters and, 102–4, 115
  electoral rules' impact on, 132–33
  incentives for making, 198–99
  Islamist parties and, 184, 186
  in Medan mayoral election (2010), 162–63
  Muslim population size and, 135, 168–69
  party-centric electoral systems and, 9
  regional head elections and, 227
  regional parties and, 190–92
  at religious group meetings, 129–30
  urban regions and, 142, 187
  viable dual-group candidates and, 155, 157–59
Islamist parties
  nationalist bridging and, 183*f*, 184–85, 186, 191*f*
  religious bonding and, 20, 180–81, 181*f*, 183*f*, 184, 186, 191*f*
Italy, 69–70

Jakarta (Indonesia)
  Action to Defend Islam demonstrations (2016) in, 200
  election posters in, 112*t*
  gubernatorial election (2017) in, 20, 197–98, 199–201
  Muslim population size in, 221–22
  regional head election rules in, 88–89
  religious polarization in, 20, 199–201, 221–22
  riots (1998) in, 76
Java
  election posters from, 110
  indigenous bonding in elections in, 207–8
  legislative seat allocations (1971) and, 73
  regional legislative elections (1957–1958) in, 72–73
  religious bonding in elections in, 207–8
  viable dual-group candidates and, 155
Javanese Indonesians, 98, 160, 165
Jokowi (Joko Widodo), 107, 200, 202–3, 211–12

Kalimantan, 14, 72–73. *See also* East Kalimantan; North Kalimantan; West Kalimantan
Kamil, Ridwan, 202–3, 220
Karolin Margret Natasa, 215–17, 222
Karo region (Indonesia), 99, 159–60
Kenya, 1, 44, 234

Lampung, 112*t*, 209*t*
Langer, Ana Ines, 24
Latinos, 23, 28, 29, 44, 46
Latuconsina, Olivia, 165–66
Liddle, Bill, 14, 74, 224, 274n.15

Lijphart, Arend, 231

Madurese, 13, 14, 214–15
Malay Indonesians, 98, 214–15
Malaysia, 1, 105
Maluku region. *See also* Ambon (Indonesia)
  Christian population in, 115, 117
  election posters from, 110–11, 112*t*, 115
  Muslim population in, 212
  regional identity appeals in, 165–66
  religious-based conflicts in, 14, 165, 218–19
  revolt (1817) in, 165
Manado (Indonesia), 107–8
Manibuy, Irene, 220
Manifesto Project dataset, 94, 95
Maranata newsletter, 99
Marzuki, 123
Masjid Raya Baiturrahman (Banda Aceh), 190
Masyumi, 71, 177, 179
Medan (Indonesia)
  Batak population in, 160–63
  Chinese population in, 98, 160, 162–63
  Christian population in, 160
  election of 2010 in, 1–3, 160–62, 161*f*, 218
  election of 2011 in, 172–74
  ethnic diversity of population in, 1–2, 98
  indigenous identity in, 142
  Javanese population in, 160
  Muslim population in, 160–62
  religious diversity of population in, 1–2
Megawati Soekarnoputri, 78–79, 173–74
Mendelberg, Tali, 27–28, 45–46
Mietzner, Marcus, 177–78, 201
Mimbar Umum (Medan newspaper), 98–99
Minangkabau, 98, 129–30, 160, 172–73, 217
mixed-member proportional systems (MMP), 77, 90
most different systems design, 163–66
most similar systems design, 167
Mount Sinabung, 159–60
Muhammadiyah, 179–80

Nahdlatul Ulama (NU), 71, 177, 179–80, 202–3

NasDem Party, 100*t*, 214–15
National Awakening Party (PKB), 100*t*, 179–80, 182*t*, 185, 189*t*, 200, 214–15, 220
nationalist bridging
  in Ambon mayoral election (2010), 165–66
  candidate-centric election systems and, 137–38
  election posters and, 114–15, 115*f*
  electoral viability of ethnic groups and, 151*f*
  Islamist parties and, 183*f*, 184–85, 186, 191*f*
  Muslim Democratic parties and, 183*f*, 185, 191*f*
  nationalist parties and, 183*f*, 184–85, 186, 191*f*
  nationalist symbols and national rhetoric as elements of, 57
  national parties and, 57
  nonviable dual-group candidates and, 154*f*, 156, 162–63
  regional parties and, 190, 191*f*
  viable dual-group candidates and, 154*f*
  viable indigenous group candidates and, 154*f*
  viable religious group candidates and, 154*f*
National Mandate Party (PAN)
  Jakarta gubernatorial election (2017) and, 200
  Muhammadiyah and, 179–80
  Muslim democratic ideology of, 182*t*, 185
  non-Muslim candidates supported by, 220
  regional head election coalition (2018) and, 202, 203
  regional press coverage in North Sumatra of, 100*t*
national parties
  ethnic bridging and, 20, 57, 58
  ethnic bypassing and, 20, 58
  in multiethnic countries, 56–57
  nationalist bridging and, 57
  nationalist parties contrasted with, 57
Nelly Armayanti, 161*f*, 162–63
The Netherlands, 70–71, 116, 165

New Order regime (Indonesia, 1965–1998)
    closed list electoral system under, 75–76
    collapse of, 12–13
    democratic institutions destroyed under, 73
    economic development as priority during, 74
    election posters in, 106–7
    legislative elections during, 12–13
    official religion requirements in, 116–17
    party-centric electoral rules under, 76, 85*t*
    press restrictions under, 99
    regional heads selected by local legislatures under, 87
Nias, 98, 115
Nigeria, 28–29, 45, 61–62
Norris, Pippa, 33–34, 104–5
North Kalimantan, 209*t*, 213*t*
North Sulawesi, 112*t*, 115, 117, 209*t*, 219–20
North Sumatra. *See also* Medan (Indonesia)
    Batak ethnic population in, 98
    Christian population in, 102–4, 115, 117, 217
    election posters from, 110–11, 112*t*
    ethnic and religious diversity of population in, 16, 97–98
    ethnic identity and, 14
    indigenous events during election seasons in, 129
    Javanese population in, 98
    legislative elections of 1971 and, 123
    overall demography of, 217
    population size of, 16, 98
    provincial newspapers in, 16
    regional head election of 2010 in, 146–47
    regional head election of 2018 in, 202, 217–18, 222, 232
    regional press in, 98–100
    religious polarization potential in, 199, 214, 218, 222
    salience of indigenous identity in, 98

Obama, Barack, 28
open lists
    candidate-centric elections and, 7, 69, 134
    Indonesian legislative elections and, 70, 79, 81–82, 83–84, 85*t*, 125–26, 227
    intraparty competition and, 229
    politicization of ethnicity and, 126–32, 227
    undermining women's representation and, 83

Pancasila, 77–78, 117–18, 123, 179–80, 279n.3
Papua. *See* Papua New Guinea; West Papua
Papua New Guinea, 43
Parkindo (Indonesian Christian Party), 117–18
Partai Aceh, 188–89, 190–92, 192*f*
Partai Bulan Bintang (PBB), 100*t*, 179, 182*t*, 185*f*, 189*t*
Partai Demokrat (PD)
    Aceh and, 192*f*
    legislative elections of 2004 and, 81
    legislative elections of 2009 and, 84
    Medan mayoral election (2010) and, 162
    nationalist bridging appeals by, 184–85
    nationalist party ideology of, 179, 182*t*
    regional press coverage in North Sumatra of, 100*t*
    religious bonding appeals by, 184–85, 186
Partai Katolik (Catholic Party), 117
Partai Keadilan Sejahtera (PKS)
    candidate recruitment by, 185
    Islamist ideology of, 179, 182*t*
    Jakarta gubernatorial election (2017) and, 200
    Medan mayoral election (2010) and, 160–62
    Muslim Brotherhood and, 179
    nationalist bridging appeals by, 185
    non-Muslim candidates supported by, 220
    North Sumatra gubernatorial election (2018) and, 218
    regional head election coalition (2018) and, 202, 203
    regional press coverage in North Sumatra of, 100*t*
    Salatiga regional head elections and, 170
    West Kalimantan gubernatorial election (2018) and, 215

partisan appeals
  Indonesian elections and, 134–35, 136, 137f, 138, 173–74
  poster imagery and, 108–9, 111–13, 114–15, 115f, 134, 171f, 173–74
party-centric elections and, 9, 50f, 133, 226
party ideology
  categorizing Indonesian parties by, 178–87, 182t
  categorizing parties in Aceh by, 188–89, 189t
  ethnic appeals and, 8f, 10, 20, 51f, 56–58
  ethnic appeals in Aceh and, 190, 191f
  Gerindra, 179, 182t
  Golkar, 179, 182t
  Hanura, 179, 182t
  historical Indonesian political parties and, 177–78
  Indonesian Democratic Party of Struggle (PDI-P), 179, 182t
  Partai Demokrat (PD), 179, 182t
  regional parties and, 58, 187–88
  religious and nationalist appeals in Indonesia and, 178–84, 181f, 183f
party-centric elections
  candidate nomination process and, 47
  closed-list systems and, 7
  electoral lists and, 47
  endorsements of candidates and, 49–50
  ethnic appeals and, 8f, 8–9, 10, 34, 51f, 56–26, 125–26, 127t, 128–32
  ethnic bridging and, 10, 57
  ethnic parties and, 58
  indigenous appeals and, 137f
  in Indonesia (1955–2004), 69f, 69–70, 76, 81, 84, 125–26
  party ideologies and, 10, 56–58, 178, 180–81
  party platforms and, 7, 9, 48, 49–50
  personal vote strategies and, 7, 46, 48
Pattimura, Kapitan, 165–66
Paulus Kastanya, 164f, 166
Pematangsiantar (Indonesia)
  Batak population in, 165
  Christian population in, 165
  demographic profile of, 163–64
  election posters in, 146–47
  indigenous identity in, 142, 146–47
  Javanese population in, 165
  mayoral election (2010), 163–65, 167
  nonviable dual-group candidates and, 163
  secular appeals in, 146–47
Pemuda Pancasila, 74
personal vote scholarship, 7, 43–46, 47–48
Peru, 70
pilkada. See regional head elections (Indonesia)
Politically Relevant Ethnic Groups (PREG) dataset, 94, 95
Pomper, Gerald, 48
Pontianak Sultanate, 215–16
Posner, Daniel, 32, 94
posters. See election posters in Indonesia
Prabowo Subianto, 179
Pranowo, Ganjar, 202–3
proportional representation (PR)
  closed-list systems and, 69–70, 73, 75, 80–81
  consociational political systems and, 33
  ethnic appeals and, 6–7, 51–52, 126–32
  ethnic politicization and, 42
  open-list systems and, 69, 70, 79
Propserous Peace Party (PDS), 100t, 117–18, 162–63, 179, 182t, 185f
Prosperous and Safe Aceh Party (PAAS), 179, 182t, 188–89, 189t
Protestants in Indonesia, 15, 26–27, 116, 146, 159
Putnam, Robert, 32–33

Rahudman Harahap, 160–63, 161f, 218
Reform Star Party (PBR), 179, 182t, 185f, 186, 189t
regional head elections (Indonesia)
  candidate-centric nature of, 136–37, 147–48
  election posters from, 109–10, 134–35
  electoral reforms (1999–2004) and, 87–89
  electoral rules for, 13, 69f, 70, 89, 90t, 147–48
  endorsements from local organizations and, 139
  ethnic appeals and, 140

introduction (2005) of, 70
nationalist bridging appeals in, 186
partisan appeals and, 134–35, 138
regional autonomy reforms (1999) and, 86–87
religious bonding appeals in, 185–86
Reilly, Benjamin, 33–34
religious bonding
  candidate-centric elections and, 136–37
  election posters and, 114–15, 115*f*
  electoral viability of religious groups and, 151*f*, 149–52
  Islamist parties and, 20, 180–81, 181*f*, 183*f*, 184, 186, 191*f*
  Muslim democratic parties and, 183*f*, 191*f*
  in Muslim-majority constituencies, 207*f*, 207–8, 209*t*, 210–11, 212–19
  nationalist parties and, 183*f*, 191*f*
  nonviable dual-group candidates and, 154*f*
  regional parties and, 190, 191*f*
  in uncompetitive elections, 175*f*, 175–76
  viable dual-group candidates and, 154*f*, 155, 156–57, 160–62, 161*f*
  viable indigenous group candidates and, 154*f*
  viable religious group candidates and, 154*f*, 156, 160–62, 161*f*
religious bridging
  election posters and, 114, 115*f*
  electoral viability of religious groups and, 151*f*, 149–52
  Islamist parties and, 183*f*
  Muslim Democratic parties and, 183*f*
  nationalist parties and, 180–81, 181*f*, 183*f*
  nonviable dual-group candidates and, 154*f*, 156, 162–63
  Pematangsiantar mayoral election (2010) and, 164
  viable dual-group candidates and, 154*f*
  viable indigenous group candidates and, 154*f*, 155–56
  viable religious group candidates and, 154*f*
religious bypassing
  election posters and, 114, 115*f*
  electoral viability of religious groups and, 151*f*, 149–52

  Islamist parties and, 183*f*
  Muslim Democratic parties and, 183*f*
  nationalist parties and, 180–81, 181*f*, 183*f*
  nonviable dual-group candidates and, 154*f*, 156, 162–63
  viable dual-group candidates and, 154*f*
  viable indigenous group candidates and, 154*f*, 155–56
  viable religious group candidates and, 154*f*
religious polarization
  in competitive elections, 208
  in elections between non-Muslim and Muslim candidates, 198–99, 205, 206*f*
  ethnic group viability and, 204
  hard-liners and, 205–6
  Jakarta gubernatorial election (2017) and, 20, 199–201, 221–22
  Muslim candidates without strong Muslim reputations and, 198–99, 205, 206*f*
  in Muslim-majority constituencies, 198–99, 204–5, 206*f*, 208–9
  in Muslim-minority constituencies, 219–20
  in two-candidate elections, 198–99, 205, 206*f*
  in West Kalimantan gubernatorial election (2018), 199, 202, 203–4, 212–14, 221
Republican Party (United States), 27–28, 46
Riau, 72–73, 209*t*, 213*t*
Riker, William, 40
Rudolf Pardede, 218
Rudyatmo, F. X. Hadi ("Rudy"), 211–12, 233

Said, H. Mohammad, 99
Salatiga (Indonesia), 109*f*, 156–59, 158*f*, 170–72, 171*f*
Salmon Sagala, 171*f*
Samosir, 146–47, 159, 167
semi-candidate centric elections, 70, 133–34
Serta Ginting, 123–25
Shair-Rosenfield, Sarah, 67

Sherlock, Stephen, 83–84
Shugart, Matthew S., 47, 68–69, 268n.14
Sigit Pramono Asri, 160–63, 161*f*, 173
Simalungun (Indonesia), 14, 217
Singkawang (Indonesia), 216–17, 221, 280n.9
single-member districts (SMDs), 45, 51–52, 77
Sitanggang, Martua, 158*f*, 159
Siti Perangin-Angin, 171*f*, 173–74
Sjahrial R. Anas, 171*f*
social constraints
   bridging appeals and, 52
   candidates ignore, 59–60
   candidates in Pameatangsiantar and Ambon and, 163–66
   defined, 9–10
   ethnic appeals and, 4, 45
   examples of, 45
   normative objections to non-Muslim candidates and, 205
   racial appeals in the U.S. and, 45–46
   religious appeals in Indonesia and, 4, 116–18, 155–56
   viable ethnic groups and, 9–10, 52, 167–69
Sofyan Tan, 161*f*, 162–63, 218, 283n.12
Solo (Indonesia), 211–12, 233
Sora Mido magazine, 99
South Africa, 69–70
South Kalimantan, 112*t*, 117
South Sulawesi, 112*t*, 117, 213*t*
South Sumatra, 72–73, 209*t*, 213*t*
Soviet Union, 86
Spain, 69–70
Stephens-Dougan, LaFleur, 28
Sudirman, 203
Sudrajat, 203
Suharto
   Asian financial crisis (1997–98) and, 76
   authoritarian nature of regime of, 73–74
   coup (1965) led by, 72–73
   democratic institutions destroyed under, 73
   election laws under, 117
   election poster restrictions under, 106–7
   ethnic politics suppressed under, 224
   fall (1998) of, 12–13
   Golkar and, 73–74, 123
   New Order regime and, 12–13
   party-centric elections under, 69–70
   press restrictions under, 99
   resignation from presidency (1998) of, 76, 91, 124
Sukarno
   coup (1965) against, 72–73
   elections of 1955 and, 12
   independence of Indonesia (1949) and, 71
   Indonesian Democratic Party and, 106–7
   Indonesian Democratic Party of Struggle and, 173–74, 179
   martial law introduced (1957) by, 72–73
   Masyumi Party banned by, 179
   Pancasila ideology and, 271n.12
Sulawesi, 14, 73. *See also* Central Sulawesi; North Sulawesi; South Sulawesi; West Sulawesi
Sulistio, Teddy, 158*f*
Sumardi, Yahya, 171*f*
Sumatra. *See* Aceh; North Sumatra; South Sumatra
Surakarta (Indonesia). *See* Solo (Indonesia)
Sutarmidji, 214–16
Switzerland, 70

Tamba, Mangiring, 158*f*
Team of Seven, 77–78, 79, 86–87, 90–91
Thailand, 26, 30–31, 105–6
Toba Samosir, 167

Ukraine, 105
Ulema National Awakening Party (PKNU), 179–80, 182*t*, 185, 189*t*
uncompetitive elections, 10–11, 59, 147, 169, 175–76
United Development Party (PPP)
   electoral reforms of 1999 and, 77
   establishment (1973) of, 74–75
   Islamist ideology of, 179, 182*t*
   Jakarta gubernatorial election (2017) and, 200
   logo of, 106–7
   non-Muslim candidates supported by, 220

INDEX   317

regional press coverage in North
  Sumatra of, 100*t*
Salatiga regional head elections and, 170
United States
  candidate-centric *versus* party-centric
    elections in, 48
  election posters in, 105–6
  national identity in, 37
  racial appeals in the elections of, 23,
    27–28, 45–46
  racial intolerance as factor limited
    ethnic appeals in, 46
Usman Siregar, 174, 174*f*

Volksraad (legislative council in colonial
  Indonesia), 70–71

Weber, Max, 60–61
West Java, 112*t*, 202–3, 209*t*, 211
West Kalimantan
  Chinese population in, 214
  Christian population in, 115, 214
  election posters in, 112*t*, 115
  ethnic diversity of, 214

religious polarization during 2018
  gubernatorial election in, 199, 202,
  203–4, 212–14, 221
West Papua
  Christian population in, 115, 117
  election posters in, 112*t*, 115
  Muslim population in, 219–20
  non-Muslim candidates supported by
    Islamist parties in, 220
  separatism in, 78, 86
West Sulawesi, 112*t*, 209*t*, 213*t*
West Sumatra, 112*t*, 209*t*
Wilson, Ian, 200–1
Wisconsin Advertising Project, 57

Yogyakarta province, 112*t*, 209*t*
Yoruba, 45, 62
Yudhoyono, Agus, 199–200
Yudhoyono, Susilo Bambang (SBY), 81,
  84, 230–31
Yugoslavia, 86
Yuliyanto, 170–72, 171*f*

Zambia, 44